ORACLE®

Oracle Press™

I0131583

Oracle Database Upgrade, Migration & Transformation Tips & Techniques

About the Authors

Edward Whalen is an Oracle ACE Director and the Chief Technologist at Performance Tuning Corporation (www.perftuning.com), a consulting company specializing in database performance, administration, virtualization, and disaster recovery solutions with over 30 years of experience. He has extensive experience in system architectural design for optimal performance. His career has consisted of hardware, OS, database, and virtualization projects for many different companies. He has written seven books on Oracle products (13 books total), the last four from Oracle Press. He has also worked on numerous benchmarks and performance tuning projects with Oracle database products.

Ed works primarily as a consultant, speaker, and part-time trainer. His specialties include Oracle Performance Tuning, High Availability, and GoldenGate. In addition, Ed is working on several new book proposals.

Jim Czuprynski has over 30 years of experience in information technology, serving diverse roles at several Fortune 1000 companies in those three decades—mainframe programmer, applications developer, business analyst, and project manager—before becoming an Oracle database administrator in 2001. He currently holds OCP certification for Oracle 9*i*, 10*g*, and 11*g*, and is an Oracle ACE Director.

Jim continues to write a steady stream of articles that focus on the myriad facets of Oracle database administration, with nearly 100 articles to his credit since 2003 for *Database Journal* (www.databasejournal.com) and IOUG's *SELECT Journal*. Jim's blog, *Generally…It Depends* (http://jimczuprynski.wordpress.com), concentrates on Oracle database technology and administration. He is the author of nearly 100 articles on Oracle Database 10*g* and Oracle Database 11*g*, with several articles on Oracle Database 12*c* appearing in *IOUG SELECT* Magazine since 2003.

Jim is also a sought-after public speaker on Oracle Database technology features. He has presented topics at Oracle OpenWorld, IOUG's COLLABORATE, Hotsos Symposium, Oracle Technology Network ACE Tours, and Oracle User Group conferences around the world.

Jim teaches core Oracle University database administration courses on behalf of Oracle and its Education Partners throughout the United States and Canada, instructing several hundred Oracle DBAs about Oracle DBA best practices since 2005. He was awarded Oracle Education Partner Instructor of the Year in 2009.

About the Technical Editor

Hans Forbrich has been programming, using, and administering computers since his first program at the University of Calgary on a DEC PSP-8i in 1969. He was involved in a number of migrations and upgrades prior to his introduction to Oracle in the mid-1980s, and has been involved in countless migrations and upgrades across many platforms in his time at a major telecom manufacturer, at an applications company, at Oracle, and over the past 12 years with his own consultancy.

Hans is an electrical engineer, holds multiple OCPs, and is an Oracle ACE Director who is well known on the Oracle speaking circuit. He consults on and teaches many classes for Oracle University on Linux, Oracle VM, Database, Middleware, GoldenGate, Database Integrator, SOA, and Integration.

ORACLE®

Oracle Press™

Oracle Database Upgrade, Migration & Transformation Tips & Techniques

Edward Whalen

Jim Czuprynski

Mc
Graw
Hill
Education

New York   Chicago   San Francisco
Athens   London   Madrid   Mexico City
Milan   New Delhi   Singapore   Sydney   Toronto

Library of Congress Cataloging-in-Publication Data

Whalen, Edward.
   Oracle database upgrade, migration & transformation tips & techniques /
Edward Whalen and Jim Czuprynski.
     pages cm
   Includes bibliographical references and index.
   ISBN 978-0-07-184605-9 (paperback)
1. Database management.   2. Oracle (Computer file)   3. Systems
migration.   I. Czuprynski, Jim.   II. Title.
   QA76.9.D3W476   2015
   005.74—dc23
                                                        2015011463

McGraw-Hill Education books are available at special quantity discounts to use as premiums and sales promotions, or for use in corporate training programs. To contact a representative, please visit the Contact Us pages at www.mhprofessional.com.

Oracle Database Upgrade, Migration & Transformation Tips & Techniques

Copyright © 2015 by McGraw-Hill Education (Publisher). All rights reserved. Printed in the United States of America. Except as permitted under the Copyright Act of 1976, no part of this publication may be reproduced or distributed in any form or by any means, or stored in a database or retrieval system, without the prior written permission of Publisher, with the exception that the program listings may be entered, stored, and executed in a computer system, but they may not be reproduced for publication.

Oracle is a registered trademark of Oracle Corporation and/or its affiliates. All other trademarks are the property of their respective owners, and McGraw-Hill Education makes no claim of ownership by the mention of products that contain these marks.

Screen displays of copyrighted Oracle software programs have been reproduced herein with the permission of Oracle Corporation and/or its affiliates.

1234567890 DOC DOC 1098765

ISBN 978-0-07-184605-9
MHID   0-07-184605-0

Sponsoring Editor Paul Carlstroem	**Technical Editor** Hans Forbrich	**Production Supervisor** Jean Bodeaux
Editorial Supervisor Janet Walden	**Copy Editor** Bill McManus	**Composition** Cenveo Publisher Services
Project Manager Sonam Arora, Cenveo® Publisher Services	**Proofreader** Claire Splan	**Illustration** Cenveo Publisher Services
Acquisitions Coordinator Amanda Russell	**Indexer** Claire Splan	**Art Director, Cover** Jeff Weeks

Information has been obtained by Publisher from sources believed to be reliable. However, because of the possibility of human or mechanical error by our sources, Publisher, or others, Publisher does not guarantee to the accuracy, adequacy, or completeness of any information included in this work and is not responsible for any errors or omissions or the results obtained from the use of such information.

Oracle Corporation does not make any representations or warranties as to the accuracy, adequacy, or completeness of any information contained in this Work, and is not responsible for any errors or omissions.

Contents at a Glance

PART IV
Optimized Upgrades/Migration

PART V
Best Practices and Tips

Contents

PART II
Cross-Platform Migration

PART III
Migration with Enhancement/Upgrade

PART IV
Optimized Upgrades/Migration

PART V
Best Practices and Tips

Acknowledgments

I would like to thank Jim Czuprynski for all of his hard work. He has done an excellent job. I would like to thank some of the people that helped with some of the many questions that I had and with suggestions to make this book great. They include Larry Carpenter, Gary Parker, Hans Forbrich, and Dan Morgan.

I would especially like to thank Hans Forbrich for his attention to detail and many great suggestions as technical editor. As an author I rely on great technical editing, and Hans was fantastic.

Finally, I would like to thank the staff at Oracle Press. Their professionalism and hard work makes writing for Oracle Press a pleasure.

–Edward Whalen

My colleague Ed Whalen's breadth and depth of experience was paramount to this book's success. Ed's foresight into what our fellow Oracle DBAs are most hungry to understand when transforming data, migrating Oracle databases between different platforms, and upgrading Oracle databases to a new release was crucial for making sure we were attacking the most pertinent points of interest.

Hans Forbrich, our technical editor, did a simply stupendous job. Hans added his perspectives based on decades of Oracle database experience, challenged our assumptions fearlessly, and provided needed encouragement to ensure we stayed on track as we tackled our thornier topics.

Paul Carlstroem and Amanda Russell, our key contacts at Oracle Press, did an excellent job guiding us through the twisting trails that a book of this breadth and complexity demands. They kept us on schedule yet never hurried us to create less than superior content.

–Jim Czuprynski

Introduction

O racle database upgrades and migrations are tasks that most DBAs must perform every few years. They become necessary because hardware gets old, applications need to have new features added, and companies grow. For these reasons and many more, you will encounter hardware refreshes, database changes, and features added such as encryption, partitioning, LOB storage, and so forth. So, what should you do when the time comes to perform an upgrade or migration? As you will see in this book, there are many ways to accomplish the same outcome. Which method is right for you depends on your specific environment, needs, and requirements. This book will provide you with many choices, tips, and techniques for performing these tasks.

We have prepared this book based upon our combined experiences during several decades in Information Technology, but we have also performed extensive research into best practices, recommendations, and pitfalls that any Oracle DBA should at least consider before beginning any project that involves migrating between different OS platforms, transforming existing databases to use different storage or enterprise systems, or upgrading databases from one Oracle release to the next. We hope that our numerous code examples and detailed checklists provide you with the confidence you and your team will need to successfully migrate, transform, and upgrade Oracle databases all the way to Oracle Database Release 12c R1 and beyond.

Chapter 1: Overview of Migration, Transformation, and Upgrade Methodologies

This chapter introduces the various methods and tools that can be used to accomplish upgrades, migrations, and transformations and provides cross references to the chapters in which they are covered—a useful feature for locating just the right information you need to start your migration, transformation, and upgrade efforts.

Chapter 2: Choosing the Right Migration Method

Chapter 2 discusses the migration methods available and provides reasons to choose the most appropriate migration method for your situation, platforms, and operating systems.

Chapter 3: Migration/Transformation/Upgrade Methodologies

Chapter 3 looks at developing the appropriate methodology to guarantee the success of your database's migration, transformation, and/or upgrade.

Chapter 4: Oracle Data Guard

Chapter 4 focuses on leveraging the features of Oracle Data Guard to migrate an Oracle database, as well as the specific circumstances that govern an effective migration using this tool set.

Chapter 5: Using Recovery Manager (RMAN) for Cross-Platform Migration

Using the Recovery Manager tool set to migrate databases between different platforms is discussed and demonstrated in Chapter 5.

Chapter 6: Transporting Tablespaces and Databases

Chapter 6 looks at two special Oracle tool sets—Transportable Tablespace Sets (TTS) and Transportable Database (TDB)—for migrating databases between platforms.

Chapter 7: Migrating Oracle Databases with Export/Import

The venerable Export/Import utility and its more recent incarnation, Data Pump Export/Import, for migrating Oracle databases are the focus of Chapter 7.

Chapter 8: Zero or Minimal Downtime Migrations with Oracle GoldenGate

Chapter 8 reviews how to leverage the features of GoldenGate to migrate databases between different environments and platforms and discusses its value for keeping data synchronized between databases for real-time data migration.

Chapter 9: Cross-Platform Transportable Tablespace Migration Utilities

Chapter 9 demonstrates how the Cross-Platform Transportable Tablespaces (XTTS) utility makes it possible to perform data migration for databases that can tolerate only an extremely brief period of read-only access.

Chapter 10: Migrating to New Storage Platforms Using ASM

Chapter 10 explains how to leverage Oracle's Automatic Storage Management (ASM) features to migrate an Oracle database between different platforms with limited downtime when both environments are using ASM storage.

Chapter 11: Database Upgrade Assistant

The Database Upgrade Assistant (DBUA) is the focus of Chapter 11, including a demonstration of how to use DBUA to upgrade an existing pre-12*c* Oracle database to Oracle 12*c*.

Chapter 12: Migrating from Microsoft SQL Server to Oracle

Chapter 12 focuses on how to migrate an entire Microsoft SQL Server database to an Oracle database using Oracle GoldenGate.

Chapter 13: Moving to Oracle Database 12*c*

Oracle Database 12*c* R1 is the focus of Chapter 13, including a summary of the key new features of this latest database release's feature set, especially its new multitenant architecture.

Chapter 14: Moving to Oracle Engineered Systems

Chapter 14 looks at the universe of Oracle Engineered Systems and lays out some special considerations and recommended best practices when migrating to these platforms.

Chapter 15: Migrating to Oracle in the Cloud

Chapter 15 discusses the recent uptrend to cloud computing and how to effectively migrate to the cloud.

Chapter 16: In Summary: Recommendations, Reminders, and Best Practices

The book concludes with a brief summary of the most valuable tips and best practices presented.

Code and Checklists Online

We have provided checklists and code examples used throughout the book online at the Oracle Press website. Please check www.OraclePressBooks.com for more details.

On with the Book

This book has been in the idea phase for several years. We are glad that we finally have the chance to bring it to reality. We hope you enjoy reading this book as much as we enjoyed writing it. Our intent was to create a book that is full of useful content to help you with your work as well as serve as a good reference.

PART
I

Planning a Smooth Migration

CHAPTER
1

Overview of Migration, Transformation, and Upgrade Methodologies

We have written this book to fill a need that we've noticed has gone quite unanswered: a practical roadmap for Oracle DBAs and their colleagues on the front lines of database migration, transformation, and upgrades to effectively plan, carefully implement, and successfully complete an upgrade, migration, or transformation project. We've classified three different types of projects within this book:

- **Data migration** This type of project involves moving data from one database to another. It's not uncommon for a data migration project to share some of the elements of a database upgrade project as well.

- **Database upgrade** We identify two key methodologies for upgrading an Oracle database: the *in-place upgrade*, in which the Oracle binary files are upgraded and scripts are executed to upgrade objects in the database itself; and the *out-of-place upgrade*, in which all the data from the previous version of the database is moved to another database that's already at a more recent version.

- **Migration with transformation** This type of project typically requires modifications to the database application *objects* as well as the database itself—for example, implementing a data partitioning scheme for a previously unpartitioned table, or migrating large objects (LOBs) from BasicFile to SecureFile format, or even encrypting previously unsecured data.

Based on our experience, however, not all projects fall into a single category, and there are often overlapping requirements during a data migration and database upgrade project. To add to the confusion, there are multiple migration methods that may or may not be appropriate for each project's requirements. One of our major goals in this book is to demystify which methods will work for different migration, upgrade, and transformation scenarios, as well as to help you identify which methods are most appropriate for your project's requirements. This book will also explain that sometimes there is only *one* option that's appropriate to accomplish a particular project's requirements.

Database Upgrade Methodologies

In essence, upgrading an Oracle database simply brings it to a newer database release from an older database release. An upgrade can involve upgrading the Oracle software and database (an *in-place upgrade*) or moving to a newer system (a *migration with upgrade*). We typically see more migration-with-upgrade projects than any other project types because many organizations want to take advantage of improved hardware and storage. Moving a database to a new storage system, operating system, or computing platform is typically an excellent opportunity to upgrade to a newer Oracle database release as well.

It's not often that an upgrade goes bad, but it does happen, so we have found that it's crucial to consider a fallback solution just in case. An advantage of migration with upgrade is that it leaves the original production system intact, thus providing a readily available fallback solution. This should be part of your project planning process, which we will cover extensively in Chapters 2 and 3; we will demonstrate the recommended best practices for using Oracle's Database Upgrade Assistant in Chapter 11.

The following represents an overview of the methods that we cover in this book for performing database upgrades or database upgrades with migrations. Each method is covered in depth in a chapter in the book.

Data Migration Methodologies

In its simplest form, a data migration involves moving data from one database to another. Depending on the method selected, a database migration can optionally include an upgrade as well as data transformation. There are multiple methods of data migration, but which method you should choose for your migration will vary based on your database and your requirements. These methods are described in the following sections.

Data Guard

Migrating with Data Guard is covered in Chapter 4. This is one of several specialty migrations that are available only under a narrow set of circumstances. However, when the requirements fit your needs, migrating with Data Guard can be a very effective and powerful method of performing a data migration. Data Guard typically requires that the platform, database version, and database are identical on both source and target systems.

In its simplest form, this migration begins with the creation of the new system as a Data Guard physical standby database. When it's time to cut over to the new system, you perform a Data Guard switchover operation. The new system becomes the primary database, and the original system is transformed into a ready-made physical standby database.

RMAN

We demonstrate how to use Recovery Manager (RMAN) to perform a database migration in Chapter 5. In an appropriate scenario, RMAN makes it simple to back up a database on one platform and restore it on another platform to complete the migration.

Transporting Tablespaces

One of the most flexible methods for data migration—transporting sets of tablespaces between databases—is covered in Chapter 6. This method allows you to move a tablespace from a source system to a destination system even when the systems are housed on completely different platforms or operating systems.

Cross-Platform Tablespace Migration

The Cross-Platform Transportable Tablespace (XTTS) migration utility—a specialized data migration method that requires extremely limited application downtime—is discussed in detail in Chapter 9.

Export/Import

Export/Import (which also includes Data Pump Export/Import) is covered in Chapter 7. In its simplest form, Export/Import takes data from one database and copies it into another database. Because of the way the export and import process works, it's also possible to perform data transformation during this process, so data can be imported into a table with a different character set, a different partitioning configuration, and so forth. Because of these properties, Export/Import is the most flexible data movement tool. Export/Import is one of the two migration-with-transformation methods that we cover in this book as well as the basis for the second one: Oracle GoldenGate.

GoldenGate

Performing a migration with Oracle GoldenGate is covered in Chapters 8 and 12. Chapter 8 shows how to perform a minimal downtime migration upgrade and transformation using Oracle GoldenGate, while Chapter 12 shows how to migrate to Oracle from a non-Oracle database—in this case, Microsoft SQL Server.

Oracle GoldenGate is a heterogeneous replication product. It enables you to set up a source system and a target system and keep them synchronized even if they are different Oracle versions, different platforms, or even completely different databases. Migration using GoldenGate is a multiphase operation. First, GoldenGate is set up to capture changes. Next, an initial migration is done. Then GoldenGate applies those changes and keeps the source and target systems in sync. Finally, the cutover is performed. With this method, the cutover is very fast. As we have observed, "It doesn't matter how long it takes to do the migration … just how long it takes to do the cutover."

Automatic Storage Management (ASM)

ASM migrations are covered in Chapter 10. This is another specialty migration method and it is only valid for migrating to new storage. It is a very simple and straightforward process and can be done with no downtime, but again, it only migrates the database to new storage. This method involves bringing in the new storage system and adding it to your system's existing ASM disk groups. After the new storage system has been added to ASM, the original disks can be dropped from the disk groups. This method works extremely well—we have performed it many times at many client sites—but it is important to note that it does not allow for any data transformation.

Migration with Transformation Methodologies

Migration with transformation usually involves improving an existing database schema. Because Oracle makes many improvements with each database release, it's often challenging to take advantage of these improvements with an existing database; sometimes the only opportunity to take advantage of them might be while you are migrating your database.

Some new features available in later Oracle database releases that you might want to consider include

- **Partitioning**   Partitioning has improved tremendously over the last few database releases, especially in Oracle 11.1.0.7, which added four new partitioning methods.

- **LOB storage**   SecureFile LOB storage is a great improvement over legacy (BasicFile) LOB storage and offers significant performance improvements as well as deduplication, compression, and encryption.

- **Security**   Encrypted tablespaces provide additional security and are fairly easy to implement.

As mentioned before, the migration process might be your only chance to make meaningful improvements to your database.

TIP & TECHNIQUE
This might be your only opportunity to make improvements. Consider the opportunity and think about how changes might improve your database.

Future Migration, Transformation, and Upgrade Techniques

Finally, this book tackles three of the newest topics in Oracle Database technology. We explore and demonstrate how data migration, data transformation, and database upgrade projects will be accomplished in the brave new world of Oracle Database 12*c* (Chapter 13), on engineered systems like Oracle's Exadata hardware line (Chapter 14), and within the realm of Oracle's Cloud Computing environment (Chapter 15).

Summary

As we have described, there are many ways to perform database migrations. Determining which method is right for your situation depends on your IT organization's needs and requirements. Remember that this migration might be the only chance that you have to make major structural changes to your database, so be sure to take advantage of this opportunity.

In this book, we provide extensive examples, checklists, and guidance on how to migrate your database from one platform to another. In Chapters 2 and 3, we'll begin the process of helping you to determine which method is most appropriate for your migration, upgrade, or transformation project, and then we'll explain how to build exactly the right plan for your impending project.

CHAPTER
2

Choosing the Right Migration Method

Chapter 1 introduced the various methods for performing data migrations. Before you can start planning your migration, you must decide on the basic method for the migration. By looking at your requirements and determining which method best meets your needs, as discussed in this chapter, you will be able to create a plan that is right for you.

Evaluating Your Environment

There is no one migration path that is right for everybody. You should choose the migration path that best meets your particular requirements. We have performed many different data migrations using different methods. In each case, we determined which method to use based on an evaluation of the following factors:

- Migration goals

- Downtime requirements

- Equipment and infrastructure availability

- Budget

- Available resources

After assessing these factors, we are able to decide which methods are available and which one best meets the specific requirements. The methods and corresponding examples that we present in this book are intended to serve as guidelines that you can use to make your own choice after assessing the preceding factors in your own environment. You might choose one of these methods, a combination of these methods, or even a method that you devise for your own particular requirements.

Our goal in this book is not to tell you which method is right for you; instead, we intend to give you solid ideas and examples upon which you can start to build your own project.

TIP & TECHNIQUE

No two migrations are the same. Every customer is different, and every migration is different. When deciding how to migrate your data, don't try to fit your plan into any of these methods exactly. Your specific needs will be different from everybody else's. This book is designed to provide you with ideas. Take these ideas and run with them. Think outside the box and do what is right for your situation.

Migration Goals

The first and most important factor in determining the best migration strategy for you is identifying what your migration goals are. Why do you want to migrate? This might seem like a very simple question, but details are important. So, let's look at several common reasons for performing a data migration. The following list is by no means comprehensive. Many other reasons exist for performing data migrations.

- **Hardware refresh**   Perhaps your hardware is out of date and you want to upgrade it to a newer, faster system. This is one of the most common reasons for performing a data migration. If you are migrating to the same hardware architecture the options and methods that are available will be different than those available if you are going to different hardware architecture, such as migrating from Oracle on AIX to Oracle on Linux or to Oracle Exadata.

- **Support requirements**   Many times migrations/upgrades are dictated by support requirements. Oracle support for very old versions of the database eventually ends. In addition, Oracle versions are tied to OS versions, which in turn lose support. Extended support can be purchased for certain time frames for a price, but eventually you must consider migrating/upgrading to a newer version of software to remain supported.

- **Consolidation**   As hardware becomes faster and more efficient, and supports more and more memory, you will often find that it is appropriate to consolidate several databases into one database. With Oracle Database 12c, you can now consolidate into a multitenant database using Oracle's pluggable databases.

- **Security requirements**   Recently we worked on a database migration/upgrade project where the motivating factor was to be able to encrypt the database using tablespace encryption using a Hardware Security Module (HSM). It is not uncommon for databases to be migrated and upgraded to support better security. In addition, security is updated on a quarterly basis via Oracle Critical Patch Updates (CPUs).

- **Performance/new features**   One of the primary reasons for migrating to a new database is to enable new database features. Each release of the Oracle database introduces a variety of new features that are designed to enhance performance and scalability.

   These new features will vary by database version and your needs. Depending on the type of features that you want to take advantage of, the method of migration might be limited.

TIP & TECHNIQUE
Determining the migration goals is important to making the overall decision as to how you are going to do the migration.

It is important to first determine all of the reasons for migrating the database before you begin the migration plan. The reasons to migrate your database will very often determine the migration methods that are available to you. As with any task, preparation and planning is key to a successful migration.

Downtime Requirements

Determining allowable downtime is another extremely important part of choosing the appropriate migration process. This requirement will determine which migration methods are viable. If you are allowed plenty of downtime and have a small database, the number of options is unlimited. Unfortunately, in many cases the amount of downtime is very limited and the size of the database is very large.

The downtime requirements will be determined by the business unit and will usually be very strict, especially if formal service-level agreements (SLAs) are in place. In several of the recent migrations that we have worked on, the downtime requirements were limited to just a few hours, whereas the database size was over 10TB. This type of scenario can limit your options to a very few. Other requirements will further limit the options that you have for your migration method.

So, what is considered downtime and what will affect that downtime? For our purposes in this book, *downtime* is considered the length of time the database is unavailable to the application servers in order to get a consistent copy of the database. Keep in mind that the methods provided in this chapter have many variations.

Transformation Goals

The transformation goals are also very important to determining the available migration methods. So, what is a transformation goal? How is a transformation different from a migration? In the simplest of terms, if you are changing the structure of the database, you are performing a transformation in addition to a migration. In this book, we pretty much call everything data migration (except for a pure upgrade).

The simplest of migration goals is to move the database from one system to another system. This is very simple and straightforward. However, many times a data migration will offer additional benefits, such as the opportunity to take advantage of new features, enhance the database, and make overall database improvements.

Here are some examples of transforming a database during a migration:

- Upgrading from one version of Oracle to a newer version. This technically does not constitute a transformation, but rather an upgrade within the data migration.

- Moving from BasicFile LOBs to SecureFile LOBs. SecureFile LOBs are first available in Oracle Database 11*g*.

- Moving from range partitioning to interval partitioning. Interval partitioning was introduced in Oracle Database 11*g*.

- Encrypting the database.

- Compressing the database.

- Moving from a non-container database to a container database with pluggable databases (first available in Oracle 12*c*).

- Partitioning the database.

- Moving to Oracle Automatic Storage Management (ASM) from non-ASM storage.

During a data migration is possibly the best time to introduce these new features.

TIP & TECHNIQUE

When you are doing any type of migration, you should carefully consider if you can enable new features and/or restructure your database. Often, your best opportunity to modify the database is during a migration.

Operational Goals

Operational goals are simply additional functionality and/or features that are needed to meet business goals. For example, your IT organization may have mandated that as part of its ongoing plans to improve its business continuity requirements, a more robust disaster recovery plan must be implemented before cutover to the new production environment, so this would be an excellent opportunity to implement Oracle Data Guard at the corresponding disaster recovery site.

Migration Methods Review

As mentioned in the previous chapter, there are several different methods for migrating a database. Each of these methods has its pros and cons, as outlined in Table 2-1. The key factor for most of these methods is how much time it takes to perform the data migration.

In this book there are many migration methods that are mentioned that are not necessarily covered in detail. This is due to the fact that many methods are subsets of each other. Therefore, you will not see a one-to-one relationship between this section and the rest of the book. In fact, many of the options listed in Table 2-1 are not entirely suited for an Oracle migration.

Method	Pros	Cons
Virtualization Migration	■ Can exactly duplicate OS and database ■ Versions of OS and Oracle remain the same ■ Basis for basic migration methodology where the system cannot be upgraded	■ Might be difficult on some older OSs ■ Can be time consuming for large systems (> 500GB)
Database Upgrade Assistant (DBUA)	■ Can be used to upgrade a database in place ■ Easy to use ■ No new hardware required	■ Can be time consuming ■ Might have to go through several iterations for older databases ■ Backing out could be time consuming
Legacy Export/ Import	■ Simple, Oracle-supplied utility ■ Can export/import DDL metadata without data ■ Import can change tablespaces ■ Basis for basic migration methodology ■ Read-only utility	■ Not viable for very large databases (VLDBs) ■ Slow
Oracle Data Pump	■ Simple, Oracle-supplied utility ■ Can export DDL ■ Import can change tablespaces ■ Can be run in phases ■ Faster than Export/Import	■ Not extremely fast ■ Requires database to be open ■ Uses the Oracle job scheduler
Oracle Data Pump over a DB link	■ Simple, Oracle supplied utility ■ Can export DDL ■ Import can change tablespaces ■ Using DBLink allows for DB to DB direct Export/Import without intermediate dump file written to disk	■ Not extremely fast ■ Speed limited by the link

Method	Pros	Cons
Data Guard	■ Oracle-supplied utility ■ Can migrate entire database	■ Database versions must be identical ■ Does not support 10*g* to 11*g* upgrade
RMAN restore	■ Oracle-supplied utility ■ Can migrate entire database	■ Database versions must be identical ■ Does not support 10*g* to 11*g* upgrade
Cross-platform tablespace migration with incremental backups	■ Oracle-supplied process ■ Uses Oracle Transportable Tablespace technology ■ Valid for 10*g* R2 upward	■ Supported only for Exadata destinations ■ Extremely complicated ■ Datafiles will need to be moved into ASM post migration ■ No fallback method available
Oracle Streams	■ Mature Oracle Utility	■ Complex to configure and maintain ■ Resource usage high when running
Quest SharePlex	■ Supports cross-platform migration ■ Supports simultaneous upgrade from 10*g* to 11*g* ■ Can replicate selective schemas ■ Minimal downtime cutover	■ Oracle-to-Oracle replication only ■ Lack of expertise on the tool ■ Initial data load may be lengthy
Oracle GoldenGate	■ Supports cross-platform migration ■ Supports simultaneous upgrade from 10*g* to higher database versions ■ Can replicate selective schemas ■ Heterogeneous database replication—supports SQL Server, Sybase, Teradata, DB2, and Oracle RDBMS ■ Minimal downtime cutover	■ Requires additional licensing ■ Initial data load may be lengthy ■ Some user-defined data types may not be supported

TABLE 2-1. *Migration Options*

Depending on your requirements, not all of these methods may work for you. In this book we will be focusing on a few methods and variations of these methods. The key methods that we will be covering are described in the following sections, along with some of their variations.

Database Upgrade Assistant (DBUA)

DBUA can be used to upgrade a database to the next major release. Using this tool can be time-consuming, and it modifies your production database. You must back up your system (as with all migration methods) before the upgrade, and the only way to back out the upgrade is to restore the original version of the database from its prior backup. DBUA performs an in-place upgrade, and it only performs upgrades, not migrations.

NOTE
Using the DBUA is the only method that we cover in this book that does not perform a migration, only an upgrade. This upgrade is done in-place.

Export/Import

The traditional Export/Import utility can still an important part of any data migration. Even if this migration method is not used as the primary method, in many cases it is used to export and import metadata such as user schemas and so forth.

This method can be used in conjunction with GoldenGate to create schema objects that are later loaded into via Export/Import or Data Pump followed by GoldenGate replication.

NOTE
Traditional Export/Import is desupported starting with Oracle Database 11g.

Data Pump

Data Pump is similar to Export/Import but is much faster. It can be used to create objects and to efficiently move data. Data Pump is very fast at moving traditional data, but transfer speeds for BasicFile LOB data tend to be dramatically slower than when transferring SecureFile LOB data.

Depending on the type of data being transferred, network throughput, and so on, it is not unusual to realize transfer speeds of over 100GB/hour using Data Pump.

RMAN

Oracle Recovery Manager (RMAN) is generally recognized as the *de facto* utility for quickly backing up and restoring a database and its data, but even though it is not specifically designed for data migration, it can be used for that purpose.

RMAN can perform both full and incremental backups. Using an incremental backup, you can reduce the length of time that the database is down during cutover to the length of time it takes to complete the incremental backup and restore.

While this method does not allow for database changes during migration, it definitely supports some basic storage changes such as tablespace relocation and endian/character set conversion.

Transportable Tablespaces

Using transportable tablespaces can be an efficient way of performing a database migration. The process is fairly fast, taking just a little longer than the time it takes to copy the tablespace's datafiles between source and target environments.

However, this method does not allow for database changes during the migration.

Cross-Platform Tablespace Migration with Incremental Backups

This is one of the primary methods used (and recommended) for migrating to Exadata systems. It essentially combines transportable tablespace methods with incremental RMAN backup methods to perform the data synchronization.

While this method does require some downtime, that downtime will be limited to the time it takes to perform the final incremental backups.

Data Guard

In certain specific cases, Oracle Data Guard can be used to migrate a source database to a different system with a similar architecture. Simply set up a physical standby database on the new system, and when you are ready to cut over, perform a Data Guard switchover operation. An additional benefit of this method is that you are left with a ready-made physical standby.

This method does not allow for database changes during the migration, and it does require the same hardware architecture on the source and target.

GoldenGate

Oracle GoldenGate is an excellent product for keeping systems in sync for a quick switchover. Since GoldenGate is a replication technology, it allows only specific tables to be replicated instead of the entire database, and that can reduce the time required to complete the cutover significantly.

GoldenGate can be used to perform migrations that include data structure changes and transformations. When used in conjunction with Oracle Flashback

Database features, the target database's performance can be tested prior to the cutover. Using GoldenGate for data migration offers many great features which we will describe later in the book.

Resources

When you consider which human resources are necessary for a data migration, you need to take into account several different factors, including the number of people needed, their skill levels, their experience, and their availability. These factors are all extremely important to performing the data migration successfully. If you don't have enough of the right resources, the project is doomed to be delayed or suffer serious setbacks.

So, what kind of resources are required? Since many different tasks need to be performed for a smooth migration, you will need a wide range of resources, including the following:

- **Project management**   Without proper project management resources, it will be very difficult to keep track of and maintain the schedule. A professional PM is absolutely needed for all but the simplest and smallest data migrations. In addition, the PM can assist with the mediation of issues that can occur before, during and after the migration.

- **Team leadership**   There must be a clear chain of command to be able to guide the project. Depending on the size of the migration, there will most likely be several teams of engineers, but they all should report to one project lead.

- **Oracle resources**   These resources must be familiar with Oracle DBA tasks and must be able to modify and/or code stored procedures and SQL scripts. They must be familiar with tools such as Export/Import and Data Pump as well as other data transport methods. They must be very familiar with the database configuration and usage as well as with the data itself.

- **GoldenGate resources**   If you are using GoldenGate for your migration method, you must have one or more skilled GoldenGate resources. Having someone who has had experience with this type of migration is important.

- **Network resources**   Any migration involves not only moving databases from one system to another, but moving application servers as well. In almost any migration, this involves opening firewalls, copying data between systems, and allowing user access, and this typically means there will be a need to modify the network configuration.

- **System administrators**   Every migration involves both database resources and OS resources. This means it is necessary to either have your DBAs perform double-duty as system administrators (if they have the skills) or have dedicated system administrators.

- **Storage administrators**   Since every database requires storage, storage administrators must be included as part of the migration project team.

- **Quality assurance and testing resources**   Before putting any new system into production, it is crucial to test it to make sure that all of the applications work properly. This involves QA analysts and testing resources. If Oracle testing tools such as Real Application Testing and Database Replay are going to be used, it's important that the QA and testing resources are familiar with how those tools will be used.

As you can see, for moderate to large migration projects, many people will be involved.

TIP & TECHNIQUE
Don't be hesitant to bring in extra help if you need it. Getting the help and expertise that you need to be successful is far better than trying to get by with available resources and failing.

In-House Resources

If the resources listed previously are available in house, that's always a good choice. In order to use in-house resources, you must make sure that they are available full-time for the migration project. If the resources are not able to be dedicated to the migration project and they are the only resources available, this often leads to delays and/or project failures. Dedicated resources are simply necessary for project success.

Additional Resources

If you are going to bring in outside resources to help with the data migration, you will need to make sure that the resources are experienced with this type of migration and have the right type of skills that are needed for the project. Additional resources are a great way to help with the database migration project because you can often find people who have already experienced the type of migration that you are performing.

There are many skilled resources or companies that you can bring on board to help with your data migration. Depending on the method that you have chosen, there are organizations that are skilled and experienced in every type of data migration. Engaging outside resources that can bring specific skills and experience to the table will increase your chance of success.

Budget

Probably the biggest deciding factor of which migration method you choose is the project's budget. The amount of time it takes to perform the migration depends on the number of staff dedicated to the project as well as any additional software and hardware resources. These all relate back to budget.

No data migration is free; there is always a cost, sometimes significant. If additional software is required, such as Oracle GoldenGate, licenses must be acquired. If additional hardware is required, both hardware and, potentially, additional licenses must be purchased.

Unfortunately, we have often seen a migration project's budget be severely underestimated, and as a result the migration ends up exhausting the planned budget. It is therefore crucial that the project's budget does take into account the project's migration goals, human resources, licensing, and hardware costs.

Additional Software

As mentioned previously, almost every migration involves the purchase (or exchange) of software licenses. When you are moving a database from one system to another system, the database licenses will most likely change, especially if the number of CPUs or cores changes. If you are migrating from one version of software to a newer one, the licensing cost will most likely change.

Database licenses are a complex issue and we will not attempt to explain them here; we simply stress that software licenses are an important component of the migration budget and their costs must be researched. Consult your software vendor for licensing costs early in the budgeting process.

Equipment Resources

Almost every data migration is done for the purpose of moving to new hardware. The new hardware may or may not match the same architecture and OS of the original system. If it does match, the migration will be much simpler, of course, but in many cases one of the primary goals of the migration is to move from one architecture to another, for any number of reasons.

Depending on whether or not the new systems are of the same hardware architecture and OS, the number of migration options will also vary. The number and type of CPU cores will dictate licensing costs; in addition, the new OS/hardware environment will most likely require additional training and staffing needs. For example, if you are migrating from Microsoft SQL Server to Oracle, you might not have the in-house resources to manage the new system without hiring additional help.

Infrastructure

Infrastructure is an important part of every migration. If you are adding new systems, you must provide sufficient network and storage connectivity to those new servers. Necessary infrastructure includes

- Rack space

- Power

- Cooling

- Network cabling

- Storage cabling

- Network switch space

- Storage switch space

- Other components, such as routing, firewalls, and so forth

Without proper infrastructure planning, your migration efforts are likely to run into unexpected problems during a crucial project phase. Remember that when migrating data, the speed of the network between the source of the migration and the target of the migration is important.

Proper infrastructure planning usually involves including the systems administration, network administration, and storage administration teams early in the planning phase alongside the database and application server groups. Our experience has shown that combining forces as early as possible during the planning stage guarantees the project will run more smoothly and efficiently.

Additional Considerations

In addition to the requirements covered previously, there are a number of other requirements that will further limit which migration methods are available in a given scenario. These include data types, database features, and so forth. If the structure of the database or the data is going to change, some options such as Data Guard cannot be used because they require an identical database on the target system.

Data Types

Typically a migration from Oracle to Oracle does not involve data type changes, unless of course changing data types is part of the reason for the migration. For example, when data type conversion from BasicFile LOBs to SecureFile LOBs is a project requirement, there can be a significant impact on project timelines, especially for testing the results of the conversion.

When moving from SQL Server to Oracle or from other databases to Oracle, it is often necessary to change data types. This is important because it will limit the choices of data migration methods. The fewer changes that will be made to the target database, the more options will be there are for data migration.

Database Features

Often data migrations are performed in order to be able to take advantage of new database features. In the past few years Oracle has added many new features that make a database upgrade worthwhile, especially when one or more new features enhance both application functionality and performance. These features might include the following:

- **Partitioning**   Oracle is constantly working to improve partitioning. In recent releases Oracle has introduced more compound partitioning types as well as new types such as interval partitioning.

- **LOBs**   SecureFile LOBs are much more efficient and extremely fast as compared to legacy LOBs. We have migrated databases and converted to SecureFile LOBs on several occasions.

- **Security**   When migrating to a new platform, it is often convenient to enhance the security model of the database. For example, during a recent upgrade/migration, we implemented encrypted tablespaces.

- **Storage**   We have found that a great time to move from non-ASM to ASM storage is during a migration, since this provides all of the additional benefits of ASM storage technology.

As discussed earlier, there are a lot of other reasons to migrate data, the most common of them being a hardware refresh.

Infrastructure Capabilities

During the data migration itself, it's important not to neglect existing infrastructure capabilities. If you do not have a sufficiently fast network as well as storage of sufficient capacity and throughput, the data migration will suffer in terms of schedule and efficiency. The infrastructure will be the conduit through which the data moves from the source to the target system. The speed will vary depending on the speed of the network and the number of components that the data must travel through.

Making Your Decision

So, how do you decide on the type of data migration that you want to perform? There are a few major factors and a number of minor factors that have been discussed in this chapter that will absolutely affect the type of database migration that you will be performing. The biggest of these factors is the downtime requirement. Because downtime requirement will vary by organization, it is important to lock down your specific needs. Let's take a look at how some of the major requirements can dictate your migration method. As always, everybody's requirements are different. Now that you are familiar with the major factors that impact your choice of database migration, it's time to make a choice by matching your specific requirements with a particular method.

How Downtime Affects Your Choice of Method

The downtime factor is very important. The shorter the downtime that you are allowed, the fewer migration options that are available to you. The migration methods in Table 2-2 are listed in the approximate order of slowest to fastest. This list takes into consideration the amount of time that the applications will be unavailable

Method	Speed
Export/Import	Slowest method; data is exported at a specific point in time.
Data Pump	Faster than Export/Import; point-in-time copy.
RMAN	Faster than Export/Import and Data Pump; point-in-time copy.
Transportable Tablespace	Faster than the previous methods; limited mainly by the time to copy the data.
Cross-Platform Tablespace Migration with Incremental Backup	Faster than the previous methods; the time for cutover is dictated by the time to do the incremental backup and restore.
Data Guard	Fast; the cutover time is limited to the time to do the switchover.
GoldenGate	Fastest, with minimal or zero downtime. Applications can be simultaneously connected to both source and target.

TABLE 2-2. *Options Listed by Downtime*

during the cutover. Note that these methods do not stand alone—as you have seen earlier in this chapter, there are many variations on these methods.

So, if your applications are restricted by a very short time frame for cutover, your options are limited to Data Guard or GoldenGate.

NOTE
GoldenGate requires an initial migration, which might be accomplished using any of the other methods.

How Versions Affect Your Choice of Method

The target Oracle version is another important factor in choosing a migration method. As Table 2-3 indicates, if the target of your migration is a different Oracle version, you can rule out using RMAN or Data Guard for the initial migration.

So, if you wish to modify the target database, you are limited to Export/Import, Data Pump, or GoldenGate. You can start to see how your decision might be made for you.

How Architecture Affects Your Choice of Method

There might be other factors involved in your decision-making process besides the downtime requirement and versioning requirement. One of these might be the architecture of the system. If you are moving to a different architecture, your options might be limited by that choice (see Table 2-4).

Method	Version Consideration
Export/Import	Target can be a different Oracle version
Data Pump	Target can be a different Oracle version
RMAN	Target must be the same version
Transportable Tablespace Sets	Limited (minor release changes)
Cross-Platform Tablespace Migration with Incremental Backup	Limited (minor release changes)
Data Guard	Target must be the same version
GoldenGate	Target can be a different Oracle version

TABLE 2-3. *Migration Options Versus Database Version Considerations*

Method	Different Architecture
Export/Import	Allowed
Data Pump	Allowed
RMAN	Not allowed
Transportable Tablespace Sets	Allowed
Cross-Platform Tablespace Migration with Incremental Backup	Allowed
Data Guard	Not allowed
GoldenGate	Allowed

TABLE 2-4. *Impact of Architecture Transition Upon Migration Methods*

How Database Transformation Affects Your Choice of Method

A database transformation occurs when you change database objects during your migration. This is a very common occurrence, and the perfect time to transform the database is when performing a migration. The following kinds of transformations are possible:

- **Partitioning** Adding partitions, converting to a different partitioning type, and so forth. This is a very common type of transformation in data migrations. During the migration itself is the best time to actually add partitioning.

- **Security** Adding encryption or a Hardware Security Module (HSM). Since adding encryption, such as encrypted tablespaces, usually requires rebuilding the tablespace structure, a migration is ideal for this type of operation.

- **LOB transformation** Changing to SecureFile LOBs. SecureFile LOBs are a new way to store LOB data, introduced in Oracle Database 11*g*. The performance of SecureFile LOBs far exceeds the performance of traditional LOB data.

- **Compression** Compressing tables or tablespaces. This can be done either within a migration or as a stand-alone task. However, compressing during a migration can be much more efficient.

- **Other** There are a number of other features that you might enable as part of the migration; some features require data transformation, while others do not.

Whether each method allows for transformation is shown in Table 2-5.

Method	Transformation Allowed
Export/Import	Yes
Data Pump	Yes
RMAN	No
Transportable Tablespace	No
Cross-Platform Tablespace Migration with Incremental Backup	No
Data Guard	No
GoldenGate	Yes

TABLE 2-5. *Options Listed by Whether Transformation Allowed*

TIP & TECHNIQUE
There are various techniques for transforming the database during a migration. They are discussed throughout this book.

Decision Summary

As you have seen, there are a number of factors that will dictate which methods are available for you to choose. Listing the factors in a table provides an easy way to see what migration methods might be eliminated, as shown in Table 2-6.

Method	Speed	Target Version	Different Architecture	Transformation
Export/Import	7 Slowest	May be different	Allowed	Yes
Data Pump	6	May be different	Allowed	Yes
RMAN	5	Must be same	Not Allowed	No
Transportable Tablespace Sets	4	Limited	Allowed	No
Cross-Platform Tablespace Migration with Incremental Backup	3	Limited	Allowed	No
Data Guard	2	Must be same	Not Allowed	No
GoldenGate	1 Fastest	May be different	Allowed	Yes

TABLE 2-6. *Migration Summary*

Now you can see how your decision is limited based on your specific criteria for migration. Depending on your requirements, the choice of migration method becomes more obvious. Of course, your specific requirements might allow for different combinations of these methods.

Hybrid Solutions

The solutions listed previously are not exclusive of each other. In fact, several of the solutions can be used together. This is especially true of Oracle GoldenGate. Oracle GoldenGate is a replication tool. It includes a facility to perform the initial data migration, but that facility is not extremely efficient. When we perform a GoldenGate migration, we combine it with other methods for doing the initial setup and migration. Let's look at an example of this.

GoldenGate Migration Example

The basic idea of using GoldenGate for a data migration is to start replicating data, perform the initial migration, and then sync up the changes that have occurred since the point in time that the initial migration occurred. Let's look at these steps in a little more detail:

1. *Start replication.* To start replication, GoldenGate extract processes mine transactions from the redo log. Once REPLICAT processes are running, all changes are being saved.

2. *Initial migration.* There are a number of options to perform the migration. You can use Export/Import, Data Pump, hardware cloning, transportable tablespaces, and so forth.

   Tablespaces were created with encryption. This encryption was set up using a hardware security module.

   Once the tablespaces were created, Export/Import was used to create the schema objects.

   The schema was then modified to include transformations such as SecureFile LOBs, partitioning, and so forth.

   The data was then migrated using an activated physical standby via Flashback Database.

3. *Sync up.* The data was synced up by enabling GoldenGate REPLICAT processes. The REPLICATs were started using the SCN that matches when the guaranteed restore point was created. This gave us the last transaction on the source database.

Once the data was synced up, both the source and target had the same data, even though they were different versions of Oracle existing on different hardware architectures and for which several database objects had been transformed.

At this point, we were then able to test the applications, perform final QA verification, and then move users to the new system.

As you can see, this is a very elegant solution using three migration methods: Export/Import, Data Pump, and GoldenGate. More details are provided later in this book.

Summary

As you have seen in this chapter, there is no one migration path that is right for everybody. You must customize your own migration path based on your needs. There are many different methods of database upgrade, migration and transformation. Each method is chosen based on your needs, which could include

- Source and target versions
- Transformation requirements
- Schedule
- Equipment and infrastructure availability
- Budget
- Available resources

All of these factors are used to determine the particular method that you need for your specific project. No two projects are exactly alike. The different methodologies and technologies can be combined to create a plan that best meets your specific needs. The methods that we have provided you with are a guideline that is used along with some examples. You might choose one of these methods, or a combination of these methods or even develop your own unique method.

Based on your requirements, your choices might be limited; however, there are always combinations that might work as well. Hybrid solutions of multiple methods usually are the best way to go.

CHAPTER
3

Migration/Transformation/
Upgrade Methodologies

I n order to begin a database upgrade, migration, and/or transformation, you must first devise a plan. This plan must include the way that you propose to attack the problem. The collection of methods or ways you intend to go about this task is the methodology. There are multiple methods and combinations of methods to perform this task. This chapter will provide examples of some of those methods and how you might use them to choose your path.

Planning the Migration Process

In the classic 1951 science fiction movie *When Worlds Collide*, the world is literally coming to an end. Astronomers have discovered that a wandering star and its habitable planet are approaching Earth swiftly on a collision course, and in a matter of months Earth will be pulverized into dust. But a few forward-thinking technocrats develop a plan: before Earth is destroyed, build spaceships that will transport enough people and supplies to the star's habitable planet in hopes of finding a new home to keep humanity alive. As the spacecraft takes shape, the camera continually focuses on a sign that says *"Waste anything but time. Time is the one thing we do not have."* As the drama reaches its peak, a group of humans makes the perilous but ultimately successful journey to the wayward planet, and humanity survives.

If this movie synopsis sounds a bit too much like your last database migration/transformation/upgrade project, then you've invested in the right book. We believe that a successful transition must address the basic fact that for any migration, transformation, or upgrade project to succeed, we must recognize that ultimately our enemy is just one thing: *time*.

TIP & TECHNIQUE
Planning the migration is the most important step in the migration process.

Determining the "Window of Inopportunity"

The most crucial obstacle to the success of your project plan is application downtime—something we prefer to view as the "window of inopportunity" for the application's user community. Of course, what is considered acceptable for this window will vary dramatically based on the type(s) of application workloads the target databases support. However, even here we can make some observations:

■ *A relatively small amount of application data is truly needed for the most crucial business operations.* Even the most complex transaction processing systems we have encountered generally house their transactional data within a few key tables; the remainder of the data needed for transactions is often quite static and housed in lookup tables—for example, U.S. postal codes, customer identifiers, transaction types, and so on. Therefore, the migration/transformation/upgrade process simply needs to focus on making data within these few tables available as soon as possible while perhaps making the other data available from alternate sources.

■ *Business users may actually be able to tolerate a reasonable length of time during which limited read-only access to application data is available.* For example, during the complex upgrade of a database from Sybase to Oracle, we discovered that the most crucial application—an audio conference reservations system—was able to tolerate several hours of read-only access. Proper coordination with the user community ensured that the database migration occurred during the quietest hours of an off-peak business cycle; users were able to record new orders via manual methods and re-enter them immediately after the most crucial application data had been loaded and validated.

■ *The older the data, the less value it holds.* In our experience, this generalization tends to hold true for most organizations. Rarely does the entire contents of a data warehouse need to be transmogrified and made immediately available in its new form; in fact, many businesses leverage the window of inopportunity to either purge or archive their oldest, least valuable data.

Application Workload Categorization

Our experience has shown that an organization's application workloads and the databases that support them tend to fall into one of just three broad categories, OLTP, hybrid, or DSS, as visualized in Figure 3-1. We'll differentiate these three categories in this section.

OLTP

For databases that support *online transaction processing (OLTP)* applications, it's crucial that any downtime is either eliminated or of such short duration that there is no disruption to your organization's business. But we contend that there's absolutely no harm in posing the following question to your organization: *What is the absolutely true minimum downtime we could accept without a serious financial penalty, including the potential loss of customer goodwill through lack of information about our planned upgrades?*

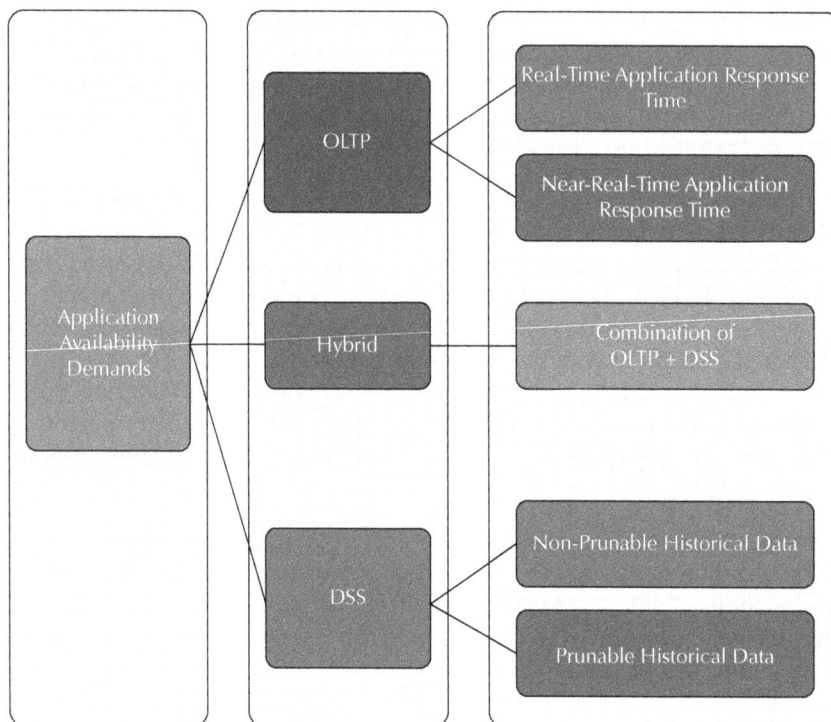

FIGURE 3-1. *Decision tree for application workloads*

Ultimately, there are only two answers:

■ **Real-time OLTP**   If your database is truly supporting any real-time OLTP application workloads—for example, a stock options trading system that's responsible for accurately recording thousands of extremely volatile financial transactions that must complete within a matter of milliseconds—then equally extreme measures and corresponding technologies must be employed to guarantee absolutely no disruption of service to the application system's customers.

■ **Near-real-time OLTP**   Any other answer from your business organization means that you have much more flexibility in deploying an appropriate migration/upgrade solution. For example, an application workload that supports a manufacturing system has peaks and valleys in its availability demands, and that means we can concentrate on leveraging those valleys as windows of opportunity for completing a migration within a more reasonable time frame: perhaps several minutes instead of mere milliseconds.

DSS

Databases that support *decision support system (DSS)* application workloads, on the other hand, will most likely be able to accept much longer outage periods than databases that support OLTP applications, simply because the applications' users already accept some reasonable outage periods during *extraction, transformation, and load (ETL)* operations. From our viewpoint, DSS workloads include

- Enterprise resource planning (ERP) systems

- Oracle Business Intelligence Enterprise Edition (OBIEE) systems

- Online analytical processing (OLAP) systems, including Oracle database's built-in OLAP capabilities or other packaged applications

- Data mining applications, including "big data" enabling tools like Hadoop or SAP/HANA

- Regional data marts or other subsets of larger DSS applications

- Ad hoc queries against time-sensitive data

- Other "home-grown" proprietary applications that produce a read-mostly workload

These databases often employ data partitioning methods to provide maximum availability to *time-sensitive* data—for example, the most recent day, week, or month of "scrubbed" sales statistics, including a running total of sales commissions about to be paid to your organization's sales force—so our focus during a migration/transformation/upgrade project is simple: *We must provide access to the most crucial recent data to our organization's application users as soon as possible.* Once that most crucial recent data has been loaded, our focus shifts to providing the *next* most crucial set of historical data, and we repeat this process until all required data has been loaded.

Fortunately, these migration activities also provide an excellent opportunity to purge truly ancient data from our DSS systems' tables, so it is equally important for us to ask our user community a simple question: Do we *really* need to load all this data? Because if there is any data we can *truly discard* forever—or at least *archive*—now would be a great time to do so.

Hybrid

Finally, the most challenging application workload environments are those in which the databases support both OLTP and DSS systems—what most Oracle DBAs typically refer to as *hybrid* databases. We suggest that—like the databases themselves—a hybrid migration/transformation/upgrade methodology must be employed, but that methodology must still focus *first* on the most time-sensitive systems—typically, the real-time OLTP (RTOLTP) application workloads. For hybrid databases, it's therefore extremely important to identify any RTOLTP systems and their relationships to any application workloads internal to the same hybrid database as well as any other external database systems that the hybrid database feeds.

Capturing Your Migration/ Transformation/Upgrade Plan: The Master Checklist

Surgeons use protocols when they perform procedures on their patients in an operating room. Commercial airline pilots use takeoff, in-flight, and landing checklists to ensure all passengers arrive safely at their destination. The information contained within our Oracle databases is often the key to life-and-death decisions (or at least important to avoiding mild inconveniences). As seasoned professionals, Oracle DBAs need checklists too. We have found this to be especially true during a complex migration/transformation/upgrade process.

We provide detailed examples of migration, transformation, and upgrade checklists throughout the upcoming chapters. These checklists are also available at www.OraclePressBooks.com, but for now let's focus on the scope of the checklist. At a minimum, it should capture the details as described in the following sections.

Milestones

Every good migration/transformation/upgrade checklist has a series of well-defined steps grouped into a set of milestones. Each milestone *must* be completed before proceeding to the next milestone. Obviously, milestones ensure that each set of tasks is performed in the proper order—but just as importantly, no task should ever be done ahead of schedule, either!

Further, each milestone should reflect its independence or dependence on other tasks in the process so that there is absolutely no confusion as to why and when something must be completed before moving on to the next milestone.

TIP & TECHNIQUE

Milestones should be reviewed in the migration status meetings at least once a week. Milestones should be assigned to particular people or groups.

Tasks, Responsibilities, and Actions

At the heart of the migration/transformation/upgrade plan are the tasks that make up each milestone. These include but are not limited to the following:

- Command scripts, SQL statements, or other database-level commands to be executed to *perform* each task

- Commands or queries to run that will *verify* a task's successful completion

- The expected *output* from a verification command or query (for example, a query that should return zero rows if a particular task has been successful)

It's also crucial to decide exactly which member of the migration/transformation/upgrade team is responsible for which task at any given point in the process. This includes listing the backup person for each primary team member in case the primary is unavailable at a crucial time.

Timelines and Expected Task Timings

As the migration/transformation/upgrade plan is refined during its recommended minimum of *three* iterations, you should record the time it takes to perform crucial individual steps. (We will explain our reasoning for three iterations of your plan shortly.) This will give you the confidence that a particular task will complete at the expected pace when it's time to perform it in the production environment. This knowledge is invaluable when you are trying to ascertain whether something may be wrong because it's taking much too long to complete—or conversely finished much too quickly.

Fallback Plans

When an airline pilot judges that a safe landing is impossible, she pushes the throttles forward, pulls back on the control yoke, and goes around for another try. Likewise, you are responsible for verifying that each milestone's detailed steps have been completed successfully and have been checked off … and then, and only then, committing to and communicating a *go/no-go decision*. This provides the opportunity to decide whether to reverse the migration/transformation/upgrade operation and fall back to the original environment.

It is critical that you ensure a *fallback plan* exists for each milestone in case there are any doubts about the success of the overall plan. In our experience, it's always the better decision to resist the urge to continue with a partially failed migration/transformation/upgrade and then clean up the mess later. And be sure to remember that falling back may also require the restoration of older database objects, removal of new data in existing tables, and reverting to prior versions of application code, especially PL/SQL objects like packages, procedures, functions, sequences, and triggers.

TIP & TECHNIQUE

We've noticed that seasoned IT professionals tend to be pessimistic by nature because they are well acquainted with Finagle's Law: Anything that can go wrong, will—at the worst possible moment. And don't forget Czuprynski's Corollary to Finagle's Law: Nothing works in production like it does in test.

Expected Results

One area that we have noticed is often neglected in a migration/transformation/ upgrade plan is the expected end results of the process. Here are some examples:

- For an Oracle database that has been *migrated* to a different physical environment—say, to a different host, a new storage array, a different RAID configuration for its database files, or perhaps even a different operating system—what are the minimum expectations of performance improvement? And if the database has been migrated to less powerful hardware, what is the maximum tolerance for comparative performance degradation?

- A database that's undergone a *transformation* will have an entirely different set of expectations that will need to be evaluated. Take the example of transforming an Oracle Database 11.2.0.3 database's existing LOBs from BasicFile to SecureFile LOBs format. The additional encryption, security, de-duplication, or compression features we've chosen to implement during the transformation should have also provided at least some performance benefits—for example, more efficient use of UNDO segments—but have there been any significant trade-offs, like unexpectedly higher CPU utilization when accessing encrypted or tightly compressed LOBs?

- Application workloads for a database that's been *upgraded* to a later release— for example, from Oracle Database 11.2.0.3 to Oracle Database 12.1.0.1— will almost certainly demonstrate performance improvement for at least some queries. But it's almost equally certain that some queries will show diminished performance as well, because the SQL statement optimizer has undergone major upgrades for Oracle Database 12*c*.

The most important decisions that need to be incorporated into this part of the plan concern what happens after the migration/transformation/upgrade has been completed, exactly how much performance degradation is tolerable based on the original baseline of acceptable application workload performance, and which tools will be used to determine any true deflections from that baseline. That will be a primary focus of the remaining sections of this chapter.

Testing Your Chosen Migration/ Transformation/Upgrade Path

We have had our share of long nights during upgrades that never completed, transformations that wouldn't transform, and migrations that failed miserably within their first few moments. Our combined experience has taught us that a minimum of *three* complete migration/transformation/upgrade "dry runs" is usually required to shake out the majority of crucial issues.

Here's why: If it appears that everything worked perfectly during the *first* cycle of testing, then you have most likely missed detecting a small but crucial failure during your post-migration verification process. If everything appears to have worked perfectly during the first *and* second test cycles, you may have just been lucky. But by the *third* iteration of the migration/transformation/upgrade process, the migration team should have accumulated an approximate metric of how much time is necessary for each step of the process, as well as the process's potential trouble spots.

TIP & TECHNIQUE

Read the fine print. This especially holds true when performing an upgrade that requires installation of patches for either Oracle Clusterware, Oracle Grid Infrastructure, or Oracle Database binaries; unfortunately, the documentation from Oracle is legendary for confusing and sometimes even contradictory instructions. And it's important to always have a fallback plan should a patch fail to install properly. Remember the immortal words of Pete Seeger: "Knowledge is what you get when you read the fine print. Experience is what you get when you don't."

Building a Migration Plan

One of the most important tasks of planning the migration is to build the migration plan. This could be a few pages for a small migration or a huge undertaking for a large migration. Small migrations might involve one or two people working closely together, whereas large migrations could involve many people, many different departments, and months of work.

The larger and more complex the migration, the more important the migration plan is. This is due to the number of people involved and the amount of work to be coordinated. Very complex migrations could take months and numerous people to make the project successful.

The migration plan must be clear and outline what tasks need to be accomplished and what resources are available to accomplish them. It must include all aspects of the project that will lead to a successful conclusion. In addition, the migration plan should be independently reviewed. With very complex plans, it would be useful to use a tool that allows resources to be scheduled, but the format is not as important as just having a workable plan.

TIP & TECHNIQUE

Several consulting firms offer migration planning services. The actual migration is performed by in-house resources, but they have the benefit of the independent views, ideas, and experiences incorporated into the migration plan.

In the next few sections we will break down the components of the migration plan into several topics. These topics are all integral pieces of the complete migration plan. They include the following:

- **Migration steps**   These are the complete steps necessary to detail the work to be done. These steps do not need to be too detailed in the high level plan, although the details should be documented in the steps that the resources will be following.

- **Resource allocation**   If you don't know who's going to be doing what, you might find yourself short on resources. It is very important to ensure that there are sufficient resources to complete the project.

TIP & TECHNIQUE

Be sure to plan for what to do if a resource becomes unavailable; for example, what alternate resources will be available should a co-worker become ill and is unable to complete the project?

- **Milestones**   How do you know if you are on target if you don't have a target? It is important to have milestones that you can strive to hit. Reporting reached milestones to management is important to show the progress of the migration.

- **Quality assurance (QA)**   It is important that you plan for QA resources in the migration plan. They are an integral part of the plan.

■ **Change requests**   As part of every project that involves doing anything related to production systems, there should be some sort of change request process. This means that everything you do that potentially affects the system must be documented and go through the change approval process. We know that this can be a pain, but it is necessary.

■ **User acceptance testing (UAT)**   There should be a description of what acceptance criteria will be accepted for approval from the testing group. This should also be detailed in the plan.

As you have seen here, there are many components of the migration documentation. Let's look at each of these components in a little more detail.

Migration Steps

The migration steps are the highest level of the migration plan. This component must include all of the major tasks needed to complete the migration. If you think of this in terms of writing a chapter in a book or writing a paper, the migration steps would be the level 1 headings. Everything else is details. This component is the high-level overview of the migration plan and must be complete in terms of the steps.

TIP & TECHNIQUE
We always write my books by laying out the level 1 headings, then filling in the level 2 and sometimes level 3 headings before even beginning to write any content. This way we have a complete outline and understand the organization of the chapter before we get started. The same approach is useful for a migration plan.

So, let's take a look at the high-level steps necessary to perform a theoretical migration. Let's make this a migration using GoldenGate for minimal downtime.

Step	Description
Planning	This step is where you work out all of the details and approvals. You address questions such as these: Why is the migration happening? What new features of Oracle are you going to take advantage of?
Core Team	The core team for the project should be documented. Who is the migration owner? Where do approvals come from?

(Continues)

Step	Description
Budget	An overall budget should be calculated. How much is the estimated cost? What budget will this come out of? What outside resources are needed, and how much will they cost?
Resources	The team should be described. What is the team going to look like? What external resources are needed, and from where will they be obtained? What roles will the teams play?
Dependencies	What other applications and/or databases does this database depend on? What other applications or databases depend on this database? The dependencies must be thoroughly documented.
Pre-Migration Steps	This is where you will look at the current database, extract metadata. What does that tell you about what changes need to be made in order to migrate successfully.
GoldenGate Setup	To begin the migration, you must start capturing transactions so that you will be able to bring the new system into synchronization with the current production system. The first step is to install, configure, and start capturing transactions with GoldenGate.
Initial Data Load	Once GoldenGate is up and running, it is necessary to do the initial data load. You can choose any of several methods to perform the initial data load.
Data Validation	After the initial data load has occurred, you should perform an initial data validation before enabling replicats. You can do this via row counts or other methods. There are numerous methods and optimizations.
Enable Replicats	Once you are satisfied with the initial data load, you can enable the replicats. Depending on how long the data load took, how many transactions occurred, and the size of the database, this might take a while.
Testing	Once the data is in sync, you have a great opportunity to perform some basic and advanced testing. How to enable flashback and test during a migration will be discussed in many of the upcoming chapters.

Step	Description
QA	At this point in the project you must conduct QA on the soon-to-be production database. Tips and techniques will be presented in subsequent chapters.
Performance Tests	In addition to testing and QA, performance tests are recommended. Tips and techniques will be presented in subsequent chapters.
Final Cutover	This is the final phase where you perform the final cutover from the old production system to the new production system. Detailed plans on how to do this are covered in the section "Production Cutover" later in this chapter.
Post-Migration Support	During the burn-in period, the migration team should monitor the new production system and be ready to address any issues that might come up immediately.
Final Report	You should prepare a report on the migration, including any issues that occurred and how they were addressed.

As you can see, this will be a fairly good-sized plan, even for fairly small migrations. By carefully planning and documenting your migration plan, your chance of a successful migration will be enhanced.

Resource Allocation

If you don't have sufficient resources both in number and in skills, your migration is destined to be unsuccessful. Depending on your migration method, you might need systems, network, storage, DBA (Oracle, SQL Server), GoldenGate, and other resources. It's not enough to just have DBA resources. If you are doing a migration with transportable tablespaces, you should have a DBA on hand who has experience performing that type of migration. If you are doing a migration using Data Pump, you should have resources who are experienced with that technology.

Outside resources are required for many data migrations, not just because the companies don't have the right in-house skills, but because they don't have enough resources. A large data migration might take a fairly large team. If you can't dedicate your own people for the number of days, weeks, or months that the migration takes, you need outside resources. In addition, outside resources can provide hands-on training and knowledge transfer to help your resources increase their skills. Having a mentor to share experiences can be extremely valuable.

TIP & TECHNIQUE
So, how do you find the trusted advisor, migration expert, and consultant that you need to help your project be successful? You can ask for recommendations from your hardware/software vendor, ask other people in your company, or even search the Internet. Look for a company with a good track record and ask for references. Make sure that these resources are not doing this type of migration for the first time with you.

Once you have pulled together your team, add them to the migration plan so that you know what resources are needed and when. Every task should have at least one resource attached to it.

Milestones

Milestones provide a great way of tracking your progress, and also provide a way to establish when you will pay your outside resources for the tasks that they have completed. A milestone should be measureable and attached to some sort of deliverable. Here are some examples of milestones:

- OS installed on new server
- Oracle installed and configured on new server
- Database built
- GoldenGate extracts and pumps running
- Metadata extracted and run on new database
- Data pump completed
- Data validation completed
- QA completed
- Documentation delivered
- Production cutover completed
- Post cutover support completed

Quality Assurance

QA is an important part of every data migration. There are several opportunities during the data migration to perform QA: at the end of the initial migration, just prior to production cutover, or during production cutover. You can perform one or more QA tests depending on your environment and requirements.

Without QA, you cannot be assured that the new environment is functioning properly. The QA tests should be thorough and complete. Most companies already have a complete QA test that can be used for this task.

TIP & TECHNIQUE
The QA test might involve a complete test just after the initial data load and a mini test just prior to production cutover.

Change Requests

Most large operations require a change request for anything that will be affecting a production system. Usually you do not have to get a change request to modify a system that is not yet in production. So, the new production system can be treated as a non-production system until such a time as it is deemed to still be production.

Because these are production systems, change requests must be submitted to the change review board for approval. These requests must be submitted well in advance of when you plan to make the actual changes. Therefore, the change requests should be scheduled in the migration plan itself, so that they are submitted in a timely manner and processed along with the rest of the migration schedule.

User Acceptance Testing

Another important component of the migration plan is user acceptance testing (UAT), which is a bit different from QA testing in that it is geared more toward the user experience. User acceptance testing can include the QA testing, if desired, as well as performance testing and functional testing. If UAT involves actual users, they should be scheduled in advance.

In many cases the functional testing component is done as part of QA testing. The same test results may be used to meet the qualifications for UAT. QA testing typically doesn't include performance testing.

Performance Testing

Performance testing is used to validate that the new platform is as fast as, or faster than, the old platform—that is, if that is your goal. Typically, a migration occurs because of the need to improve the performance of the application. If this is the case, performance testing should be performed. Performance tests can be very complex and take a significant time to run, which means getting baseline performance results sometimes might be difficult to achieve.

TIP & TECHNIQUE

To gauge how well the new system is performing, you must have something to compare against. This means running a performance baseline against the current production machine. This can sometimes be difficult to do. Tools such as Oracle's Real Application Testing package, which includes Database Replay and SQL Performance Analyzer, can be extremely helpful.

A performance baseline involves running performance tests against the current production hardware. In a 24×7 production environment, this may be difficult to do, but if possible, a performance baseline should be taken. These results can be used to compare performance with the new platform.

Performance tests should be run against the new platform. These results should be compared with the performance baseline taken from the existing production platform. Once these two have been compared and reported on, you will be assured that the new system should perform as required. Of course, you never really know until you go into production, so close monitoring for the first few weeks is necessary.

Functional Testing

Functional testing is basically testing the functionality of the system. This involves creating test scenarios and validating that the application is returning the correct data. Functional testing and QA testing are sometimes the same. If the QA testing is comprehensive, the results can satisfy the UAT functional testing requirements. If not, a separate set of tests must be run.

As you can see from this section, the migration plan is critical to planning a successful migration. Planning is not enough: you must thoroughly document what you intend to accomplish, thereby creating a migration plan.

Production Cutover

You've created the migration checklist; all required resources have been retained, assigned their duties, and stand ready to assist in the migration/transformation/upgrade operation; and the final iteration of the minimum three executions of your migration plan has been completed successfully. Now all that's left to do is complete the task at hand: It's time to execute the plan in production.

Planning the Cutover to Production

Based on our experience, it's not uncommon to spend *two months* planning in advance for a production cutover that might take less than *20 minutes*. The goal of the production cutover—besides, of course, the obvious goal of a completely successful migration/transformation/upgrade accomplished within the target "window of inopportunity"—is that the application users notice *absolutely nothing different* about how their application workloads execute.

Database Verification

The most crucial aspect of a production cutover, of course, is that the target Oracle database itself has been migrated/transformed/upgraded according to the planned migration checklist. Verifying the successful production cutover includes checking the sources described in the following sections.

The Usual Suspects: Diagnostic and Trace Files

The target database's *alert log* provides a reliable and unequivocal source of validation for a successful production cutover, especially after a database upgrade operation has been completed. If any of the crucial components of the database are not performing correctly, the alert log is usually the first place to look for evidence of an impending failure. If any issues are related to user sessions' server processes or database background processes, the alert log will also contain references to corresponding trace files, dump files, or core dumps that should be investigated for more detailed diagnostic information and retained for eventual shipment to Oracle Technical Support for their diagnosis and solution recommendations.

If the target database has been upgraded to Oracle Database Release 11.1.0.7 or later, don't neglect to check the Automatic Diagnostic Repository (ADR) for any unexpected problems and their corresponding incidents. ADR information can always be accessed through the ADR command interface (ADRCI); however, if Oracle Database 11*g* Grid Control, Oracle Database 11*g* Database Control, or Oracle Database 12*c* Cloud Control has been configured, then consider using the Oracle Enterprise Manager Support Workbench to access ADR information.

Often Neglected: Logs for Data Migration and Transformation

Depending on the migration/transformation/upgrade method(s) that you have selected for moving data between the source and target databases, it's also important to verify *all* of the log files for the data transfer utilities that may have been used:

- Oracle SQL*Loader records the number of records that were successfully processed, inserted, rejected due to specific filter conditions, and—most importantly—tossed out as bad rows due to formatting errors.

- Likewise, Oracle Data Pump creates a log of which operations were completed successfully—including remapping and transformation of data, tables, and tablespaces—as well as any operations that may have failed.

- The success or failure of Transportable Tablespace operations is recorded in at least two places: within the corresponding DataPump log for the migration of the tablespace objects' metadata, and within the database's alert log for the successful plug-in of the migrated tablespaces. And don't forget to verify Recovery Manager (RMAN) logs if any of the target database's tablespaces were migrated from a source database of different *endianness*.

NOTE
We'll cover these different migration/transformation/ upgrade techniques in thorough detail throughout the chapters that follow.

Ensuring the Database's Data Integrity

In our experience, this part of the post-cutover verification can be the most tedious and nerve-wracking step of the process. However, if the minimum of three successful tests of the migration plans have been accomplished, it's much more unlikely that any data integrity issues will arise.

Static Verification

As an Oracle DBA, you should have full access to the expected row counts for each table within the source database(s) through either simple SELECT COUNT(*) FROM <schema>.<table_name> queries or queries against the query optimizer's statistics views (e.g., DBA_TABLES, DBA_INDEXES, and DBA_TAB_PARTITIONS). Remember that optimizer statistics may vary between source and target databases because of differences in the frequency at which they have been gathered; however, these crude counting methods are an excellent way to identify that a table, table partition, or index has not been loaded or created properly. Ideally, the expected results of these counts should have already been recorded in a simple SPOOLed text file so that they can be quickly cross-verified with your organization's preferred file-comparison tool.

Live Verification

The same resources who have been working alongside you as the migration/ transformation/upgrade process was developed, tested, and implemented are often the most valuable people to verify the success of the production cutover. Once you are satisfied with the results of all static verification methods, it's time to call in your most trusted allies—the Q/A resources, subject matter experts (SMEs), and any other trusted application users—and task them with deeper verification of their data.

Don't forget to inform the evaluation team testers that application performance may initially appear to be degraded if additional optimizer statistics (e.g., histograms) are still being gathered at this stage of the production cutover. Also, if some secondary indexes either are in the process of being created, have been made invisible, or have not even been created, the evaluation team may encounter unexpectedly poorer query performance. This variance against expected application performance should most certainly be noted, especially when the target database has just been migrated to an engineered platform. (We'll discuss the special ramifications of not creating secondary indexes on tables in the upcoming chapter on migrating to engineered platforms like Oracle Exadata.)

Automated Verification
Finally, to mitigate the time and expense of developing and implementing these mainly manual processes, you might consider an automated database comparison tool like Oracle GoldenGate Veridata that can compare and contrast the contents of the original source versus the contents of the target database. Note that Oracle *does* require separate licensing for Veridata, but you may be able to negotiate a lower cost for its one-time use during your migration/transformation/upgrade process.

Application Server Migration
Just about any client that needs to connect to an upgraded database will most likely perform better with—and even may require installation of!—the appropriate Oracle Client software. It may seem to be a minor step, but implementing new client connectivity software may actually introduce additional variables into your migration/transformation/upgrade testing plan, especially when applications need to take advantage of some of the newer *security* features first available in Oracle Database 11*g* R1 and/or the latest Transaction Guard features that were recently made available in Oracle Database 12*c* R1. And don't forget that—depending on the relative age and operating system requirements of the application server—it may even be necessary to install the 32-bit Oracle Client version instead of the 64-bit version.

Evaluating Application Performance
Our experiences have shown us that complaints from users about post-cutover application performance issues are often quite subjective, may have nothing to do with the cutover at all, and can lead even the most experienced Oracle DBAs down blind alleys in an attempt to prove that there is truly nothing wrong with the database. But the good news is that the same tools and techniques we use to analyze application performance issues in day-to-day "firefighting" against poorly written SQL statements can be brought to bear to eliminate finger-pointing exercises during the post-cutover period.

Metrics: ADDM, AWR, ASH, and StatsPack

Gathering satisfactory metrics to back up your contention that the application is actually performing *no worse* than before the cutover is one of the best ways to alleviate any confrontations with application users, developers, and especially management personnel:

- If your organization has licensed the Diagnostic Pack for the source and target database environments, comparing Automatic Workload Repository (AWR) reports from the source and target databases for similar application workload periods is an excellent way to obtain objective analyses of how much better or worse the target database is performing versus the source database. Likewise, Oracle's Automatic Database Diagnostic Monitor (ADDM) tool can provide expert advice for tuning the target database based on AWR data … and it may even make several recommendations that identify problems that the user community hasn't even identified yet.

- For more detailed analysis, Active Session History (ASH) provides valuable data on database performance, often at a second-by-second interval. ASH also requires licensing the Diagnostic Pack for its use.

- If your organization has not licensed the Diagnostic Pack, you can use the venerable StatsPack tool without any additional licensing costs to assist in potential problem diagnosis. However, be aware that StatsPack's ability to analyze application performance issues is effectively limited to a minimum of a 15-minute window; only ASH in concert with AWR and ADDM provides deeper metric granularity, especially for Oracle Database 12*c* databases.

Automation: Real Application Testing Suite

Introduced in Oracle Database 11*g* R1, Oracle also offers the Real Application Testing Suite. This separately licensed package includes two sub-suites:

- **SQL Performance Analyzer (SPA)**   Offers the capability to compare actual SQL statement performance between the original source database and the new target database configuration.

- **Database Workload Capture and Replay**   Permits the capture of actual application workloads on the source system's database with virtually no penalty during those applications' execution. The applications' execution profiles thus captured are then replayable immediately against the eventual target system's environment so that any significant performance differences can be immediately discovered and the appropriate root cause(s) of the variances can be tracked down.

For Oracle Database 11*g* R2, these two sub-suites cooperate even more closely together to provide a simpler workflow for discovering the true causes of performance degradation well before a new system is deployed. And for Oracle Database 12*c* R1, there are extended cross-platform migration reporting and analysis features available. (We'll cover these tools in more details in an upcoming chapter.)

TIP & TECHNIQUE

If the goal of the migration/transformation/upgrade was to increase the performance of application workload(s), don't be surprised if you never receive an unsolicited compliment from the general user community about how much faster their data entry screens are now loading or how much more quickly their reports are executing. Of course, if even the slightest poor performance should unexpectedly result, don't be surprised that you will hear about it immediately.

Summary

Here's a quick summary of what we've covered in this chapter:

- No matter what type of migration/transformation/upgrade process you are involved with, it's important to remember that your enemy is always time, and it's the one thing you simply cannot waste.

- Choosing the right methodology for a migration/transformation/upgrade process is crucial, and the choice always depends on the application workload(s) that requires the least amount of downtime for your users.

- OLTP applications typically require much shorter outage time windows than DSS applications, so it's important to identify the most crucial OLTP application(s) in the system being converted.

- Migrating systems that support DSS applications likely permit longer outage periods but usually need a lot more time for loading data; therefore, it's usually best to concentrate on migrating/transforming/upgrading whichever DSS data that will be needed immediately once the system has been made available again, and transfer the less time-sensitive data later.

- No single migration/transformation/upgrade methodology fits all projects, so it's important to plan with maximum flexibility and a determination to use the right tool for the right job to guarantee success.

PART

II

Cross-Platform
Migration

CHAPTER
4

Oracle Data Guard

I n the previous chapter you were introduced to a number of different methods for performing data migrations and some of the pros and cons of those methods. In this chapter we will begin to look at some of those migration methods. When looking at the typical migration methods, many people don't consider Data Guard at all. Migrating databases with Data Guard is very restrictive, but if you are able to use this method, it is quite effective.

Data Guard Overview

Data Guard is Oracle's premier disaster recovery tool. By replicating log records and using the very efficient and fast recovery mechanism, one or more standby systems are maintained in either a local location or a remote location. The evolution of Data Guard has added features to maintain the standby system, detect errors, and even allow the standby to be used for read-only reporting while maintaining it as a standby in real time.

The primary and intended task of Data Guard is disaster recovery. While maintaining a standby system, additional benefits of Oracle Data Guard allow for reporting, testing, backups (instead of the primary server), and more. Data Guard was not really designed for data migration, but because of the efficiency and speed (and reliability) of the failover operation, Data Guard is ideal for data migration under certain strict criteria. Before we look at the criteria for migrating with Data Guard, let's look at a brief overview of Data Guard and its features.

What Is Data Guard?

Oracle Data Guard is a high availability and disaster recovery feature of the Oracle database. Data Guard is included with the Enterprise Edition of the database server and is an integral part of the Oracle Maximum Availability Architecture (MAA). Data Guard is essentially a built-in replication feature designed to allow for up to 30 standby databases from one primary database.

By replicating the entire database and keeping it in sync, the standby database can instantly take over in the event of the loss of the primary database server. This allows your business to keep running even in the event of a catastrophic failure. The mechanisms built into the Oracle database server are the result of many years of evolution, making it rock solid. How it works and the features it includes are covered in the next few sections.

How Does Data Guard Work?

Whenever a change is made to the Oracle database, records are placed into the redo logs. The primary purpose of the redo log is for database recovery. Since changes to the database are cached, in the event of a system failure, the changes would be lost except for the redo log records. So, if a failure were to happen, the redo log would be read, any committed transactions would be replayed (rolled forward), and any noncommitted transactions would be rolled back.

Data Guard takes these redo records and constantly replays them on the standby system, thus keeping the primary and standby databases in sync. Data Guard can be configured in a number of different modes, depending on your needs.

- **Oracle Physical Standby**   The standby server is kept completely in sync with the primary. No changes can be made to the standby, and the database is a block-for-block equivalent of the primary.

- **Data Guard Logical Standby**   Uses Oracle LogMiner technology to convert log records to DML statements and applies them to an open copy of the database. Because Logical Standby is not an exact copy of the primary, it may not be appropriate for data migration. There is, however, a method where Logical Standby can be used for a short period of time to assist with database upgrades. This chapter covers only Physical Standby.

So, how does Data Guard work? Oracle automatically extracts and transports redo records from the primary database to the standby database using one of three methods: the Log Writer process (LGWR); its recent successor, the Log Writer Network Service process (LNS); or the Archiver process (ARCH). The log writer will send each log record to the standby to be written into the standby redo logs on the standby system as they are being written to the redo logs on the primary. The Archiver process waits until a log switch and copies the entire archive log file to the standby database. A separate process on the standby reads, and applies, the redo to the standby database exactly as it was written to the primary.

- **Data Guard with LGWR or LNS**   Using the Log Writer process or the Log Writer Network Service process, each log record is written into the local redo log file and the standby redo log file on the standby database simultaneously. This is known as *synchronous mode*. This provides a mechanism where the standby database is kept entirely in sync with the primary database. This is also known as *zero data loss mode*. If the primary were to fail, the standby would take over with absolutely no loss of data.

    So, what is the downside of zero data loss mode? Because the LGWR process has to write to both the primary and standby before a transaction is considered committed, there is a performance hit on the primary database. So, zero data loss mode is typically only used with a standby database that is local to the primary database. Data Guard over long distances is discouraged with zero data loss mode.

Synchronous Mode and Latency

The concepts of bandwidth and latency are often confused. While an environment may have sufficient bandwidth, it may not be usable because of poor latency. *Latency* is the time between an event and a response. In terms of Data Guard synchronous mode, latency is the time between when the log record started writing and a response was returned from the OS. When you write to a remote location, the latency is the time it takes to write there and receive confirmation that it has been written. The problem with synchronous mode and long distances is the response time, not how much data per second you can write (throughput).

The theoretical maximum speed to send data from New York to Los Angeles based on the speed of light is 13 ms. This is nowhere near what you will actually achieve, since you have to deal with routers, firewalls, and so forth. So, the theoretical speed-of-light round-trip is 26 ms, meaning every log write to a remote system across the country will add 26 ms to each commit. Even this is a long time, but after adding additional components and latencies, you are actually going to see round-trips of hundreds of milliseconds or even thousands of milliseconds. This might be considered unacceptable in your environment.

TIP & TECHNIQUE

A new feature in Oracle Database 12c is far sync, which is designed to allow a hybrid Data Guard configuration that combines the features of zero data loss mode and a remote standby configuration. See My Oracle Support (MOS) Note 1565071, Data Guard 12c New Feature: Far Sync Standby, *for the most recent information on this feature.*

■ **Data Guard with ARCH**   Using the Archiver process, the redo information is shipped more efficiently because it is shipped in bulk, one archive log at a time. The upside of this is that it is much more efficient, especially for long distances. This is because throughput is now the concern rather than latency.

The problem with using archive logs for Data Guard is that now the standby system is not kept in sync; it is up to an entire archive log behind. In the event of a failure, this might be unacceptable in your environment.

TIP & TECHNIQUE
In most environments where high availability and disaster recovery are required, both a local standby and a remote standby are configured. This gives you maximum protection as well as the ability to host a standby system offsite. If you are using Oracle Database 12c, you can use far sync as well.

Data Guard Components

Data Guard is made up of three main services: Redo Transport Services, Apply Services, and Role Transitions. They each serve an integral part of the Data Guard process. Redo Transport Services consists of the movement of redo data. Apply Services is responsible for applying the data to the standby, and Role Transitions is used to manage the role changes in the Data Guard environment.

Redo Transport Services

Redo Transport Services consists of two types of transport methods and is responsible for transmitting redo data from the primary to the standby systems, managing and resolving missing data or gaps, and detecting missing archived log files on the standby and replacing them. As mentioned in the previous section, the redo transport services can use either of the following three mechanisms:

- **LGWR**   The Log Writer process will write redo log information into both the local and standby redo log files. This provides the highest level of protection.

- **ARCH**   The Archiver will archive the online redo log file into both the local location and all configured standby locations.

- **LNS**   The Log Writer Network Service Process (LNS) sends the redo information via the network. This process is specifically designed to ship redo information over the network.

Redo Transport Services is responsible for the redo data going from the primary to the standby but is not responsible for applying that data.

Apply Services

Apply Services is responsible for taking the redo information that has been copied to the standby and applying it to the standby database. The mechanism used is either Redo Apply or Log Apply, for Physical Standby and Logical Standby respectively.

- **Redo Apply**   The Redo Apply mechanism is used when running as a Physical Standby database and uses the recovery mechanism that is built into the database. This is extremely efficient and fast.

- **Log Apply** The Log Apply mechanism is used for Logical Standby and converts log records to INSERT, UPDATE, and DELETE statements that are applied to the open database. While potentially slower, this method does allow some flexibility, such as database version mismatch, and you can exploit this during some migration processes.

Apply Services can be enabled and disabled as desired and is independent of Transport Services. This allows the standby environment to receive the redo changes while allowing delays in applying updates, which may be useful for configuring and testing the standby database itself.

Role Transitions

Role Transitions allows Data Guard systems to switch roles from primary to standby. There are two types of Role Transitions: Switchover and Failover. Switchover changes roles between a primary and a standby, whereas a Failover makes the standby the primary when communication between the primary and standby has been lost. Failover implies that the "record of last transmission" *may* be incorrect, and therefore blocks the possibility of switching back to the original configuration, whereas Switchover ensures sufficient consistency that we may "switch back" to the original primary-standby configuration. For data migrations, the Switchover mechanism will be used.

Data Guard Modes

Data Guard supports three protection modes: Maximum Protection Mode, Maximum Availability Mode, and Maximum Performance Mode. Which mode you should choose depends on your environment and your particular needs.

Maximum Protection Mode

Maximum Protection Mode or zero data loss mode is used to guarantee that no data loss will occur if the primary database were to fail. This mode uses the synchronous redo transport mode. No transactions are considered committed until the redo data has been written to both the primary and the standby redo logs.

If the communication between the primary and standby systems is interrupted, the primary will shut down rather than continue in an unprotected mode. This is why this mode is only used in specific circumstances.

Maximum Availability Mode

Maximum Availability Mode provides the highest level of protection without affecting the primary database. It works the same as Maximum Protection Mode unless it is unable to write data to the standby redo logs. If that case were to occur, the Maximum Protection Mode would downgrade itself to Maximum Performance Mode. Once caught up, it will revert to Maximum Protection Mode.

TIP & TECHNIQUE
Oracle Database 12c has introduced a new feature called fast sync that is available for Maximum Availability Mode. This allows the standby to return receipt of the standby redo write when it is received in memory, rather than when it is written to disk. This provides higher performance with little risk.

Maximum Performance Mode

Maximum Performance Mode is the default protection mode and has the least impact on the primary database. It minimizes the impact by allowing transactions to commit as soon as all of the redo log that has been generated for the transaction has been written to the local (primary) online redo log. Redo log data will also be written to all of the standby databases, but the commit does not wait for that to happen on the primary.

In this mode, there is little performance impact on the primary database while still providing a high level of performance.

Data Guard Broker

The Data Guard Broker is an included utility that is used to control and manage Data Guard configurations. The Data Guard Broker allows you to easily and efficiently maintain and monitor Data Guard with a single utility that works across all systems in the Data Guard Configuration. The use of the Data Guard Broker is optional, but is highly recommended.

We recommend using the Data Guard Broker because of the additional functionality and because it is required to integrate Data Guard into an Oracle Enterprise Manager Cloud Control configuration. For more information, see the Oracle Data Guard documentation or *Oracle Enterprise Manager Cloud Control 12c Deep Dive*, by Michael New and Ed Whalen, also from Oracle Press (2013).

Requirements for Migrating with Data Guard

Using Data Guard for a data migration really has only one requirement, but it is a big one: the database version and database must be the same. You cannot perform any transformations or version upgrades. Data Guard does support limited data migration in environments with heterogeneous primary and standby databases, but that will not be covered in this book. For the purpose of this book we will consider the requirement that the same version of Oracle must be used on the primary and standby and that only limited changes are allowed.

The following list represents the changes between primary and standby that are allowed:

- **Different hardware** Since the Data Guard system is a database product and the database is keyed to a specific OS and hardware architecture, as long as the architecture and endian are the same and the database software is the same, Data Guard will work between different server hardware.

  So, for example, as long as you are setting up Data Guard using Version 12.1.0.1, you can have your primary database on an Exadata X3 and the standby on an Exadata X4.

- **Different OS version** Since the Data Guard system is a database product and the database is keyed to a specific OS and hardware architecture, as long as the architecture is the same and the database software is the same, Data Guard will work between different versions of the operating system.

  So, for example, as long as you are setting up Data Guard using Version 12.1.0.1, you can have your primary database on an Exadata X3 and the standby on an Exadata X4.

- **Different storage** The storage can be different between the primary and standby systems. Often we will find that the storage on the standby is not as robust or as fast as the storage on the primary system.

  When performing an upgrade, the opposite is often true; the storage and server hardware is usually better on the standby.

- **Filesystem to ASM** Data Guard is an easy way to move from a database running on a filesystem or NFS and convert to Automatic Storage Management (ASM). Data Guard is perfectly capable of handling databases of different storage types on the primary and standby systems.

TIP & TECHNIQUE

Any of these items can be different between the primary system and the physical standby. This is what makes Data Guard capable of being used for a data migration.

As you will see later in the chapter, using Data Guard for a data migration involves creating the new system as the physical standby and simply doing a switchover. The new system becomes the primary, and you have the additional benefit of a physical standby that is all ready to go.

Configuring Data Guard

Configuring Data Guard is a fairly straightforward task. It involves the following steps:

1. Set up the primary and standby in preparation of Data Guard.

2. Modify init.ora parameters on the primary.

3. Create the standby system.

4. Duplicate the database to the standby.

5. Configure the Data Guard Broker and enable Data Guard.

6. Test and validate.

These steps are outlined in the following sections.

Set Up the Primary and Standby in Preparation of Data Guard

To create a standby database, it is necessary to perform a few changes both within and outside the database. You need to set several parameters in the database and modify a number of other database support structures, mainly the password file, listeners, network configuration entries, and some directory structures. In addition, you must modify the listeners, modify the tnsnames.ora file, and create password files.

Create Standby Redo Log Files

If you are using Oracle Managed Files (OMF), creating standby redo log files is very easy. Find the number of log files and then create that many standby redo log files. You must do this for each instance. Use the following syntax:

```
SQL> alter database add standby logfile thread 1 size 50M;
SQL> alter database add standby logfile thread 1 size 50M;
    Repeat until all the standby logfiles are created….
SQL> alter database add standby logfile thread 2 size 50M;
SQL> alter database add standby logfile thread 2 size 50M;
SQL> alter database add standby logfile thread 1 size 50M;
    Repeat until all the standby logfiles are create….
```

NOTE
Each node in a RAC cluster has a different log thread, hence the thread qualifier.

You should add a standby log file for each log file plus one additional standby log file to accommodate the finite time between the redo information being received from the primary and the time it is applied to the standby. It is critical that the standby redo log files be the same size as (or greater than) the largest primary redo log files, and it is strongly recommended that all primary redo log files be the same size. In order to check the log files and the standby log files, use the following syntax:

```
SQL> select group#, bytes from v$log;
SQL> select group#, bytes from v$standby_log;
```

The standby log files are an important part of the Data Guard setup.

Listener Configuration

The listener configuration is very important both for the initial RMAN DUPLICATE DATABASE command (discussed later in the chapter) and for the Data Guard Broker to be able to properly perform a switchover operation. The standby system must have a static registration for the database, and both the standby and primary must have a static registration for the Data Guard Broker to function properly.

Data Guard Listener or No Data Guard Listener

It is often recommended to create a separate listener specifically for Data Guard traffic. We have mixed feelings about this. If the connectivity between the primary and standby is via the same network card as normal traffic, then we feel that there is no need to create a dedicated listener. If there is a separate network card for Data Guard traffic, then we highly recommend a separate listener.

In a RAC or ASM configuration, the listener should be configured in the Grid Infrastructure home. Here are a few examples of listener.ora files:

Primary Database:

```
LISTENER=(DESCRIPTION=(ADDRESS_LIST=(ADDRESS=(PROTOCOL=IPC)(KEY=LISTENER))))
# line added by Agent
LISTENER_SCAN3=(DESCRIPTION=(ADDRESS_LIST=(ADDRESS=(PROTOCOL=IPC)(KEY=LISTENER_
SCAN3))))                # line added by Agent
LISTENER_SCAN2=(DESCRIPTION=(ADDRESS_LIST=(ADDRESS=(PROTOCOL=IPC)(KEY=LISTENER_
SCAN2))))                # line added by Agent
LISTENER_SCAN1=(DESCRIPTION=(ADDRESS_LIST=(ADDRESS=(PROTOCOL=IPC)(KEY=LISTENER_
SCAN1))))                # line added by Agent
ENABLE_GLOBAL_DYNAMIC_ENDPOINT_LISTENER_SCAN1=ON                    # line added by Agent
ENABLE_GLOBAL_DYNAMIC_ENDPOINT_LISTENER_SCAN2=ON                    # line added by Agent
ENABLE_GLOBAL_DYNAMIC_ENDPOINT_LISTENER_SCAN3=ON                    # line added by Agent
```

```
ENABLE_GLOBAL_DYNAMIC_ENDPOINT_LISTENER=ON                    # line added by Agent
SID_LIST_LISTENER=
  (SID_LIST=
    (SID_DESC=
      (GLOBAL_DBNAME=rac04db_DGMGRL)
      (ORACLE_HOME=/u01/app/oracle/product/11.2.0.4/dbhome_1)
      (SID_NAME=rac04db1)
    )
  )
```

Since the listener will be sharing the same network adapter, we simply added the _DGMGRL entry to the standard LISTENER that was created by netca (Network Configuration Assistant). The second node in the cluster will have similar entries.

Standby Database:

```
LISTENER=(DESCRIPTION=(ADDRESS_LIST=(ADDRESS=(PROTOCOL=IPC)(KEY=LISTENER))))
# line added by Agent
LISTENER_SCAN3=(DESCRIPTION=(ADDRESS_LIST=(ADDRESS=(PROTOCOL=IPC)(KEY=LISTENER_
SCAN3))))                # line added by Agent
LISTENER_SCAN2=(DESCRIPTION=(ADDRESS_LIST=(ADDRESS=(PROTOCOL=IPC)(KEY=LISTENER_
SCAN2))))                # line added by Agent
LISTENER_SCAN1=(DESCRIPTION=(ADDRESS_LIST=(ADDRESS=(PROTOCOL=IPC)(KEY=LISTENER_
SCAN1))))                # line added by Agent
ENABLE_GLOBAL_DYNAMIC_ENDPOINT_LISTENER_SCAN1=ON                  # line added by Agent
ENABLE_GLOBAL_DYNAMIC_ENDPOINT_LISTENER_SCAN2=ON                  # line added by Agent
ENABLE_GLOBAL_DYNAMIC_ENDPOINT_LISTENER_SCAN3=ON                  # line added by Agent
ENABLE_GLOBAL_DYNAMIC_ENDPOINT_LISTENER=ON                  # line added by Agent
SID_LIST_LISTENER=
  (SID_LIST=
    (SID_DESC=
      (GLOBAL_DBNAME=rac04sb_DGMGRL)
      (ORACLE_HOME=/u01/app/oracle/product/11.2.0.4/dbhome_1)
      (SID_NAME=rac04sb1)
    )
    (SID_DESC=
      (GLOBAL_DBNAME=rac04sb)
      (ORACLE_HOME=/u01/app/oracle/product/11.2.0.4/dbhome_1)
      (SID_NAME=rac04sb1)
    )
  )
```

Notice that this entry also uses the standard listener. In addition, this listener also includes a static entry for the rac04sb (standby) database.

NOTE
This configuration will register only with the local listener. The entries shown here will not register with the RAC SCAN listeners. That is as intended.

tnsnames.ora Configuration

On both the primary and standby nodes, the tnsnames.ora file will be similar. Here is an example of the tnsnames.ora file:

```
# tnsnames.ora Network Configuration File: /u01/app/oracle/
product/11.2.0.4/dbhome_1/network/admin/tnsnames.ora
# Generated by Oracle configuration tools.

RAC04DB =
  (DESCRIPTION =
    (ADDRESS = (PROTOCOL = TCP)(HOST = rac04-scan)(PORT = 1521))
    (CONNECT_DATA =
      (SERVER = DEDICATED)
      (SERVICE_NAME = rac04db)
    )
  )

RAC04DB1 =
  (DESCRIPTION =
    (ADDRESS = (PROTOCOL = TCP)(HOST = rac04a-vip)(PORT = 1521))
    (CONNECT_DATA =
      (SERVER = DEDICATED)
      (SID = rac04db1)
    )
  )

RAC04DB2 =
  (DESCRIPTION =
    (ADDRESS = (PROTOCOL = TCP)(HOST = rac04b-vip)(PORT = 1521))
    (CONNECT_DATA =
      (SERVER = DEDICATED)
      (SID = rac04db2)
    )
  )

RAC04SB =
  (DESCRIPTION =
    (ADDRESS = (PROTOCOL = TCP)(HOST = rac05-scan)(PORT = 1521))
    (CONNECT_DATA =
      (SERVER = DEDICATED)
      (SERVICE_NAME = rac04sb)
    )
  )

RAC04SB1 =
  (DESCRIPTION =
    (ADDRESS = (PROTOCOL = TCP)(HOST = rac05a-vip)(PORT = 1521))
    (CONNECT_DATA =
```

```
        (SERVER = DEDICATED)
        (SID = rac04sb1)
    )
  )

RAC04SB2 =
  (DESCRIPTION =
    (ADDRESS = (PROTOCOL = TCP)(HOST = rac05b-vip)(PORT = 1521))
    (CONNECT_DATA =
      (SERVER = DEDICATED)
      (SID = rac04sb2)
    )
  )
```

Notice that the tnsnames.ora file contains both RAC SCAN addresses and direct vip addresses. Since the broker is RAC aware, it knows which instance to connect to directly.

TIP & TECHNIQUE

Entries for RAC and Data Guard in the tnsnames.ora file should not be propagated to tiers other than the database tier.

Password File

Since Data Guard ships logs and communicates directly between the databases, user connectivity is required. In order for this to work, an Oracle password file is required. The password file allows SQL*Plus to communicate as SYSDBA with a database that is not currently running. This allows SQL*Plus to start a database. There is most likely already a password file on the primary. This file can be copied to the standby. It goes in the $ORACLE_HOME/dbs directory and should be renamed to reflect the name of the standby database.

Create Directories on the Standby System

Since the standby database is not created with the Oracle Database Configuration Assistant (DBCA), some of the necessary directories will not be created. You need to create the following directories manually:

- **adump**   This is the audit dump directory. It is usually defined as $ORACLE_BASE/admin/<DATABASE>/adump.

- **Datafiles**   If you are not using ASM, you must create the directory where the datafiles will reside.

- **FRA (Fast Recovery Area)**   If you are not using ASM, you must create the recovery file directory.

Modify init.ora Parameters on the Primary

There are a number of init.ora parameters that are necessary for Data Guard to function correctly. There are also a few settings that must be set at the database level. In many cases, Data Guard can be enabled on a production database without any downtime. The exception is with the database settings.

The database must be running in ARCHIVELOG mode. If the database is not running in ARCHIVELOG mode, it must be enabled before you can proceed. It is very rare to find any production database that is not running in ARCHIVELOG mode, so this usually is not a problem. The database must also be running the FORCE LOGGING option, which disallows any nonlogged operations. Since Data Guard works off of the redo log, any nonlogged operations would not be able to be replicated. It is necessary to run all logged operations. FORCE LOGGING enables this.

> **NOTE**
> *FORCE LOGGING overrides developer, dictionary, and session settings related to NOLOGGING mode.*

The rest of the Data Guard configuration involves setting Oracle initialization parameters. The primary parameters that enable and configure Data Guard are as follows:

- **log_archive_config** This is used to set the databases involved in the Data Guard configuration.

- **db_unique_name** This parameter sets the unique name of the database. Since all databases in a Data Guard configuration share the same database name, this uniquely identifies each primary or standby database.

- **log_archive_dest_*n*** The log_archive_dest_*n* parameters are used to configure 1 to 30 standby databases. Typically, log_archive_dest_1 is used to configure the local redo log location.

  This parameter is used to specify exactly how Data Guard is configured to work. The large number of options for configuring the log_archive_dest_*n* parameters can be found in the Oracle documentation.

> **TIP & TECHNIQUE**
> *We have found that the best way to configure Data Guard is to use the basic parameters to configure Data Guard and then let the Data Guard Broker manage the configuration.*

- **standby_file_management** When this parameter is set to AUTO, a datafile created on the primary will be created on the standby. This makes standby management much easier.

- **fal_server** On a standby system, this parameter specifies the database to fill log gaps from. FAL stands for Fetch Archive Log.

There are also a number of optional parameters that can be set. They include

- **archive_lag_target** Specifies a minimum amount of time between log switches. The log switch will occur either when normally required or when the number of seconds specified by archive_lag_target is reached, whichever is sooner.

- **db_file_name_convert** This parameter is used to convert the location of datafiles from the primary to the standby. It uses pattern matching to substitute patterns.

- **log_file_name_convert** This parameter is used to convert the location of datafiles from the primary to the standby. It uses pattern matching to substitute patterns.

There are a few other optional parameters that are beyond the scope of this book, since we are primarily concerned with using Data Guard for data migration. The easiest way to change the parameters is to simply create a SQL script to set the parameters by modifying the spfile (server parameter file).

In the following example, the primary database is a two-node RAC named rac04db. The standby database that will be created is a RAC cluster to be named rac04sb. The following script will set the parameters for the primary database:

SQL Script set_primary_parameters.sql:

```
alter system set archive_lag_target=1800 scope=both
alter system set db_unique_name='rac04db' scope=both;
alter system set log_archive_config='DG_CONFIG=(rac04db,rac04sb)' scope=both;
alter system set log_archive_dest_1='LOCATION=USE_DB_RECOVERY_FILE_DEST
VALID_FOR=(ALL_LOGFILES,ALL_ROLES) DB_UNIQUE_NAME=rac04db' scope=both;
alter system set log_archive_dest_2='SERVICE=rac04sb ASYNC VALID_FOR=(ONLINE_
LOGFILES,PRIMARY_ROLE) DB_UNIQUE_NAME=rac04sb' scope=both;
alter system set standby_file_management='AUTO' scope=both;
```

NOTE
You will probably already have log_archive_dest_1 or equivalent set. The existing parameter should be set to reflect the VALID_FOR and DB_UNIQUE_NAME settings shown in the code.

Running this SQL will set the required Data Guard parameters in the primary database. None of these parameters require a database restart.

Once you have modified the parameter file on the primary, you need to create a parameter file for the standby database. Since most of the parameters should be the same on the primary and the standby, the best way to proceed is to create a pfile from the spfile and use this to create the standby system.

Creating a pfile from the primary spfile is done with the following command:

```
SQL> CREATE PFILE='$HOME/initstdby.ora' FROM SPFILE;
```

The parameter file should be modified with the database names reversed so that the primary is configured as the standby. This way the switchover will work properly and the initial primary can become the standby.

Create the Standby System

The standby database is created using the following steps:

1. *Verify directories.* Make sure that the audit directory has been created and, if necessary, create the datafile and recovery area directories.

2. *Set up the parameter file.* If this is a RAC system or a stand-alone system, or if you want to be able to run the Data Guard Broker, an spfile must be created. In RAC this file is created in ASM and referred to by a pfile in the $ORACLE_HOME/dbs directory.

    The spfile was taken from the spfile on the primary and modified to reflect that this is the standby system. The primary should be set up in the log_archive_dest_2 parameter as the standby for this standby.

3. *Start up in nomount.* The standby instance must be started in nomount mode in order to have the basic functionality to perform the RMAN operations.

Duplicate the Database to the Standby

To get started, you must duplicate the primary database to the standby. You have a number of choices here. You can use RMAN with a DUPLICATE DATABASE command (our preference for small databases) or you can use any other method that is available, such as using hardware snapshot and clone features.

If you choose to use RMAN, here is the procedure:

1. Set the environment to the primary database.

2. Create the spfile.

3. Configure the database into the cluster.

Set the Environment to the Primary Database

To set the environment to the primary database, use the following:

```
$ rman target / auxiliary sys/<pwd>@<standby>
RMAN>  duplicate target database for standby from active database dorecover;
```

Create the spfile

When using DUPLICATE DATABASE FOR STANDBY, the spfile will be created in the $ORACLE_HOME/dbs directory with the name spfile<SID>.ora. This is fine if you are in a non-RAC environment; however, for RAC the spfile should reside in ASM. To copy the spfile into ASM, the best way we've found it to use an intermediate pfile.

Create two scripts: one to create the pfile and one to create the spfile.

> **TIP & TECHNIQUE**
> *Create the pfile by using the command*
> `CREATE PFILE='filespec' FROM SPFILE;`
> *Create the spfile by using the command*
> `CREATE SPFILE='filespec' FROM`
> `PFILE='filespec';`

Once the spfile is in place, set your Oracle SID either by using the ORACLE_SID and ORACLE_HOME environment variables or by editing /etc/oratab and adding an entry for the standby database and instance.

In order for the spfile to be used, you need to set up the pfile or spfile. If using filesystems, it is okay to create an spfile in $ORACLE_HOME/dbs. If you are using ASM, you will set up a pfile in $ORACLE_HOME/dbs that points to the ASM spfile. For example:

initrac04sb1.ora:

```
SPFILE='+DATA/rac0db/spfilerac04db.ora'
```

This will give you enough to start the database using the spfile. The final database setup step is to add the database and instances into the Clusterware.

Configure the Database into the Cluster

To register the database into the Clusterware, you need to run `srvctl` with the `add database` and `add instance` commands. First, add the database:

```
$ srvctl add database -d <db_unique_name> -o <oracle home> -c RAC -p
'<spfile>' -r physical_standby -n <db_name>
```

Next, add the instances:

```
$ srvctl add instance -d <db_unique_name> -i <instance_name> -n <node>
```

The following is an example of a shell script to add both of these.

add__db.sh:

```
srvctl add database -d rac00sb -o /u01/app/oracle/product/11.2.0.4/dbhome_1
-c RAC -p '+DATA/rac00sb/spfilerac00sb.ora' -r physical_standby -n rac0db
srvctl add instance -d rac00sb -i rac00sb1 -n rac01a
srvctl add instance -d rac00sb -i rac00sb2 -n rac01b
```

To start Data Guard, you can do it manually or you can add the Data Guard Broker and let the broker start managed recovery. We prefer to let the broker do its job.

Configure the Data Guard Broker

To configure the broker, you must put a few parameters into the initialization parameters. You need two broker config files (in ASM) and to start the broker. The parameters for the broker config files are dg_broker_config_file1 and dg_broker_config_file2. The parameter to start the broker is dg_broker_start. The following is an example script to enable these.

enable_broker.sh:

```
alter system set dg_broker_config_file1=' +DATA/dr1rac04db.dat';
alter system set dg_broker_config_file1=' +FRA/dr2rac04db.dat';
alter system set dg_broker_start=TRUE;
```

Once the broker is started on both systems (primary and standby), you must configure the broker.

Configuring the broker is done via the dgmgrl utility, which is the command-line utility to access the broker. The steps to configure the broker are to create a configuration, add the standby, and enable the configuration. This is shown in the following syntax:

```
$ dgmgrl sys/<password>
```

> **TIP & TECHNIQUE**
> *Don't be tempted to use the syntax* dgmgrl /.
> *This will result in the inability to connect to the standby, and the second step will fail with an invalid username/password error.*

```
DGMGRL> create configuration rac04
> as primary database is rac04db connect identifier is rac04db;
DGMGRL> add database rac04sb as connect identifier is 'rac04sb';
DGMGRL> enable configuration rac04;
```

It is possible to enable redo transport and redo apply from sqlplus using `alter system` commands, but once the broker is enabled it will do that for you. There are a few commands you can use to check, such as `show configuration`:

```
DGMGRL> show configuration

Configuration - rac00

  Protection Mode: MaxPerformance
  Databases:
    rac0db  - Primary database
    rac00sb - Physical standby database

Fast-Start Failover: DISABLED

Configuration Status:
SUCCESS
```

This shows that the configuration is up and running. There are many more commands that will validate the configuration and operation of Data Guard. There is also information in the alert log to validate Data Guard.

Test and Validate

If you are running in a production environment, there are not a lot of tests that you can do that will not affect the primary.

TIP & TECHNIQUE
A test such as a switchover will affect the primary database, whereas a test such as a snapshot standby will not.

You should do some testing to make sure that the Data Guard replication is working properly, but keep in mind that Data Guard has been around for a long time and is very reliable and stable if properly configured.

Migrating with Data Guard

Migrating with Data Guard is the easiest task in this entire chapter. There are only two steps:

1. Configure the new system as a Physical Standby database.

2. Perform a switchover operation.

This leaves the new system, formerly the physical standby, as the new primary database and the newly migrated database. As an extra bonus, you now have a premade physical standby that is ready in case of any problem with the new primary database.

The actual migration process could take some time. Depending on how long it takes to migrate the applications, this could be a matter of minutes or hours. As mentioned before, it doesn't matter how long it takes to do the migration, what matters is how long it takes to cutover to the new system. That is the step that involves losing access to the database. The switchover should only take a few seconds.

Summary

In this chapter you have seen that Data Guard is not just for disaster recovery and high availability. Under very specific circumstances where only a hardware refresh is being done or very specific changes are being made, Data Guard can be a quite effective migration tool. As a review, only a few changes can be made. They include

- **Different hardware** You can upgrade the hardware by going to new hardware as long as the OS architecture and database version are constant.

- **Different OS version** As long as the architecture is the same and the database software is the same, Data Guard will work between different versions of the operating system.

- **Different storage** The storage can be different between the primary and standby systems. Often we will find that the storage on the standby is not as robust or as fast as the storage on the primary system.

- **Filesystem to ASM** Data Guard is an easy way to move from a database running on filesystem or NFS and convert to ASM. Data Guard is perfectly capable of handling a database of different storage types on the primary and standby system.

Data Guard is a very fast and effective way of migrating a database without causing significant load on the primary system. In fact, in many cases, a physical standby is probably already in use.

CHAPTER
5

Using Recovery Manager (RMAN) for Cross-Platform Migration

Oracle Recovery Manager (RMAN) is one of the most flexible yet sophisticated methods for migrating data between operating systems and storage systems. This chapter delves into how you can leverage RMAN to quickly and powerfully move massive amounts of data from one platform to another in just about every migration scenario.

RMAN: Intrinsic Benefits

Whether it's an entire database that needs to be completely (or incompletely) recovered or just a single database block that has been corrupted and needs immediate recovery, our experience tells us that most Oracle DBAs have already acknowledged RMAN as the industry standard for handling these scenarios. In case your organization is still in the minority that leverages user-managed backup and recovery techniques, this section presents some benefits of shifting over to RMAN as you migrate, transform, or upgrade your Oracle databases.

Reliability

Over the years, RMAN has evolved to become one of the most reliable backup, recovery, and storage migration tools available. When it first appeared in Oracle8*i* Database, it was a bit flaky; for example, in RMAN's earliest incarnations, Oracle strongly recommended maintaining a Recovery Catalog to make sure that RMAN backup information was always available during restore and recovery operations—a recommendation that wasn't really reversed until Oracle9*i* Database, when NOCATALOG mode became the default for backup operations. Oracle9*i* essentially stabilized RMAN but didn't make any significant improvements. As a result, many hard-core Oracle DBAs completely abandoned its use, returning to their tried-and-true backup solutions—usually a set of user-managed backup scripts that invoked `BEGIN BACKUP` and `END BACKUP` commands to perform full database backups one tablespace at a time.

However, Oracle Database 10*g* introduced a much more reliable version of RMAN that included several excellent game-changing features, most notably the *Flash Recovery Area*—what in later releases is called the *Fast Recovery Area*, or *FRA* for short—as well as significant improvements to RMAN's flexibility, granularity, and performance. However, the damage to RMAN's reputation had been done, and some Oracle shops waited until Oracle Database 11*g* R1 to revisit RMAN as a preferred backup method.

To RMAN or Not to RMAN: Is This Even a Question?

We occasionally encounter Oracle shops that have still shied away from using RMAN to back up, restore, and recover their Oracle databases. In some cases, Oracle DBAs have been forced to use hardware-based backup solutions that their storage administration (SA) team has mandated for use across the entire corporation. While this may alleviate any political infighting between SAs and DBAs, we still encourage a DBA in this situation to ask their SA the following question:

> *Are you going to be standing right next to me when I have a serious database outage to explain to our CIO why this database isn't available yet, especially when it turns out that if we had used RMAN for our backup/restore/recovery strategy, we could have restored only a few datafiles or maybe even just a few database blocks, and we could have already brought this database back online?*

If the answer is either a blank look or a dismissive shrug of the SA's shoulders, then we suggest the DBA kindly but firmly remind the SA that since he is not going to assist during a database's restoration and recovery, he should not be dictating a backup policy that could hamper the DBA's ability to bring the database back from the brink of disaster via the simplest, fastest, and most reliable methods possible.

Processing Efficiency

Every RMAN operation is performed over an I/O path called a *channel*. Via its `ALLOCATE CHANNEL` or `CONFIGURE CHANNEL` commands, RMAN can dedicate one or more channels to processing either the data that is being backed up or the data being accessed during a migration effort. By using multiple channels to parallelize backup and restore operations, RMAN can drastically reduce the amount of time necessary to access, transfer, and migrate data between databases, storage systems, or platforms—especially when the source and/or destination system has a large number of CPUs to allow parallelized data transfer operations to continue apace while normal database operations continue unabated.

Oracle usually recommends keeping the maximum number of channels to no more than four during any backup, restore, or recovery operation, but in an extreme case—like a massive data migration, of course!—this limit can be sensibly ignored so that the amount of work that needs to be done can be spread evenly across all I/O channels. In fact, in a Real Application Clusters (RAC) database environment, we have often seen Oracle DBAs deploy a single database service dedicated only to RMAN processing so that multiple database instances can partake in backup, restore, and recovery operations in parallel.

NOTE
We will explore how to monitor RMAN processing for any throughput "back pressure" in an upcoming section.

Security

If your organization's security administrator hasn't reminded you this week that as much as 80 percent of data theft occurs within the firewall, then she simply isn't doing her job. However, it's that last 20 percent—sending data beyond the firewall—that many Oracle DBAs often overlook as a potential vector for data theft.

Oracle Database 10g R2 was the first release that made it possible to encrypt RMAN backup files using its new Transparent Data Encryption (TDE) capabilities. TDE offers four different backup encryption methods—3DES168, AES128, AES192, and AES256—that comply with Federal Information Processing Standards (FIPS). While TDE must be separately licensed as part of the Advanced Security pack, it's also extremely simple to implement and can be used in concert with a normal password-based method to ensure that an RMAN backup is completely unusable if it should fall into the wrong hands. Oracle Database 11g R1 also added the capability to leverage a Hardware Security Module (HSM) device so that the maintenance of the TDE master key is essentially removed from human tampering.

Unit 61398: The Mandiant Report

Organizations that doubt if the additional cost of data encryption is worth its considerable price tag would do well to read "APT1: Exposing One of China's Cyber Espionage Units," a report by Mandiant, a company that is constantly on the lookout for threats to data security. Published in March 2013, Mandiant's publicly available 73-page report detailed some frightening, pernicious threats to intellectual property.

Mandiant identified a shadowy organization known only as Unit 61398 as Advanced Persistent Threat One (APT1). Mandiant reported that Unit 61398 had stolen hundreds of terabytes of information—especially the intellectual property of over 140 U.S.- and European-based businesses—since 2006. Most of the attacks were mounted against countries in which English is the native language; in one especially egregious case, Unit 61398 stole over 6.5TB from just one company in just 10 months. Mandiant also stated that the reason that it's difficult to know just how much data has been taken is that even though the Chinese government denies its involvement, Unit 61398 appears to be a unit of the Chinese People's Liberation Army dedicated to cyber-espionage.

On May 16, 2014, in an unprecedented case, U.S. Attorney General Eric Holder issued indictments against five Chinese army officers—all of them members of Unit 61398—for their hacking activities and thefts of intellectual property conducted against U.S. businesses since 2006. John Carlin, head of the Department of Justice's National Security Division, stated that "[w]hile the men and women of our American businesses spent their business days innovating, creating, and developing strategies to compete in the global marketplace, these members of unit 61398 spent their business days in Shanghai stealing the fruits of our labor."

RMAN Backup, Restore, and Recovery Techniques

RMAN is a vital tool for performing database migrations, so it is important to first understand how advances in RMAN—especially as of Oracle Database 10*g*—have laid the groundwork for all future RMAN capabilities. First and foremost, you should never forget that the RMAN executable is really nothing more than a command shell, very much like SQL*Plus, that constructs backup, restore, and recovery operations and then simply hands off those operations to the DBMS_BACKUP_RESTORE package, where the RMAN master and shadow processes actually perform the work.

Fundamental Changes

Oracle Database 10*g* R1's RMAN improvements focused on what was most important to Oracle DBAs and the organizations they support: the ability to back up even a relatively large database as quickly as possible while expanding the capability to quickly restore and recover that database to any desired point in time within the database's defined Recovery Point Objective (RPO).

RPO and RTO: Why Should I Care?

If you have not heard these two terms in the IT industry, you haven't been to enough Oracle user conferences or sat through sales presentations from storage vendors and purveyors of backup appliances lately. So here's a brief clarification:

- A database's *Recovery Point Objective (RPO)* is the required point-in-time recovery window. For example, if a database's RPO is 72 hours, then the DBA must be able to guarantee that the database could be recovered to any point in time in the last three days. However, most database application users do not understand that this implies that at least some—if not all—data that was captured *after* the point-in-time recovery has been completed will be discarded. This is quite different from the ability to *see* data from a prior point in time…which is why Oracle Database 10*g* R1 introduced the ability to execute a Flashback Version Query to view data from *well before* the RPO.

- A database's *Recovery Time Objective (RTO)* is the time it will take to achieve the database's RPO. In short, how long will it take to perform recovery to bring the database to the desired point in time within the RPO? More practically, the RTO is the time period during which the managers of the database's application users will be screaming about the database being unavailable.

Fast Incremental Level 1 Backups: Block Change Tracking

One of the most welcome changes for RMAN in Oracle Database 10*g* R1 was the elimination of multiple layers of incremental backups in favor of just two levels: `INCREMENTAL LEVEL 0` (the base backup that must be present for all future incremental backups) and `INCREMENTAL LEVEL 1` (as part of either a `DIFFERENTIAL` or `CUMULATIVE` backup strategy). Oracle 10*g* R1 also introduced the Block Change Tracking (BCT) feature, described in more detail in an upcoming section.

Archived Redo Logs and RESETLOG Identifiers

Oracle 10*g* R1 also resolved a persistent issue with classification and retention of a database's archived redo logs after the database has been opened via the `ALTER DATABASE OPEN RESETLOGS;` command during an incomplete recovery. As of that release, a RESETLOG identifier—essentially, the SCN of the database when it last was opened in RESETLOG mode—is attached to every archived redo log during its creation. Since `ALTER DATABASE OPEN RESETLOGS;` resets the sequence number of all online redo logs back to a value of 1, there had been a danger in prior releases that an archived redo log with relatively low sequence numbers from a previous database incarnation could have been overwritten inadvertently by a new archived redo log from the present incarnation.

Recovery Through RESETLOGS

Hopefully, incomplete recovery operations are not needed very often for databases, mainly because they are so time-consuming. (Recall that any incomplete recovery of a database requires the restoration of *all* database files from a prior backup, followed by a *careful* recovery to the prior point in time within the specified RPO.) Since Oracle 10*g* R1 implemented the RESETLOG identifier strategy, each backup, image copy, and archived redo log now intrinsically knows which database incarnation it is a part of. Known as *Recovery Through RESETLOGS*, this feature makes it possible to return a database to a *prior* incarnation, before an incomplete recovery occurred, and even roll the database's state further forward using that *prior* incarnation's RMAN backup files before opening the database once again with the `ALTER DATABASE OPEN RESETLOGS;` command to construct a new incarnation. We'll discuss another way this feature can be leveraged in an upcoming section on the `FLASHBACK DATABASE` command.

Fast Recovery Area

Perhaps the most significant improvement for RMAN in Oracle Database 10*g* R1 was the introduction of the Flash Recovery Area, now named the Fast Recovery Area. Even though the concept of the FRA has been around since 2003, we have often found that many shops do not truly understand its power and capabilities. This section provides a brief rundown of which FRA features most Oracle DBAs need to understand intrinsically.

> **NOTE**
> *In Oracle Database 10g R2, Oracle renamed the Flash Recovery Area to the* Fast Recovery Area, *so to avoid any confusion, we'll use the acronym FRA throughout the rest of this chapter.*

One Place to Store All Recovery Files

The FRA provides a single location for all files needed for any database's recovery, including archived redo logs, datafile backup sets (and their corresponding backup pieces), datafile image copies, and Flashback Logs. The FRA therefore functions as the central warehouse for all database files needed for a database's complete recovery.

Intelligent Space Management Through Planned Obsolescence

One of the best features of the FRA is its dedication to retaining only the files that are *absolutely necessary* to meet a database's RPO, which RMAN enforces via its RETENTION POLICY attribute and which the DBA sets through the RMAN CONFIGURE command. For example, if the DBA and the database users have agreed upon an RPO of three days, the DBA would instruct RMAN to honor this policy by issuing the command CONFIGURE RETENTION POLICY TO RECOVERY WINDOW OF 3 DAYS; within an RMAN session, which stores the retention policy within the database's control file. RMAN will then police the FRA to ensure that any file that is no longer needed for database recovery within the RPO's range is automatically marked as OBSOLETE. Should there be sufficient space pressure within the FRA—for example, when a backup file will not fit within it—RMAN will then automatically delete the obsoleted file(s).

> **TIP & TECHNIQUE**
> *We will discuss Flashback Logs and their extreme usefulness in more detail in the upcoming chapter that covers Flashback Database. For now, it's important to know that Flashback Logs can only be stored within the FRA.*

Centralized Storage for All Oracle Database Recovery Files

The FRA can be placed on just about any storage device—a normal OS file system, Oracle's Automatic Storage Management (ASM) file system, an NFS mount point, or even Oracle's ZFS Storage Appliance (especially useful with the Oracle Exadata Database Machine and the Oracle Database Appliance)—so that a single large mount point can be defined for numerous databases. The space allocated for each database's FRA is controlled through the DB_RECOVERY_FILE_DEST_SIZE initialization parameter, which functions as a database usage quota for each database so that it can allocate just the space it needs for recovery. Each database can monitor the space it has already used and how much free space remains within its FRA quota by querying the GV$RECOVERY_AREA_USAGE dynamic view.

However, the *total* space needed for *all* Oracle database backups can be managed strategically by allocating the sum of all required recovery space for all databases to the underlying file system. This also provides the unique opportunity for DBAs and storage administrators to construct a global plan for the space required for all Oracle databases and their required backup needs while still taking into account the RPO of each Oracle database individually.

Elements of Oracle's Recommended Backup Strategy

It should not come as any great surprise that Oracle's recommended database backup strategy leverages the extensive RMAN features detailed previously, so let's take a look at how these features contribute to a robust database restoration and recovery plan, especially when dealing with databases that support real-time OLTP or near-real-time OLTP application workloads (introduced in Chapter 3).

Block Change Tracking

As we mentioned earlier, Oracle Database 10*g* R1 introduced the concept of Block Change Tracking (BCT). When an Oracle DBA implements this feature, a new background process called the Change Tracking Writer (CTWR) records each datafile block that the Database Writer (DBW0) background process has written to a datafile. CTWR flips a corresponding bit in a Block Change Tracking File (BCTF), initially sized at 10MB, to record up to 300GB worth of changed database blocks. If necessary, the BCTF will automatically grow by 10MB increments to accommodate the recording of even larger amounts of incrementally modified database blocks. Whenever a new INCREMENTAL LEVEL 1 backup has been taken, the bitmaps for all datafile blocks are automatically reset so that RMAN can take advantage of the BCTF yet again during the next incremental backup cycle.

> **NOTE**
> *BCTF is especially important for BIGFILE tablespaces because they can grow to enormous sizes. Keep in mind that a BIGFILE tablespace with database blocks sized at 32KB can potentially grow to 128TB before all space is exhausted.*

The biggest advantage of the BCTF is that RMAN does not have to read through all database blocks in a datafile to first ascertain which blocks have changed since the last differential backup. (Prior releases had required a complete re-read of each block header in every datafile being backed up to ascertain which blocks had changed since the last backup.) For datafiles that contain relatively few changed blocks when compared to the total of all blocks in the file, BCT means it takes considerably less time to identify and back up changed blocks.

BCT is activated by simply instructing the Oracle database exactly where the BCTF should reside, as shown in Listing 5-1. Note that if no filename is specified, Oracle will name the file based on Oracle Managed Files (OMF) naming conventions to store the BCTF within the directory specified by the DB_FILE_CREATE_DEST initialization parameter.

Listing 5-1 *Implementing Block Change Tracking*

```
ALTER DATABASE ENABLE BLOCK CHANGE TRACKING
USING FILE '+DATA/PROD_AP/bctf.f' REUSE;
```

Recover Forward Forever

Though many Oracle DBAs haven't even heard of it, Oracle recommends using a strategy called *Incrementally Updateable Image Copies (IUIC)* for backing up crucial databases. This strategy is especially useful when there are tight time windows during which database backups as well as recovery must occur. The strategy relies upon taking an INCREMENTAL LEVEL 0 image copy of every datafile in the database—once, and *only* once!—storing that image copy within the database's FRA, and then, from that point forward, only taking INCREMENTAL LEVEL 1 (that is, differential) backups at least once per day for the remainder of the database's existence.

The advantage of this strategy is that datafile contents generally do not change dramatically between each nightly backup cycle, so the time it will take to create an INCREMENTAL LEVEL 1 backup set will be dramatically shorter as well. And when the aforementioned Block Change Tracking strategy has been implemented, the time it takes to create the differential backups for each datafile is reduced even more dramatically.

In the following example, we are assuming that the database's Recovery Point Objective is only 24 hours, which is established via the RMAN CONFIGURE command:

```
CONFIGURE RETENTION POLICY TO RECOVERY WINDOW OF 1 DAY;
```

Listing 5-2 shows a basic implementation of this IUIC strategy via an RMAN script. It lists the result of the first day's backup strategy, assuming the aforementioned 24-hour RPO.

Listing 5-2 *IUIC Backup Strategy, Cycle 1*

```
#####
# Results from 1st run:
# - Incremental Level 0 image copies of datafiles 1 - 5 now exist
#   because even though a Level 1 incremental backup was requested,
#   no Level 0 incremental backup has yet been created with the tag
#   of img_cpy_upd.
#####

RMAN> RUN {
################################################################################
# RMAN Script: IncrementallyUpdatedImageCopyBackups.rcv
#
# Creates a daily image copy of all datafiles and Level 1 incremental backups
# for use by the daily image copies. Note that the PLUS ARCHIVELOG command
# will handle archival of any archived redo logs.
#
################################################################################

# Roll forward any available changes to image copy files from the previous
# set of incremental Level 1 backups
RECOVER
    COPY OF DATABASE
    WITH TAG 'img_cpy_upd';

# Create incremental level 1 backup of all datafiles in the database for
# roll-forward application against image copies
BACKUP
    INCREMENTAL LEVEL 1
    FOR RECOVER OF COPY WITH TAG 'img_cpy_upd'
    DATABASE
    PLUS ARCHIVELOG;
}
2> 3> 4> 5> 6> 7> 8> 9> 10> 11> 12> 13> 14> 15> 16> 17> 18> 19> 20> 21> 22> 23> 24>
Starting recover at 2009-05-05.12:35:50
using target database control file instead of recovery catalog
allocated channel: ORA_DISK_1
channel ORA_DISK_1: SID=117 device type=DISK
no copy of datafile 1 found to recover
no copy of datafile 2 found to recover
no copy of datafile 3 found to recover
no copy of datafile 4 found to recover
no copy of datafile 5 found to recover
Finished recover at 2009-05-05.12:35:55

Starting backup at 2009-05-05.12:35:56
current log archived
using channel ORA_DISK_1
channel ORA_DISK_1: starting archived log backup set
channel ORA_DISK_1: specifying archived log(s) in backup set
input archived log thread=1 sequence=29 RECID=18 STAMP=686061359
channel ORA_DISK_1: starting piece 1 at 2009-05-05.12:36:16
channel ORA_DISK_1: finished piece 1 at 2009-05-05.12:36:17
piece handle=+FRA/orcl/backupset/2009_05_05/annnf0_tag20090505t123559_0.263.686061377
tag=TAG20090505T123559 comment=NONE
channel ORA_DISK_1: backup set complete, elapsed time: 00:00:02
Finished backup at 2009-05-05.12:36:18
```

```
Starting backup at 2009-05-05.12:36:18
using channel ORA_DISK_1
no parent backup or copy of datafile 1 found
no parent backup or copy of datafile 2 found
no parent backup or copy of datafile 3 found
no parent backup or copy of datafile 5 found
no parent backup or copy of datafile 4 found
channel ORA_DISK_1: starting datafile copy
input datafile file number=00001 name=+DATA/orcl/datafile/system.257.685971885
output file name=+FRA/orcl/datafile/system.264.686061393 tag=IMG_CPY_UPD RECID=14
STAMP=686061458
channel ORA_DISK_1: datafile copy complete, elapsed time: 00:01:15
channel ORA_DISK_1: starting datafile copy
input datafile file number=00002 name=+DATA/orcl/datafile/sysaux.258.685971937
output file name=+FRA/orcl/datafile/sysaux.265.686061485 tag=IMG_CPY_UPD RECID=15
STAMP=686061549
channel ORA_DISK_1: datafile copy complete, elapsed time: 00:01:16
channel ORA_DISK_1: starting datafile copy
input datafile file number=00003 name=+DATA/orcl/datafile/undotbs1.259.685971971
output file name=+FRA/orcl/datafile/undotbs1.274.686061573 tag=IMG_CPY_UPD RECID=16
STAMP=686061588
channel ORA_DISK_1: datafile copy complete, elapsed time: 00:00:26
channel ORA_DISK_1: starting datafile copy
input datafile file number=00005 name=+DATA/orcl/datafile/example.260.685971993
output file name=+FRA/orcl/datafile/example.276.686061613 tag=IMG_CPY_UPD RECID=17
STAMP=686061625
channel ORA_DISK_1: datafile copy complete, elapsed time: 00:00:16
channel ORA_DISK_1: starting incremental level 1 datafile backup set
channel ORA_DISK_1: specifying datafile(s) in backup set
including current control file in backup set
including current SPFILE in backup set
channel ORA_DISK_1: starting piece 1 at 2009-05-05.12:40:46
channel ORA_DISK_1: finished piece 1 at 2009-05-05.12:40:50
piece handle=+FRA/orcl/backupset/2009_05_05/ncsnn1_tag20090505t123619_0.277.686061647
tag=TAG20090505T123619 comment=NONE
channel ORA_DISK_1: backup set complete, elapsed time: 00:00:04
channel ORA_DISK_1: starting datafile copy
input datafile file number=00004 name=+DATA/orcl/datafile/users.262.685972137
output file name=+FRA/orcl/datafile/users.278.686061661 tag=IMG_CPY_UPD RECID=18
STAMP=686061663
channel ORA_DISK_1: datafile copy complete, elapsed time: 00:00:04
Finished backup at 2009-05-05.12:41:05

Starting backup at 2009-05-05.12:41:05
current log archived
using channel ORA_DISK_1
channel ORA_DISK_1: starting archived log backup set
channel ORA_DISK_1: specifying archived log(s) in backup set
input archived log thread=1 sequence=30 RECID=20 STAMP=686061669
channel ORA_DISK_1: starting piece 1 at 2009-05-05.12:41:21
channel ORA_DISK_1: finished piece 1 at 2009-05-05.12:41:25
piece handle=+FRA/orcl/backupset/2009_05_05/annnf0_tag20090505t124110_0.280.686061681
tag=TAG20090505T124110 comment=NONE
channel ORA_DISK_1: backup set complete, elapsed time: 00:00:04
Finished backup at 2009-05-05.12:41:25
```

Note that since no `INCREMENTAL LEVEL 0` image copy nor any `INCREMENTAL LEVEL 1` backups yet existed for the specified backup tag (`img_cpy_upd`), RMAN had no choice but to create an image copy `INCREMENTAL LEVEL 0` backup of each datafile.

On the second day in this cycle, the same script is run again, but this time RMAN created a new `INCREMENTAL LEVEL 1` backup set containing just the blocks that have changed since the `INCREMENTAL LEVEL 0` image copies have been created, as shown in Listing 5-3.

Listing 5-3   *IUIC Backup Strategy, Cycle 2*

```
#####
# Results from 2nd run:
# - Incremental Level 0 image copies of datafiles 1 - 5 now exist
#   but since no Incremental Level 1 image copy backups yet exist
#   with a tag of img_cpy_upd, none will be applied to the existing
#   Level 0 backups.
# - Incremental Level 1 backups of datafiles 1 - 5 will be taken
#   because Incremental Level 0 backups (their eventual "parents")
#   now exist.
# - Datafile 6 is a new datafile, so RMAN will create an Incremental
#   Level 0 backup for it.
#####

RMAN> RUN {
##############################################################################
# RMAN Script: IncrementallyUpdatedImageCopyBackups.rcv
#
# Creates a daily image copy of all datafiles and Level 1 incremental backups
# for use by the daily image copies. Note that the PLUS ARCHIVELOG command
# will handle archival of any archived redo logs.
#
##############################################################################

# Roll forward any available changes to image copy files from the previous
# set of incremental Level 1 backups
RECOVER
    COPY OF DATABASE
    WITH TAG 'img_cpy_upd';

# Create incremental level 1 backup of all datafiles in the database for
# roll-forward application against image copies
BACKUP
    INCREMENTAL LEVEL 1
    FOR RECOVER OF COPY WITH TAG 'img_cpy_upd'
    DATABASE
    PLUS ARCHIVELOG;
}
2> 3> 4> 5> 6> 7> 8> 9> 10> 11> 12> 13> 14> 15> 16> 17> 18> 19> 20> 21> 22> 23> 24>
Starting recover at 2009-05-05.12:49:33
using channel ORA_DISK_1
no copy of datafile 1 found to recover
no copy of datafile 2 found to recover
no copy of datafile 3 found to recover
```

```
no copy of datafile 4 found to recover
no copy of datafile 5 found to recover
no copy of datafile 6 found to recover
Finished recover at 2009-05-05.12:49:35


Starting backup at 2009-05-05.12:49:36
current log archived
using channel ORA_DISK_1
channel ORA_DISK_1: starting archived log backup set
channel ORA_DISK_1: specifying archived log(s) in backup set
input archived log thread=1 sequence=29 RECID=18 STAMP=686061359
input archived log thread=1 sequence=30 RECID=20 STAMP=686061669
input archived log thread=1 sequence=31 RECID=22 STAMP=686062181
channel ORA_DISK_1: starting piece 1 at 2009-05-05.12:50:07
channel ORA_DISK_1: finished piece 1 at 2009-05-05.12:50:11
piece handle=+FRA/orcl/backupset/2009_05_05/annnf0_tag20090505t124942_0.282.686062209
tag=TAG20090505T124942 comment=NONE
channel ORA_DISK_1: backup set complete, elapsed time: 00:00:04
Finished backup at 2009-05-05.12:50:11

Starting backup at 2009-05-05.12:50:12
using channel ORA_DISK_1
no parent backup or copy of datafile 6 found
channel ORA_DISK_1: starting incremental level 1 datafile backup set
channel ORA_DISK_1: specifying datafile(s) in backup set
input datafile file number=00001 name=+DATA/orcl/datafile/system.257.685971885
input datafile file number=00002 name=+DATA/orcl/datafile/sysaux.258.685971937
input datafile file number=00003 name=+DATA/orcl/datafile/undotbs1.259.685971971
input datafile file number=00005 name=+DATA/orcl/datafile/example.260.685971993
input datafile file number=00004 name=+DATA/orcl/datafile/users.262.685972137
channel ORA_DISK_1: starting piece 1 at 2009-05-05.12:50:27
channel ORA_DISK_1: finished piece 1 at 2009-05-05.12:52:02
piece handle=+FRA/orcl/backupset/2009_05_05/nnndn1_tag20090505t125012_0.283.686062227
tag=TAG20090505T125012 comment=NONE
channel ORA_DISK_1: backup set complete, elapsed time: 00:01:35
channel ORA_DISK_1: starting datafile copy
input datafile file number=00006 name=+DATA/orcl/datafile/data1.261.686061729
output file name=+FRA/orcl/datafile/data1.284.686062335 tag=IMG_CPY_UPD RECID=19
STAMP=686062338
channel ORA_DISK_1: datafile copy complete, elapsed time: 00:00:08
channel ORA_DISK_1: starting incremental level 1 datafile backup set
channel ORA_DISK_1: specifying datafile(s) in backup set
including current control file in backup set
including current SPFILE in backup set
channel ORA_DISK_1: starting piece 1 at 2009-05-05.12:52:38
channel ORA_DISK_1: finished piece 1 at 2009-05-05.12:52:42
piece handle=+FRA/orcl/backupset/2009_05_05/ncsnn1_tag20090505t125012_0.285.686062359
tag=TAG20090505T125012 comment=NONE
channel ORA_DISK_1: backup set complete, elapsed time: 00:00:04
Finished backup at 2009-05-05.12:52:42

Starting backup at 2009-05-05.12:52:42
current log archived
using channel ORA_DISK_1
channel ORA_DISK_1: starting archived log backup set
channel ORA_DISK_1: specifying archived log(s) in backup set
input archived log thread=1 sequence=32 RECID=24 STAMP=686062365
```

```
channel ORA_DISK_1: starting piece 1 at 2009-05-05.12:52:58
channel ORA_DISK_1: finished piece 1 at 2009-05-05.12:53:02
piece handle=+FRA/orcl/backupset/2009_05_05/annnf0_tag20090505t125246_0.287.686062379
tag=TAG20090505T125246 comment=NONE
channel ORA_DISK_1: backup set complete, elapsed time: 00:00:04
Finished backup at 2009-05-05.12:53:02
```

Finally, on the third (and all subsequent) days in this cycle, RMAN will at last begin processing the IUIC strategy and will recover the image copy of each datafile by one day using the oldest INCREMENTAL LEVEL 1 backup set, as shown in Listing 5-4.

Listing 5-4 *IUIC Backup Strategy, Cycle 3*

```
#####
# Results from 3rd run:
# - The previous night's Incremental Level 1 backups for datafiles 1 - 5
#   will now be applied to their Incremental Level 0 image copy "parents."
# - Incremental Level 1 backups of datafiles 1 - 6 will be taken.
# - The Incremental Level 0 image copy backup of datafile 6 will not yet
#   be updated from Incremental Level 1 backups until the next run.
#####

RMAN> RUN {
###############################################################################
# RMAN Script: IncrementallyUpdatedImageCopyBackups.rcv
#
# Creates a daily image copy of all datafiles and Level 1 incremental backups
# for use by the daily image copies. Note that the PLUS ARCHIVELOG command
# will handle archival of any archived redo logs.
#
###############################################################################

# Roll forward any available changes to image copy files from the previous
# set of incremental Level 1 backups
RECOVER
    COPY OF DATABASE
    WITH TAG 'img_cpy_upd';

# Create incremental level 1 backup of all datafiles in the database for
# roll-forward application against image copies
BACKUP
    INCREMENTAL LEVEL 1
    FOR RECOVER OF COPY WITH TAG 'img_cpy_upd'
    DATABASE
    PLUS ARCHIVELOG;
}
2> 3> 4> 5> 6> 7> 8> 9> 10> 11> 12> 13> 14> 15> 16> 17> 18> 19> 20> 21> 22> 23> 24>
Starting recover at 2009-05-05.13:28:26
using channel ORA_DISK_1
no copy of datafile 6 found to recover
channel ORA_DISK_1: starting incremental datafile backup set restore
channel ORA_DISK_1: specifying datafile copies to recover
recovering datafile copy file number=00001 name=+FRA/orcl/datafile/
```

```
system.264.686061393
recovering datafile copy file number=00002 name=+FRA/orcl/datafile/
sysaux.265.686061485
recovering datafile copy file number=00003 name=+FRA/orcl/datafile/
undotbs1.274.686061573
recovering datafile copy file number=00004 name=+FRA/orcl/datafile/users.278.686061661
recovering datafile copy file number=00005 name=+FRA/orcl/datafile/
example.276.686061613
channel ORA_DISK_1: reading from backup piece +FRA/orcl/backupset/2009_05_05/nnndn1_ta
g20090505t125012_0.283.686062227
channel ORA_DISK_1: piece handle=+FRA/orcl/backupset/2009_05_05/nnndn1_tag2009050
5t125012_0.283.686062227 tag=TAG20090505T125012
channel ORA_DISK_1: restored backup piece 1
channel ORA_DISK_1: restore complete, elapsed time: 00:00:08
Finished recover at 2009-05-05.13:28:37

Starting backup at 2009-05-05.13:28:39
current log archived
using channel ORA_DISK_1
channel ORA_DISK_1: starting archived log backup set
channel ORA_DISK_1: specifying archived log(s) in backup set
input archived log thread=1 sequence=29 RECID=18 STAMP=686061359
input archived log thread=1 sequence=30 RECID=20 STAMP=686061669
input archived log thread=1 sequence=31 RECID=22 STAMP=686062181
input archived log thread=1 sequence=32 RECID=24 STAMP=686062365
input archived log thread=1 sequence=33 RECID=26 STAMP=686064523
channel ORA_DISK_1: starting piece 1 at 2009-05-05.13:29:00
channel ORA_DISK_1: finished piece 1 at 2009-05-05.13:29:01
piece handle=+FRA/orcl/backupset/2009_05_05/annnf0_tag20090505t132844_0.289.686064541
tag=TAG20090505T132844 comment=NONE
channel ORA_DISK_1: backup set complete, elapsed time: 00:00:02
Finished backup at 2009-05-05.13:29:02

Starting backup at 2009-05-05.13:29:02
using channel ORA_DISK_1
channel ORA_DISK_1: starting incremental level 1 datafile backup set
channel ORA_DISK_1: specifying datafile(s) in backup set
input datafile file number=00001 name=+DATA/orcl/datafile/system.257.685971885
input datafile file number=00002 name=+DATA/orcl/datafile/sysaux.258.685971937
input datafile file number=00003 name=+DATA/orcl/datafile/undotbs1.259.685971971
input datafile file number=00005 name=+DATA/orcl/datafile/example.260.685971993
input datafile file number=00006 name=+DATA/orcl/datafile/data1.261.686061729
input datafile file number=00004 name=+DATA/orcl/datafile/users.262.685972137
channel ORA_DISK_1: starting piece 1 at 2009-05-05.13:29:14
channel ORA_DISK_1: finished piece 1 at 2009-05-05.13:30:50
piece handle=+FRA/orcl/backupset/2009_05_05/nnndn1_tag20090505t132902_0.290.686064555
tag=TAG20090505T132902 comment=NONE
channel ORA_DISK_1: backup set complete, elapsed time: 00:01:36
channel ORA_DISK_1: starting incremental level 1 datafile backup set
channel ORA_DISK_1: specifying datafile(s) in backup set
including current control file in backup set
including current SPFILE in backup set
channel ORA_DISK_1: starting piece 1 at 2009-05-05.13:31:05
channel ORA_DISK_1: finished piece 1 at 2009-05-05.13:31:09
piece handle=+FRA/orcl/backupset/2009_05_05/ncsnn1_tag20090505t132902_0.291.686064665
tag=TAG20090505T132902 comment=NONE
```

```
channel ORA_DISK_1: backup set complete, elapsed time: 00:00:04
Finished backup at 2009-05-05.13:31:09

Starting backup at 2009-05-05.13:31:09
current log archived
using channel ORA_DISK_1
channel ORA_DISK_1: starting archived log backup set
channel ORA_DISK_1: specifying archived log(s) in backup set
input archived log thread=1 sequence=34 RECID=28 STAMP=686064673
channel ORA_DISK_1: starting piece 1 at 2009-05-05.13:31:26
channel ORA_DISK_1: finished piece 1 at 2009-05-05.13:31:29
piece handle=+FRA/orcl/backupset/2009_05_05/annnf0_tag20090505t133114_0.293.686064687
tag=TAG20090505T133114 comment=NONE
channel ORA_DISK_1: backup set complete, elapsed time: 00:00:03
Finished backup at 2009-05-05.13:31:30
```

The oldest INCREMENTAL LEVEL 1 backup sets and archived redo logs that are now prior to the RPO are eligible to be marked with a status of OBSOLETE and, when the FRA encounters space pressure, will be automatically deleted. However, note that the incrementally updated image copies of each datafile that have been recovered forward by one day using this process will *never* be deleted; in fact, they will continue to be used as the basis of all backup operations. Best of all, since these incrementally recovered image copies are retained in the FRA, they are available for immediate restoration and recovery operations should a datafile become damaged, corrupted, or even deleted due to human error.

TIP & TECHNIQUE
The IUIC strategy can also be expanded for a RPO that is greater than one day. See My Oracle Support (MOS) Note 351455.1, Oracle Suggested Strategy & Backup Retention, *for complete information.*

Advanced RMAN Features

Some other RMAN features that were first introduced in Oracle Database 11*g* R1 and 12*c* R1 offer some potentially extreme benefits for increasing both the efficiency and speed of migration techniques that we have already discussed.

RMAN Enhancements in Oracle 11*g*: Multi-Piece Backup Sets

Oracle Database 11*g* R1 introduced the concept of *multi-piece backup sets*, which permits RMAN to back up extremely large datafiles in parallel via one or more I/O channels, storing each section of the datafile's blocks as smaller pieces of the whole. Listing 5-5 shows an example of how to use this feature—specified via the SECTION SIZE directive—to back up a larger datafile in 25MB "chunks" over multiple channels.

Listing 5-5 *Creating Multi-Piece Backup Sets*

```
RMAN> BACKUP AS BACKUPSET
      SECTION SIZE 25M
      TABLESPACE UNDOTBS1;
Starting backup at 26-MAY-14
using channel ORA_DISK_1
using channel ORA_DISK_2
channel ORA_DISK_1: starting full datafile backup set
channel ORA_DISK_1: specifying datafile(s) in backup set
input datafile file number=00003 name=+DATA/orcl/datafile/undotbs1.261.848415217
backing up blocks 1 through 3200
channel ORA_DISK_1: starting piece 1 at 26-MAY-14
channel ORA_DISK_2: starting full datafile backup set
channel ORA_DISK_2: specifying datafile(s) in backup set
input datafile file number=00003 name=+DATA/orcl/datafile/undotbs1.261.848415217
backing up blocks 3201 through 6400
channel ORA_DISK_2: starting piece 2 at 26-MAY-14
channel ORA_DISK_1: finished piece 1 at 26-MAY-14
piece
. . .
channel ORA_DISK_1: specifying datafile(s) in backup set
input datafile file number=00003 name=+DATA/orcl/datafile/undotbs1.261.848415217
backing up blocks 44801 through 46080
channel ORA_DISK_1: starting piece 15 at 26-MAY-14
channel ORA_DISK_2: finished piece 14 at 26-MAY-14
piece handle=/u01/app/oracle/fast_recovery_area/ORCL/backupset/2014_05_26/o1_mf_nnndf_
TAG20140526T175413_9r7kjrp6_.bkp tag=TAG20140526T175413 comment=NONE
channel ORA_DISK_2: backup set complete, elapsed time: 00:00:00
channel ORA_DISK_1: finished piece 15 at 26-MAY-14
piece handle=/u01/app/oracle/fast_recovery_area/ORCL/backupset/2014_05_26/o1_mf_nnndf_
TAG20140526T175413_9r7kjrv5_.bkp tag=TAG20140526T175413 comment=NONE
channel ORA_DISK_1: backup set complete, elapsed time: 00:00:01
Finished backup at 26-MAY-14
```

RMAN Enhancements in Oracle 12*c*

Oracle Database 12*c* R1 expanded upon 11*g*'s new features and added several of
its own:

- **Multi-piece image copies**   Like 11*g* R1's ability to split up any enormous
  datafile into a series of multiple pieces, 12*c* now makes it possible to create
  image copies of very large datafiles. This means it's now possible to use
  multiple RMAN channels to parallelize image copy creation.

- **Smarter active database cloning**   In prior releases, DUPLICATE DATABASE
  operations against an active database always used image copies to push
  information from the source database to the destination. Oracle 12*c* has
  improved the intelligence of DUPLICATE DATABASE to allow it to choose
  to use either RMAN image copies or backup sets during the cloning, as well
  as the opportunity for the destination database to pull the data from the
  source instead of having the source database push the backups to its eventual
  destination.

- **Full transportable exports**   Perhaps the most impressive new migration tool is the integration of Data Pump, `DBMS_FILE_TRANSFER`, and RMAN Transportable Tablespace Sets (TTS) under a single set of commands. We will cover this new *Full Transportable Export* feature in extensive detail in Chapters 9 and 13 when we review the available alternatives for database transformation and upgrade when an Oracle 12*c* database is the eventual destination.

Migrating Between ASM and Other File Systems

Now that we have firmly established the multiple reasons for why any "post-10*g*" Oracle DBA should strongly consider using RMAN for all of her Oracle database backup and recovery requirements, let us consider its powerful capabilities for migration between traditional file systems—for example, Linux EXT3 and EXT4, Microsoft's NTFS, and other OS-specific file systems—and Oracle's proprietary Automatic Storage Management (ASM) file system.

If the database can tolerate sufficient downtime while the database is migrated to ASM storage, and there is sufficient disk space on the target ASM disk groups, then RMAN can complete the migration in an extremely short time. Note that this same migration strategy can be readily adapted to handle situations in which the physical disk space needed to complete the migration must first be reclaimed from existing storage devices. The final migration method selected will depend on both the amount of downtime that the non-ASM system can tolerate and the amount of disk space available on the ASM file system for migration of the entire database.

Non-ASM to ASM Migration: Complete Migration

Our first migration scenario will leverage RMAN to perform a complete migration of a database from a non-ASM storage system to an ASM storage system. Consider the following scenario for the database that is the target of the migration operation:

- The operating system is Oracle Linux Version 6 Update 3 (the kernel is 2.6.39-400.17.1.el6uek.x86_64).

- Oracle Grid Infrastructure has already been installed and there is an active ASM instance configured.

- The database to be migrated has been upgraded to Oracle Database Release 11.2.0.4.

- The database is approximately 2.5GB in size and is already in ARCHIVELOG mode.

- All database files—including the server parameter file (SPFILE), control files, datafiles, temp files, online redo logs, archived redo logs, and all backup files—are currently retained on Linux's proprietary EXT4 file system.

- There is sufficient space in the +DATA ASM disk group for the database's SPFILE, control files, permanent tablespace datafiles, temporary tablespace files, and online redo logs.

- There is sufficient space in the +FRA ASM disk group for all archived redo logs.

Phase 1: Migration Preparation

The first phase in the migration effort is to prepare the database and its largest physical files—the datafiles for all its tablespaces—for migration. Checklist 5-1 lays out the required steps to complete this phase, which are presented in detail in the following subsections.

Step	Operation	Description	Done?
1	Capture database file metadata	Capture metadata for all database files about to be migrated.	
2	Verify COMPATIBLE setting	If COMPATIBLE is < 11.0.0.0, then it will be necessary to change any READ ONLY transportable tablespaces to READ WRITE mode.	
3	Create INCREMENTAL LEVEL 0 image copy backups of all datafiles	Back up all datafiles as INCREMENTAL LEVEL 0 image copy backups, routing them to their eventual ASM disk group(s).	
4	Create INCREMENTAL LEVEL 1 backups of all datafiles	Create INCREMENTAL LEVEL 1 differential backups for all datafiles.	

CHECKLIST 5-1 *Migration Preparation Operations*

Capture Database File Metadata   The SQL commands in Listing 5-6 capture all the metadata about all of the database files for the database about to be migrated. This metadata is especially useful to confirm the state of the migrated database at any point in time during the migration. Listing 5-7 shows the resulting output from the commands issued in Listing 5-6.

Listing 5-6 *Pre-Migration—Database File Metadata*

```
SET LINESIZE 110
SET PAGESIZE 20000
TTITLE "Control File Status"
COL name                    FORMAT A80      HEADING "Control File Name" WRAP
COL status                  FORMAT A07      HEADING "Status"
COL rcvydest                FORMAT A04      HEADING "Made|Via|FRA?"
SELECT
     name
    ,status
    ,is_recovery_dest_file rcvydest
  FROM v$controlfile
;
TTITLE OFF


TTITLE "Online Redo Log Groups File Status"
COL group#                  FORMAT 9999     HEADING "Log|File|Grp#"
COL member                  FORMAT A80      HEADING "File Name" WRAP
COL type                    FORMAT A07      HEADING "Type"
COL status                  FORMAT A07      HEADING "Status"
COL rcvydest                FORMAT A04      HEADING "Made|Via|FRA?"
SELECT
     group#
    ,member
    ,status
    ,type
    ,is_recovery_dest_file rcvydest
  FROM v$logfile
;
TTITLE OFF


TTITLE "DataFile Status"
COL file#                   FORMAT 9999     HEADING "Data|File|#"
COL name                    FORMAT A80      HEADING "DataFile Name" WRAP
COL status                  FORMAT A07      HEADING "Status"
SELECT
     file#
    ,name
    ,status
  FROM v$datafile
;
TTITLE OFF


TTITLE "TempFile Status"
COL file#                   FORMAT 9999     HEADING "Temp|File|#"
COL name                    FORMAT A80      HEADING "TempFile Name" WRAP
COL status                  FORMAT A07      HEADING "Status"
SELECT
     file#
    ,name
    ,status
  FROM v$tempfile
;
TTITLE OFF
```

Listing 5-7   *Captured Database File Metadata*

```
                            Control File Status

Control File Name
--------------------------------------------------------------------------------
/u01/app/oracle/oradata/ORCL/controlfile/o1_mf_9qpv1761_.ctl
/u01/app/oracle/fast_recovery_area/ORCL/controlfile/o1_mf_9qpv179q_.ctl

                        Online Redo Log Groups File Status
   Log
  File
  Grp# File Name                                                          Type
  ----- --------------------------------------------------------------    ------
     1 /u01/app/oracle/oradata/ORCL/onlinelog/o1_mf_1_9qpv19kr_.log        ONLINE
     1 /u01/app/oracle/fast_recovery_area/ORCL/onlinelog/o1_mf_1_9qpv19nj_.log  ONLINE
     2 /u01/app/oracle/oradata/ORCL/onlinelog/o1_mf_2_9qpv1c0s_.log        ONLINE
     2 /u01/app/oracle/fast_recovery_area/ORCL/onlinelog/o1_mf_2_9qpv1c39_.log  ONLINE
     3 /u01/app/oracle/oradata/ORCL/onlinelog/o1_mf_3_9qpv1dgj_.log        ONLINE
     3 /u01/app/oracle/fast_recovery_area/ORCL/onlinelog/o1_mf_3_9qpv1djw_.log  ONLINE

                              DataFile Status
  Data
  File
    # DataFile Name                                                       Status
  ----- --------------------------------------------------------------    ------
     1 /u01/app/oracle/oradata/ORCL/datafile/o1_mf_system_9qptyxl7_.dbf    SYSTEM
     2 /u01/app/oracle/oradata/ORCL/datafile/o1_mf_sysaux_9qptyxmo_.dbf    ONLINE
     3 /u01/app/oracle/oradata/ORCL/datafile/o1_mf_undotbs1_9qptyxms_.dbf  ONLINE
     4 /u01/app/oracle/oradata/ORCL/datafile/o1_mf_users_9qptyxnm_.dbf     ONLINE
     5 /u01/app/oracle/oradata/ORCL/datafile/o1_mf_example_9qpv1kqg_.dbf   ONLINE
     6 /u01/app/oracle/oradata/ORCL/ap_data.dbf                            ONLINE
     7 /u01/app/oracle/oradata/ORCL/ap_idx.dbf                             ONLINE
     8 /u01/app/oracle/oradata/ORCL/ado_hot_data.dbf                       ONLINE
     9 /u01/app/oracle/oradata/ORCL/ado_hot_idx.dbf                        ONLINE
    10 /u01/app/oracle/oradata/ORCL/ado_warm_data.dbf                      ONLINE
    11 /u01/app/oracle/oradata/ORCL/ado_warm_idx.dbf                       ONLINE
    12 /u01/app/oracle/oradata/ORCL/ado_cool_data.dbf                      ONLINE
    13 /u01/app/oracle/oradata/ORCL/ado_cool_idx.dbf                       ONLINE
    14 /u01/app/oracle/oradata/ORCL/ado_cold_data.dbf                      ONLINE
    15 /u01/app/oracle/oradata/ORCL/ado_cold_idx.dbf                       ONLINE

                              TempFile Status
  Temp
  File
    # TempFile Name                                                       Status
  ----- --------------------------------------------------------------    ------
     1 /u01/app/oracle/oradata/ORCL/datafile/o1_mf_temp_9qpv1jll_.tmp      ONLINE
```

Verify COMPATIBLE Setting   If a database's COMPATIBLE initialization parameter is still set to a value of less than 11.0.0.0, it will be necessary to bring each transportable tablespace into READ WRITE mode so that RMAN can construct a backup of these tablespaces' datafile(s). Since this database was created via the Database Configuration Assistant (DBCA) under Oracle Release 11.2.0.4, there is no need to do this. However, it is indeed possible that a database that has been migrated from earlier releases may still have its COMPATIBLE setting at an earlier release level, so it's important to verify this:

```
SQL> SHOW PARAMETER COMPATIBLE
NAME                                 TYPE        VALUE
------------------------------------ ----------- ----------
compatible                           string      11.2.0.4.0
```

Create INCREMENTAL LEVEL 0 Image Copy Backups of All Datafiles   This step is crucial to a speedy migration to a different file system. We will construct INCREMENTAL LEVEL 0 image copy backups of all datafiles, but instead of creating them on the *original* file system, we will create these backups on the target ASM disk group(s), as shown in Listing 5-8. This makes extremely short work of these datafiles' recovery in the final phase of the migration process.

Listing 5-8   *Creating INCREMENTAL LEVEL 0 Image Copy Backups*

```
RMAN> BACKUP
      INCREMENTAL LEVEL 0
      AS COPY
      FORMAT '+DATA'
      DATABASE;

Starting backup at 24-MAY-14
using target database control file instead of recovery catalog
allocated channel: ORA_DISK_1
channel ORA_DISK_1: SID=18 device type=DISK
channel ORA_DISK_1: starting datafile copy
input datafile file number=00001 name=/u01/app/oracle/oradata/ORCL/datafile/o1_mf_
system_9qptyxl7_.dbf
output file name=+DATA/orcl/datafile/system.258.848415125 tag=TAG20140524T145200
RECID=3 STAMP=848415164
channel ORA_DISK_1: datafile copy complete, elapsed time: 00:00:45
channel ORA_DISK_1: starting datafile copy
input datafile file number=00002 name=/u01/app/oracle/oradata/ORCL/datafile/o1_mf_
sysaux_9qptyxmo_.dbf
output file name=+DATA/orcl/datafile/sysaux.259.848415167 tag=TAG20140524T145200
RECID=4 STAMP=848415194
channel ORA_DISK_1: datafile copy complete, elapsed time: 00:00:35
channel ORA_DISK_1: starting datafile copy
input datafile file number=00006 name=/u01/app/oracle/oradata/ORCL/ap_data.dbf
output file name=+DATA/orcl/datafile/ap_data.260.848415201 tag=TAG20140524T145200
RECID=5 STAMP=848415212
channel ORA_DISK_1: datafile copy complete, elapsed time: 00:00:15
channel ORA_DISK_1: starting datafile copy
input datafile file number=00003 name=/u01/app/oracle/oradata/ORCL/datafile/o1_mf_
undotbs1_9qptyxms_.dbf
output file name=+DATA/orcl/datafile/undotbs1.261.848415217 tag=TAG20140524T145200
RECID=6 STAMP=848415225
channel ORA_DISK_1: datafile copy complete, elapsed time: 00:00:15
channel ORA_DISK_1: starting datafile copy
```

```
input datafile file number=00005 name=/u01/app/oracle/oradata/ORCL/datafile/o1_mf_
example_9qpv1kqg_.dbf
output file name=+DATA/orcl/datafile/example.262.848415231 tag=TAG20140524T145200
RECID=7 STAMP=848415249
channel ORA_DISK_1: datafile copy complete, elapsed time: 00:00:25
channel ORA_DISK_1: starting datafile copy
input datafile file number=00010 name=/u01/app/oracle/oradata/ORCL/ado_warm_data.dbf
output file name=+DATA/orcl/datafile/ado_warm_data.263.848415257
tag=TAG20140524T145200 RECID=8 STAMP=848415261
channel ORA_DISK_1: datafile copy complete, elapsed time: 00:00:07
channel ORA_DISK_1: starting datafile copy
input datafile file number=00011 name=/u01/app/oracle/oradata/ORCL/ado_warm_idx.dbf
output file name=+DATA/orcl/datafile/ado_warm_idx.264.848415263 tag=TAG20140524T145200
RECID=9 STAMP=848415268
channel ORA_DISK_1: datafile copy complete, elapsed time: 00:00:07
channel ORA_DISK_1: starting datafile copy
input datafile file number=00012 name=/u01/app/oracle/oradata/ORCL/ado_cool_data.dbf
output file name=+DATA/orcl/datafile/ado_cool_data.265.848415271
tag=TAG20140524T145200 RECID=10 STAMP=848415276
channel ORA_DISK_1: datafile copy complete, elapsed time: 00:00:07
channel ORA_DISK_1: starting datafile copy
input datafile file number=00013 name=/u01/app/oracle/oradata/ORCL/ado_cool_idx.dbf
output file name=+DATA/orcl/datafile/ado_cool_idx.266.848415279 tag=TAG20140524T145200
RECID=11 STAMP=848415283
channel ORA_DISK_1: datafile copy complete, elapsed time: 00:00:07
channel ORA_DISK_1: starting datafile copy
input datafile file number=00014 name=/u01/app/oracle/oradata/ORCL/ado_cold_data.dbf
output file name=+DATA/orcl/datafile/ado_cold_data.267.848415285
tag=TAG20140524T145200 RECID=12 STAMP=848415290
channel ORA_DISK_1: datafile copy complete, elapsed time: 00:00:07
channel ORA_DISK_1: starting datafile copy
input datafile file number=00015 name=/u01/app/oracle/oradata/ORCL/ado_cold_idx.dbf
output file name=+DATA/orcl/datafile/ado_cold_idx.268.848415293 tag=TAG20140524T145200
RECID=13 STAMP=848415297
channel ORA_DISK_1: datafile copy complete, elapsed time: 00:00:07
channel ORA_DISK_1: starting datafile copy
input datafile file number=00007 name=/u01/app/oracle/oradata/ORCL/ap_idx.dbf
output file name=+DATA/orcl/datafile/ap_idx.269.848415299 tag=TAG20140524T145200
RECID=14 STAMP=848415304
channel ORA_DISK_1: datafile copy complete, elapsed time: 00:00:07
channel ORA_DISK_1: starting datafile copy
input datafile file number=00008 name=/u01/app/oracle/oradata/ORCL/ado_hot_data.dbf
output file name=+DATA/orcl/datafile/ado_hot_data.270.848415307 tag=TAG20140524T145200
RECID=15 STAMP=848415307
channel ORA_DISK_1: datafile copy complete, elapsed time: 00:00:03
channel ORA_DISK_1: starting datafile copy
input datafile file number=00009 name=/u01/app/oracle/oradata/ORCL/ado_hot_idx.dbf
output file name=+DATA/orcl/datafile/ado_hot_idx.271.848415309 tag=TAG20140524T145200
RECID=16 STAMP=848415310
channel ORA_DISK_1: datafile copy complete, elapsed time: 00:00:03
channel ORA_DISK_1: starting datafile copy
copying current control file
output file name=+DATA/orcl/controlfile/backup.272.848415313 tag=TAG20140524T145200
RECID=17 STAMP=848415313
channel ORA_DISK_1: datafile copy complete, elapsed time: 00:00:01
channel ORA_DISK_1: starting datafile copy
```

```
input datafile file number=00004 name=/u01/app/oracle/oradata/ORCL/datafile/o1_mf_
users_9qptyxnm_.dbf
output file name=+DATA/orcl/datafile/users.273.848415313 tag=TAG20140524T145200
RECID=18 STAMP=848415314
channel ORA_DISK_1: datafile copy complete, elapsed time: 00:00:01
channel ORA_DISK_1: starting incremental level 0 datafile backup set
channel ORA_DISK_1: specifying datafile(s) in backup set
including current SPFILE in backup set
channel ORA_DISK_1: starting piece 1 at 24-MAY-14
channel ORA_DISK_1: finished piece 1 at 24-MAY-14
piece handle=+DATA/orcl/backupset/2014_05_24/nnsnn0_tag20140524t145200_0.274.848415315
tag=TAG20140524T145200 comment=NONE
channel ORA_DISK_1: backup set complete, elapsed time: 00:00:01
Finished backup at 24-MAY-14
```

Create INCREMENTAL LEVEL 1 Backups of All Datafiles   As shown in Listing 5-9, we will also create differential INCREMENTAL LEVEL 1 backups for all datafiles so that we can capture any additional changes to the database's contents after the initial INCREMENTAL LEVEL 0 backups have been created. This is an extremely effective method of capturing just the blocks that have changed since the last backups were created, and we can repeat this process several times before we decide to officially migrate the database to ASM.

Listing 5-9   *Creating INCREMENTAL LEVEL 1 Backup Sets*

```
>> First INCREMENTAL LEVEL 1 backup:
RMAN> BACKUP INCREMENTAL LEVEL 1 FORMAT '+DATA' DATABASE;
Starting backup at 24-MAY-14
using target database control file instead of recovery catalog
allocated channel: ORA_DISK_1
channel ORA_DISK_1: SID=24 device type=DISK
channel ORA_DISK_1: starting incremental level 1 datafile backup set
channel ORA_DISK_1: specifying datafile(s) in backup set
input datafile file number=00001 name=/u01/app/oracle/oradata/ORCL/datafile/o1_mf_system_9qptyxl7_.dbf
input datafile file number=00002 name=/u01/app/oracle/oradata/ORCL/datafile/o1_mf_sysaux_9qptyxmo_.dbf
input datafile file number=00006 name=/u01/app/oracle/oradata/ORCL/ap_data.dbf
input datafile file number=00003 name=/u01/app/oracle/oradata/ORCL/datafile/o1_mf_undotbs1_9qptyxms_.dbf
input datafile file number=00005 name=/u01/app/oracle/oradata/ORCL/datafile/o1_mf_example_9qpv1kqg_.dbf
input datafile file number=00010 name=/u01/app/oracle/oradata/ORCL/ado_warm_data.dbf
input datafile file number=00011 name=/u01/app/oracle/oradata/ORCL/ado_warm_idx.dbf
input datafile file number=00012 name=/u01/app/oracle/oradata/ORCL/ado_cool_data.dbf
input datafile file number=00013 name=/u01/app/oracle/oradata/ORCL/ado_cool_idx.dbf
input datafile file number=00014 name=/u01/app/oracle/oradata/ORCL/ado_cold_data.dbf
input datafile file number=00015 name=/u01/app/oracle/oradata/ORCL/ado_cold_idx.dbf
input datafile file number=00007 name=/u01/app/oracle/oradata/ORCL/ap_idx.dbf
input datafile file number=00008 name=/u01/app/oracle/oradata/ORCL/ado_hot_data.dbf
input datafile file number=00009 name=/u01/app/oracle/oradata/ORCL/ado_hot_idx.dbf
input datafile file number=00004 name=/u01/app/oracle/oradata/ORCL/datafile/o1_mf_users_9qptyxnm_.dbf
channel ORA_DISK_1: starting piece 1 at 24-MAY-14
channel ORA_DISK_1: finished piece 1 at 24-MAY-14
piece handle=+DATA/orcl/backupset/2014_05_24/nnndn1_tag20140524t150949_0.275.848416189
tag=TAG20140524T150949 comment=NONE
channel ORA_DISK_1: backup set complete, elapsed time: 00:00:03
channel ORA_DISK_1: starting incremental level 1 datafile backup set
channel ORA_DISK_1: specifying datafile(s) in backup set
```

```
including current control file in backup set
including current SPFILE in backup set
channel ORA_DISK_1: starting piece 1 at 24-MAY-14
channel ORA_DISK_1: finished piece 1 at 24-MAY-14
piece handle=+DATA/orcl/backupset/2014_05_24/ncsnn1_tag20140524t150949_0.276.848416193
tag=TAG20140524T150949 comment=NONE
channel ORA_DISK_1: backup set complete, elapsed time: 00:00:01
Finished backup at 24-MAY-14


>> Second INCREMENTAL LEVEL 1 backup:
RMAN> BACKUP INCREMENTAL LEVEL 1 FORMAT '+DATA' DATABASE;
Starting backup at 24-MAY-14
using target database control file instead of recovery catalog
allocated channel: ORA_DISK_1
channel ORA_DISK_1: SID=143 device type=DISK
channel ORA_DISK_1: starting incremental level 1 datafile backup set
channel ORA_DISK_1: specifying datafile(s) in backup set
input datafile file number=00001 name=/u01/app/oracle/oradata/ORCL/datafile/o1_mf_system_9qptyxl7_.dbf
input datafile file number=00002 name=/u01/app/oracle/oradata/ORCL/datafile/o1_mf_sysaux_9qptyxmo_.dbf
input datafile file number=00006 name=/u01/app/oracle/oradata/ORCL/ap_data.dbf
input datafile file number=00003 name=/u01/app/oracle/oradata/ORCL/datafile/o1_mf_undotbs1_9qptyxms_.dbf
input datafile file number=00005 name=/u01/app/oracle/oradata/ORCL/datafile/o1_mf_example_9qpv1kqg_.dbf
input datafile file number=00007 name=/u01/app/oracle/oradata/ORCL/ap_idx.dbf
input datafile file number=00010 name=/u01/app/oracle/oradata/ORCL/ado_warm_data.dbf
input datafile file number=00011 name=/u01/app/oracle/oradata/ORCL/ado_warm_idx.dbf
input datafile file number=00012 name=/u01/app/oracle/oradata/ORCL/ado_cool_data.dbf
input datafile file number=00013 name=/u01/app/oracle/oradata/ORCL/ado_cool_idx.dbf
input datafile file number=00014 name=/u01/app/oracle/oradata/ORCL/ado_cold_data.dbf
input datafile file number=00015 name=/u01/app/oracle/oradata/ORCL/ado_cold_idx.dbf
input datafile file number=00008 name=/u01/app/oracle/oradata/ORCL/ado_hot_data.dbf
input datafile file number=00009 name=/u01/app/oracle/oradata/ORCL/ado_hot_idx.dbf
input datafile file number=00004 name=/u01/app/oracle/oradata/ORCL/datafile/o1_mf_users_9qptyxnm_.dbf
channel ORA_DISK_1: starting piece 1 at 24-MAY-14
channel ORA_DISK_1: finished piece 1 at 24-MAY-14
piece handle=+DATA/orcl/backupset/2014_05_24/nnndn1_tag20140524t151405_0.277.848416449
tag=TAG20140524T151405 comment=NONE
channel ORA_DISK_1: backup set complete, elapsed time: 00:00:25
channel ORA_DISK_1: starting incremental level 1 datafile backup set
channel ORA_DISK_1: specifying datafile(s) in backup set
including current control file in backup set
including current SPFILE in backup set
channel ORA_DISK_1: starting piece 1 at 24-MAY-14
channel ORA_DISK_1: finished piece 1 at 24-MAY-14
piece handle=+DATA/orcl/backupset/2014_05_24/ncsnn1_tag20140524t151405_0.278.848416473
tag=TAG20140524T151405 comment=NONE
channel ORA_DISK_1: backup set complete, elapsed time: 00:00:01
Finished backup at 24-MAY-14
```

Phase 2: Prerequisites Immediately Prior to Migration

Once you have completed all Phase 1 checklist items, you need to decide whether it is truly time to finish the migration or to wait because significant additional changes to the existing contents of the database's datafiles are likely. If significant changes are likely, then we recommend taking another set of INCREMENTAL LEVEL 1 backups using the code in Listing 5-9. However, once you have taken the final set of INCREMENTAL LEVEL 1 backups, it's time to make a go/no go decision to complete the migration. Checklist 5-2 outlines the final set of prerequisites that must be completed before proceeding with the final migration. The steps are described in the subsections that follow.

Step	Operation	Description	Done?
1	Archive online redo log	Issue `ALTER SYSTEM SWITCH LOGFILE;` command to archive the most current online redo log.	
2	Disable unnecessary recovery settings	Turn off BCT. Turn off Flashback Database logging. Remove any restore points.	
3	Perform consistent database shutdown	Issue `SHUTDOWN IMMEDIATE` command to ensure no uncommitted changes remain and that all dirtied database buffers are checkpointed.	

CHECKLIST 5-2   *Immediate Pre-Migration Prerequisites*

Archive Online Redo Log   As shown in Listing 5-10, issuing the `ALTER SYSTEM ARCHIVE LOG CURRENT;` command ensures two things: the database is indeed in ARCHIVELOG mode (otherwise, this command will fail) and the most current online redo log has been archived.

Listing 5-10   *Archiving Current Online Redo Logs*

```
SQL> ALTER SYSTEM ARCHIVE LOG CURRENT;
. . .
ALTER SYSTEM ARCHIVE LOG
Sat May 24 14:48:14 2014
Thread 1 advanced to log sequence 50 (LGWR switch)
  Current log# 2 seq# 50 mem# 0: /u01/app/oracle/oradata/ORCL/onlinelog/o1_mf_2_9qpv1c0s_.log
  Current log# 2 seq# 50 mem# 1: /u01/app/oracle/fast_recovery_area/ORCL/onlinelog/o1_mf_2_9qpv1c39_.log
Archived Log entry 4 added for thread 1 sequence 49 ID 0x5201b6d7 dest 1:
. . .
```

Disable Unnecessary Recovery Settings   This step includes the removal of database recovery settings that are simply unnecessary while completing the migration, as shown in Listing 5-11.

Listing 5-11 *Disabling Unnecessary Recovery Settings*

```
-- Disable Block Change Tracking (BCT):
SQL> ALTER DATABASE DISABLE BLOCK CHANGE TRACKING;

ERROR at line 1:
ORA-19759: block change tracking is not enabled


-- Disable Flashback Database logging:
SQL> ALTER DATABASE FLASHBACK OFF;

Database altered.

-- Delete any RESTORE POINTs (if any exist, via DROP RESTORE POINT <rp_name>:
SQL> SELECT * FROM v$restore_point;
no rows selected

>> From database's alert log:
. . .
alter database flashback off
Flashback Database Disabled
Completed: alter database flashback off
Sat May 24 15:38:18 2014
alter database disable block change tracking
ORA-19759 signalled during: alter database disable block change tracking...
. . .
```

Perform Consistent Database Shutdown   The final step in Phase 2 is to cleanly shut down the database that is about to be migrated using the SHUTDOWN IMMEDIATE; command, as shown in Listing 5-12. This ensures that all pending transactions are either committed or rolled back; it also guarantees that the Oracle database has taken a complete checkpoint for all database files before beginning the final phase of the migration process.

Listing 5-12 *Performing a Consistent Database Shutdown*

```
SQL> SHUTDOWN IMMEDIATE;
From database's alert log:
. . .
Shutting down archive processes
Archiving is disabled
Sat May 24 15:43:38 2014
Stopping background process VKTM
ARCH: Archival disabled due to shutdown: 1089
Shutting down archive processes
Archiving is disabled
Sat May 24 15:43:41 2014
Instance shutdown complete
. . .
```

Phase 3: Completing the Migration

Once a successful consistent database shutdown has been achieved, the clock is ticking to complete the migration to ASM. The good news with using this strategy is that most of the work has already been completed through Step 3 of Phase 1; in other words, all of the database's datafiles *have already been migrated to ASM*. All that is left to complete is the migration of the remaining SPFILE, control files, online redo logs, and temporary files to ASM, and this takes an extremely short time, as shown in the examples following the summary checklist in Checklist 5-3.

Step	Operation	Description	Done?
1	Migrate modified SPFILE to ASM	■ Build a PFILE from the current SPFILE. ■ Modify the PFILE's initialization parameters to point to ASM disk group(s) for *all* files. ■ Test the PFILE. ■ Rebuild an ASM-based SPFILE. ■ Restart the instance.	
2	Migrate control files to ASM	Restore the database's control files to the chosen ASM disk group(s).	
3	Mount the database	Mount the database using the newly migrated control files.	
4	Switch to previously migrated datafiles	Use the SWITCH DATABASE TO COPY; RMAN command to switch all datafiles to ASM-based storage.	
5	Recover the database	Perform complete recovery on the migrated datafiles using differential INCREMENTAL LEVEL 1 backups, archived redo logs, and currently online redo logs.	
6	Open the database in RESETLOGS mode	Issue the ALTER DATABASE OPEN RESETLOGS; command to open the database.	
7	Migrate online redo logs to ASM	Re-create all members for the online redo log groups on the chosen ASM disk group(s).	

Step	Operation	Description	Done?
8	Migrate temporary tablespace temp file(s) to ASM	Create a new temp file for all temporary tablespace(s) on the chosen ASM disk group(s).	
9	Switch FRA to ASM	Modify DB_RECOVERY_FILE_ DEST to ASM storage.	
10	Restore/rebuild database backups to FRA on ASM	Optionally, restore any existing backup files to the FRA on its new ASM disk group(s).	
11	Validate the migration	Validate that all database files have been successfully migrated per expectations.	

CHECKLIST 5-3   *Complete Migration to ASM*

Migrate Modified SPFILE to ASM   The first step in the migration process is to update the current database's SPFILE so that it will point to ASM disk groups instead of its current file system for the new database files that will be created during the migration. To satisfy this we'll create a new PFILE from the existing SPFILE, modify the parameters that control the creation of Oracle Managed Files (OMF) so they reference the appropriate ASM disk groups, and then re-create a new SPFILE from that PFILE. Listing 5-13 shows this process.

Listing 5-13   *Creating the New SPFILE*

```
-- Build a new PFILE from the contents of the current SPFILE:
SQL> CREATE PFILE='/home/oracle/init_orcl.ora' FROM SPFILE;
-- Modify these initialization parameters in the PFILE to point to ASM locations:
*.control_files='+DATA','+FRA'
*.db_create_file_dest = "+DATA"
*.db_create_online_log_dest_1= "+DATA"
*.db_create_online_log_dest_2= "+FRA"
-- Test these changes by attempting to restart the database instance with the new PFILE:
SQL> SHUTDOWN IMMEDIATE;
SQL> STARTUP NOMOUNT PFILE='/home/oracle/init_orcl.ora';
. . .
System parameters with non-default values:
  processes              = 150
  sga_target             = 1536M
  control_files          = "+DATA"
  control_files          = "+FRA"
  db_block_size          = 8192
  compatible             = "11.2.0.4.0"
  db_create_file_dest    = "+DATA"
  db_create_online_log_dest_1= "+DATA"
  db_create_online_log_dest_2= "+FRA"
  db_recovery_file_dest  = "/u01/app/oracle/fast_recovery_area". . .
. . .
```

```
-- The instance restart was successful, then rebuild the SPFILE in its new ASM-based location
SQL> SHUTDOWN IMMEDIATE;
SQL> CREATE SPFILE='+DATA/ORCL/spfileorcl.ora'
     FROM PFILE='/home/oracle/init_orcl.ora';
-- Add a new PFILE named $ORACLE_HOME/dbs/initorcl.ora that points to
-- the ASM-based SPFILE. It only contains one line:
*.SPFILE='+DATA/ORCL/spfileorcl.ora'
```

Migrate Control Files to ASM   Now that the control file parameter has been modified in the SPFILE and the database instance has been started—that is, the database is in NOMOUNT mode—we will migrate the control files to ASM via the commands in Listing 5-14.

Listing 5-14   *Migrating Control Files to ASM*

```
RMAN> RESTORE CONTROLFILE FROM '/u01/app/oracle/oradata/ORCL/controlfile/o1_mf_9qpv1761_.ctl;

. . .
Starting restore at 24-MAY-14
using target database control file instead of recovery catalog
allocated channel: ORA_DISK_1
channel ORA_DISK_1: SID=12 device type=DISK
channel ORA_DISK_1: copied control file copy
output file name=+DATA/orcl/controlfile/current.280.848420839
output file name=+FRA/orcl/controlfile/current.256.848420839
Finished restore at 24-MAY-14
SUCCESS: diskgroup DATA was mounted
Sat May 24 16:27:19 2014
NOTE: dependency between database orcl and diskgroup resource ora.DATA.dg is established
SUCCESS: diskgroup FRA was mounted
Spfile +DATA/orcl/spfileorcl.ora is in old pre-11 format and compatible >= 11.0.0; converting
to new H.A.R.D. compliant format.
NOTE: dependency between database orcl and diskgroup resource ora.FRA.dg is established
. . .
```

Mount the Database   As shown in Listing 5-15, it is time to bring the database into MOUNT mode since the control files have been successfully restored to their new ASM disk group.

Listing 5-15   *Mounting the Database*

```
RMAN> ALTER DATABASE MOUNT;
. . .
Sun May 25 08:19:20 2014
alter database mount
Sun May 25 08:19:24 2014
Successful mount of redo thread 1, with mount id 1376245384
Database mounted in Exclusive Mode
Lost write protection disabled
Completed: alter database mount
. . .
```

Switch to Previously Migrated Datafiles   Since all of the datafiles have already been transferred to their new locations on ASM storage, it is time to instruct the database's control file to stop using the original datafiles and start using the ASM-based ones instead via the `SWITCH DATABASE TO COPY` RMAN command, as shown in Listing 5-16.

Listing 5-16   *Switching Datafiles to ASM Storage*

```
RMAN> SWITCH DATABASE TO COPY;
. . .
using target database control file instead of recovery catalog
datafile 1 switched to datafile copy "+DATA/orcl/datafile/system.258.848415125"
datafile 2 switched to datafile copy "+DATA/orcl/datafile/sysaux.259.848415167"
datafile 3 switched to datafile copy "+DATA/orcl/datafile/undotbs1.261.848415217"
datafile 4 switched to datafile copy "+DATA/orcl/datafile/users.273.848415313"
datafile 5 switched to datafile copy "+DATA/orcl/datafile/example.262.848415231"
datafile 6 switched to datafile copy "+DATA/orcl/datafile/ap_data.260.848415201"
datafile 7 switched to datafile copy "+DATA/orcl/datafile/ap_idx.269.848415299"
datafile 8 switched to datafile copy "+DATA/orcl/datafile/ado_hot_data.270.848415307"
datafile 9 switched to datafile copy "+DATA/orcl/datafile/ado_hot_idx.271.848415309"
datafile 10 switched to datafile copy "+DATA/orcl/datafile/ado_warm_data.263.848415257"
datafile 11 switched to datafile copy "+DATA/orcl/datafile/ado_warm_idx.264.848415263"
datafile 12 switched to datafile copy "+DATA/orcl/datafile/ado_cool_data.265.848415271"
datafile 13 switched to datafile copy "+DATA/orcl/datafile/ado_cool_idx.266.848415279"
datafile 14 switched to datafile copy "+DATA/orcl/datafile/ado_cold_data.267.848415285"
datafile 15 switched to datafile copy "+DATA/orcl/datafile/ado_cold_idx.268.848415293"
. . .
```

Recover the Database   Since all datafiles have essentially been restored, the next step is to recover the database. RMAN will leverage all available `INCREMENTAL LEVEL 1` backups generated since the original image copy backups of the datafiles were created as well as any archived redo logs and the current online redo log to complete their recovery, as shown in Listing 5-17.

Listing 5-17   *Recovering the Database*

```
RMAN> RECOVER DATABASE;
Starting recover at 25-MAY-14
allocated channel: ORA_DISK_1
channel ORA_DISK_1: SID=135 device type=DISK
channel ORA_DISK_1: starting incremental datafile backup set restore
channel ORA_DISK_1: specifying datafile(s) to restore from backup set
destination for restore of datafile 00001: +DATA/orcl/datafile/system.258.848415125
destination for restore of datafile 00002: +DATA/orcl/datafile/sysaux.259.848415167
destination for restore of datafile 00003: +DATA/orcl/datafile/undotbs1.261.848415217
destination for restore of datafile 00004: +DATA/orcl/datafile/users.273.848415313
destination for restore of datafile 00005: +DATA/orcl/datafile/example.262.848415231
```

```
destination for restore of datafile 00006: +DATA/orcl/datafile/ap_data.260.848415201
destination for restore of datafile 00007: +DATA/orcl/datafile/ap_idx.269.848415299
destination for restore of datafile 00008: +DATA/orcl/datafile/ado_hot_data.270.848415307
destination for restore of datafile 00009: +DATA/orcl/datafile/ado_hot_idx.271.848415309
destination for restore of datafile 00010: +DATA/orcl/datafile/ado_warm_data.263.848415257
destination for restore of datafile 00011: +DATA/orcl/datafile/ado_warm_idx.264.848415263
destination for restore of datafile 00012: +DATA/orcl/datafile/ado_cool_data.265.848415271
destination for restore of datafile 00013: +DATA/orcl/datafile/ado_cool_idx.266.848415279
destination for restore of datafile 00014: +DATA/orcl/datafile/ado_cold_data.267.848415285
destination for restore of datafile 00015: +DATA/orcl/datafile/ado_cold_idx.268.848415293
channel ORA_DISK_1: reading from backup piece +DATA/orcl/backupset/2014_05_24/nnndn1_tag20140
524t150949_0.275.848416189
channel ORA_DISK_1: piece handle=+DATA/orcl/backupset/2014_05_24/nnndn1_tag2014052
4t150949_0.275.848416189 tag=TAG20140524T150949
channel ORA_DISK_1: restored backup piece 1
channel ORA_DISK_1: restore complete, elapsed time: 00:00:01
channel ORA_DISK_1: starting incremental datafile backup set restore
channel ORA_DISK_1: specifying datafile(s) to restore from backup set
destination for restore of datafile 00001: +DATA/orcl/datafile/system.258.848415125
destination for restore of datafile 00002: +DATA/orcl/datafile/sysaux.259.848415167
destination for restore of datafile 00003: +DATA/orcl/datafile/undotbs1.261.848415217
destination for restore of datafile 00004: +DATA/orcl/datafile/users.273.848415313
destination for restore of datafile 00005: +DATA/orcl/datafile/example.262.848415231
destination for restore of datafile 00006: +DATA/orcl/datafile/ap_data.260.848415201
destination for restore of datafile 00007: +DATA/orcl/datafile/ap_idx.269.848415299
destination for restore of datafile 00008: +DATA/orcl/datafile/ado_hot_data.270.848415307
destination for restore of datafile 00009: +DATA/orcl/datafile/ado_hot_idx.271.848415309
destination for restore of datafile 00010: +DATA/orcl/datafile/ado_warm_data.263.848415257
destination for restore of datafile 00011: +DATA/orcl/datafile/ado_warm_idx.264.848415263
destination for restore of datafile 00012: +DATA/orcl/datafile/ado_cool_data.265.848415271
destination for restore of datafile 00013: +DATA/orcl/datafile/ado_cool_idx.266.848415279
destination for restore of datafile 00014: +DATA/orcl/datafile/ado_cold_data.267.848415285
destination for restore of datafile 00015: +DATA/orcl/datafile/ado_cold_idx.268.848415293
channel ORA_DISK_1: reading from backup piece +DATA/orcl/backupset/2014_05_24/nnndn1_tag20140
524t151405_0.277.848416449
channel ORA_DISK_1: piece handle=+DATA/orcl/backupset/2014_05_24/nnndn1_tag2014052
4t151405_0.277.848416449 tag=TAG20140524T151405
channel ORA_DISK_1: restored backup piece 1
channel ORA_DISK_1: restore complete, elapsed time: 00:00:36

starting media recovery
media recovery complete, elapsed time: 00:00:01
Finished recover at 25-MAY-14
```

Open the Database   Because the database's control files were simply relocated rather than restored from a backup of the control file, the database can be opened with the ALTER DATABASE OPEN; command, as shown in Listing 5-18.

Listing 5-18   *Opening the Database*

```
RMAN> ALTER DATABASE OPEN;
RMAN> alter database open;
database opened
>> Detail from alert log:
Sun May 25 08:27:55 2014
```

```
alter database open
Sun May 25 08:27:56 2014
LGWR: STARTING ARCH PROCESSES
Sun May 25 08:27:56 2014
ARC0 started with pid=26, OS id=20320
ARC0: Archival started
LGWR: STARTING ARCH PROCESSES COMPLETE
ARC0: STARTING ARCH PROCESSES
Sun May 25 08:27:57 2014
ARC1 started with pid=27, OS id=20322
Thread 1 opened at log sequence 58
  Current log# 1 seq# 58 mem# 0: /u01/app/oracle/oradata/ORCL/onlinelog/o1_mf_1_9qpv19kr_.log
  Current log# 1 seq# 58 mem# 1: /u01/app/oracle/fast_recovery_area/ORCL/onlinelog/o1_
mf_1_9qpv19nj_.log
Successful open of redo thread 1
MTTR advisory is disabled because FAST_START_MTTR_TARGET is not set
Sun May 25 08:27:57 2014
ARC2 started with pid=28, OS id=20324
Sun May 25 08:27:57 2014
SMON: enabling cache recovery
Sun May 25 08:27:57 2014
ARC3 started with pid=29, OS id=20326
ARC1: Archival started
ARC2: Archival started
ARC1: Becoming the 'no FAL' ARCH
ARC1: Becoming the 'no SRL' ARCH
ARC2: Becoming the heartbeat ARCH
ARC3: Archival started
ARC0: STARTING ARCH PROCESSES COMPLETE
[20271] Successfully onlined Undo Tablespace 2.
Undo initialization finished serial:0 start:656616204 end:656617064 diff:860 (8 seconds)
Verifying file header compatibility for 11g tablespace encryption..
Verifying 11g file header compatibility for tablespace encryption completed
SMON: enabling tx recovery
Database Characterset is AL32UTF8
No Resource Manager plan active
replication_dependency_tracking turned off (no async multimaster replication found)
Starting background process QMNC
Sun May 25 08:28:01 2014
QMNC started with pid=30, OS id=20328
Sun May 25 08:28:09 2014
Completed: alter database open
Sun May 25 08:28:09 2014
Starting background process CJQ0
Sun May 25 08:28:09 2014
CJQ0 started with pid=35, OS id=20348
Setting Resource Manager plan SCHEDULER[0x32DF]:DEFAULT_MAINTENANCE_PLAN via scheduler window
Setting Resource Manager plan DEFAULT_MAINTENANCE_PLAN via parameter
Sun May 25 08:28:13 2014
Starting background process VKRM
Sun May 25 08:28:13 2014
VKRM started with pid=33, OS id=20359
```

Migrate Online Redo Logs to ASM   You may have noted in Listing 5-18 that, at this point, the database is still using the online redo logs from the non-ASM storage. The next order of business is to convert all online redo logs to use ASM storage. This can be accomplished one of two ways: programmatically or manually.

Programmatic Migration of Online Redo Logs to ASM   Listing 5-19 shows a simple anonymous PL/SQL block (AutoRedoLogMigration.sql) that will automatically build new online disk groups on ASM storage, switch each non-ASM disk group to use ASM, and then automatically delete the original online redo log groups.

Listing 5-19   *Automatically Creating New Online Redo Logs*

```
/*
|| SQL Script:  AutomaticRedoLogMigration.sql
|| Purpose:     Handles automatic migration of all online redo logs (ORLs) for
||              a database when it's being converted from one storage environment
||              to another
|| Author:      Jim Czuprynski (Zero Defect Computing, Inc.)
|| Provenance:  Oracle 11gR2 Automatic Storage Management Guide (E18951-03)
*/

SET SERVEROUTPUT ON;
DECLARE
    CURSOR curORLG IS
        SELECT
             group# grp
            ,thread# thr
            ,bytes
            ,'NO' srl
          FROM v$log
        UNION
        SELECT
             group# grp
            ,thread# thr
            ,bytes
            ,'YES' srl
          FROM v$standby_log
         ORDER BY 1;
    stmt VARCHAR2(2048);

BEGIN
    FOR rec IN curORLG
        LOOP
            -----
            -- Is the online redo log actually a standby redo log (SRL) because
            -- this is a physical standby database? If so, then rebuild it
            -- as such and drop the original SRL group ...
            -----
            IF (rec.srl = 'YES') THEN
                stmt := 'ALTER DATABASE ADD STANDBY LOGFILE THREAD ' ||
                        rec.thr || ' SIZE ' || rec.bytes;
                EXECUTE IMMEDIATE stmt;
                stmt := 'ALTER DATABASE DROP STANDBY LOGFILE GROUP ' || rec.grp;
                EXECUTE IMMEDIATE stmt;
            ELSE
                -----
                -- ... otherwise, it must be a normal ORL, so handle it as such,
                -- being sure to checkpoint the system when the ORL encountered
                -- is the +current+ ORL.
```

```
       -----
           stmt := 'ALTER DATABASE ADD LOGFILE THREAD ' ||
                   rec.thr || ' SIZE ' || rec.bytes;
           EXECUTE IMMEDIATE stmt;
           BEGIN
               stmt := 'ALTER DATABASE DROP LOGFILE GROUP ' || rec.grp;
               DBMS_OUTPUT.PUT_LINE(stmt);
               EXECUTE IMMEDIATE stmt;
           EXCEPTION
               WHEN OTHERS THEN
                   EXECUTE IMMEDIATE 'ALTER SYSTEM SWITCH LOGFILE';
                   EXECUTE IMMEDIATE 'ALTER SYSTEM CHECKPOINT GLOBAL';
                   EXECUTE IMMEDIATE stmt;
           END;
         END IF;
       END LOOP;
END;
/
```

Manual Migration of Online Redo Logs to ASM   Listing 5-20 offers the manual approach to accomplishing the migration of online redo logs. While more tedious than the method shown in Listing 5-19, it does offer the flexibility of creating the online redo logs with a larger size and does accommodate the newer 4KB sector size disks introduced in recent years.

4KB Sector Size Disks, Native vs. Emulation Mode, and Online Redo Logs

If the physical disks that underlie the new ASM disk groups utilize a 4KB sector size, then the new online redo log groups must be created using the BLOCKSIZE parameter as shown in Listing 5-20. It's also important to find out if the 4KB sector size disks are using *native* versus *emulation* mode for writing out data from the Logical Byte Addresses (LBAs) in the disks' cache. Be aware that disk drives using emulation mode instead of native mode can have an unexpectedly negative performance impact when online redo log entries are written to those devices!

Listing 5-20   *Manually Creating New Online Redo Logs*

```
-- Create three new online redo log groups
SQL> ALTER DATABASE ADD LOGFILE THREAD 1;
SQL> ALTER DATABASE ADD LOGFILE THREAD 1;
SQL> ALTER DATABASE ADD LOGFILE THREAD 1;
-- Confirm current state and location of all online redo log groups
SQL> COL member FORMAT A50 WRAP
```

```
SQL> SELECT group#, member FROM v$logfile ORDER BY 1,2;
    GROUP# MEMBER
---------- --------------------------------------------------
         1 /u01/app/oracle/fast_recovery_area/ORCL/onlinelog/
           o1_mf_1_9qpv19nj_.log
         1 /u01/app/oracle/oradata/ORCL/onlinelog/o1_mf_1_9qp
           v19kr_.log
         2 /u01/app/oracle/fast_recovery_area/ORCL/onlinelog/
           o1_mf_2_9qpv1c39_.log
         2 /u01/app/oracle/oradata/ORCL/onlinelog/o1_mf_2_9qp
           v1c0s_.log
         3 /u01/app/oracle/fast_recovery_area/ORCL/onlinelog/
           o1_mf_3_9qpv1djw_.log
         3 /u01/app/oracle/oradata/ORCL/onlinelog/o1_mf_3_9qp
           v1dgj_.log
         4 +DATA/orcl/onlinelog/group_4.282.848687267
         4 +FRA/orcl/onlinelog/group_4.258.848687269
         5 +DATA/orcl/onlinelog/group_5.281.848687277
         5 +FRA/orcl/onlinelog/group_5.257.848687279
         6 +DATA/orcl/onlinelog/group_6.283.848687297
         6 +FRA/orcl/onlinelog/group_6.259.848687299

-- Switch logs 3 times and then take complete checkpoint:
SQL> ALTER SYSTEM ARCHIVE LOG CURRENT;
SQL> ALTER SYSTEM ARCHIVE LOG CURRENT;
SQL> ALTER SYSTEM ARCHIVE LOG CURRENT;
SQL> ALTER SYSTEM CHECKPOINT;
SQL> SELECT group#, status,
       (bytes/(1024*1024)) size_mb, blocksize
       FROM v$log ORDER BY 1;

    GROUP# STATUS              SIZE_MB  BLOCKSIZE
---------- ----------------  ---------- ----------
         1 INACTIVE                  50        512
         2 INACTIVE                  50        512
         3 INACTIVE                  50        512
         4 INACTIVE                 100        512
         5 INACTIVE                 100        512
         6 CURRENT                  100        512

-- Now drop original online redo log groups
SQL> ALTER DATABASE DROP LOGFILE GROUP 1;
Database altered.
SQL> ALTER DATABASE DROP LOGFILE GROUP 2;
Database altered.
SQL> ALTER DATABASE DROP LOGFILE GROUP 3;
Database altered.
>> Details from database's alert log:
. . .
Completed: alter database drop logfile group 5
Tue May 27 18:27:47 2014
ALTER DATABASE ADD LOGFILE THREAD 1
Completed: ALTER DATABASE ADD LOGFILE THREAD 1
Tue May 27 18:27:57 2014
ALTER DATABASE ADD LOGFILE THREAD 1
Completed: ALTER DATABASE ADD LOGFILE THREAD 1
Tue May 27 18:28:16 2014
```

```
ALTER DATABASE ADD LOGFILE THREAD 1
Completed: ALTER DATABASE ADD LOGFILE THREAD 1
Tue May 27 18:31:05 2014
ALTER SYSTEM ARCHIVE LOG
Tue May 27 18:31:05 2014
Thread 1 advanced to log sequence 63 (LGWR switch)
  Current log# 4 seq# 63 mem# 0: +DATA/orcl/onlinelog/group_4.282.848687267
  Current log# 4 seq# 63 mem# 1: +FRA/orcl/onlinelog/group_4.258.848687269
Archived Log entry 17 added for thread 1 sequence 62 ID 0x5201b6d7 dest 1:
Tue May 27 18:31:22 2014
ALTER SYSTEM ARCHIVE LOG
Tue May 27 18:31:22 2014
Thread 1 advanced to log sequence 64 (LGWR switch)
  Current log# 5 seq# 64 mem# 0: +DATA/orcl/onlinelog/group_5.281.848687277
  Current log# 5 seq# 64 mem# 1: +FRA/orcl/onlinelog/group_5.257.848687279
Archived Log entry 18 added for thread 1 sequence 63 ID 0x5201b6d7 dest 1:
ALTER SYSTEM ARCHIVE LOG
Thread 1 advanced to log sequence 65 (LGWR switch)
  Current log# 6 seq# 65 mem# 0: +DATA/orcl/onlinelog/group_6.283.848687297
Thread 1 advanced to log sequence 65 (LGWR switch)
  Current log# 6 seq# 65 mem# 1: +FRA/orcl/onlinelog/group_6.259.848687299
Archived Log entry 19 added for thread 1 sequence 64 ID 0x5201b6d7 dest 1:
Tue May 27 18:32:50 2014
ALTER DATABASE DROP LOGFILE GROUP 1
Deleted Oracle managed file /u01/app/oracle/oradata/ORCL/onlinelog/o1_mf_1_9qpv19kr_.log
Deleted Oracle managed file /u01/app/oracle/fast_recovery_area/ORCL/onlinelog/o1_mf_1_9qpv19nj_.log
Completed: ALTER DATABASE DROP LOGFILE GROUP 1
ALTER DATABASE DROP LOGFILE GROUP 2
Deleted Oracle managed file /u01/app/oracle/oradata/ORCL/onlinelog/o1_mf_2_9qpv1c0s_.log
Deleted Oracle managed file /u01/app/oracle/fast_recovery_area/ORCL/onlinelog/o1_mf_2_9qpv1c39_.log
Completed: ALTER DATABASE DROP LOGFILE GROUP 2
Tue May 27 18:33:08 2014
ALTER DATABASE DROP LOGFILE GROUP 3
Deleted Oracle managed file /u01/app/oracle/oradata/ORCL/onlinelog/o1_mf_3_9qpv1dgj_.log
Deleted Oracle managed file /u01/app/oracle/fast_recovery_area/ORCL/onlinelog/o1_mf_3_9qpv1djw_.log
Completed: ALTER DATABASE DROP LOGFILE GROUP 3
. . .
```

Migrate Temporary Tablespace Temp File(s) to ASM   Moving an existing temp
file from non-ASM to ASM-based storage is quite trivial because a temporary
tablespace is typically only used when large amounts of temporary disk space are
needed for SQL statements that require huge sort work areas or for storage of global
temporary table (GTT) segments. Listing 5-21 shows how simple it is to add an
ASM-based temp file to an existing temporary tablespace.

Listing 5-21   *Migrating Temporary Tablespace Temp File(s) to ASM*

```
SQL> ALTER DATABASE
     TEMPFILE '/u01/app/oracle/oradata/ORCL/datafile/o1_mf_temp_9qpv1jll_.tmp' DROP;
SQL> ALTER TABLESPACE temp ADD TEMPFILE;
...
```

Switch FRA to ASM Next, it's time to switch the current non-ASM storage location to its new ASM home:

```
SQL> ALTER SYSTEM SET DB_RECOVERY_FILE_DEST='+FRA';
System altered.
```

NOTE
Now would be a good time to verify the size of the FRA—set via DB_RECOVERY_FILE_DEST_SIZE— to ensure that it's an even multiple of the FRA ASM disk group's Allocation Unit (AU).

Restore/Rebuild Database Backups to FRA on ASM The penultimate task to accomplish is the migration of any existing RMAN backups and other files needed for database recovery to their new home in the ASM-based FRA. To accomplish this, we can either simply allow the next scheduled backup cycle to run, or we can migrate all existing backup files to the new FRA with just a few RMAN commands as shown in Listing 5-22.

Listing 5-22 *Migrating Existing RMAN Backups to ASM-Based FRA*

```
RMAN> BACKUP DATAFILECOPY ALL FORMAT '+FRA';
RMAN> BACKUP BACKUPSET ALL FORMAT '+FRA';
RMAN> BACKUP COPY OF ARCHIVELOG ALL FORMAT '+FRA';
```

Validate the Migration Finally, it's crucial to validate that no Oracle database file has been left behind inadvertently and that the migration has been 100 percent completed. The query in Listing 5-6 that we ran at the outset of the migration effort is an excellent way to verify that all database files have indeed been migrated. Listing 5-23 shows the output from that same query once the migration had been completed on our test system.

Listing 5-23 *Post-Migration—Captured Database File Metadata*

```
                              Control File Status

                                                              Made
                                                              Via
Control File Name                                    Status   FRA?
--------------------------------------------------- -------- ----
+DATA/orcl/controlfile/current.280.848420839                  NO
+FRA/orcl/controlfile/current.256.848420839                   NO
```

```
                         Online Redo Log Groups File Status

  Log                                                                         Made
 File                                                                         Via
 Grp#  File Name                                            Status  Type   FRA?
 -----  --------------------------------------------------  ------  ------  ----
    4   +DATA/orcl/onlinelog/group_4.282.848687267           ONLINE  NO
    4   +FRA/orcl/onlinelog/group_4.258.848687269            ONLINE  NO
    5   +DATA/orcl/onlinelog/group_5.281.848687277           ONLINE  NO
    5   +FRA/orcl/onlinelog/group_5.257.848687279            ONLINE  NO
    6   +DATA/orcl/onlinelog/group_6.283.848687297           ONLINE  NO
    6   +FRA/orcl/onlinelog/group_6.259.848687299            ONLINE  NO

                              DataFile Status
 Data
 File
    #  DataFile Name                                         Status
 -----  --------------------------------------------------  ------
    1   +DATA/orcl/datafile/system.258.848415125             SYSTEM
    2   +DATA/orcl/datafile/sysaux.259.848415167             ONLINE
    3   +DATA/orcl/datafile/undotbs1.261.848415217           ONLINE
    4   +DATA/orcl/datafile/users.273.848415313             ONLINE
    5   +DATA/orcl/datafile/example.262.848415231           ONLINE
    6   +DATA/orcl/datafile/ap_data.260.848415201           ONLINE
    7   +DATA/orcl/datafile/ap_idx.269.848415299            ONLINE
    8   +DATA/orcl/datafile/ado_hot_data.270.848415307       ONLINE
    9   +DATA/orcl/datafile/ado_hot_idx.271.848415309        ONLINE
   10   +DATA/orcl/datafile/ado_warm_data.263.848415257      ONLINE
   11   +DATA/orcl/datafile/ado_warm_idx.264.848415263       ONLINE
   12   +DATA/orcl/datafile/ado_cool_data.265.848415271      ONLINE
   13   +DATA/orcl/datafile/ado_cool_idx.266.848415279       ONLINE
   14   +DATA/orcl/datafile/ado_cold_data.267.848415285      ONLINE
   15   +DATA/orcl/datafile/ado_cold_idx.268.848415293       ONLINE
```

Non-ASM to ASM Migration: Phased Migration

A phased migration scenario is not radically different from a complete migration
scenario. What distinguishes a *phased* migration from a *complete* migration,
however, is the point in time at which the Oracle DBA decides to migrate the
source database's SPFILE, control files, online redo logs, the datafiles for the
SYSTEM, UNDOTBS, and SYSAUX tablespaces, and any temp files to their new
destination on ASM. The phased migration approach is especially useful in at least
four situations:

- **Tight migration time windows**   When there is a very narrow timeframe
  during which the migration to ASM must be completed, a phased migration
  approach restricts potential system downtime to how long it will take to
  complete the final migration of the database's SPFILE, control files, and the
  critical tablespaces (especially SYSTEM and UNDOTBS).

- **Extremely large datafiles**   A phased migration approach also allows
  migration of tablespace sets that are composed of extremely large datafiles.
  The time it will take to migrate these files can be mitigated by performing
  RMAN image copy backups in parallel.

■ **Insufficient disk space on target platform** This approach works extremely well when the target platform doesn't have sufficient surplus disks for the database files being migrated and the storage between both source and target are "shareable." Once the datafiles have been migrated from the source platform to the target platform, the disks that originally contained the source database files can be wiped clean and added into the ASM disk groups on the target, thus expanding the ASM storage gradually over time.

■ **Consolidated database migration** If a hybrid database is supporting several database applications, and if those applications' tablespaces are self-contained in tablespace sets, it may make sense to adopt a phased migration approach. Applications can be migrated to ASM storage individually over a period of time to limit excessive downtime, and the least critical application(s) can be migrated before the most crucial application(s).

The alternate checklists for Phases 1 and 3 of a phased migration approach are highlighted in Checklists 5-1A and 5-3A; note that the checklist for Phase 2 is unchanged.

Step	Operation	Description	Done?
1	Capture database file metadata	Capture metadata for all database files about to be migrated.	
2	Verify `COMPATIBLE` setting	If `COMPATIBLE` is < 11.0.0.0, then it will be necessary to change any READ ONLY transportable tablespaces to READ WRITE mode.	
3	Create `INCREMENTAL LEVEL 0` image copy backups of datafiles for selected tablespaces	Back up selected tablespaces as `INCREMENTAL LEVEL 0` image copy backups, routing them to their eventual ASM disk group(s).	
4	Create `INCREMENTAL LEVEL 1` backups of datafiles for selected tablespaces	Create `INCREMENTAL LEVEL 1` differential backups for selected tablespaces.	
5	Recover selected tablespaces to image copies	Use the `SWITCH TABLESPACE <tablespace name> TO COPY;` RMAN command to switch all datafiles for selected tablespaces to ASM-based storage.	

Step	Operation	Description	Done?
6	Move non-ASM mount points to ASM disk groups	Once all database files have been moved from one or more set(s) of LUNs, those LUNs can be wiped clean of any file system and then added as new ASM disks into an existing ASM disk group. This can also be done from SQL*Plus while connected to the ASM instance via the `ALTER DISKGROUP <diskgroup name> ADD <disk_name_1, disk_name_2, …> REBALANCE POWER n;` command, where n can range from 1 to 1024 in Oracle 11.2.0.2.	
7	Rebalance ASM disk groups	Once old mount points are added via Step 6 to the ASM disk groups, ASM should automatically rebalance them, thus spreading all ASM AUs across all available ASM disks. This can also be done from SQL*Plus while connected to the ASM instance via the `ALTER DISKGROUP <diskgroup name> REBALANCE POWER n;` command.	

CHECKLIST 5-1A *Phased Migration from Non-ASM to ASM Storage: Preparations*

Step	Operation	Description	Done?
1	Migrate modified SPFILE to ASM	■ Build a PFILE from the current SPFILE. ■ Modify the PFILE's initialization parameters to point to ASM disk group(s) for *all* files. ■ Test the PFILE. ■ Rebuild an ASM-based SPFILE. ■ Restart the instance.	

CHECKLIST 5-3A *Phased Migration from Non-ASM to ASM Storage: Completion*

Step	Operation	Description	Done?
2	Migrate control files to ASM	Restore the database's control files to the chosen ASM disk group(s).	
3	Mount the database	Mount the database using the newly migrated control files.	
4	Create `INCREMENTAL LEVEL 0` image copy backups of datafiles for remaining tablespaces	Back up datafiles for any remaining tablespaces—that is, `SYSTEM`, `UNDOTBS`, `SYSAUX`, and any others—as `INCREMENTAL LEVEL 0` image copy backups, routing them to their eventual ASM disk group(s).	
5	Switch to remaining datafiles	Use the `SWITCH DATABASE TO COPY;` RMAN command to switch all remaining datafiles to ASM-based storage.	
6	Recover the database	Perform complete recovery on the migrated datafiles using differential `INCREMENTAL LEVEL 1` backups, archived redo logs, and currently online redo logs.	
7	Open database In RESETLOGS mode	Issue the `ALTER DATABASE OPEN RESETLOGS;` command to open the database.	
8	Migrate online redo logs to ASM	Re-create all members for the online redo log groups on the chosen ASM disk group(s).	
9	Migrate temporary tablespace temp file(s) to ASM	Create a new temp file for all temporary tablespace(s) on the chosen ASM disk group(s).	
10	Switch FRA to ASM	Modify `DB_RECOVERY_FILE_DEST` to ASM storage.	
11	Restore/rebuild database backups to FRA on ASM	Optionally, restore any existing backup files to the FRA on its new ASM disk group(s).	
12	Validate the migration	Validate that all database files have been successfully migrated per expectations	

CHECKLIST 5-3A   *Phased Migration from Non-ASM to ASM Storage: Completion* (Continued)

In this migration scenario, the major difference is that instead of migrating the database in one pass, we will use a set of incremental backups of *some* of the database's datafiles to migrate only the selected tablespaces, and we will migrate the remaining tablespaces at a later date. This means we can complete the migration in an iterative fashion to accommodate one or more of the four limiting situations we mentioned in the introduction to this section.

Create INCREMENTAL LEVEL 0 Image Copy Backups of Selected Tablespaces As in the original Step 3 of Checklist 5-1, we will construct INCREMENTAL LEVEL 0 image copy backups of the datafiles for only the tablespaces we wish to migrate to the target ASM disk group(s), as shown in Listing 5-24.

Listing 5-24 *Creating INCREMENTAL LEVEL 0 Image Copy Backups for Specific Tablespaces*

```
RMAN> BACKUP
        INCREMENTAL LEVEL 0
        AS COPY
        FORMAT '+DATA'
        TABLESPACES ap_data, ap_idx, ap_hot_data, ap_hot_idx;
```

Create INCREMENTAL LEVEL 1 Backups of Datafiles for Selected Tablespaces
Listing 5-25 shows how to create differential INCREMENTAL LEVEL 1 backups for just the selected tablespaces' datafiles to capture any additional changes to those tablespaces after the initial INCREMENTAL LEVEL 0 backups have been created.

Listing 5-25 *Creating INCREMENTAL LEVEL 1 Backup Sets for Selected Tablespaces*

```
RMAN> BACKUP INCREMENTAL LEVEL 1 FORMAT '+DATA'
        TABLESPACES ap_data, ap_idx, ap_hot_data, ap_hot_idx;
Starting backup at 24-MAY-14
using target database control file instead of recovery catalog
```

Create INCREMENTAL LEVEL 0 Backups for Remaining Tablespaces We will construct INCREMENTAL LEVEL 0 image copy backups of the datafiles for only the tablespaces that are remaining so that we can migrate them to the target ASM disk group(s), as shown in Listing 5-26.

Listing 5-26 *Creating INCREMENTAL LEVEL 0 Image Copy Backups for Remaining Tablespaces*

```
RMAN> BACKUP
        INCREMENTAL LEVEL 0
        AS COPY
        FORMAT '+DATA'
        TABLESPACES system, sysaux, undotbs1, users, example;
```

Migrating from ASM to Non-ASM File Systems

The previous sections established that RMAN is an excellent tool for migrating a database from other file systems to ASM. Likewise, RMAN is the obvious choice for migrating a database from ASM to other file systems as well. Essentially, the same steps used to migrate to ASM can be used in reverse to migrate from ASM to any other non-ASM file system.

Monitoring RMAN Performance During Database Migration

We like to think of RMAN as really nothing more than a *database block movement engine*...because that is all that RMAN does when it makes calls to the DBMS_ BACKUP_RESTORE PL/SQL package, which itself is making extremely low-level calls to the appropriate Oracle database(s) to copy or move a series of database blocks between source and destination. This offers a unique opportunity for monitoring how RMAN is actually performing during any operation.

GV$SESSION_LONGOPS

The venerable GV$SESSION_LONGOPS dynamic view (or V$SESSION_LONGOPS for non-RAC database instances) records any database operation that is consuming either five seconds of CPU or five seconds of physical I/O. Because of its intense physical I/O activity, RMAN falls into this category naturally when it is performing backup and restore operations.

The query shown in Listing 5-27 is extremely useful for keeping an eye on long-running RMAN operations. It reports all RMAN operations based on the estimated number of database blocks that each channel needs to back up or restore, as well as the number of operations that have been completed so far. This yields quite a bit of valuable information, including an approximate amount of time that it will take to finally complete the operation. It's also helpful for isolating RMAN operations that seem to be taking forever as compared to other executions of the same script, or for identifying I/O channels that are underperforming when compared to other channels used during the same RMAN job.

Listing 5-27   *Monitoring Long-Running RMAN Tasks*

```
COL opname        FORMAT A20           HEADING "Operation Name"
COL context       FORMAT 9999999       HEADING "RMAN|Operation"
COL totalwork     FORMAT 999,999,999   HEADING "Total|Work"
COL sofar         FORMAT 999,999,999   HEADING "Done|So Far"
COL pct_done      FORMAT 999.99        HEADING "Pct|Done"
TTITLE 'Devices Available For RMAN Utilization'
SELECT
    opname
   ,context
   ,totalwork
```

```
  ,sofar
  ,ROUND(SOFAR/TOTALWORK*100,2) pct_done
FROM v$session_longops
WHERE opname LIKE 'RMAN%'
  AND opname NOT LIKE '%aggregate%'
  AND totalwork != 0
  AND sofar <> totalwork;
```

```
              Progress of Ongoing RMAN Backup/Restore Operations
                                   RMAN       Total       Done    Pct
Operation Name                 Operation       Work     So Far   Done
------------------------------ --------- ------------ ---------- -------
RMAN: full datafile backup             1       52,880     52,862  99.97
RMAN: full datafile backup             1       99,840     66,302  66.41
RMAN: full datafile backup             1       86,400     53,758  62.22
```

Oracle Enterprise Manager

Any of the various incarnations of Oracle Enterprise Manager provides similar
insight into what is happening during a long-running RMAN operation. For
example, Figure 5-1 shows a screenshot of Enterprise Manager Cloud Control 12*c*'s

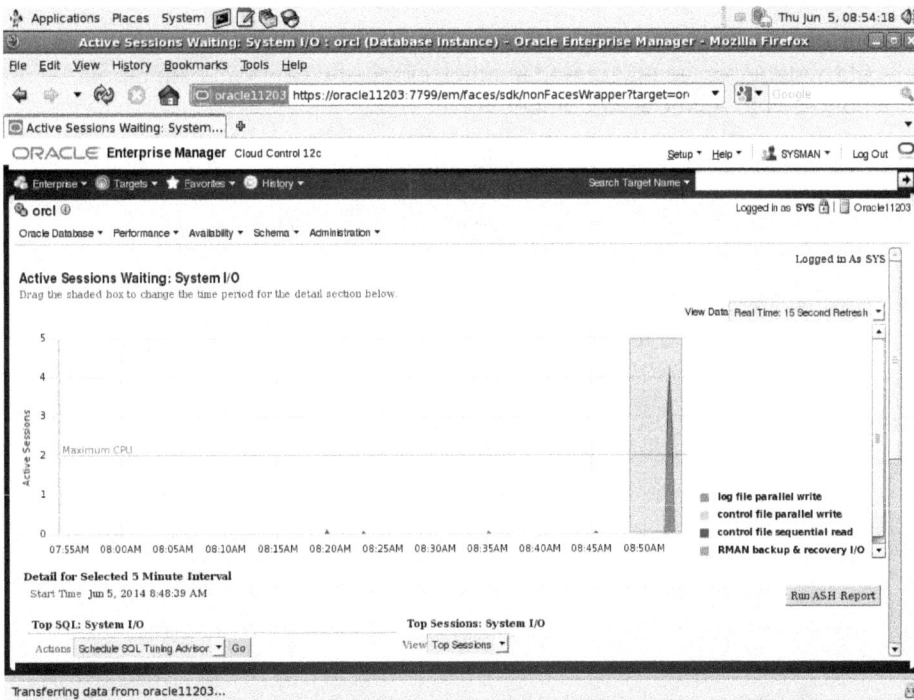

FIGURE 5-1. *Enterprise Manager Cloud Control 12c RMAN-related wait events*

Performance panel that displays the corresponding wait events as RMAN is performing backup operations similar to what we monitored in the prior section with GV$SESSION_LONGOPS. Unfortunately, this information is not as meaningful as the query and its corresponding results shown in Listing 5-27.

Summary

Here's a quick summary of what we've covered in this chapter:

- RMAN is a robust tool for backing up, restoring, and recovering any Oracle database, and Oracle Releases 10*g*, 11*g*, and 12*c* have contributed significant power and flexibility for faster and more reliable backup and recovery operations than can be achieved via user-managed backup strategies.

- The Fast Recovery Area (FRA) is an excellent choice for long-term retention of backup files for database recovery, yet many Oracle DBAs are unaware of RMAN's capability to provide long-term backup strategies—especially the strongly recommended Incrementally Updateable Image Copy (IUIC) strategy!—for OLTP systems.

- RMAN is also an excellent tool for migrating database files from one file system/storage platform to another, especially when migrating from non-ASM to ASM-based storage.

- RMAN makes short work of complex migration strategies, even when insufficient disk space is immediately available on the targeted ASM disk groups and existing storage must be migrated simultaneously to those disk groups.

- Oracle offers several methods for monitoring the progress of ongoing RMAN backup and recovery operations, including SQL queries against GV$SESSION_LONGOPS and Enterprise Manager.

CHAPTER

6

Transporting Tablespaces and Databases

I n Chapter 5, we discussed how to leverage the features of Recovery Manager (RMAN) to migrate databases in whole or in part between completely different *file systems*—say, for example, from non-ASM to ASM storage. While that is not an unusual scenario, it is equally common for organizations to migrate between completely different *operating system* platforms as older hardware is retired or as corporate policies evolve. We have found this to be exceptionally true during the 2014–2015 IT business cycle—what we like to think of as the onset of the *Age of Consolidation*—as extremely powerful engineered systems like Oracle's Exadata Database Machine, Oracle's SPARC SuperCluster M6-32, and IBM's POWER8 Systems attract more interest and market share.

However, migrating Oracle databases to new and completely different platforms brings a special set of challenges for an Oracle DBA because, in most cases, significant differences exist between the original source database's OS and the OS of its final destination. So, while the Oracle database software shelters the developers who build the applications that generate workloads against the database, the Oracle DBA, unfortunately, is granted no such quarter.

Migrating Between Operating Systems

This chapter therefore focuses on two distinct methods of data migration:

- Migrating one or more Transportable Tablespace Sets (TTS) between different OS platforms

- Migrating a complete Transportable Database (TDB) between different OS platforms

TTS and TDB migrations have similar prerequisites and utilize essentially the same methods. As you will soon see, however, each method has some special benefits and disadvantages to consider before you choose which is the most appropriate method for you, especially when you are deciding whether to transport an entire *database* between different OS platforms.

TIP & TECHNIQUE
While the TTS and TDB methods are quite obviously aimed at migrating all or part of a source database to its new destination database in an extremely short time period, don't neglect the fact that these methods are also excellent methods for migrating data from non-ASM file systems to ASM disk groups.

TTS Migration vs. TDB Migration: Variables to Consider

Table 6-1 lays out a brief history of which TTS and TDB features were made available in which release of Oracle Database, and Table 6-2 lists the variables that you must take into account whenever planning partial or full database migration via TTS and TDB. The tables are followed by a more in-depth discussion of these techniques' benefits and drawbacks.

Oracle Database Release	Feature Description
10.1	Transportable Tablespace Sets (TTS) introduced. Transportable Database (TDB) introduced.
10.2	TTS versioning capabilities introduced.
11.1	TDB now permitted between Linux and Windows platforms. TTSs can be backed up whether they are left in READ ONLY mode or READ WRITE mode (earlier releases required READ WRITE mode). Partitions and subpartitions are now fully transportable (that is, there is no need to move the whole table or exchange out any partitions or subpartitions first).
11.2	Now possible to skip unnecessary datafiles during TDB operations.
12.1	Full Transportable Export (FTE) introduced—a "munging together" of Data Pump, DBMS_FILE_TRANSFER, and TTS.

TABLE 6-1. *TTS and TDB Feature List*

Benefits and Drawbacks	Transportable Tablespace Sets (TTS)	Transportable Database (TDB)
Cross-platform transportability	Yes	Yes
Permits different endianness between source and destination databases	Yes	No
Requires source tablespaces/databases to be open in READ ONLY mode	Yes	Yes
Requires compatible character sets between source and destination databases	Yes	Yes
Requires source database shutdown and restart	No	Yes
Can leverage existing RMAN backups	Yes	No

TABLE 6-2. *TTS vs. TDB: Benefits and Drawbacks*

NOTE
We will delve into the unique features of Full Transportable Export features as part of our extensive review of Oracle Database 12c R1 features in Chapter 13.

Cross-Platform Migration and Endian Concerns

TDB and TTS are most likely the fastest ways to migrate all or part of a database between dissimilar OS platforms—for example, between Windows and Linux. However, cross-platform migration is also hampered by the fact that not all operating systems share the same endianness. While it is impossible to migrate databases between platforms of different endianness via TDB, TTS makes relatively short work of migrating data between different platforms because it has the ability to convert a database's datafiles from one endian format to another. (See the sidebar on endianness a bit later in the chapter for a discussion of how endianness impacts data migration.)

Character Set Compatibility

One of the most often overlooked issues for TTS and TDB operations is that the character sets of the source and destination databases must be strict supersets of each other. This means that even if the source database's character set is ISO 8859-15 West European (WEISO8859P15) and the destination database's character set is 32-bit Unicode (AL32UTF8), it is impossible to perform a migration using either TTS or TDB migration techniques.

TIP & TECHNIQUE
The limitation of identical character sets may appear to be a serious irritant in this scenario. However, it may be worthwhile to consider character set conversion of the source database and/or destination database before any migration activities. This is especially important if you are planning to eventually upgrade the destination database to Oracle Database 12c, because in that release the character scan utility (CSCAN) has been deprecated in favor of a new utility, Oracle Database Migration Assistant for Unicode (DMU), which we will discuss in more detail in Chapter 9. Also, be aware that if you are considering implementing the new multitenant architecture when you migrate your database to Oracle 12c, it requires that every pluggable database (PDB) within the same container database (CDB) must utilize the same character set.

Window of Inopportunity

By far the most crucial factor between choosing TDB or TTS over other data migration methods is what we have labeled in Chapter 3 as the *window of inopportunity*: the degree to which the source database can tolerate *any* application downtime at all. For example, if the entire contents of a 4TB production database are required to determine the impact of a crucial OS patch, the Oracle database release, or even the latest version of application software, and those data must be replicated completely to a QA database server for testing purposes, then choosing the fastest possible method to transfer data between production and QA database platforms is crucial.

While Data Pump Export has improved dramatically the speed at which data can be dumped from the source database, the amount of time it takes to reload the data into the destination database via Data Pump Import may also be a crucial factor in the evaluation process. Therefore, TTS or TDB may offer dramatic improvements in migration turnaround times—as long as the source database can tolerate a complete or partial reduction in DML activity when the database or selected tablespaces are opened in `READ ONLY` mode.

Cross-Platform Migration: The Triumvirate

Three Oracle features enable TTS and TDB to *capture, convert, register,* and *transport* all required database components between source and destination environments: RMAN, Data Pump, and `DBMS_FILE_TRANSFER`. Since these applications all run within the database kernel and use database server processes to perform their work, they can potentially take advantage of Oracle database parallel processing features as well.

RMAN

RMAN is at the heart of TTS and TDB operations. It is used to construct backups of tablespaces and to convert them to the proper endianness. An Oracle DBA can decide whether the source OS platform or destination OS platform is most appropriate to perform endian conversion based on the server's processing capacity as well as whether applications accessing the TTS's data can tolerate that data being accessible in `READ ONLY` mode.

Data Pump

Data Pump has been available since Oracle Database 10*g* R1 and is used during TTS and TDB operations to capture, transport, and deliver database object metadata between source and destination OS platforms using these features:

- *Data Pump Export* captures metadata about the database objects that comprise the tablespaces that are going to be migrated from the database on the source OS platform into the database on the destination OS platform.

This makes it possible to make a copy of all datafiles for a TTS and then essentially "unplug" that TTS in a consistent and recoverable state for transport to a different platform.

■ *Data Pump Import* is used to load metadata about the database objects that comprise the tablespaces that have been migrated from the database on the source OS platform into the database on the destination OS platform. Once the metadata has been imported into the destination database, all that needs to be done is to plug the transported datafiles into the destination database's control file(s) to associate them with their corresponding tablespaces. The tablespaces can then be opened in either READ ONLY or READ WRITE mode as appropriate to the post-migration strategy.

DBMS_FILE_TRANSFER

Finally, the DBMS_FILE_TRANSFER package is an extremely important component of TTS and TDB because it enables any Oracle database to transfer the appropriate database files between source and destination OS platforms efficiently, effectively, and securely. Best of all, because DBMS_FILE_TRANSFER uses database protocols rather than OS protocols to transfer data, any potential security concerns for transporting sensitive data via OS tools like telnet or ftp are reduced or eliminated.

Overcoming Endian Boundaries

Oracle Database 10*g* R1 introduced the CONVERT command for RMAN operations. CONVERT gives RMAN the power to literally transform a datafile that has been created on any supported *source* OS platform—say, for example, a Microsoft Windows 32-bit x86 server—to any other supported *destination* OS platform—for example, a Linux x86 64-bit server—*without the need to reload any data*.

Fortunately, the only prerequisite before CONVERT can be used against a tablespace set's datafiles is simple: all of the datafiles for the tablespace set must have been opened *at least once* in READ WRITE mode with the database's COMPATIBLE initialization parameter set to at least 10.0.0.0. When a datafile is opened in this manner, Oracle automatically stamps the datafile header as an Oracle 10*g*–compatible datafile. Note that even if a tablespace had been opened previously in READ ONLY mode, it's only necessary to open it once in READ WRITE mode after COMPATIBLE has been raised to at least 10.0.0.0; the tablespace can then immediately be placed back into READ ONLY mode.

Why You Need to Care About Endianness: Big Endian, Little Endian, and Numbers

It's a term that's thrown around a lot within the IT industry, but the concept of *endianness* is actually rooted deeply within a liberal arts agenda. The British author Jonathan Swift, well known for his deeply satirical prose in pamphlets like "A Modest Proposal," which suggested a reasonable way to overcome Ireland's famine through cannibalism, is probably most famous for his 1726 political satire *Gulliver's Travels*. Swift described the 100-year-long conflict between the inhabitants of Lilliput and Blefuscu that was triggered by a disagreement over which end of their boiled eggs should be opened first: the *little end* or the *big end*. Swift's satire was aimed squarely at the disagreements between English Protestants and Scottish Catholics of his times.

As the legend goes, two IT engineers were having an argument about what to call an OS platform that stores data in memory by placing the *highest* part of the number—the *big end*—first, versus placing the *lowest* byte first, or the *little end*. One of the engineers—most likely a recovering English major—hit upon the Jonathan Swift reference, thereby introducing several generations of IT professionals to arcane yet classic British literature.

Determining Which Platforms Support TTS and TDB Migration Operations

The list of OS platforms that Oracle Database supports for TTS and TDB operations is actually internalized in the kernel of the database release itself. Dynamic view V$TRANSPORTABLE_PLATFORM contains the current list of platforms that are supported, as well as each platform's endianness. When linked to the V$DATABASE dynamic view, it is equally simple to determine the endianness of the current database's OS platform, as shown in Listings 6-1 and 6-2.

Listing 6-1 *Determining Platform Support for TTS/TDB Database Migration Operations*

```
SET LINESIZE 80
COL endian_format    FORMAT A12     HEADING "Endian|Format"
COL platform_name    FORMAT A60     HEADING "Platform Name" WRAP
TTITLE "Platforms Currently Supported for TTS / TDB Operations|(from V$TRANSPORTABLE_PLATFORM)"
SELECT
    endian_format
   ,platform_name
  FROM v$transportable_platform
 ORDER BY endian_format, platform_name
;
TTITLE OFF
```

```
             Platforms Currently Supported for TTS / TDB Operations
                         (from V$TRANSPORTABLE_PLATFORM)

Endian
Format        Platform Name
-----------   --------------------------------------------------------
Big           AIX-Based Systems (64-bit)
Big           Apple Mac OS
Big           HP-UX (64-bit)
Big           HP-UX IA (64-bit)
Big           IBM Power Based Linux
Big           IBM zSeries Based Linux
Big           Solaris[tm] OE (32-bit)
Big           Solaris[tm] OE (64-bit)
Little        Apple Mac OS (x86-64)
Little        HP IA Open VMS
Little        HP Open VMS
Little        HP Tru64 UNIX
Little        Linux IA (32-bit)
Little        Linux IA (64-bit)
Little        Linux x86 64-bit
Little        Microsoft Windows IA (32-bit)
Little        Microsoft Windows IA (64-bit)
Little        Microsoft Windows x86 64-bit
Little        Solaris Operating System (x86)
Little        Solaris Operating System (x86-64)

20 rows selected.
```

Listing 6-2   *Discovering Current Platform Details*

```
SET LINESIZE 60
TTITLE "Current Database Platform Endianness|(from V$DATABASE + V$TRANSPORTABLE_PLATFORM)"
COL name            FORMAT A16      HEADING "Database Name"
COL endian_format   FORMAT A12      HEADING "Endian|Format"
SELECT
     D.name
    ,TP.endian_format
  FROM
     v$transportable_platform TP
    ,v$database D
 WHERE TP.platform_name = D.platform_name
;
TTITLE OFF


          Current Database Platform Endianness
        (from V$DATABASE + V$TRANSPORTABLE_PLATFORM)

                   Endian
Database Name      Format
----------------   ------------
ORCL               Little
```

Transporting Tablespace Sets: The Basics

Our first TTS migration scenario will utilize RMAN, Data Pump, and DBMS_FILE_
TRANSFER to transport two tablespaces—AP_DATA and AP_IDX—which can be
brought into READ ONLY mode for a brief period of time while being transported

from one database to another. Here are the pertinent details for the source and destination databases:

■ The source database (ORA10G) is running under Oracle Database Release 10.2.0.1 on host ORA10A, an Oracle Linux Version 6 Update 3 platform (the kernel is 2.6.39-400.17.1.el6uek.x86_64).

■ The ORA10G database contains two tablespaces.

■ The destination database (ORCL) is running under Oracle Database 11.2.0.4 on host OEL01, an Oracle Linux Version 6 Update 3 platform (the kernel is 2.6.39-400.17.1.el6uek.x86_64).

■ Both the source and destination databases were created with the AL32UTF8 character set.

■ There is sufficient space in the +DATA ASM disk group on OS platform OEL01 to accommodate tablespaces AP_DATA and AP_IDX.

TTS Operations: Prerequisites

Checklist 6-1 lists the necessary prerequisites to performing a TTS operation.

Step	Operation	Description	Done?
1	Determine source and destination platform endianness	Verify source and platform endianness. If different endianness is detected, decide where the RMAN CONVERT command will be executed.	
2	Verify transportability of selected tablespace set	Confirm that ■ Tablespaces selected are indeed part of self-contained set. ■ Database character set is identical (or at least that the destination database's character set is a superset of the source database).	

CHECKLIST 6-1 *TTS Pre-Migration Preparations*

Step	Operation	Description	Done?
3	Create transportability infrastructure	Build any directories needed for temporary storage of Data Pump Export and Import parameter files and dump sets and grant appropriate permissions to directory objects.	
		Build a database link to permit transmission of files via DBMS_FILE_TRANSFER.	
		Prepare Data Pump Export and Import scripts and parameter files for metadata capture and transport.	

CHECKLIST 6-1   *TTS Pre-Migration Preparations* (Continued)

Deciding Where to Convert Endian Formatting: The Source or the Destination?

Unfortunately, endian transformation is required when performing a migration between big-endian and little-endian hosts. But the decision as to where to perform the endian conversion is a crucial one that depends on several factors that go beyond the scope of this book. Some considerations include

- How many *CPU cycles* are available on the source host versus the destination host?

- What is the current application or processing *workload* on the source host during the migration as compared to the destination host?

- Are there any *security concerns* about converting on the destination host versus performing the conversion on the source host?

- Finally—and perhaps most crucially!—on which host will the endian conversion *take the least time*? Since the tablespaces being transported *must* remain in READ ONLY mode until their datafiles have been successfully transferred to the destination platform, the sooner the conversion has completed, the sooner that they can be reverted to READ WRITE mode on the source and/or destination platform.

Determine Source and Destination Platform Endianness

The first prerequisite is to determine the endianness of the source and destination platforms using the query shown previously in Listing 6-2. In this case, we have identified that both platforms are little endian (Linux x86), so there will be no need to perform any conversions via the RMAN CONVERT command in the next phase of the migration process.

Verify Transportability of Selected Tablespace Set

To confirm that the selected tablespaces are truly transportable, we leverage the DBMS_TTS.SET_CHECK procedure to ensure that there are no extraneous object dependencies for the tablespace set. To illustrate both a failed and a successful transportability check, Listing 6-3 shows two iterations of this procedure—one *excluding* the AP_IDX tablespace from the tablespace set, and one *including* it so that all referenced objects are included.

Listing 6-3 *Verifying Tablespace Set Transportability*

```
BEGIN
    DBMS_TTS.TRANSPORT_SET_CHECK(
        ts_list => 'AP_DATA'
        ,incl_constraints => TRUE
        ,full_check => TRUE
    );
END;
/
SELECT * FROM transport_set_violations;

Index AP.VENDORS_PK_IDX in tablespace AP_IDX enforces primary constriants of table
AP.VENDORS in tablespace AP_DATA
Index AP.INVOICES_PK_IDX in tablespace AP_IDX enforces primary constriants of table
AP.INVOICES in tablespace AP_DATA
Index AP.INVOICE_ITEMS_PK_IDX in tablespace AP_IDX enforces primary constriants of
table AP.INVOICE_ITEMS in tablespace AP_DATA
Index AP.INVOICE_ITEMS_PROD_IDX in tablespace AP_IDX points to table AP.INVOICE_ITEMS
in tablespace AP_DATA

-----
-- Include AP_IDX in the verification process to reverify
-- if TTS set is now truly self-contained
-----
BEGIN
    DBMS_TTS.TRANSPORT_SET_CHECK(
        ts_list => 'AP_DATA,AP_IDX'
        ,incl_constraints => TRUE
        ,full_check => TRUE
    );
END;
/
SELECT * FROM transport_set_violations;

no rows selected
```

Create Transportability Infrastructure

To complete the prerequisites for tablespace transportability, we will build the appropriate database links and create all required directory objects on both the source and destination databases, as shown in Listing 6-4.

Listing 6-4 *Creating Transportability Infrastructure*

```
-----
-- Prepare the source database
-----

$> mkdir /home/oracle/TTS

DROP DATABASE LINK oel01;
CREATE DATABASE LINK oel01
    CONNECT TO system IDENTIFIED BY "oracle_4U"
    USING 'orcl11g';

CREATE OR REPLACE DIRECTORY ora10g_dbf
    AS '/u02/app/oracle/oradata/ora10g';
CREATE OR REPLACE DIRECTORY ttsfiles
    AS '/home/oracle/TTS';
GRANT READ, WRITE ON DIRECTORY ttsfiles TO PUBLIC;


-----
-- Prepare the target database
-----
$> mkdir /home/oracle/TTS

CREATE OR REPLACE DIRECTORY oel01_dg_data
    AS '+DATA/ORCL/DATAFILE';
CREATE OR REPLACE DIRECTORY ttsfiles
    AS '/home/oracle/TTS';
GRANT READ, WRITE ON DIRECTORY ttsfiles TO PUBLIC;
```

TTS: Performing the Migration Operation

Checklist 6-2 describes the steps required to migrate a TTS from the source database to its corresponding destination platform. Note that in this scenario, the source and destination *both have the same endianness*.

Step	Operation	Description	Done?
1	Switch selected tablespaces to READ ONLY mode on source database	From SQL*Plus on the source database, issue ALTER TABLESPACE <tablespace name> READ ONLY; for each tablespace about to be transported.	

Step	Operation	Description	Done?
2	Capture source tablespace metadata via Data Pump	Via Data Pump Export, capture the metadata for all objects in each tablespace about to be transported.	
3	Transport datafiles and metadata from source platform to destination platform	Use `DBMS_FILE_TRANSFER` to copy all datafiles and Data Pump dump set from source to destination platform.	
4	Perform endian conversion at destination	If necessary, convert the tablespace's datafiles to the endian format on the destination OS platform.	
5	Import source tablespace metadata via Data Pump Export	Via Data Pump Import, import the metadata for each transported tablespace.	
6	Switch transported tablespaces to `READ WRITE` mode at destination	Issue `ALTER TABLESPACE` *<tablespace name>* `READ WRITE;` for each tablespace that has been incorporated into the destination database.	
7	Revert selected tablespaces to `READ WRITE` mode at source	If desired, issue `ALTER TABLESPACE` *<tablespace name>* `READ WRITE;` for each tablespace transported from the source platform.	

CHECKLIST 6-2 *Example TTS Operation*

Switch Selected Tablespaces to READ ONLY Mode on Source Database

The first step in the migration process is to restrict the ability of applications to modify the data in the tablespaces selected for migration by bringing those tablespaces into `READ ONLY` mode as shown in Listing 6-5.

Listing 6-5 *Switching Tablespaces to READ ONLY Mode*

```
ALTER TABLESPACE ap_data READ ONLY;
Tablespace altered.
ALTER TABLESPACE ap_idx READ ONLY;
Tablespace altered.
```

Capture Source Tablespace Metadata via Data Pump

Next, we will utilize Data Pump Export to export a list of all the metadata in these two tablespaces. Listing 6-6 shows the Data Pump Export parameter file we will use to capture just the desired metadata, and Listing 6-7 shows the invocation of the Data Pump Export operation.

Listing 6-6   *Data Pump Export Parameter File*

```
JOB_NAME = TTS_1
DIRECTORY = TTSFILES
DUMPFILE = tts_1.dmp
LOGFILE = tts_1.log
TRANSPORT_TABLESPACES = "ap_data,ap_idx"
TRANSPORT_FULL_CHECK = TRUE
```

Listing 6-7   *Results of Data Pump Export Invocation*

```
$> expdp system/oracle_4U PARFILE=/home/oracle/TTS/TTS_1.dpectl

Export: Release 10.2.0.1.0 - 64bit Production on Friday, 13 June, 2014 18:33:40

Copyright (c) 2003, 2005, Oracle.  All rights reserved.

Connected to: Oracle Database 10g Enterprise Edition Release 10.2.0.1.0 - 64bit Production
With the Partitioning, OLAP and Data Mining options
Starting "SYS"."SYS_EXPORT_TRANSPORTABLE_01":  userid="/********@(DESCRIPTION=(ADDRESS=(PRO
TOCOL=beq)(PROGRAM=/u01/app/oracle/product/10.2.0/db_1/bin/oracle)(ARGV0=oraclefxkl)(ARGS=\
(DESCRIPTION=\(LOCAL=YES\)\(ADDRESS=\(PROTOCOL=beq\)\)\))(ENVS=ORACLE_SID=fxkl))(CONNECT_
DATA=(SID=fxkl))) AS SYSDBA" transport_tablespaces= AP_DATA, AP_IDX dumpfile=tts_2.dmp
directory=TTSFILES logfile=tts_2.log Processing object type TRANSPORTABLE_EXPORT/PLUGTS_BLK
Processing object type TRANSPORTABLE_EXPORT/TABLE
Processing object type TRANSPORTABLE_EXPORT/GRANT/OWNER_GRANT/OBJECT_GRANT
Processing object type TRANSPORTABLE_EXPORT/INDEX
Processing object type TRANSPORTABLE_EXPORT/CONSTRAINT/CONSTRAINT
Processing object type TRANSPORTABLE_EXPORT/INDEX_STATISTICS
Processing object type TRANSPORTABLE_EXPORT/CONSTRAINT/REF_CONSTRAINT
Processing object type TRANSPORTABLE_EXPORT/TABLE_STATISTICS
Processing object type TRANSPORTABLE_EXPORT/POST_INSTANCE/PLUGTS_BLK
Master table "SYS"."SYS_EXPORT_TRANSPORTABLE_01" successfully loaded/unloaded
```

Transport Datafiles and Metadata from Source Platform to Destination Platform

Now that the transportability metadata has been generated, it is time to migrate the transportable tablespaces' datafiles and their metadata to the destination platform and place the files in their final destination directories. Listing 6-8 shows how to leverage the PUT_FILE procedure of the Oracle-supplied DBMS_FILE_TRANSFER package to move the Data Pump Export dump set and both datafiles to their destinations. Note that the OEL01_DG_DATA directory object actually maps to the DATAFILE directory for the ORCL database in the +DATA ASM disk group.

Listing 6-8 *Invoking DBMS_FILE_TRANSFER.PUT_FILE*

```
BEGIN
    DBMS_FILE_TRANSFER.PUT_FILE(
        source_directory_object => 'ORA10G_DBF'
        ,source_file_name => 'ap_data.dbf'
        ,destination_directory_object => 'OEL01_DG_DATA'
        ,destination_file_name => 'AP_DATA.DBF'
        ,destination_database => 'OEL01'
    );
    DBMS_FILE_TRANSFER.PUT_FILE(
        source_directory_object => 'ORA10G_DBF'
        ,source_file_name => 'ap_idx.dbf'
        ,destination_directory_object => 'OEL01_DG_DATA'
        ,destination_file_name => 'AP_IDX.DBF'
        ,destination_database => 'OEL01'
    );
    DBMS_FILE_TRANSFER.PUT_FILE(
        source_directory_object => 'TTSFILES'
        ,source_file_name => 'tts_1.dmp'
        ,destination_directory_object => 'TTSFILES'
        ,destination_file_name => 'tts_1.dmp'
        ,destination_database => 'OEL01'
    );
END;
/
```

Listing 6-9 shows the resulting filenames that ASM selected for the files transferred via `DBMS_FILE_TRANSFER`; note that the original filenames are preserved as aliases for the new ASM files.

Listing 6-9 *Results of File Transference to +DATA ASM Disk Group*

```
asmcmd ls -ls DATA/ORCL/DATAFILE
Type        Redund  Striped  Time            Sys  Block_Size  Blocks       Bytes
Space  Name
DATAFILE  MIRROR  COARSE   JUN 15 18:00:00  Y       8192    25601   209723392
424673280  ADO_COLD_DATA.267.848415285
DATAFILE  MIRROR  COARSE   JUN 15 18:00:00  Y       8192    25601   209723392
424673280  ADO_COLD_IDX.268.848415293
. . .
                                            N
AP_DATA.DBF => +DATA/ORCL/DATAFILE/FILE_TRANSFER.269.850329875
                                            N
AP_IDX.DBF => +DATA/ORCL/DATAFILE/FILE_TRANSFER.260.850329877
. . .
DATAFILE  MIRROR  COARSE   JUN 15 18:00:00  Y       8192    12801   104865792
214958080  FILE_TRANSFER.260.850329877
DATAFILE  MIRROR  COARSE   JUN 15 18:00:00  Y       8192    12801   104865792
214958080  FILE_TRANSFER.269.850329875
DATAFILE  MIRROR  COARSE   JUN 15 18:00:00  Y       8192    89601
734011392  1473249280  SYSAUX.259.848415167
. . .
```

Perform Endian Conversion at Destination

All datafiles for the transported tablespace have now been transferred successfully. Had these files been transferred from a big-endian database, it would now be necessary to run the RMAN CONVERT command to create brand-new datafiles in a little-endian format. Listing 6-10 shows an example of how to accomplish this if it were indeed necessary.

Listing 6-10 *Using RMAN CONVERT to Convert Endianness*

```
RMAN> CONVERT TABLESPACE ap_data
      TO PLATFORM='Linux x86 64-bit'
      FORMAT='+DATA';
```

Import Source Tablespace Metadata via Data Pump

Now that transport and conversion are completed for all tablespaces, all that is required to complete the migration is to plug the transported tablespaces into the destination database via Data Pump Import, as shown in Listings 6-11 and 6-12.

Listing 6-11 *Data Pump Import Parameter File*

```
JOB_NAME = TTS_1
DIRECTORY = TTSFILES
DUMPFILE = tts_1.dmp
LOGFILE = tts_1.log
TRANSPORT_DATAFILES = '+DATA/ORCL/DATAFILE/AP_DATA.DBF','+DATA/ORCL/DATAFILE/AP_IDX.DBF'
```

Listing 6-12 *Plugging Transported Tablespaces into Destination Database*

```
$> impdp system/oracle_4U PARFILE=tts_1.dpictl

>> Results of successful transportable tablespace import at destination
>> (from destination database's alert log)

. . .
Thu Jun 12 18:32:18 2014
DM00 started with pid=36, OS id=2269, job SYSTEM.TTS_1
Thu Jun 12 18:32:19 2014
DW00 started with pid=37, OS id=2271, wid=1, job SYSTEM.TTS_1
Plug in tablespace AP_IDX with datafile
  '+DATA/ORCL/DATAFILE/AP_IDX.DBF'
Plug in tablespace AP_DATA with datafile
 ,'+DATA/ORCL/DATAFILE/AP_DATA.DBF'
. . .
```

Switch Transported Tablespaces to READ WRITE Mode at Destination

Now that all tablespaces have been successfully transported from the source to the destination database, it is time to open them in READ WRITE mode so that applications can access their data, as shown in Listing 6-13.

Listing 6-13 *Switching Transported Tablespaces to READ WRITE Mode*

```
SQL> ALTER TABLESPACE ap_data READ WRITE;
Tablespace altered.

SQL> ALTER TABLESPACE ap_idx READ WRITE;
Tablespace altered.
```

Revert Selected Tablespaces to READ WRITE Mode on Source Database

Finally, the same commands in Listing 6-13 can be issued on the source database to bring the source of the transported tablespaces back into READ WRITE mode.

> **NOTE**
> *This final step is definitely optional, especially if the application or applications accessing the transported tablespaces need to perform DML activity against them. However, this is a valuable method for a final comparison of the contents of the newly transported tablespaces between the source and destination platforms.*

TTS: Advanced Techniques

In the TTS migration scenario discussed in this section, we explore yet another way to transport the same two tablespaces—AP_DATA and AP_IDX—from the source ORA10G (10.2.0.1) database to the destination ORCL (11.2.0.4) database. This time, however, we will leverage RMAN's *Tablespace Point-In-Time Recovery (TSPITR)* capability to transport the tablespaces as of an earlier SCN from the source to the destination.

Checklist 6-3 describes the steps necessary to transport the AP_DATA and AP_IDX tablespaces from the ORA10G (10.2.0.1) database on the ORA10A Linux x86-64 platform to the ORCL (11.2.0.4) database on the OEL01 Linux x86-64 platform. The same prerequisite verification steps listed in Checklist 6-1 are still required, while the steps necessary to complete the tablespace migration in Checklist 6-3 are quite similar to those in Checklist 6-2.

Step	Operation	Description	Done?
1	Create Transportable Tablespace Set as of specific point in time	Use RMAN TRANSPORTABLE TABLESPACE command to build a TTS for a specific point in time.	

CHECKLIST 6-3 *Point-in-Time TTS*

Step	Operation	Description	Done?
2	Transport datafiles and metadata from source platform to destination platform	Use `DBMS_FILE_TRANSFER` to copy all datafiles and Data Pump dump set from the source to the destination platform.	
3	Perform endian conversion at destination	If necessary, convert the tablespace's datafiles to the endian format on the destination OS platform.	
4	Import source tablespace metadata via Data Pump Export	Via Data Pump Import, import the metadata for each transported tablespace.	
5	Switch transported tablespaces to `READ WRITE` mode at destination	Issue `ALTER TABLESPACE <tablespace name> READ WRITE;` for each tablespace that has been incorporated into the destination database	
6	Revert tablespaces to `READ WRITE` mode at source	If desired, issue `ALTER TABLESPACE <tablespace name> READ WRITE;` for each tablespace transported from the source platform.	

CHECKLIST 6-3 *Point-in-Time TTS* (Continued)

Create Transportable Tablespace Set as of Specific SCN

Listing 6-14 shows the `RMAN TRANSPORT TABLESPACE` command we constructed to create a consistent copy of the `AP_DATA` and `AP_IDX` tablespaces on the source OS platform as of a specific SCN. Note that it is also possible to specify a *timestamp*, a *log sequence number*, or even a *restore point* as the desired point in time to recover the tablespace set.

Listing 6-14 *Point-in-Time TRANSPORT TABLESPACE Command*

```
TRANSPORT TABLESPACE ap_data, ap_idx
   TABLESPACE DESTINATION '/home/oracle/TTS'
   AUXILIARY DESTINATION '/home/oracle/TTS'
   DATAPUMP DIRECTORY TTSFILES
   DUMP FILE 'tts_2.dmp'
   IMPORT SCRIPT 'tts_2_impsql'
   EXPORT LOG 'tts_2.log'
   UNTIL SCN 2145863;
```

Note that it is unnecessary to bring the tablespaces into READ ONLY mode because that happens automatically during the invocation of the TRANSPORT TABLESPACE command. Listing 6-15 shows the results of this operation.

Listing 6-15 *Point-in-Time TRANSPORT TABLESPACE Recovery: Results*

```
using target database control file instead of recovery catalog
RMAN-05026: WARNING: presuming following set of tablespaces applies to specified point in time

List of tablespaces expected to have UNDO segments
tablespace SYSTEM
tablespace UNDOTBS1

Creating automatic instance, with SID='fxkl'

initialization parameters used for automatic instance:
db_name=ORA10G
compatible=10.2.0.1.0
db_block_size=8192
db_files=200
db_unique_name=tspitr_ORA10G_fxkl
large_pool_size=1M
shared_pool_size=110M
#No auxiliary parameter file used
db_create_file_dest=/home/oracle/TTS
control_files=/home/oracle/TTS/cntrl_tspitr_ORA10G_fxkl.f


starting up automatic instance ORA10G

Oracle instance started

Total System Global Area      201326592 bytes

Fixed Size                      2019576 bytes
Variable Size                 146804488 bytes
Database Buffers               50331648 bytes
Redo Buffers                    2170880 bytes
Automatic instance created

contents of Memory Script:
{
# set the until clause
set until  scn 2145863;
# restore the controlfile
restore clone controlfile;
# mount the controlfile
sql clone 'alter database mount clone database';
# archive current online log for tspitr to a resent until time
sql 'alter system archive log current';
# avoid unnecessary autobackups for structural changes during TSPITR
sql 'begin dbms_backup_restore.AutoBackupFlag(FALSE); end;';
}
executing Memory Script

executing command: SET until clause

Starting restore at 15-JUN-14
allocated channel: ORA_AUX_DISK_1
```

```
channel ORA_AUX_DISK_1: sid=37 devtype=DISK

channel ORA_AUX_DISK_1: restoring control file
channel ORA_AUX_DISK_1: copied control file copy
input filename=/u02/app/oracle/flash_recovery_area/ORA10G/controlfile/o1_mf_
TAG20140615T105734_9svjn8hx_.ctl
output filename=/home/oracle/TTS/cntrl_tspitr_ORA10G_fxkl.f
Finished restore at 15-JUN-14

sql statement: alter database mount clone database

sql statement: alter system archive log current

sql statement: begin dbms_backup_restore.AutoBackupFlag(FALSE); end;
released channel: ORA_AUX_DISK_1

contents of Memory Script:
{
# generated tablespace point-in-time recovery script
# set the until clause
set until  scn 2145863;
# set an omf destination filename for restore
set newname for clone datafile  1 to new;
# set an omf destination filename for restore
set newname for clone datafile  2 to new;
# set an omf destination filename for restore
set newname for clone datafile  3 to new;
# set an omf destination tempfile
set newname for clone tempfile  1 to new;
# set a destination filename for restore
set newname for datafile  6 to
 "/home/oracle/TTS/ap_data.dbf";
# set a destination filename for restore
set newname for datafile  7 to
 "/home/oracle/TTS/ap_idx.dbf";
# rename all tempfiles
switch clone tempfile all;
# restore the tablespaces in the recovery set plus the auxilliary tablespaces
restore clone datafile  1, 2, 3, 6, 7;
switch clone datafile all;
#online the datafiles restored or flipped
sql clone "alter database datafile  1 online";
#online the datafiles restored or flipped
sql clone "alter database datafile  2 online";
#online the datafiles restored or flipped
sql clone "alter database datafile  3 online";
#online the datafiles restored or flipped
sql clone "alter database datafile  6 online";
#online the datafiles restored or flipped
sql clone "alter database datafile  7 online";
# make the controlfile point at the restored datafiles, then recover them
recover clone database tablespace  "AP_DATA", "AP_IDX", "SYSTEM", "UNDOTBS1", "SYSAUX" delete
archivelog;
alter clone database open resetlogs;
# PLUG HERE the creation of a temporary tablespace if export fails due to lack
# of temporary space.
# For example in Unix these two lines would do that:
#sql clone "create tablespace aux_tspitr_tmp
#          datafile ''/tmp/aux_tspitr_tmp.dbf'' size 500K";
}
```

```
executing Memory Script

executing command: SET until clause

executing command: SET NEWNAME

executing command: SET NEWNAME

executing command: SET NEWNAME

executing command: SET NEWNAME

executing command: SET NEWNAME

executing command: SET NEWNAME

renamed temporary file 1 to /home/oracle/TTS/TSPITR_ORA10G_FXKL/datafile/o1_mf_temp_%u_.tmp in
control file

Starting restore at 15-JUN-14
allocated channel: ORA_AUX_DISK_1
channel ORA_AUX_DISK_1: sid=39 devtype=DISK

channel ORA_AUX_DISK_1: restoring datafile 00001
input datafile copy recid=2 stamp=850301860 filename=/u02/app/oracle/flash_recovery_area/
ORA10G/datafile/o1_mf_system_9svjmgtv_.dbf
destination for restore of datafile 00001: /home/oracle/TTS/TSPITR_ORA10G_FXKL/datafile/o1_mf_
system_%u_.dbf
channel ORA_AUX_DISK_1: copied datafile copy of datafile 00001
output filename=/home/oracle/TTS/TSPITR_ORA10G_FXKL/datafile/o1_mf_system_9svlnxnx_.dbf recid=9
stamp=850303955
channel ORA_AUX_DISK_1: restoring datafile 00002
input datafile copy recid=7 stamp=850301879 filename=/u02/app/oracle/flash_recovery_area/
ORA10G/datafile/o1_mf_undotbs1_9svjn6c6_.dbf
destination for restore of datafile 00002: /home/oracle/TTS/TSPITR_ORA10G_FXKL/datafile/o1_mf_
undotbs1_%u_.dbf
channel ORA_AUX_DISK_1: copied datafile copy of datafile 00002
output filename=/home/oracle/TTS/TSPITR_ORA10G_FXKL/datafile/o1_mf_undotbs1_9svlo4om_.dbf
recid=10 stamp=850303957
channel ORA_AUX_DISK_1: restoring datafile 00003
input datafile copy recid=3 stamp=850301865 filename=/u02/app/oracle/flash_recovery_area/
ORA10G/datafile/o1_mf_sysaux_9svjmoy2_.dbf
destination for restore of datafile 00003: /home/oracle/TTS/TSPITR_ORA10G_FXKL/datafile/o1_mf_
sysaux_%u_.dbf
channel ORA_AUX_DISK_1: copied datafile copy of datafile 00003
output filename=/home/oracle/TTS/TSPITR_ORA10G_FXKL/datafile/o1_mf_sysaux_9svlo5p8_.dbf
recid=11 stamp=850303961
channel ORA_AUX_DISK_1: restoring datafile 00006
input datafile copy recid=5 stamp=850301873 filename=/u02/app/oracle/flash_recovery_area/
ORA10G/datafile/o1_mf_ap_data_9svjn045_.dbf
destination for restore of datafile 00006: /home/oracle/TTS/ap_data.dbf
channel ORA_AUX_DISK_1: copied datafile copy of datafile 00006
output filename=/home/oracle/TTS/ap_data.dbf recid=12 stamp=850303965
channel ORA_AUX_DISK_1: restoring datafile 00007
input datafile copy recid=6 stamp=850301876 filename=/u02/app/oracle/flash_recovery_area/
ORA10G/datafile/o1_mf_ap_idx_9svjn370_.dbf
destination for restore of datafile 00007: /home/oracle/TTS/ap_idx.dbf
channel ORA_AUX_DISK_1: copied datafile copy of datafile 00007
output filename=/home/oracle/TTS/ap_idx.dbf recid=13 stamp=850303967
Finished restore at 15-JUN-14
```

```
datafile 1 switched to datafile copy
input datafile copy recid=14 stamp=850303967 filename=/home/oracle/TTS/TSPITR_ORA10G_FXKL/
datafile/o1_mf_system_9svlnxnx_.dbf
datafile 2 switched to datafile copy
input datafile copy recid=15 stamp=850303967 filename=/home/oracle/TTS/TSPITR_ORA10G_FXKL/
datafile/o1_mf_undotbs1_9svlo4om_.dbf
datafile 3 switched to datafile copy
input datafile copy recid=16 stamp=850303967 filename=/home/oracle/TTS/TSPITR_ORA10G_FXKL/
datafile/o1_mf_sysaux_9svlo5p8_.dbf
datafile 6 switched to datafile copy
input datafile copy recid=17 stamp=850303967 filename=/home/oracle/TTS/ap_data.dbf
datafile 7 switched to datafile copy
input datafile copy recid=18 stamp=850303967 filename=/home/oracle/TTS/ap_idx.dbf

sql statement: alter database datafile  1 online

sql statement: alter database datafile  2 online

sql statement: alter database datafile  3 online

sql statement: alter database datafile  6 online

sql statement: alter database datafile  7 online

Starting recover at 15-JUN-14
using channel ORA_AUX_DISK_1

starting media recovery

archive log thread 1 sequence 15 is already on disk as file /u02/app/oracle/flash_recovery_
area/ORA10G/archivelog/2014_06_15/o1_mf_1_15_9svjncxb_.arc
archive log thread 1 sequence 16 is already on disk as file /u02/app/oracle/flash_recovery_
area/ORA10G/archivelog/2014_06_15/o1_mf_1_16_9svljjfw_.arc
archive log filename=/u02/app/oracle/flash_recovery_area/ORA10G/archivelog/2014_06_15/o1_
mf_1_15_9svjncxb_.arc thread=1 sequence=15
archive log filename=/u02/app/oracle/flash_recovery_area/ORA10G/archivelog/2014_06_15/o1_
mf_1_16_9svljjfw_.arc thread=1 sequence=16
media recovery complete, elapsed time: 00:00:01
Finished recover at 15-JUN-14

database opened

contents of Memory Script:
{
#mark read only the tablespace that will be exported
sql clone "alter tablespace AP_DATA read only";
#mark read only the tablespace that will be exported
sql clone "alter tablespace AP_IDX read only";
# export the tablespaces in the recovery set
host 'expdp userid=\"/@\(DESCRIPTION=\(ADDRESS=\(PROTOCOL=beq\)\(PROGRAM=/u01/app/oracle/
product/10.2.0/db_1/bin/oracle\)\(ARGV0=oraclefxkl\)\(ARGS=^'\(DESCRIPTION=\(LOCAL=YES\)\
(ADDRESS=\(PROTOCOL=beq\)\)\)^'\)\)\(ENVS=^'ORACLE_SID=fxkl^'\)\)\(CONNECT_DATA=\(SID=fxkl\)\)\)
as sysdba\" transport_tablespaces=
 AP_DATA,
 AP_IDX dumpfile=
tts_2.dmp directory=
TTSFILES logfile=
tts_2.log';
}
executing Memory Script
```

```
sql statement: alter tablespace AP_DATA read only

sql statement: alter tablespace AP_IDX read only


Export: Release 10.2.0.1.0 - 64bit Production on Sunday, 15 June, 2014 11:32:51

Copyright (c) 2003, 2005, Oracle.  All rights reserved.

Connected to: Oracle Database 10g Enterprise Edition Release 10.2.0.1.0 - 64bit Production
With the Partitioning, OLAP and Data Mining options
Starting "SYS"."SYS_EXPORT_TRANSPORTABLE_01":  userid="/********@(DESCRIPTION=(ADDRESS=(PROTOCO
L=beq)(PROGRAM=/u01/app/oracle/product/10.2.0/db_1/bin/oracle)(ARGV0=oraclefxkl)(ARGS=\
(DESCRIPTION=\(LOCAL=YES\)\(ADDRESS=\(PROTOCOL=beq\)\)\))(ENVS=ORACLE_SID=fxkl))(CONNECT_
DATA=(SID=fxkl))) AS SYSDBA" transport_tablespaces= AP_DATA, AP_IDX dumpfile=tts_2.dmp
directory=TTSFILES logfile=tts_2.log
Processing object type TRANSPORTABLE_EXPORT/PLUGTS_BLK
Processing object type TRANSPORTABLE_EXPORT/TABLE
Processing object type TRANSPORTABLE_EXPORT/GRANT/OWNER_GRANT/OBJECT_GRANT
Processing object type TRANSPORTABLE_EXPORT/INDEX
Processing object type TRANSPORTABLE_EXPORT/CONSTRAINT/CONSTRAINT
Processing object type TRANSPORTABLE_EXPORT/INDEX_STATISTICS
Processing object type TRANSPORTABLE_EXPORT/CONSTRAINT/REF_CONSTRAINT
Processing object type TRANSPORTABLE_EXPORT/TABLE_STATISTICS
Processing object type TRANSPORTABLE_EXPORT/POST_INSTANCE/PLUGTS_BLK
Master table "SYS"."SYS_EXPORT_TRANSPORTABLE_01" successfully loaded/unloaded
******************************************************************************
Dump file set for SYS.SYS_EXPORT_TRANSPORTABLE_01 is:
  /home/oracle/TTS/tts_2.dmp
Job "SYS"."SYS_EXPORT_TRANSPORTABLE_01" successfully completed at 11:33:02

host command complete
/*
   The following command may be used to import the tablespaces.
   Substitute values for <logon> and <directory>.
   impdp <logon> directory=<directory> dumpfile= 'tts_2.dmp' transport_datafiles= /home/oracle/
TTS/ap_data.dbf, /home/oracle/TTS/ap_idx.dbf
*/
------------------------------------------------------------
-- Start of sample PL/SQL script for importing the tablespaces
------------------------------------------------------------
-- creating directory objects
CREATE DIRECTORY STREAMS$DIROBJ$1 AS  '/home/oracle/TTS/';
/* PL/SQL Script to import the exported tablespaces */
DECLARE
  -- the datafiles
  tbs_files      dbms_streams_tablespace_adm.file_set;
  cvt_files      dbms_streams_tablespace_adm.file_set;
  -- the dumpfile to import
  dump_file      dbms_streams_tablespace_adm.file;
  dp_job_name    VARCHAR2(30) := NULL;
  -- names of tablespaces that were imported
  ts_names        dbms_streams_tablespace_adm.tablespace_set;
BEGIN
  -- dump file name and location
  dump_file.file_name :=  'tts_2.dmp';
  dump_file.directory_object := 'TTSFILES';
  -- forming list of datafiles for import
  tbs_files( 1).file_name :=  'ap_data.dbf';
  tbs_files( 1).directory_object :=  'STREAMS$DIROBJ$1';
```

```
  tbs_files( 2).file_name := 'ap_idx.dbf';
  tbs_files( 2).directory_object := 'STREAMS$DIROBJ$1';
  -- import tablespaces
  dbms_streams_tablespace_adm.attach_tablespaces(
    datapump_job_name      => dp_job_name,
    dump_file              => dump_file,
    tablespace_files       => tbs_files,
    converted_files        => cvt_files,
    tablespace_names       => ts_names);
  -- output names of imported tablespaces
  IF ts_names IS NOT NULL AND ts_names.first IS NOT NULL THEN
    FOR i IN ts_names.first .. ts_names.last LOOP
      dbms_output.put_line('imported tablespace '|| ts_names(i));
    END LOOP;
  END IF;
END;
/
-- dropping directory objects
DROP DIRECTORY STREAMS$DIROBJ$1;
------------------------------------------------------------
-- End of sample PL/SQL script
------------------------------------------------------------


Removing automatic instance
shutting down automatic instance
Oracle instance shut down
Automatic instance removed
auxiliary instance file /home/oracle/TTS/cntrl_tspitr_ORA10G_fxkl.f deleted
auxiliary instance file /home/oracle/TTS/TSPITR_ORA10G_FXKL/datafile/o1_mf_system_9svlnxnx_.dbf
deleted
auxiliary instance file /home/oracle/TTS/TSPITR_ORA10G_FXKL/datafile/o1_mf_undotbs1_9svlo4om_.
dbf deleted
auxiliary instance file /home/oracle/TTS/TSPITR_ORA10G_FXKL/datafile/o1_mf_sysaux_9svlo5p8_.dbf
deleted
auxiliary instance file /home/oracle/TTS/TSPITR_ORA10G_FXKL/datafile/o1_mf_temp_9svlolfm_.tmp
deleted
auxiliary instance file /home/oracle/TTS/TSPITR_ORA10G_FXKL/onlinelog/o1_mf_1_9svloj68_.log
deleted
auxiliary instance file /home/oracle/TTS/TSPITR_ORA10G_FXKL/onlinelog/o1_mf_2_9svlojw6_.log
deleted
auxiliary instance file /home/oracle/TTS/TSPITR_ORA10G_FXKL/onlinelog/o1_mf_3_9svlokl8_.log
deleted
```

Transport Datafiles and Metadata from Source Platform to Destination Platform

As in the first scenario, it is still incumbent upon the Oracle DBA to transport the two tablespaces' datafiles and the Data Pump Export dump set from the source to the destination platform; in this scenario, however, the datafiles will be copied from the directory specified during the previous TRANSPORT TABLESPACE operation. Listing 6-16 shows the invocation of the DBMS_FILE_TRANSFER utility to complete the transfer of these files between platforms ORA10A and OEL01.

Listing 6-16 *Transferring Datafiles and Metadata from Source to Destination Platforms*

```
BEGIN
    DBMS_FILE_TRANSFER.PUT_FILE(
         source_directory_object => 'TTSFILES'
         ,source_file_name => 'ap_data.dbf'
         ,destination_directory_object => 'OEL01_DG_DATA'
         ,destination_file_name => 'AP_DATA.DBF'
         ,destination_database => 'OEL01'
    );
    DBMS_FILE_TRANSFER.PUT_FILE(
         source_directory_object => 'TTSFILES'
         ,source_file_name => 'ap_idx.dbf'
         ,destination_directory_object => 'OEL01_DG_DATA'
         ,destination_file_name => 'AP_IDX.DBF'
         ,destination_database => 'OEL01'
    );
    DBMS_FILE_TRANSFER.PUT_FILE(
         source_directory_object => 'TTSFILES'
         ,source_file_name => 'tts_2.dmp'
         ,destination_directory_object => 'TTSFILES'
         ,destination_file_name => 'tts_2.dmp'
         ,destination_database => 'OEL01'
    );
END;
/
```

Perform Endian Conversion at Destination

If endian conversion of the transported tablespace is still required, it can be performed on the destination database in the same manner as shown in Listing 6-10 in the first scenario.

Import Source Tablespace Metadata via Data Pump

The same mechanism we used in the first scenario to import tablespace metadata into the destination database can be leveraged in this step as well, as shown in Listing 6-17.

Listing 6-17 *Plugging Transported Tablespaces into Destination Database*

```
$> impdp system/oracle_4U directory=TTSFILES dumpfile='tts_2.dmp' TRANSPORT_
DATAFILES=+DATA/ORCL/DATAFILE/ap_data.dbf, +DATA/ORCL/DATAFILE/ap_idx.dbf

. . .
Thu Jun 12 18:32:18 2014
DM00 started with pid=36, OS id=2269, job SYSTEM.TTS_1
Thu Jun 12 18:32:19 2014
DW00 started with pid=37, OS id=2271, wid=1, job SYSTEM.TTS_1
Plug in tablespace AP_IDX with datafile
  '+DATA/ORCL/DATAFILE/AP_IDX.DBF'
Plug in tablespace AP_DATA with datafile
  '+DATA/ORCL/DATAFILE/AP_DATA.DBF'
. . .
```

Switch Transported Tablespaces to READ WRITE Mode at Destination

Again, the identical SQL*Plus commands in Listing 6-13 in the first scenario are used here to bring the tablespaces just imported into the destination database into READ WRITE mode, if so desired.

Revert Selected Tablespaces to READ WRITE Mode on Source Database

Note that it is also unnecessary to revert any of the tablespaces transported in Step 1 on the source database into READ WRITE mode, as the TRANSPORT TABLESPACE command *automatically reopens them* in READ WRITE mode as soon as that command has completed successfully.

TDB: Transporting Entire Databases

Oracle Database 10*g* Release 2 (10*g* R2) was the first release to provide the capability to migrate an entire Oracle *database* from one source OS platform to a completely different destination OS platform. Like TTS operations, Transportable Database (TDB) operations make it possible to migrate a complete database, even if the source and destination databases reside on different *physical hardware platforms*, use completely different *storage devices* to retain database files, and even utilize different *operating systems*. The downtime required to migrate a database between its current source platform and its future destination platform is thus limited to the time it takes to migrate the datafiles of the database's tablespaces between source and destination platforms. And there is one other unfortunate limitation that holds true for TDB operations, even for Oracle Database 12*c* R1: *Transport between different endian architectures is not supported.*

TDB: Advantages and Drawbacks

Several aspects of TDB make it extremely attractive as compared to the migration methods discussed in Chapter 5.

Source Database Must Be in READ ONLY Mode

TDB requires that the entire database must be placed in READ ONLY mode before a database transport operation can proceed, so that all tablespaces—including the "core" tablespaces like SYSTEM, SYSAUX, and UNDOTBS—can be transported from the source OS platform to the destination OS platform. This makes it much simpler to complete a migration in a timely fashion, especially when a database can tolerate the minimal downtime to transfer all necessary database files between source and destination platforms.

Simplified Script Generation

TDB minimizes the complexity that other migration methods demand because it automatically constructs all scripts—including those necessary for SPFILE creation, control file re-creation, and RMAN conversion operations—required to complete the transport of the database to its new destination OS platform. This also makes it simple to adjust for any serious differences in computing power or storage configuration between source and destination servers. For example, if the destination OS platform has twice as much memory as its corresponding source OS platform, or if the source OS platform uses non-ASM storage but the destination OS platform is leveraging ASM storage, the database transport script can be modified just once to accommodate these differences.

Endianness Limitations

Unfortunately, TDB has one glaring limitation: it can *only* be used to transport databases between source and destination platforms when both platforms have *identical endianness.*

TDB: A Practical Example

This final migration scenario leverages TDB's features to perform a complete migration of an Oracle Database 10*g* R2 database between two little-endian platforms. The scenario presented is becoming a common occurrence as more IT organizations contemplate the migration of smaller, non-mission-critical (but still *important*) databases out of Microsoft Windows environments and into one of the various flavors of the Linux operating system:

- The source OS platform is Microsoft Windows 2003, and all database files are stored in Microsoft's proprietary NTFS file system.

- The source database is Oracle 10.2.0.1, is approximately 2.5GB in size, and is already in ARCHIVELOG mode.

- The destination OS platform is Red Hat Enterprise Linux Version 5 Update 2.

- The destination database will use the Linux EXT3 file system for storage of all database files, including the SPFILE, control files, datafiles, tempfiles, online redo logs, archived redo logs, and all backup files.

- There is sufficient space in the destination database's platform to store the database's SPFILE, control files, permanent tablespace datafiles, temporary tablespace files, and online redo logs.

- There is sufficient space in the destination database's Fast Recovery Area (FRA) mount point for all archived redo logs.

These platforms obviously do not share the same operating system, but that is not an issue because TDB automatically generates the proper RMAN `CONVERT` commands to translate the source database's components so they can be used at the destination. This, of course, makes extremely short work of all conversion efforts, and it is also possible to decide to convert the database's datafiles on the destination server instead of the source platform in order to limit the time required to complete the conversion.

Checklist 6-4 describes the steps necessary to leverage TDB to transport the entire source database from its original Microsoft Windows 2003 platform to its new destination, a RHEL Linux x86-64 platform.

Step	Operation	Description	Done?
1	Perform consistent shutdown of source database	From SQL*Plus on the source database, issue `SHUTDOWN IMMEDIATE;` and wait for shutdown to complete cleanly.	
2	Reopen source database in `READ ONLY` mode	From SQL*Plus on the source database, issue `STARTUP READ ONLY;` to open the database in `READ ONLY` mode.	
3	Verify database transportability	Execute procedures to verify the database is in the proper state for transportability: ■ DBMS_TTS.CHECK_DB ■ DBMS_TTS.CHECK_EXTERNAL	
4	Prepare source database for transport to destination	Prepare for conversion: ■ If conversion is done on the *source* platform, then RMAN generates and retains appropriate converted versions on the source platform for eventual transport to the destination. ■ If conversion is done on the destination, then RMAN generates a conversion script that is shipped to the destination database for eventual execution there.	

Step	Operation	Description	Done?
5	Transport source database to destination database OS platform	Ship all necessary scripts and database files to the destination server via either `scpy`, `sftp`, or the `DBMS_FILE_TRANSFER` utility.	
6	Open destination database	From SQL*Plus on the destination database, issue `ALTER DATABASE OPEN RESETLOGS;` to open the database in a new incarnation.	

CHECKLIST 6-4   *TDB Migration: A Practical Example*

Perform Consistent Shutdown of Source Database

First, the Oracle DBA shuts down the database to ensure that all of the database's control files and datafiles are "frozen" temporarily so that the database can be transported.

Reopen Source Database in READ ONLY Mode

Next, we will reopen the source database itself in READ ONLY mode. Of course, this does mean that the source database will be available only for limited queries until the transport preparations are completed, and DML against the database will be completely forbidden.

Verify Database Transportability

Next, we will verify that the database is indeed currently transportable via the DBMS_ TTS.CHECK_DB and DBMS_TTS.CHECK_EXTERNAL packaged procedures. These procedures will determine if the entire database can now be transported; conversely, if there are any external objects—BFILEs, directory objects, or external tables—that need to be moved separately to complete the migration, these two procedures will report what objects will need to be migrated separately to the destination database once all standard TDB operations have completed. Listing 6-18 shows the invocation of and the output from these two procedures.

Listing 6-18   *Verifying Database Transportability*

```
-----
-- Using DBMS_TDB to validate if a database is ready for transport
-----
SET SERVEROUTPUT ON
DECLARE
```

```
    db_check BOOLEAN;
BEGIN

    -----
    -- Can this database be transported to the specified target platform?
    -----
    db_check :=
        DBMS_TDB.CHECK_DB(
            target_platform_name => 'Linux IA (32-bit)'
            ,skip_option => DBMS_TDB.SKIP_OFFLINE
        );
    IF db_check
        THEN DBMS_OUTPUT.PUT_LINE('Database can be transferred to target platform.');
        ELSE DBMS_OUTPUT.PUT_LINE('Warning!!! Database CANNOT be transported to target
platform.');
    END IF;

    -----
    -- Are there any directories or external objects that need to be
    -- transferred separately after these tablespace(s) have been
    -- transported to the target platform?
    -----
    db_check := DBMS_TDB.CHECK_EXTERNAL;
    IF db_check
        THEN DBMS_OUTPUT.PUT_LINE('Database can be transferred to target platform.');
        ELSE DBMS_OUTPUT.PUT_LINE('Warning!!! Database CANNOT be transported to target
platform.');
    END IF;

END;
/
```

Prepare Source Database for Transport to Destination

Now it's time to execute the appropriate RMAN CONVERT command script to prepare the database to be cloned at the destination platform:

- If the Oracle DBA desires to convert the database's datafiles at the *source* platform, Oracle will automatically create the converted datafiles in a specified directory on the source platform; otherwise, Oracle will generate the appropriate scripts that the DBA will later execute on the *destination* server to perform the datafile conversion there.

- Oracle also creates a script for the creation of the new database on the destination platform; the script prepares the migrated database's control file to reflect the completely new location of all datafiles and online redo logs on the destination server.

Listing 6-19 illustrates the results of preparing the database for transport and eventual conversion on the *target* platform.

Listing 6-19 *Preparing Source Database for Transport when Conversion Will Occur on the Target Platform*

```
-----
-- RMAN session that prepares database for transport and conversion
-----


C:\WINDOWS\system32>rman target /

Recovery Manager: Release 10.2.0.1.0 - Production on Wed Apr 19 18:39:28 2006
Copyright (c) 1982, 2005, Oracle.  All rights reserved.
connected to target database: ORCL102 (DBID=3040314982)

RMAN> RUN {
2>      #####
3>      # Converting a database on target platform
4>      #####
5>      CONVERT DATABASE
6>      ON TARGET PLATFORM
7>      CONVERT SCRIPT 'c:\oracle\rptrepos\rptrepos.cnv'
8>      TRANSPORT SCRIPT 'c:\oracle\rptrepos\rptrepos.txp'
9>      NEW DATABASE 'rptrepos'
11>     DB_FILE_NAME_CONVERT =
                'c:\oracle\oradata\orcl102'
                'c:\oracle\rptrepos';
12> }

Starting convert at 14-JUN-14
using channel ORA_DISK_1

External table HR.XT_EMPLOYEE_PAYCHECKS found in the database
External table HR.XT_EMPLOYEE_SECURED found in the database
External table SH.XT_MIDWEST_SALES found in the database
External table SH.SALES_TRANSACTIONS_EXT found in the database

Directory SYS.TTXPORTS found in the database
Directory SYS.FTP_SECURED found in the database
Directory SYS.EXTERNAL_DIR found in the database
Directory SYS.DATA_PUMP_DIR found in the database
Directory SYS.SUBDIR found in the database
Directory SYS.XMLDIR found in the database
Directory SYS.MEDIA_DIR found in the database
Directory SYS.LOG_FILE_DIR found in the database
Directory SYS.DATA_FILE_DIR found in the database
Directory SYS.WORK_DIR found in the database
Directory SYS.ADMIN_DIR found in the database

BFILE PM.PRINT_MEDIA found in the database

User SYS with SYSDBA and SYSOPER privilege found in password file
channel ORA_DISK_1: starting to check datafiles
input datafile fno=00001 name=C:\ORACLE\ORADATA\ORCL102\SYSTEM01.DBF
channel ORA_DISK_1: datafile checking complete, elapsed time: 00:00:01
channel ORA_DISK_1: starting to check datafiles
input datafile fno=00003 name=C:\ORACLE\ORADATA\ORCL102\SYSAUX01.DBF
channel ORA_DISK_1: datafile checking complete, elapsed time: 00:00:00
channel ORA_DISK_1: starting to check datafiles
```

```
input datafile fno=00002 name=C:\ORACLE\ORADATA\ORCL102\UNDOTBS01.DBF
channel ORA_DISK_1: datafile checking complete, elapsed time: 00:00:00
channel ORA_DISK_1: starting to check datafiles
input datafile fno=00005 name=C:\ORACLE\ORADATA\ORCL102\EXAMPLE01.DBF
channel ORA_DISK_1: datafile checking complete, elapsed time: 00:00:00
channel ORA_DISK_1: starting to check datafiles
input datafile fno=00015 name=C:\ORACLE\ORADATA\ORCL102\LMT_XACT01.DBF
channel ORA_DISK_1: datafile checking complete, elapsed time: 00:00:00
channel ORA_DISK_1: starting to check datafiles
input datafile fno=00004 name=C:\ORACLE\ORADATA\ORCL102\USERS01.DBF
channel ORA_DISK_1: datafile checking complete, elapsed time: 00:00:01
channel ORA_DISK_1: starting to check datafiles
input datafile fno=00016 name=C:\ORACLE\ORADATA\ORCL102\LMT_REF01.DBF
channel ORA_DISK_1: datafile checking complete, elapsed time: 00:00:00
Run SQL script C:\ORACLE\RPTREPOS\RPTREPOS.TXP on the target platform to create database
Edit init.ora file C:\ORACLE\INIT_RPTREPOS.ORA. This PFILE will be used to create the
database on the target platform

Run RMAN script C:\ORACLE\RPTREPOS\RPTREPOS.CNV on target platform to convert datafiles
To recompile all PL/SQL modules, run utlirp.sql and utlrp.sql on the target platform
To change the internal database identifier, use DBNEWID Utility
Finished backup at 14-JUN-14
```

Alternatively, Listing 6-20 shows how to convert the database's datafiles on the *source* platform before transporting the datafiles to the target platform.

Listing 6-20 *Preparing Source Database for Transport When Conversion Will Occur on the Source Platform*

```
C:\WINDOWS\system32>rman target /
Recovery Manager: Release 10.2.0.1.0 - Production on Sun Apr 16 14:16:38 2006
Copyright (c) 1982, 2005, Oracle.  All rights reserved.
connected to target database: ORCL102 (DBID=3040314982)

RMAN> RUN {
2>      CONVERT DATABASE
3>      NEW DATABASE 'rptrepos'
4>      TRANSPORT SCRIPT 'c:\oracle\rptrepos\rptrepos.sql'
5>      TO PLATFORM 'Linux IA (32-bit)'
6>      db_file_name_convert 'c:\oracle\oradata\orcl102' 'c:\oracle\rptrepos';
7> }

Starting convert at 13-JUN-14
using target database control file instead of recovery catalog
allocated channel: ORA_DISK_1
channel ORA_DISK_1: sid=153 devtype=DISK

External table HR.XT_EMPLOYEE_PAYCHECKS found in the database
External table HR.XT_EMPLOYEE_SECURED found in the database
External table SH.XT_MIDWEST_SALES found in the database
External table SH.SALES_TRANSACTIONS_EXT found in the database

Directory SYS.TTXPORTS found in the database
Directory SYS.FTP_SECURED found in the database
```

```
Directory SYS.EXTERNAL_DIR found in the database
Directory SYS.DATA_PUMP_DIR found in the database
Directory SYS.SUBDIR found in the database
Directory SYS.XMLDIR found in the database
Directory SYS.MEDIA_DIR found in the database
Directory SYS.LOG_FILE_DIR found in the database
Directory SYS.DATA_FILE_DIR found in the database
Directory SYS.WORK_DIR found in the database
Directory SYS.ADMIN_DIR found in the database

BFILE PM.PRINT_MEDIA found in the database

User SYS with SYSDBA and SYSOPER privilege found in password file
channel ORA_DISK_1: starting datafile conversion
input datafile fno=00001 name=C:\ORACLE\ORADATA\ORCL102\SYSTEM01.DBF
converted datafile=C:\ORACLE\RPTREPOS\SYSTEM01.DBF
channel ORA_DISK_1: datafile conversion complete, elapsed time: 00:01:26
channel ORA_DISK_1: starting datafile conversion
input datafile fno=00003 name=C:\ORACLE\ORADATA\ORCL102\SYSAUX01.DBF
converted datafile=C:\ORACLE\RPTREPOS\SYSAUX01.DBF
channel ORA_DISK_1: datafile conversion complete, elapsed time: 00:00:45
channel ORA_DISK_1: starting datafile conversion
input datafile fno=00002 name=C:\ORACLE\ORADATA\ORCL102\UNDOTBS01.DBF
converted datafile=C:\ORACLE\RPTREPOS\UNDOTBS01.DBF
channel ORA_DISK_1: datafile conversion complete, elapsed time: 00:00:25
channel ORA_DISK_1: starting datafile conversion
input datafile fno=00005 name=C:\ORACLE\ORADATA\ORCL102\EXAMPLE01.DBF
converted datafile=C:\ORACLE\RPTREPOS\EXAMPLE01.DBF
channel ORA_DISK_1: datafile conversion complete, elapsed time: 00:00:26
channel ORA_DISK_1: starting datafile conversion
input datafile fno=00015 name=C:\ORACLE\ORADATA\ORCL102\LMT_XACT01.DBF
converted datafile=C:\ORACLE\RPTREPOS\LMT_XACT01.DBF
channel ORA_DISK_1: datafile conversion complete, elapsed time: 00:00:03
channel ORA_DISK_1: starting datafile conversion
input datafile fno=00004 name=C:\ORACLE\ORADATA\ORCL102\USERS01.DBF
converted datafile=C:\ORACLE\RPTREPOS\USERS01.DBF
channel ORA_DISK_1: datafile conversion complete, elapsed time: 00:00:03
channel ORA_DISK_1: starting datafile conversion
input datafile fno=00016 name=C:\ORACLE\ORADATA\ORCL102\LMT_REF01.DBF
converted datafile=C:\ORACLE\RPTREPOS\LMT_REF01.DBF
channel ORA_DISK_1: datafile conversion complete, elapsed time: 00:00:02
```

Run SQL script C:\ORACLE\RPTREPOS\RPTREPOS.SQL on the target platform to create database
Edit init.ora file C:\ORACLE\PRODUCT\10.2.0\DB_1\DATABASE\INIT_00HGLPN4_1_0.ORA. This
PFILE will be used to **create the database** on the target platform
To recompile all PL/SQL modules, run **utlirp.sql** and **utlrp.sql** on the target platform
To change the internal database identifier, use **DBNEWID** Utility
Finished backup at 13-JUN-14

Transport Source Database Files to Destination Database OS Platform

At last, it is time to complete the transfer of all source database components, plus
any required conversion scripts, to the destination OS platform to complete the
migration. Either OS commands, Secure Copy (SCP), Secure FTP (SFTP), or the

DBMS_FILE_TRANSFER procedure can be used to "push" or "pull" copies of all necessary datafiles from the source database platform into the appropriate directories on the destination platform.

Create New Control Files on Destination Platform   Once all files have been transferred to the destination OS platform, the DBA runs the previously generated CREATE CONTROLFILE script at the destination server (see Listing 6-21) to create the new database's control file and mount the database.

Listing 6-21   *Creating New Control File for Destination Database*

```
-----
-- Use this PFILE to open the database:
-----

#####
# Edited PFILE for use during creation of new database
#####

# Please change the values of the following parameters:
  control_files           = "/u01/app/oracle/oradata/RPTREPOS/control01.ctl"
  db_recovery_file_dest   = "/u01/app/oracle/flash_recovery_area"
  db_recovery_file_dest_size= 2147483648
  audit_file_dest         = "/u01/app/oracle/admin/RPTREPOS/adump"
  background_dump_dest     = "/u01/app/oracle/admin/RPTREPOS/bdump"
  user_dump_dest          = "/u01/app/oracle/admin/RPTREPOS/udump"
  core_dump_dest          = "/u01/app/oracle/admin/RPTREPOS/cdump"
  db_name                 = "RPTREPOS"
# Please review the values of the following parameters:
  __shared_pool_size      = 54525952
  __large_pool_size       = 4194304
  __java_pool_size        = 4194304
  __streams_pool_size     = 4194304
  __db_cache_size         = 46137344
  remote_login_passwordfile= "EXCLUSIVE"
  db_domain               = ""
# The values of the following parameters are from source database:
  processes               = 150
  sga_max_size            = 134217728
  sga_target              = 117440512
  db_block_size           = 8192
  compatible              = "10.2.0.1.0"
  db_file_multiblock_read_count= 16
  undo_management         = "AUTO"
  undo_tablespace         = "UNDOTBS1"
  shared_servers          = 2
  max_shared_servers      = 5
  job_queue_processes     = 10
  open_cursors            = 300
  pga_aggregate_target    = 33554432
```

```
/*
|| Script: RPTREPOS.TXP
|| Edited control file creation script to create database on
|| target platform
*/

-- The following commands will create a new control file and use it
-- to open the database.
-- Data used by Recovery Manager will be lost.
-- The contents of online logs will be lost and all backups will
-- be invalidated. Use this only if online logs are damaged.
-- After mounting the created controlfile, the following SQL
-- statement will place the database in the appropriate
-- protection mode:
--   ALTER DATABASE SET STANDBY DATABASE TO MAXIMIZE PERFORMANCE

STARTUP NOMOUNT PFILE='/u01/app/oracle/oradata/RPTREPOS/INIT_RPTREPOS.ORA'
CREATE CONTROLFILE REUSE SET DATABASE "RPTREPOS" RESETLOGS  ARCHIVELOG
    MAXLOGFILES 16
    MAXLOGMEMBERS 3
    MAXDATAFILES 100
    MAXINSTANCES 8
    MAXLOGHISTORY 292
LOGFILE
  GROUP 1 '/u01/app/oracle/oradata/RPTREPOS/redo01.log'  SIZE 50M,
  GROUP 2 '/u01/app/oracle/oradata/RPTREPOS/redo02.log'  SIZE 50M,
  GROUP 3 '/u01/app/oracle/oradata/RPTREPOS/redo03.log'  SIZE 50M
DATAFILE
  '/u01/app/oracle/oradata/RPTREPOS/SYSTEM01.DBF',
  '/u01/app/oracle/oradata/RPTREPOS/UNDOTBS01.DBF',
  '/u01/app/oracle/oradata/RPTREPOS/SYSAUX01.DBF',
  '/u01/app/oracle/oradata/RPTREPOS/USERS01.DBF',
  '/u01/app/oracle/oradata/RPTREPOS/EXAMPLE01.DBF',
  '/u01/app/oracle/oradata/RPTREPOS/LMT_XACT01.DBF',
  '/u01/app/oracle/oradata/RPTREPOS/LMT_REF01.DBF'
CHARACTER SET AL32UTF8
;
```

Execute Conversion Scripts on Destination Database   The final step in the transport phase is to execute all the conversion scripts (if any exist) on the destination database to complete datafile conversion, as shown in Listing 6-22.

Listing 6-22 *Converting TDB Tablespaces on Destination Platform*

```
$> rman target /

Recovery Manager: Release 10.2.0.1.0 - Production on Wed Apr 19 19:49:26 2006
Copyright (c) 1982, 2005, Oracle.  All rights reserved.
connected to target database: RPTREPOS (DBID=3040314982, not open)

RUN {
  CONVERT DATAFILE '/u01/app/oracle/oradata/RPTREPOS/SYSTEM01.DBF'
    FROM PLATFORM 'Microsoft Windows IA (32-bit)'
```

```
    FORMAT '/u01/app/oracle/oradata/RPTREPOS/system01.dbf';
  CONVERT DATAFILE '/u01/app/oracle/oradata/RPTREPOS/SYSAUX01.DBF'
    FROM PLATFORM 'Microsoft Windows IA (32-bit)'
    FORMAT '/u01/app/oracle/oradata/RPTREPOS/sysaux01.dbf';
  CONVERT DATAFILE '/u01/app/oracle/oradata/RPTREPOS/UNDOTBS01.DBF'
    FROM PLATFORM 'Microsoft Windows IA (32-bit)'
    FORMAT '/u01/app/oracle/oradata/RPTREPOS/sysaux01.dbf';
  CONVERT DATAFILE '/u01/app/oracle/oradata/RPTREPOS/EXAMPLE01.DBF'
    FROM PLATFORM 'Microsoft Windows IA (32-bit)'
    FORMAT '/u01/app/oracle/oradata/RPTREPOS/example01.dbf';
  CONVERT DATAFILE '/u01/app/oracle/oradata/RPTREPOS/LMT_XACT01.DBF'
    FROM PLATFORM 'Microsoft Windows IA (32-bit)'
    FORMAT '/u01/app/oracle/oradata/RPTREPOS/lmt_xact01.dbf';
  CONVERT DATAFILE '/u01/app/oracle/oradata/RPTREPOS/USERS01.DBF'
    FROM PLATFORM 'Microsoft Windows IA (32-bit)'
    FORMAT '/u01/app/oracle/oradata/RPTREPOS/users01.dbf';
  CONVERT DATAFILE '/u01/app/oracle/oradata/RPTREPOS/LMT_REF01.DBF'
    FROM PLATFORM 'Microsoft Windows IA (32-bit)'
    FORMAT '/u01/app/oracle/oradata/RPTREPOS/lmt_ref01.dbf';
}
2> 3> 4> 5> 6> 7> 8> 9> 10> 11> 12> 13> 14> 15> 16> 17> 18> 19> 20> 21> 22> 23> 24> 25> 26>
Starting backup at 14-JUN-14
using target database control file instead of recovery catalog
allocated channel: ORA_DISK_1
channel ORA_DISK_1: sid=155 devtype=DISK
channel ORA_DISK_1: starting datafile conversion
input filename=/u01/app/oracle/oradata/RPTREPOS/SYSTEM01.DBF
converted datafile=/u01/app/oracle/oradata/RPTREPOS/system01.dbf
channel ORA_DISK_1: datafile conversion complete, elapsed time: 00:04:19
Finished backup at 14-JUN-14

Starting backup at 14-JUN-14
using channel ORA_DISK_1
channel ORA_DISK_1: starting datafile conversion
input filename=/u01/app/oracle/oradata/RPTREPOS/SYSAUX01.DBF
converted datafile=/u01/app/oracle/oradata/RPTREPOS/sysaux01.dbf
channel ORA_DISK_1: datafile conversion complete, elapsed time: 00:03:07
Finished backup at 14-JUN-14

using channel ORA_DISK_1
channel ORA_DISK_1: starting datafile conversion
input filename=/u01/app/oracle/oradata/RPTREPOS/UNDOTBS01.DBF
converted datafile=/u01/app/oracle/oradata/RPTREPOS/undotbs01.dbf
channel ORA_DISK_1: datafile conversion complete, elapsed time: 00:00:59
Finished backup at 14-JUN-14

Starting backup at 14-JUN-14
using channel ORA_DISK_1
channel ORA_DISK_1: starting datafile conversion
input filename=/u01/app/oracle/oradata/RPTREPOS/EXAMPLE01.DBF
converted datafile=/u01/app/oracle/oradata/RPTREPOS/example01.dbf
channel ORA_DISK_1: datafile conversion complete, elapsed time: 00:00:55
Finished backup at 14-JUN-14
```

```
Starting backup at 14-JUN-14
using channel ORA_DISK_1
channel ORA_DISK_1: starting datafile conversion
input filename=/u01/app/oracle/oradata/RPTREPOS/LMT_XACT01.DBF
converted datafile=/u01/app/oracle/oradata/RPTREPOS/lmt_xact01.dbf
channel ORA_DISK_1: datafile conversion complete, elapsed time: 00:00:08
Finished backup at 14-JUN-14

Starting backup at 14-JUN-14
using channel ORA_DISK_1
channel ORA_DISK_1: starting datafile conversion
input filename=/u01/app/oracle/oradata/RPTREPOS/USERS01.DBF
converted datafile=/u01/app/oracle/oradata/RPTREPOS/users01.dbf
channel ORA_DISK_1: datafile conversion complete, elapsed time: 00:00:08
Finished backup at 14-JUN-14

Starting backup at 14-JUN-14
using channel ORA_DISK_1
channel ORA_DISK_1: starting datafile conversion
input filename=/u01/app/oracle/oradata/RPTREPOS/LMT_REF01.DBF
converted datafile=/u01/app/oracle/oradata/RPTREPOS/lmt_ref01.dbf
channel ORA_DISK_1: datafile conversion complete, elapsed time: 00:00:03
Finished backup at 14-JUN-14
```

Open Destination Database

After the transfer phase is complete, only the following few tasks remain, as shown in Listing 6-23:

- Open the transported database via the `ALTER DATABASE OPEN RESETLOGS;` command.

- Add temp files for any temporary tablespace(s).

- Recompile all PL/SQL code via `utlrp.sql`.

Listing 6-23 *Final Results: TDB Operations Completed*

```
SQL> alter database open resetlogs;

Database altered.

SQL> ALTER TABLESPACE TEMP
    ADD TEMPFILE '/u01/app/oracle/oradata/RPTREPOS/temp01.tmp'
    SIZE 202375168
    AUTOEXTEND ON
    NEXT 655360
    MAXSIZE 32767M;  2    3    4    5    6
```

```
Tablespace altered.

SQL> shutdown immediate;
Database closed.
Database dismounted.
ORACLE instance shut down.

SQL> STARTUP UPGRADE PFILE='C:\ORACLE\INIT_RPTREPOS.ORA'
SQL> @@ ?/rdbms/admin/utlirp.sql

<<< Results edited for brevity >>>

SQL> DOC
DOC>#########################################################################
DOC>#########################################################################
DOC>   utlirp.sql completed successfully. All PL/SQL objects in the
DOC>   database have been invalidated.
DOC>
DOC>   Shut down and restart the database in normal mode and run utlrp.sql to
DOC>   recompile invalid objects.
DOC>#########################################################################
DOC>#########################################################################

SQL> shutdown immediate;
Database closed.
Database dismounted.
ORACLE instance shut down.

SQL> STARTUP PFILE='/u01/app/oracle/oradata/RPTREPOS/INIT_RPTREPOS.ORA'
ORACLE instance started.

Total System Global Area   134217728 bytes
Fixed Size                   1218148 bytes
Variable Size               83888540 bytes
Database Buffers            46137344 bytes
Redo Buffers                 2973696 bytes
Database mounted.
Database opened.
SQL> @@ ?/rdbms/admin/utlrp.sql

TIMESTAMP
----------------------------------------------------------------------------
COMP_TIMESTAMP UTLRP_BGN  2014-06-15 20:53:24

<<< Results edited for brevity >>>

TIMESTAMP
----------------------------------------------------------------------------
COMP_TIMESTAMP UTLRP_END  2014-06-15 21:18:24
```

Summary

Let's briefly recap the key points we've covered in this chapter:

- Oracle's Transportable Tablespace Set (TTS) features make it quite simple to migrate tablespace sets between source and destination platforms. However, we cannot ignore the "window of inopportunity"—the amount of downtime that can be tolerated by any applications dependent on the data in the tablespaces being transported—when considering if TTS is an appropriate method for migrating those data, because the source tablespaces must briefly remain in READ ONLY mode until the TTS operations are completed.

- Likewise, Oracle's Transportable Database (TDB) features makes short work of migrating entire *databases* between source and destination platforms, as long as (a) the platforms have the same endianness, and (b) the applications that the databases support can tolerate the necessary downtime while the entire source database remains in READ ONLY mode during the initial migration steps.

PART
III

Migration with Enhancement/Upgrade

CHAPTER
7

Migrating Oracle Databases with Export/Import

O ne of the most basic and simplest tools for performing data migrations is Export/Import. The Export/Import tools have gone through several iterations, but all versions essentially perform the same function: extract data from an Oracle database into a binary file, known as the dump file, and load that data into an Oracle database. Legacy Export/Import has evolved into Data Pump Export/Import, but they are essentially the same function, though the latter has some major enhancements. These tools can move data from one database to another but can perform only minor transformations.

Oracle Export and Import can be categorized into two different sets of tools: Legacy Export/Import and Data Pump Export/Import. Both perform a similar basic function and sometimes data is interchangeable, but internally they are different tools. This chapter covers the use of both Legacy Export/Import and Data Pump Export/Import.

TIP & TECHNIQUE
Use Data Pump Export/Import whenever you are moving from an Oracle Database 10g or later database. Legacy Export/Import should be used only when moving from an Oracle9i or earlier database.

Introduction to Export/Import

Legacy Export/Import has been a part of Oracle for many versions, replaced by Data Pump Export/Import in Oracle Database 10*g*. Legacy Export/Import has been desupported by Oracle Support since the release of Oracle Database 11*g*. However, it still can be used for some specific purposes, such as migrations from Oracle9*i* or earlier. For the purpose of this book, the coverage will mainly focus on Data Pump Export/Import, simply referred to as Data Pump where appropriate.

NOTE
For this chapter, unless specifically referenced as Legacy Export/Import or Data Pump Export/Import, the use of the term Export/Import refers to both.

Both Legacy Export/Import and Data Pump serve a singular purpose: to copy data from an Oracle database into a binary file system file that can then be used to copy the data into another Oracle database. Unlike Oracle RMAN, which is covered later in this book, Export/Import copies row data rather than block data.

Both Legacy Export/Import and Data Pump Export/Import take Oracle row data and put it into a binary file, referred to in this chapter as an *export file*. This export file can be very large (depending on the file system) and can be read only by the Oracle Import utilities. Data Pump Import can read Legacy Export files, but Legacy Import cannot read Data Pump Export files.

When Data Pump Export/Import was introduced, its significant performance improvement over Legacy Export/Import was one of the main reasons why it became the preferred Export/Import utility. These days, the ongoing support for new Oracle features is perhaps the biggest reason to stick with Data Pump Export/Import.

Overview of Migrating a Database with Export/Import

We often use the following high-level steps to migrate databases:

1. *Export metadata.* This allows us to capture all of the objects, schemas, and so forth.

2. *Create target database.* In addition to creating the target database, we create tablespaces using the new structure, such as ASM or encrypted tablespaces.

3. *Import metadata.* We use this metadata in the next step to create objects and use them as a template for any modifications that we choose to do.

TIP & TECHNIQUE

Careful planning can be important at this stage. You can choose what type of metadata to import. You can import table definitions, constraints, triggers, and so forth. It is much more efficient to rebuild indexes after all the data has been loaded. It is also a good idea to see if the index is really still needed as well. Sometimes obsolete indexes aren't removed from the system. So, you can import some constraints now, such as NOT NULL or primary key and wait to import indexes and foreign key constraints until after data has been loaded.

4. *Modify objects.* A data migration is the best possible time to make improvements to the structure of your database, such as making partitioning changes, moving to SecureFile LOBs, enabling compression, encrypting tablespaces, and so on.

5. *Load data*. We do this via the `DATA_ONLY` option of Data Pump.

TIP & TECHNIQUE
Loading data with indexes disabled and building indexes later will enhance performance of data loads. Be careful. Disabling indexes used for foreign keys while leaving the constraints enabled can cause some performance issues.

6. *Import optional structures.* Depending on your needs you can import additional structures such as constraints, indexes, and so forth if you have not already imported them when you imported the metadata. Depending on the migration, we may or may not enable some constraints before loading data.

TIP & TECHNIQUE
We usually prefer to enable primary key constraints before importing data. However, using either import tool, you must disable referential integrity constraints because of the order of loading data. This can be a problem with existing tables and multiple imports. If you try to load a table that has an enabled foreign key constraint to a table that hasn't been loaded yet, you will have a problem.

Planning is very important in determining the method of migration, what you want to migrate at each stage, and how you are going to assign resources. Good planning can make or break a data migration.

Transformations and Export/Import

Since the export file holds row data, when importing into an Oracle database using Import you can easily transform data as long as the tables are the same. So, what kinds of transformation can take place? Here are a few of them:

- **Upgrade** An export from Oracle 10*g* or 9*i* can be imported into an Oracle 11*g* database, thus performing an upgrade and migration at the same time.

- **Structural transformations** Since export files contain row data, underlying tablespaces can be different, and even column sizes and order.

- **Storage transformation** Storage can easily be converted from non-ASM to ASM storage.

- **Partitioning transformations**   Since data is loaded into the database by row, it is easy to load data from a nonpartitioned source into a partitioned target.

- **Security**   Data can be encrypted during import at the target.

- **Compression**   Data can be compressed as it is imported into the target.

Import is one of the few methods of migration that allows so much flexibility during the migration. This is usually the catch-all when changes are being made. Other methods of migration, such as migrating using Oracle GoldenGate, will often use Data Pump as part of the process.

Using Export/Import for Backup and Recovery and Data Movement

Export/Import can also be a useful tool for backing up a specific table, schema, or tablespace at the dictionary-only, data-only, or dictionary-data level. Unlike using RMAN, you can back up very specific pieces of data. Often Export/Import is used to back up very specific data before doing an upgrade, data load, or other operations so that the data can quickly be replaced in the event of a failure. Export/Import is also used to move data between databases. These other uses of Export/Import can be very useful but are beyond the scope of this book. Please see the Oracle Utilities guide for further information.

Types of Exports

Both Legacy and Data Pump Export offer a number of different modes for moving data out of an Oracle database. The various modes allow for different data sets to be exported:

- **Full**   Allows for the complete database to be exported. This includes all objects, including all system objects. This mode is normally not used for migrations unless you are moving to the same architecture system and not transforming data.

- **Tablespace**   Allows for the complete tablespace export. This will export all objects in a tablespace. This does not include system objects.

- **Transportable Tablespaces**   Available with Data Pump. This mode also allows for transportable tablespaces data movement. Transportable tablespaces are covered separately in this book.

- **User/Schema**   This mode allows for all of the objects belonging to a user to be exported. With proper privileges you can also export schema objects belonging to another user. User mode is used for Legacy Export and Schema mode is used with Data Pump.

- **Table/Partition**   This mode allows for specific tables and/or partitions to be exported. During a recent migration we used this mode to export database partitions individually in parallel. LOB data often experiences performance problems during export. By exporting LOB partitions in parallel, performance can be enhanced.

- **System Change Number (SCN)**   With both Legacy Export/Import and Data Pump Export/Import, you have the option to export to a specific SCN using the FLASHBACK_SCN parameter. This can be very valuable for creating a consistent version of data. You will see how this can be important in the next chapter.

Depending on the type of migration that meets your needs, you will most likely use one or more of the preceding modes.

TIP & TECHNIQUE

Data Pump can supplement other migration methods, because you can use it to move one or more tables that might need to be moved at cutover.

Using Export/Import to Migrate Metadata

During some types of migrations, such as zero downtime migrations using Oracle GoldenGate (covered in Chapter 8), there is a need to create an Oracle database before beginning the migration. In addition, if you plan to perform transformations, it is useful to create an empty database before performing the migration. In this manner you can import the object definitions, modify the database structure, and then migrate the data.

Using Export to Generate Metadata

Both Legacy and Data Pump Export can be used to generate metadata. Many of us are used to doing this, because this is the way we have done metadata generation for a long time. However, there are other ways of generating metadata. Tools such as the DBMS_METADATA package, Oracle SQL Developer, and Oracle Enterprise Manager (OEM) can generate metadata to be used to set up the target database. These tools are quite effective, quite useful, and, in some cases, very easy to use.

Exporting and importing metadata is the first step. After you have created the database structure, you can modify objects and import the data. The last step is to create indexes, enable constraints and triggers, and then create statistics.

Using Legacy Export/Import to Migrate Oracle Databases

Legacy Export/Import is typically used only when specific circumstances require some of its features that are not available in Data Pump. In particular, Data Pump cannot be used against a read-only database, whereas Legacy Export/Import can, because Data Pump Export uses the internal job scheduler in the Oracle database. In addition, on occasion we have found it easier to use Legacy tools for metadata migration.

Exporting Metadata with Legacy Export/Import

During some types of migrations, such as zero downtime migrations using Oracle GoldenGate (covered in Chapter 8), there is a need to create an Oracle database before beginning the migration. In addition, if you plan to perform transformations, it is useful to create a shell database before performing the migration. In this manner you can import the object definitions, modify the database structure, and then migrate the data.

Don't underestimate the value of exporting and importing metadata. This allows you to create the database structure, modify it, and then continue with your data migration. This is one of the best ways to perform data transformations, since you are starting with the source database structure, then moving to a newer, more optimal structure.

So, how do you migrate the database structure without migrating the data? That is one of the features of Export and Import. Legacy Export and Import include specific options to migrate specific pieces of data.

Legacy Export has several options for migrating metadata. These options, if chosen correctly, will export the object definitions without migrating the actual data. The options that are important to metadata are

- **CONSTRAINTS**   Setting CONSTRAINTS=y specifies that Export will export the constraints, which can then be imported into the target database.

- **FULL**   Setting FULL=y specifies that a full export should be done. You can further limit to no data by using the ROWS=n parameter.

TIP & TECHNIQUE
To export metadata that includes user definitions, use
FULL=y and ROWS=n.

- **GRANTS**   When GRANTS=y is specified, permissions will be exported.

- **INDEXES**   INDEXES=y indicates that indexes should be exported.

- **OWNER**   Specifies the owner of the objects to be exported. This specifies a user mode export.

- **PARFILE** Specifies a parameter file to be used for the export parameter definitions. This parameter file can hold all of the other options.

- **ROWS** By default, ROWS=y is set, specifying that data is exported. If you want to export metadata only, specify ROWS=n.

- **STATISTICS** Specifies whether statistics should be exported and, if so, whether they should be computed or estimated.

- **TRIGGERS** When TRIGGERS=y is set, trigger definitions will be exported.

- **TABLES** Specifies a list of tables to be exported and specifies table mode export.

- **TABLESPACES** Specifies tablespace mode export.

TIP & TECHNIQUE
Use a parameter file when doing exports and imports. This can avoid creating a more repeatable and self-documenting process.

You can choose any of several ways to export the metadata using Legacy Export. With some options user definitions are not allowed, so some tasks, such as the creation of users, must be done manually. The following are a few examples.

TIP & TECHNIQUE
We prefer to create the user account and security manually. We will use Export/Import for creating object metadata only.

- Full metadata export:

  ```
  exp full=y rows=n statistics=none file=ora10g.dmp log=ora10g.log
  ```
- User mode for user scott:

  ```
  exp owner=scott file=exp1.dmp log=exp1.log
  ```

TIP & TECHNIQUE
The export log is a valuable piece of data. We always like to compare our export logs to our import logs to make sure that the number of rows per table matches.

Exporting with Legacy Export/Import

After creating the objects on the target system, you are ready to migrate the actual table data. You do so by exporting the database using one of several methods: tablespace mode, table mode, or user mode. Which mode you should choose typically depends on the amount and type of data that you are exporting.

If you are exporting a small amount of data, you can simply choose user mode and perform an export for each user. If you have large partitioned tables, you will probably want to perform the export in parallel using individual exports to create individual export files. You can even take this a step further and export on a partition-by-partition basis, thus increasing the concurrency. When doing this, you should disable indexes or create them later.

The various exports can be done using the command line directly or using a parameter file. In many cases where we have split up exports into several pieces, we have created the shell script for doing the export from a database query. This is done by a SELECT statement that can generate the script with table mode or partition mode exports.

Once you have determined the mode of export, you have to implement the export. Since the import must use the export files that are generated, you must plan on how to share this data. There are several ways:

■ **File Copy** Once you've completed the export, you can copy the export files to the remote system where they can be imported.

■ **NFS Mount (NAS)** Export the dump files to an NFS mount that is mounted from both the source system and target system. This allows you to share the dump files on both source and target without having to duplicate the files. Since you will be crossing the network in both directions, there is a potential for performance degradation.

■ **NFS Mount (local)** You can export the files locally and remotely mount the export directories from the target system. This will reduce one network transmission.

■ **NFS Mount (remote)** You can export the files to an NFS mount that is a disk on the remote (target) system. We prefer this method because it does the import optimally.

Exporting is fairly straightforward. Depending on the mode you choose, you will have different parameters to set. The following sections present a few examples of various export techniques.

User Mode Export

In user mode export, you specify the OWNER parameter in the export. This export only exports data belonging to the users specified in the parameter.

```
$ exp OWNER=scott,ewhalen,jczuprynski FILE=exp1.dmp LOG=exp1.log
```

NOTE
Be careful when naming the dump file. It is possible
to overwrite the dump file with simultaneous exports.

Table Mode Export

In table mode export, you specify the specific tables using the TABLES parameter. This export only exports the specified objects.

```
$ exp TABLES=(scott.emp,ewhalen.tab1,jczuprynski.tab2) FILE=exp2.dmp LOG=exp2.log
```

Partition Mode Export

In partition mode export, you specify the specific tables and partitions using the TABLES parameter. This export only exports the specified objects.

```
$ exp OWNER=scott TABLES=(emp.part1, emp.part2, emp.part3) FILE=exp3.dmp LOG=exp3.log
```

Importing with Legacy Export/Import

Importing can be accomplished with a two-step process: first import the table data, then import the indexes, constraints, and triggers. Optionally, you can import the indexes, constraints, and triggers during the metadata process and disable them during import.

When importing data, the behavior of Import will vary based on whether the target object exists. If a table does not exist in the target database, it will be created. If a table already exists, it will not be re-created. Thus, it is possible to transform the target database by pre-creating the objects in the manner that you desire. This is true of both Legacy Import and Data Pump Import.

Why Disable Constraints, Triggers, and Indexes?

During the import some problems will occur. Because Import runs serially, foreign key constraints will be violated because the dependent tables are not populated yet. In addition, indexes are more efficiently built after the data has been imported.

Triggers   When importing data, you are importing tables that are modified by user applications as well as the data that is generated by triggers. You don't want triggers to fire during the import, since essentially you will be re-firing the trigger.

Constraints   You should disable referential integrity constraints because the import almost certainly will not run in the correct order to ensure that all referenced tables are loaded before the table that references them. Once you are finished, you should carefully enable and validate the constraint.

Indexes It is more efficient to build the index after the data is loaded than to build it during the load.

You can import the data by using the `imp` command and specifying the import file, the user and/or table, and a log file. You can run multiple imports at the same time, thus creating some parallelism. The following sections present a few examples of importing with Legacy Import.

Import Special Parameters

When using Legacy Import, you can use several special parameters to change the behavior of the import. These parameters apply to all modes and include the following:

- **DATA_ONLY** When you specify DATA_ONLY, the table data is imported and no metadata is imported. Any metadata parameters such as INDEXES, CONSTRAINTS, and so on are ignored.

- **FROMUSER/TOUSER** The FROMUSER and TOUSER parameters allow you to change the name of the user that is in the dump file to a new user. These commands are used as a set.

- **ROWS** The ROWS parameter specifies whether table data is imported or not.

User Mode Import

In user mode import, you specify the user or users to export in the export parameters, although if you want to import all of the users that have been exported to the dump file, it is not necessary to specifically identify them.

NOTE
User mode import does not export the user definitions and permissions. That information is only available in a full export.

Although you don't need to specify users if you are importing all the users, if you want to *change* the name of a user, you need to use the FROMUSER/TOUSER parameters set:

```
$ imp FROMUSER=ewhalen TOUSER=kwilliams DUMPFILE=exp1.dmp LOGFILE=imp1.log
```

This will import the data from the exp1.dmp file and convert data that was exported from ewhalen to the kwilliams user.

Table Mode Import

In table mode import, you specify the tables using the `TABLES` parameter. This import only imports the specified objects. If you used the `TABLES` option in the export and now want to import all of these tables, you don't need to specify any parameters.

```
$ imp TABLES=(ewhalen.tab1) DUMPFILE=exp2.dmp LOGFILE=imp2.log
```

Partition Mode Import

In partition mode import, you specify the partitions using the `TABLES` parameter. This import only imports the specified objects. If you used the `PARTITIONS` option in the export and now want to import all of these partitions, you don't need to specify any parameters.

```
$ imp OWNER=scott TABLES=(emp.part1, emp.part2, emp.part3)
DUMPFILE=exp3.dmp LOGFILE=imp3.log
```

The partition mode export/import can be effective on very large tables to increase the amount of parallelism.

Legacy Export/Import Summary

Legacy Export/Import can be used when migrating from a database that is of a version prior to Oracle Database 10*g*, where Data Pump Export/Import was introduced. As mentioned earlier, Legacy Export/Import is just one way to move metadata. The method used to move the metadata and method used to move the data can be different. These are individual operations.

Using Data Pump Export/Import to Migrate Oracle Databases

If you are using a version of Oracle that is 10*g* or newer, Data Pump Export/Import is preferred over Legacy Export/Import. Although there are still several reasons why Legacy tools might be used, if at all possible you should use Data Pump. Data Pump is much faster and more flexible and efficient.

Data Pump has been enhanced since it was introduced in Oracle Database 10*g*, but a 10*g* Data Pump dump file can be read from any newer version of the Oracle Data Pump utility. Data Pump can be used for both metadata and data. The concepts are the same as they are for the legacy tools, but the syntax is different.

Unlike the legacy tools, Data Pump runs inside the database rather than as an external utility. The expdp and impdp commands actually create jobs that run inside the database, thus eliminating the need to go through the network layer. This is one of the reasons why Data Pump is so much faster than Legacy Export/Import.

NOTE
In Legacy Export the data is moved from the database to the Export utility, potentially across the network, and is formatted in the utility. With Data Pump Export the formatting and processing are done in the PL/SQL engine in the server process on the database machine, eliminating the network, and potentially eliminating other SQL parsing overhead. Legacy Import and Data Pump Import behave the same way. The Data Pump method can be orders of magnitude faster, and there are several other benefits, such as the capability to suspend and resume.

Data Pump Export/Import Directory Objects

Unlike Legacy Export/Import, Data Pump Export/Import runs inside the database as mentioned previously. Data Pump is a server-side utility rather than a client utility. Data Pump accesses the export files and log files via a directory object in Oracle. This directory object must exist and must be accessible to the user performing the export/import. In a RAC cluster this should be a shared directory using Oracle Database File System (DBFS), Oracle Automatic Storage Management Cluster File System (ACFS), or Network File System (NFS). To determine which directory objects exist, use the following query:

```
set linesize 200 pagesize 200;
COLUMN OWNER FORMAT a8;
COLUMN DIRECTORY_NAME FORMAT a15;
COLUMN DIRECTORY_PATH FORMAT a70;

SELECT * FROM dba_directories;
OWNER DIRECTORY_NAME  DIRECTORY_PATH
----- --------------- ------------------------------------------------------------
SYS   ADMIN_DIR       /ade/aime_ship_10gR2_050630.0022/oracle/md/admin
SYS   DATA_PUMP_DIR   /u01/app/oracle/product/10.2.0/db_1/admin/ora10g/dpdump/
SYS   DATA_FILE_DIR
      /u01/app/oracle/product/10.2.0/db_1/demo/schema/sales_history/
SYS   WORK_DIR        /ade/aime_ship_10gR2_050630.0022/oracle/work
SYS   LOG_FILE_DIR    /u01/app/oracle/product/10.2.0/db_1/demo/schema/log/
SYS   MEDIA_DIR
      /u01/app/oracle/product/10.2.0/db_1/demo/schema/product_media/
SYS   XMLDIR
      /u01/app/oracle/product/10.2.0/db_1/demo/schema/order_entry/
SYS   SUBDIR
      /u01/app/oracle/product/10.2.0/db_1/demo/schema/order_entry//2002/Sep
```

To create a new directory object and grant permissions, use this:

```
SQL> CREATE OR REPLACE DIRECTORY exp_dir AS '/home/oracle/exp';
Directory created.
SQL> GRANT READ,WRITE ON DIRECTORY exp_dir TO scott;
Grant succeeded.
```

When using Data Pump, it is necessary to specify the directory object to be used during the export and import process. Here is an example:

```
expdp schemas=scott directory=exp_dir dumpfile=exp1.dmp logfile=exp1.log
```

Exporting Metadata with Data Pump Export/Import

Exporting metadata with Data Pump Export is similar to exporting metadata with Legacy Export but the parameters are different. To specify a metadata-only export, use the CONTENT=METADATA_ONLY parameter. This parameter specifies that only the metadata will be exported, with no table data. Thus, this is an easy way to export the object definitions. This parameter works in any mode except transportable tablespaces mode and query mode.

Here are a few examples of how to use Data Pump Export to export metadata only. The first example exports the definitions of all objects owned by the scott, hr, and oe schemas:

```
expdp schemas=scott,hr,oe directory=exp_dir dumpfile=exp2.dmp
logfile=exp2.log content=metadata_only
```

The second example shows how you can export all metadata. You can choose the metadata for a specific schema by using the SCHEMAS parameter with impdp.

```
expdp full=y directory=exp_dir dumpfile=exp3.dmp logfile=exp3.log
content=metadata_only
```

Once you have exported the metadata, you can still specify additional options on the Data Pump Import to exclude or include specific objects or schemas.

Exporting with Data Pump

After creating the objects on the target system, you are ready to migrate the actual table data. This is done via Data Pump by exporting the database using one of several methods: tablespace mode, table mode, schema mode, or transportable tablespace mode. Which mode you should choose typically depends on the amount and type of data that you are exporting.

TIP & TECHNIQUE

Transportable tablespace mode is very efficient if no transformations are being done to the target database.

As with Legacy Export, if you are exporting a small amount of data you can simply choose schema mode and perform an export for each schema. If you have large partitioned tables, you will probably want to perform the export in parallel using individual exports to create individual export files of each table or partition.

The various exports can be done using the command line directly or using a parameter file. In many cases where we have split up exports into several pieces, we have created the shell script for doing the export from a database query. This is done by a SELECT statement that can generate the script with table mode or partition mode exports.

Once you have determined the mode of export, you have to implement the export. Since the import must use the export files that are generated, you must plan on how to share this data. There are several ways to do this:

- **File Copy**   Once you've completed the export, you can copy the export files to the remote system where they can be imported. This is inefficient and requires double the storage.

- **NFS Mount (NAS)**   Export the dump files to an NFS mount that is mounted from both the source system and target system. This allows you to share the dump files on both source and target without having to duplicate the files. You must have a fast network and a fast NAS to be efficient.

- **NFS Mount (local)**   You can export the files locally and remotely mount the export directories from the target system. This is not recommended because you are mounting an NFS file system on the production server.

- **NFS Mount (remote)**   You can export the files to an NFS mount that is a disk on the remote (target) system. We prefer this method because it does the import optimally and offloads the NFS to a server currently not in production.

- **DB Link**   Using the NETWORK_LINK parameter, you can perform an import from another system using a database link.

Exporting is fairly straightforward. Depending on the mode you choose, you will have different parameters to set. The following sections present examples of various export techniques.

Schema Mode Export

In schema mode export, you specify the SCHEMAS parameter in the export. This export only exports data belonging to the schemas specified in the parameter.

```
$ expdp schemas=scott,ewhalen,jczuprynski directory=exp_dir
dumpfile=exp1.dmp logfile=exp1.log
```

Table Mode Export

In table mode export, you specify the tables using the TABLES parameter. This export only exports the specified objects.

```
$ expdp tables=(scott.emp,ewhalen.tab1,jczuprynski.tab2) directory=exp_
dir dumpfile=exp2.dmp logfile=exp2.log
```

Partition Mode Export

In partition mode export, you specify the tables and partitions using the TABLES parameter with the partition qualifier. This export only exports the specified objects.

```
$ expdp schemas=scott tables=(emp.part1, emp.part2, emp.part3)
directory=exp_dir dumpfile=exp3.dmp logfile=exp3.log
```

Importing with Data Pump Import

Importing can be accomplished with a two-step process: first import the table row data, then import the indexes, constraints, and triggers either together or separately. Optionally, you can import the indexes, constraints, and triggers during the metadata process and disable them during import.

When importing data, the behavior of Data Pump will vary based on whether the target object exists. If a table does not exist in the target database, it will be created. If a table already exists, it will not be re-created. Thus, it is possible to transform the target database by pre-creating the objects in the manner that you desire. This is true of both Legacy Import and Data Pump Import.

You can import the data using the impdp command by specifying the import file, the schema and/or table, or partition and a log file. You can run multiple imports at the same time, thus creating some parallelism; however, there are some limitations.

When doing a table import using direct path import, the entire table will be locked. If you are running multiple imports, only one will run at a time, thus nullifying the attempt at parallelism.

TIP & TECHNIQUE

When importing into a partitioned table with parallelism, import into multiple tables and use the Partition Exchange Load (PEL) technique to populate the partitions.

Import Special Parameters

When using Data Pump Import, you can use several special parameters to change the behavior of the import. These parameters apply to all modes and include the following:

- **CONTENT**   When CONTENT=DATA_ONLY is specified, the table data is imported and no metadata is imported. Any metadata parameters such as INDEXES, CONSTRAINTS, and so on are ignored. When CONTENT=METADATA_ONLY is specified, only the metadata (definitions) are imported. No data is imported.

- **REMAP_SCHEMA**   This parameter allows you to change the name of the schema that is in the dump file to a new schema. This is similar to the legacy FROMUSER/TOUSER mode.

- **REMAP_TABLE**   This parameter allows you to change the name of tables as they are imported.

- **TABLE_EXISTS_ACTION**   This parameter specifies what to do if the table already exists. Options include truncate, append, skip, and replace. If you are loading into multiple partitions separately you must set this to append, otherwise the entire table would be truncated.

Schema Mode Import

In schema mode import, you specify the schema or schemas to be imported in the parameters; however, if you want to import all of the schemas that have been exported to the dump file, it is not necessary to specifically identify them. This does not import the user definitions and permissions. That information is only available in a full export.

Although you don't need to specify schemas if you are importing all the schemas, if you want to *change* the name of a schema, you need to use the REMAP_SCHEMA parameter.

```
$ impdp directory=exp_dir dumpfile=exp1.dmp logfile=imp1.log
REMAP_SCHEMA=ewhalen:kwilliams
```

This will import the data from the exp1.dmp file and convert data that was exported from ewhalen to the kwilliams schema.

Table Mode Import

In table mode import, you specify the tables using the TABLES parameter. This import only imports the specified objects. If you used the TABLES option in the export and now want to import all of these tables, you don't need to specify any parameters.

```
$ impdp directory=exp_dir tables=(ewhalen.tab1) dumpfile=exp2.dmp
logfile=imp2.log
```

Partition Mode Import

In partition mode import, you specify the partitions using the TABLES parameter. This import only imports the specified objects. If you used the PARTITIONS option in the export and now want to import all of these partitions, you don't need to specify any parameters.

```
$ impdp owner=scott tables=(emp.part1, emp.part2, emp.part3)
directory=exp_dir dumpfile=exp3.dmp logfile=imp3.log
```

The partition mode export/import can be effective on very large tables to increase the amount of parallelism.

Data Pump Export/Import Summary

You can use Data Pump Export/Import when migrating from an Oracle Database 10*g* or later database. As mentioned earlier, Data Pump Export/Import is just one way to move metadata. The method used to move the metadata and the method used to move the data can be different. Data Pump Export/Import performs much better than Legacy Export/Import and should be used if at all possible.

Point-in-Time Export Using FLASHBACK_SCN

When performing an export for use with a data migration, if the database is not currently active you will not get a consistent view of the database. One way to get a consistent view is to export as of a specific System Change Number (SCN). This is particularly useful when the database is active and you want to use something like Oracle GoldenGate in conjunction with the data migration.

The SCN is an identifier of every change to the database. This is used to keep track of the changes made to the database. Because there can be many changes going on at once, and with some migrations such as with GoldenGate it is desired to know the last transaction that has occurred, you can start processing changes with the SCN after when the export was taken.

One way to do this (if possible) is to capture a recent SCN and use that for the export and for the starting point with GoldenGate replication. With both Legacy and Data Pump Export/Import you can export to a specific SCN using the FLASHBACK_SCN option. This exports (in any mode) data to that specific SCN.

More information on using this option is presented in the next chapter, which covers data migration with GoldenGate.

Summary

This chapter has covered both Legacy Export/Import and Data Pump Export/Import. If you are running on Oracle Database 10*g* or later, you are better off using Data Pump; however, there are still a number of people migrating a legacy system from Oracle9*i*, in which case Data Pump is not available.

NOTE
As of Oracle Database 11g R2, Legacy Export is desupported.

In either case, both Legacy and Data Pump Export/Import can be used to move data from one system to another. The advantage of Export/Import over other methods is the ability to transform data. Some other methods, such as Data Guard, Transportable Tablespaces, and RMAN, do not allow for transformations.

As you will see in the next chapter, Export/Import can be an important step in doing a zero downtime migration with Oracle GoldenGate.

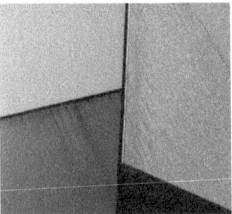

CHAPTER
8

Zero or Minimal Downtime Migrations with Oracle GoldenGate

Of the various migration techniques and methods described in this book, migration using Oracle GoldenGate is the only true way to do a migration with little or no downtime. This is because Oracle GoldenGate allows for the source and target systems to be kept completely in sync during the cutover using bidirectional replication. In fact, for a true zero downtime migration, it is possible to move applications from source to target while both systems are still being used. This allows for each application to be moved from the source to the target individually, thus incurring no downtime.

TIP & TECHNIQUE
Use Oracle GoldenGate if you have a requirement for little or no downtime during the migration and cutover.

In contrast, a near-zero downtime migration uses almost the same technique with unidirectional replication. At cutover, only the applications have to be moved; the database is already in sync and ready to be used. We prefer the near-zero downtime migration over zero downtime migration because it is a bit less complex and enables us to perform a few more verifications before the cutover is complete. This chapter describes both methods.

Introduction to Oracle GoldenGate

GoldenGate Software was founded in 1995 and was acquired by Oracle in 2009. GoldenGate is a leading heterogeneous replication technology that is used for many different purposes, including data migration.

Uses of Oracle GoldenGate

As mentioned, Oracle GoldenGate is a heterogeneous replication technology. In this case, heterogeneous means that neither the database technology (version or OS) nor the endian technology of the source and target systems needs to be the same. GoldenGate can be used in a number of different configurations including unidirectional (one source, one target), bidirectional (source replicates to target and target replicates back to source), mesh (multiple systems replicating to each other), broadcast (one source, multiple targets), and consolidation (multiple sources, one target). GoldenGate can be either end-to-end or cascade.

How Does GoldenGate Work?

GoldenGate replication works by capturing log information and mining that information. The mined log information is transformed into INSERT, UPDATE, and DELETE statements, which are then applied on the target database. This technology works for a number of database and system platforms and is not limited to Oracle technology. There are several modes of accessing database Oracle log information, which include reading from the redo log directly, using a connection into the ASM instance to read the log, reading the log via an API, or using an integrated process that reads the log information internally to the database.

Which method you should use to read the log will vary based on your own individual configuration and requirements. The available log reading options will vary based on the database that you are running and your version of Oracle GoldenGate.

GoldenGate Components

GoldenGate consists of three different processes that control various parts of the replication process:

- **Manager**   The controlling process.

- **Extract**   The process that reads data from a data source and writes it to the GoldenGate trail file.

- **Replicat**   The process that reads trail file data and writes it to the target database. (The word *replicate* is shortened to *replicat* in GoldenGate because of the original eight-character legacy.)

As described next, these processes work together to move data from one system/ database to another.

Manager Process

The manager process is the controlling process of the GoldenGate system. The manager process is also responsible for starting the collector process, which does not show up in GoldenGate but can be seen in the OS processes. The collector process is the process that receives data from the pump process (see the next section).

Extract Process

The extract process is responsible for taking data from a data source (such as the Oracle redo log files) and writing that data into the GoldenGate trail file. The GoldenGate trail file is a platform-independent, GoldenGate-specific file that contains transactional information from the source. The extract can source its data from many different sources, such as database log files or other trail files.

Typically, a GoldenGate system is set up with two extracts. The first extracts data from the source database and writes the trail file locally. The second extract is used to take that trail file as its source and write it to the target system. This second extract is known as the *pump process*. By writing the first trail file locally, there is little chance of interrupting log mining in the event of a network error.

Replicat Process

The replicat process takes trail file data and writes it into the target database. This is done via `INSERT`, `UPDATE`, and `DELETE` statements. If there is a performance problem with GoldenGate, it is usually found on the replicat side because of the serial nature of the replicat process. GoldenGate version 12 introduced more parallelism into the replicat process.

So, how do these processes work together? That information is provided in the next section.

GoldenGate Workflow

GoldenGate works by taking redo information from the source system, converting it into `INSERT`, `UPDATE`, and `DELETE` statements, and applying those statements on the target system. As you have seen earlier, in addition to the manager process, there are two types of processes—extracts and replicats. And typically there are two extracts—one to extract data from the log into a local trail file, and one to copy that data remotely to the remote trail file.

The reason to use the second extract (aka pump) is to isolate the reading of the database log from the network. By having the extract process local, there is less chance of log reads being delayed due to the inability to write to a remote file.

Planning a Migration with GoldenGate

GoldenGate can replicate many object types and table types but not all. Therefore, you must do a little planning and pre-replication work to determine if the desired tables are supported. The best way to determine this is to run the GoldenGate check script. This script is available for multiple platforms and is downloadable from the Oracle Support website; see MOS Note 1298562.1, *Oracle GoldenGate database Complete Database Profile check script (All Schemas)*, for an example.

> **NOTE**
> *GoldenGate cannot replicate all objects. Running the GoldenGate check script or profile script is recommended during the planning phase in order to determine which, if any, objects cannot be replicated so that you can make other arrangements.*

If the check script identifies objects that are not supported with GoldenGate, those objects must be migrated separately, either at cutover or at an earlier point if the data is static. The tables that you will be replicating will be included in the extract parameter file.

In addition to planning the migration, you must plan to have enough storage for GoldenGate trail files. The size of the trail files will depend on how busy the database is and how long you want to retain the trail files. It is important that you plan this ahead of time and be prepared.

Migrating a Database with GoldenGate

At the highest level, a minimal downtime migration using GoldenGate involves the following main steps:

1. Set up GoldenGate.

2. Configure and validate the database.

3. Enable replication by starting the extract and pump processes on the schemas and/or tables that are to be migrated.

4. Activate a physical standby for GoldenGate Export/Import.

5. Sync the database by enabling the replicat process (at the proper place).

6. Monitor until cutover.

7. Perform pre-cutover validation.

8. Perform the cutover.

9. (Optional) Clean up GoldenGate.

This is the high-level overview. Let's look at the detailed steps involved in performing a zero or near-zero downtime migration using GoldenGate. This narrative outlines the general steps for performing a migration/upgrade from Oracle 10*g* to Oracle 11*g* using GoldenGate version 11.2.

TIP & TECHNIQUE
*When migrating from one system to another, you might be asked by management to enable reverse replication, so that the old system can be used as a failback in case any application failures occur. See the sidebar "Setup for 11*g* to 10*g* GoldenGate Replication" later in this chapter.*

Set Up GoldenGate

Before you can configure and enable GoldenGate to replicate from the 10*g* system to the 11*g* system, GoldenGate must be installed on the source and target systems.

NOTE
GoldenGate software can be downloaded from the Oracle Software Delivery Cloud at http://edelivery .oracle.com. The latest version is usually found at http://support.oracle.com. You must have a My Oracle Support (MOS) account to download the latest version from support.

GoldenGate setup includes the following steps:

1. Install the GoldenGate software on both the source and target.

    a. Create a directory to be used for GoldenGate: **/app/oracle/goldengate**

    b. Unzip and untar the GG distribution files (11.2.1.0.16 for Oracle 10*g* or 11*g*, depending on the system).

    c. Set the environment variable for GGHOME to point to that directory.

    d. Set the environment variable for LD_LIBRARY_PATH.

    e. Add an alias for $GGHOME to point to the goldengate home directory.

TIP & TECHNIQUE
Create an alias to cd to $GGHOME and enable ggsci. For example, `alias ggsci="cd $GGHOME; ./ggsci"`

    f. Change the directory to GGHOME and invoke ggsci:

    ```
    $ cd $GGHOME
    $ ggsci
    ```

    g. Create subdirs. This creates the subdirectories that you need for GoldenGate.

    ```
    GGSCI> create subdirs
    ```

    h. Manually create subdirectories for dirdsc and diroby. These are optional for the discard directory and for the obey files.

    i. Link dirdat to a large file system for trail files. This is so that the trail files don't fill up your regular file systems.

TIP & TECHNIQUE
The Bequeath interface is an interface into the Oracle database that bypasses the listener. When using the Bequeath interface, the Oracle server automatically spawns a dedicated server process and does not go through the network layers. The Bequeath protocol is only available when connecting to the instance locally. Because the Bequeath interface does not go through the network layers, there is a performance advantage.

2. If you are using a database configured with ASM as the target database, you should add an entry in the tnsnames.ora file for the ASM instance in order to connect via the Bequeath interface.

   a. Modify the tnsnames.ora file and add the following entry. Add a Bequeath entry for the ASM instance.

   ```
   ASM_BEQ =
       (DESCRIPTION =
           (ADDRESS = (PROTOCOL = BEQ)
           (PROGRAM = /u01/app/oracle/product/10.2.0/db_1/bin/oracle)
            (ARGV0 = oracle+ASM1)
            (ARGS = '(DESCRIPTION=(LOCAL=YES)
   (ADDRESS=(PROTOCOL=BEQ))) ')
            (ENVS =  'ORACLE_HOME=/u01/app/oracle/product/10.2.0/
   asm,ORACLE_SID=+ASM1')
       )
       (CONNECT_DATA =
           (SERVICE_NAME = +ASM)
           (INSTANCE_NAME = +ASM1)
       )
   )
   ```

   b. Verify connectivity to the ASM instance:

   ```
   $ sqlplus sys@asm_beq as SYSDBA
   ```

3. Create a GoldenGate Administrator account (GGADMIN) defined in the source and target databases.

   a. Create a unique tablespace for the GGADMIN user (ggadmin):

   ```
   SQL> create tablespace ggadmin;
   ```

   b. Create the ggadmin user:

   ```
   SQL> create user ggadmin identified by "ggadmin" default
   tablespace ggadmin temporary tablespace temp;
   ```

    c. Grant DBA privilege to the GGADMIN user. This is the easiest way to handle the ggadmin user; however, if you need to be more restrictive, the GoldenGate documentation specifies the necessary permissions.

```
SQL> grant dba to ggadmin;
```

    d. Grant an unlimited quota on the ggadmin to ggadmin:

```
SQL> alter user ggadmin quota unlimited on ggadmin;
```

4. Create encryption keys for both the ggadmin and sys (ASM instance) users. This allows you to encrypt the passwords, so that there are no cleartext passwords in the parameter or obey files.

    a. Change the directory to GGHOME.

    b. Create an ENCKEYS file.

> **NOTE**
> *The only encryption protocol supported on many older systems is Blowfish, which is 128-bit encryption.*

    ■ On 10*g*:

```
$ ./keygen 128 3 > ENCKEYS
```

    ■ On 11*g*:

```
$ ./keygen 256 3 > ENCKEYS
$ cat ENCKEYS
```

    c. Edit the ENCKEYS file to include securekey1, securekey2, and securekey3 identifiers and the header as follows:

```
#Key Name          Encryption Key
securekey1          0x71B220C07D3FBE9F7B6C86320F0369A8
securekey2          0x55366B9165EDEA51682B6DB947555024
securekey3          0x38C00BB807833292095DE3966206D325
```

    d. Create a backup copy of the ENCKEYS file. This file is crucial for encryption/decryption purposes.

5. Encrypt the ggadmin and sys passwords on 10*g*:

```
GGSCI>  encrypt password ggadmin BLOWFISH encryptkey securekey1
GGSCI>  encrypt password <ASM Sys pwd> BLOWFISH encryptkey securekey2
```

6. Encrypt the ggadmin and sys passwords on 11*g*:

```
GGSCI>  encrypt password ggadmin AES256 encryptkey securekey1
GGSCI>  encrypt password <ASM Sys pwd> AES256 encryptkey securekey2
```

TIP & TECHNIQUE
*Encrypt the ggadmin password with securekey2
and use that password for ASM. Replace the ASM
password file with the database password file. The
ggadmin user can now be used for access into the
ASM instance.*

7. On 10*g*, use the encrypted password in the parameter files. Use the following format:

```
USERID ggadmin@source, PASSWORD "AADAAAAAAAAAAAGAJELEDHEAHJTHZF ¬
LGJIZIQHDHTGGENIDISDWACIHFGADFKJUHCEBIUJACNADHYIGJ", BLOWFISH, ¬
EncryptKey securekey1

TRANLOGOPTIONS ASMUSER sys@ASM_BEQ, ASMPASSWORD "AADAAAAAAAAAAAG ¬
AJELEDHEAHJTHZFLGJIZIQHDHTGGENIDISDWACIHFGADFKJUHCEBIUJACNADHY ¬
IGJ" BLOWFISH EncryptKey securekey2
```

8. On 11*g*, use the encrypted password in the parameter files. Use the following format:

```
USERID ggadmin@source, PASSWORD "AADAAAAAAAAAAAGAJELEDHEAHJTHZF ¬
LGJIZIQHDHTGGENIDISDWACIHFGADFKJUHCEBIUJACNADHYIGJ", AES256, ¬
EncryptKey securekey1
```

NOTE
*Connectivity to the ASM instance on 11g is via
the DBLOGREADER API rather than connecting to
the ASM instance. The DBLOGREADER API is not
supported on Oracle 10g (10.2.0.4) or earlier.*

Configure and Validate the Database

Now that GoldenGate is configured, you need to configure and validate the database to make sure that it is ready to run GoldenGate.

1. Prepare the source and target databases (replicate in both directions).

   a. Verify that the database is in ARCHIVELOG mode.

   b. Disable the recycle bin.

   ■ On 10*g*:
   ```
   SQL> alter system set recyclebin=OFF sid='*';
   ```

   ■ On 11*g*:
   ```
   SQL> alter system set recyclebin=OFF deferred sid='*';
   ```

    c. Enable database-level supplemental logging. Table-level supplemental logging will be enabled a little later.

```
SQL> alter database add supplemental log data;
```

TIP & TECHNIQUE
It is a good idea to have the database shut down for enabling database-level supplemental logging.

    d. Enable force logging:

```
SQL> alter database force logging;
```

    e. Make sure the DBMS_SHARED_POOL package is installed for DDL trigger performance:

```
SQL> @?/rdbms/admin/dbmspool.sql;
```

    f. On any database that is 11.2.0.4 or newer, set the following parameter:

```
SQL> ALTER SYSTEM SET ENABLE_GOLDENGATE_REPLICATION = TRUE SCOPE=BOTH SID='*';
```

2. Enable checkpoint tables on both the source and target.

    a. Run ggsci on both systems:

```
GGSCI> dblogin userid ggadmin , password ggadmin
GGSCI> add checkpointtable ggadmin.checkpoint
```

    b. Add the following to the GLOBALS file:

```
CHECKPOINTTABLE ggadmin.checkpoint
```

3. Add table-level supplemental logging (10*g*) for applicable schemas. You can do this for one table at a time or for all tables in a schema.

```
GGSCI> add trandata <schema>.*
GGSCI> info trandata <schema>.*
```

This has been scripted and can be run for each group:

```
GGSCI>  obey diroby/add_tg01.oby
```

TIP & TECHNIQUE
If `add trandata` fails on a table due to an "ORA-00054: resource busy and acquire with NOWAIT specified" error, run that `add trandata` again until it succeeds.

4. Optionally, add schema-level supplemental logging (11*g*) for applicable schemas. You can do this for one group at a time or for all groups.

```
GGSCI> add schematrandata <schema>
GGSCI> info schematrandata <schema>
```

TIP & TECHNIQUE

Script the add trandata *and* info trandata *in obey files. Place them in the diroby directory. If* add schematrandata *fails on a table due to an "ORA-00054: resource busy and acquire with NOWAIT specified" error, run that* add schematrandata *again until it succeeds.*

5. On 11*g* systems, if using Transparent Data Encryption (TDE), you must do the following step:

```
$ cd $GGHOME
$ sqlplus / as SYSDBA
SQL> @prvtclkm.plb
SQL> grant execute on sys.dbms_internal_clkm to ggadmin;
```

6. On 11*g* systems, you should disable the automatic space advisor since it can create compressed tables. Because we are using classic extract (not integrated extract), compressed tables are not supported.

   a. To disable the automatic space advisor, run the following from SQL*Plus:

   ```
   BEGIN
     DBMS_AUTO_TASK_ADMIN.disable(
       client_name => 'auto space advisor',
       operation   => NULL,
       window_name => NULL);
   END;
   /
   ```

   b. To re-enable it, run the following from SQL*Plus:

   ```
   BEGIN
     DBMS_AUTO_TASK_ADMIN.enable(
       client_name => 'auto space advisor',
       operation   => NULL,
       window_name => NULL);
   END;
   /
   ```

Enable GoldenGate Replication

The first step of the actual migration (assuming the databases are in place and operational) is to configure and enable GoldenGate to replicate from the 10*g* system to the 11*g* system. We will assume that this is a RAC cluster on both source and target. In addition, you should set up DDL replication. Optionally, you can set up sequence replication if needed for testing. If you will not be doing any testing involving sequences that step is not needed.

Set Up DDL Replication

Setting up DDL replication ensures that any changes to the database are replicated to the new system. This is not necessary if there is a freeze on the source system; however, it is a good idea to do this just in case.

1. Set up DDL triggers on the source system or, if replicating in both directions, on both systems, but only activate on the source. You should do this while the system is quiesced during a maintenance window.

   a. Grant permission to ggadmin for DDL processing as SYSDBA:

   ```
   SQL> grant execute on utl_file to ggadmin;
   SQL> @marker_setup.sql
   SQL> @ddl_setup.sql
   SQL> @role_setup.sql
   SQL> grant ggs_ggsuser_role to ggadmin;
   SQL> @ddl_enable.sql;    Note: Do not run this on the target until it
   becomes the source.
   SQL> @ddl_pin.sql ggadmin;
   ```

   b. If all scripts have been run, disable DDL replication on the target as SYSDBA so that there is no duplication of DDL operations:

   ```
   SQL> @ddl_disable.sql;
   ```

2. Configure the GLOBALS file as shown here:

   ```
   GGSCHEMA ggadmin
   CHECKPOINTTABLE ggadmin.checkpoint
   ```

3. Create the manager parameter file. The manager parameter file mgr.prm is shown here:

   ```
   PORT 7809
   DYNAMICPORTLIST 7850-7860
   LAGINFOMINUTES 0
   LAGREPORTMINUTES 10
   LAGCRITICALMINUTES 60
   AUTORESTART EXTRACT E*, RETRIES 10, WAITMINUTES 5, RESETMINUTES 1440
   AUTORESTART EXTRACT P*, RETRIES 10, WAITMINUTES 5, RESETMINUTES 1440
   AUTORESTART REPLICAT R*, RETRIES 10, WAITMINUTES 5, RESETMINUTES 1440
   PURGEOLDEXTRCTS /u01/app/oracle/goldengate/dirdat/*, USECHECKPOINTS,
   MINKEEPDAYS 10, FREQUENCYMINUTES 15
   ```

TIP & TECHNIQUE
The ports listed in the manager parameter file (mgr.prm) must be opened in any firewall that you have between the source and target systems.

4. Create the extract parameter file. Exclude unsupported and problematic tables. A sample is shown here:

```
EXTRACT EXT01
SETENV (ORACLE_SID=MYSID)
SETENV (ORACLE_HOME=/u01/app/oracle/product/10.2.0/db_1)
SETENV (NLS_LANG="AMERICAN_AMERICA.AL32UTF8")
USERID ggadmin PASSWORD "AACAAAAAAAAAAAHAWEMIDDFIFGHEFCRA" BLOWFISH
EncryptKey securekey1
TRANLOGOPTIONS EXCLUDEUSER ggadmin
--TRANLOGOPTIONS LOGRETENTION DISABLED
TRANLOGOPTIONS LOGRETENTION SR
TRANLOGOPTIONS ASMUSER ggadmin@ASM_BEQ, ASMPASSWORD
"AACAAAAAAAAAAAHAWEMIDDFIFGHEFCRA" BLOWFISH EncryptKey securekey1
WARNLONGTRANS 3H CHECKINTERVAL 30m
REPORTCOUNT EVERY 10 MINUTES, RATE
DISCARDFILE /u01/app/oracle/goldengate/dirdsc/ext01.dsc, APPEND
DISCARDROLLOVER ON SUNDAY
GETUPDATEBEFORES
DDL INCLUDE MAPPED
DDLOPTIONS ADDTRANDATA RETRYOP RETRYDELAY 10 MAXRETRIES 10

EXTTRAIL /u01/app/oracle/goldengate/dirdat/la

TABLE SCHEMA1.* ;
TABLE SCHEMA2.* ;
TABLE SCHEMA3.* ;
TABLE SCHEMA4.* ;
```

5. Create the pump parameter file. This parameter file is shown here:

```
EXTRACT PUMP01
SETENV (ORACLE_SID=MYSID)
SETENV (ORACLE_HOME=/u01/app/oracle/product/10.2.0/db_1)
SETENV (NLS_LANG="AMERICAN_AMERICA.AL32UTF8")
PASSTHRU
RMTHOST targetsystem.targetdomain, MGRPORT 7809, COMPRESS,
TCPBUFSIZE 262144, TCPFLUSHBYTES 262144
STATOPTIONS REPORTFETCH
REPORTCOUNT EVERY 10 MINUTES, RATE
DISCARDFILE /u01/app/oracle/goldengate/dirdsc/pump01.dsc, APPEND
DISCARDROLLOVER ON SUNDAY

RMTTRAIL /u01/app/oracle/goldengate/dirdat/ra

TABLE SCHEMA1.* ;
TABLE SCHEMA2.* ;
TABLE SCHEMA3.* ;
TABLE SCHEMA4.* ;
```

6. Add extract and pump.

> **NOTE**
> *These steps should be scripted in the diroby directory as add_ext01.oby, add_pump01.oby, and so on.*

   a. Create the add_ext01.oby obey file:

```
dblogin userid ggadmin password "AACAAAAAAAAAAAIANGKIRANBMHJCEBYG",
BLOWFISH, EncryptKey securekey1
add extract ext01, tranlog, begin now, threads 2
add exttrail /u01/app/oracle/goldengate/dirdat/aa, extract ext01,
megabytes 200
```

   b. Create the add_pump.oby obey file:

```
dblogin userid ggadmin password "AACAAAAAAAAAAAIANGKIRANBMHJCEBYG",
BLOWFISH, EncryptKey securekey1
add extract pump, exttrailsource /u01/app/oracle/goldengate/dirdat/ba,
extseqno 0, extrba 0
add rmttrail /u01/app/oracle/goldengate/dirdat/ra, extract pump,
megabytes 200
```

7. Start the extract on the source.

8. If desired, enable log retention. Log retention is used to make sure RMAN does not delete archivelog files that are needed for GoldenGate. It is not necessary if you are maintaining and monitoring archivelogs manually.

   a. Run the following SQL statements as SYSDBA:

```
SQL> exec dbms_streams_auth.grant_admin_privilege('ggadmin');
SQL> grant insert on system.logmnr_restart_ckpt$ to ggadmin;
SQL> grant update on sys.streams$_capture_process to ggadmin;
SQL> grant become user to ggadmin;
```

   b. Add the following to the extract parameter file:

```
TRANLOGOPTIONS LOGRETENTION SR
```

Set Up Sequence Replication

Sequence replication should be added if you will be performing testing on the target system using sequences. If this is not the case, then sequences do not need to be replicated, however, it is advisable to reset sequences just prior to the cutover in order to have the source and target sequences in sync.

1. Set up sequence replication.

   a. On both the source database and the target database, run the following as SYSDBA from the GGHOME directory:

```
SQL> @sequence
```

    b. On the source system, run the following as SYSDBA:

```
SQL> grant execute on ggadmin.updateSequence to ggadmin;
```

    c. On the target system, run the following as SYSDBA:

```
SQL> grant execute on ggadmin.replicateSequence to ggadmin;
```

    d. On the source system, run the following:

```
SQL> alter table sys.seq$ add supplemental log data (primary
key) columns;
```

    e. Restart the extract:

```
GGSCI> stop ext <ext>
GGSCI> start ext <ext>
```

    f. On the source, run ggsci and flush the sequences:

```
GGSCI> flush sequence <schema>.*
```

2. Set up the manager parameter file on the target and start it.

3. Start the pump on the source. It is at this point that you must check the target to make sure that trail files are getting written there.

TIP & TECHNIQUE

If trail files aren't showing up on the target system, the issue is probably either that the manager isn't running or that you have a firewall problem.

Activate a Physical Standby for GoldenGate Export/Import

If you are exporting from a physical standby, create a guaranteed restore point before you activate the database. This serves two purposes: it gives you a place to flash back to in order to become a physical standby again, and it provides you with the SCN to use in the replicat.

You can use the following steps to activate a physical standby to use for your initial migration. This process describes how to configure and manage a Data Guard physical standby as a source of a GoldenGate source database for Data Pump Export/ Import. It assumes that you are using Data Guard Broker.

1. Enable Flashback Database on the physical standby.

2. Validate that there is sufficient storage in the FRA to store flashback logs.

3. Cancel managed recovery.

    ■ Using SQL statements:

```
SQL> ALTER DATABASE RECOVER MANAGED STANDBY DATABASE CANCEL;
```

Optionally, cancel log shipping on the primary:

```
SQL> ALTER SYSTEM SET log_archive_dest_state_2=DEFER SID='*';
```

■ Using the Broker:

```
DGMGRL> EDIT DATABASE <sby> SET STATE='APPLY-OFF';
DGMGRL> EDIT DATABASE <sby> SET STATE='LOG-TRANSPORT-OFF'
```

Optionally, you can start the Data Guard Broker using the following command:

```
SQL> ALTER system SET dg_broker_start=FALSE;
```

4. Get the current SCN.

```
SQL> SELECT current_scn FROM v$database;
$ sqlplus / as SYSDBA @get_scn
```

CAUTION
Obtaining the SCN before activating the physical standby is critical. This SCN is used for both starting the replicat and exporting the data.

5. Create a guaranteed restore point:

```
SQL> CREATE RESTORE POINT phys_sby GUARANTEE FLASHBACK DATABASE;
```

6. Verify the SCN:

```
SQL> SELECT scn, time, name from v$restore_point;
```

or:

```
SQL> SELECT scn, time, name from v$restore_point WHERE
name='phys_sby';
```

7. Activate the database:

```
SQL> ALTER DATABASE ACTIVATE STANDBY DATABASE;
SQL> STARTUP MOUNT FORCE;
SQL> ALTER DATABASE OPEN;
```

8. Create MIGRATE directory object if applicable.

9. Export schema groups, using the SCN obtained in step 4. This will guarantee that only the data as it existed in the physical standby at the time of activation will be used.

10. Flash back to the guaranteed restore point:

```
SQL> SHUTDOWN IMMEDIATE;
SQL> FLASHBACK DATABASE TO RESTORE POINT phys_sby;
SQL> ALTER DATABASE CONVERT TO PHYSICAL STANDBY;
SQL> STARTUP MOUNT FORCE;
```

11. Re-enable recovery mode.

- Using SQL statements:

   ```
   SQL> ALTER DATABASE RECOVER MANAGED STANDBY DATABASE DISCONNECT;
   ```

   Optionally, cancel log shipping on the primary:

   ```
   SQL> ALTER SYSTEM SET log_archive_dest_state_2=ENABLE SID='*';
   ```

- Using the Broker:

   ```
   DGMGRL> EDIT DATABASE <sby> SET STATE='APPLY-ON';
   DGMGRL> EDIT DATABASE <sby> SET STATE='LOG-TRANSPORT-ON';
   ```

   Optionally, you can stop the Data Guard Broker using the following command:

   ```
   SQL> ALTER system SET dg_broker_start=FALSE;
   ```

12. Validate that the system is applying logs from the alert log.

13. Drop the restore point:

   ```
   SQL> DROP RESTORE POINT phys_sby;
   ```

TIP & TECHNIQUE

It is important to know the last SCN of the static copy of the database that you are using for the initial replication. This allows you to start processing the replicat just after that SCN.

14. Prepare to export and import the data using the SCN.

TIP & TECHNIQUE

Prior to importing any data, verify that all database and crontab jobs are disabled on the target system. Also, verify that all triggers and foreign key constraints are disabled on the target system.

a. Document the SCN of the source of the initial migration.

b. Use this SCN in the export parameter file.

15. Export using the SCN. The Data Pump Export parameter file should include the following options:

   ```
   FLASHBACK_SCN=<scn number from above>
   CONTENT=DATA_ONLY
   SCHEMAS=<group schemas>
   ```

16. Import into the target database.

    a. Disable foreign-key constraints on the target database.

    b. Disable triggers on the target database.

    c. The Data Pump Import parameter file should include the following options:
    ```
    CONTENT=DATA_ONLY
    TABLE_EXISTS_ACTION=TRUNCATE
    SCHEMAS=<group schemas>
    ```

    d. Gather schema stats on the newly imported objects.

    e. Enable foreign-key constraints that were disabled previously.

    f. Enable triggers that were enabled previously.

17. Disable scheduler jobs on the target database and generate a new script to enable the jobs.

18. Check invalid objects using the following:

    a. Run the following SQL:
    ```
    SELECT owner,
           object_type,
           object_name,
           status
    FROM   dba_objects
    WHERE  status = 'INVALID'
    ORDER BY owner, object_type, object_name;
    ```

    b. Fix invalid objects. This can be done with the Oracle package UTLRP.SQL.

Sync Target with Source

Once you have configured and started the extract and pump processes in GoldenGate, and completed the initial migration, it is necessary to bring the source and target databases in sync and keep them that way. This is done with GoldenGate.

1. Enable the SUPPRESSTRIGGERS option on the target.

2. Set up the manager and replicat processes on the target. The replicat parameter file is shown here:
   ```
   REPLICAT REP01
   SETENV (ORACLE_HOME=/app/oracle/product/11.2.0.4/dbhome_1)
   SETENV (NLS_LANG="AMERICAN_AMERICA.AL32UTF8")
   USERID ggadmin, PASSWORD "AADAAAAAAAAAAAIABJZDQCFAXIEEFCVJQBDGMCWITEFCQ ¬
   ```

```
FBFNBDAXEWHTHPHCCRJNHVCHIBBTCBCHBSHSCAJLBQFYEEBNAIFNBIDJCIAKEBCNAPC" ¬
AES256 ENCRYPTKEY securekey1
ASSUMETARGETDEFS
REPORTCOUNT EVERY 10 MINUTES, RATE
DISCARDFILE /app/oracle/goldengate/dirdsc/rep01.dsc, APPEND, MEGABYTES 100
DISCARDROLLOVER ON SUNDAY
REPERROR (default, abend)
DDLERROR default, abend
DYNAMICRESOLUTION
GROUPTRANSOPS 2000
DBOPTIONS SUPPRESSTRIGGERS
DDL INCLUDE MAPPED
DDLOPTIONS REPORT


MAP SCHEMA01.*, TARGET SCHEMA01.*;
MAP SCHEMA02.*, TARGET SCHEMA02.*;
MAP SCHEMA03.*, TARGET SCHEMA03.*;
MAP SCHEMA04.*, TARGET SCHEMA04.*;
```

3. Add the replicat to the target using the following syntax. This should be scripted in an obey file.

```
dblogin userid ggadmin password "AADAAAAAAAAAAAIABJZDQCFAXIEEFCVJQBDGMC ¬
WITEFCQFBFNBDAXEWHTHPHCCRJNHVCHIBBTCBCHBSHSCAJLBQFYEEBNAIFNBIDJCIAKEBCNAPC", ¬
AES256, EncryptKey securekey1
add replicat rep01, exttrail /app/oracle/goldengate/dirdat/ra , extseqno 0, ¬
extrba 0
```

4. Start the manager and target. This should already have been done. Check the target and make sure it is running without error.

```
GGSCI> start mgr
GGSCI> start replicat rep aftercsn <SCN>
```

Monitor Until Cutover

At this point, GoldenGate should be up and running. After a while, the source and target will become in sync. You will usually want to synchronize several days before going live so that you have time to prepare for the cutover. And you can monitor GoldenGate with the `info all` command in GGSCI. The lag shown is the amount of time that the target is behind the source. Fix issues as they arise.

TIP & TECHNIQUE
We often tell people that when using GoldenGate for migration, it doesn't matter how long the migration takes; what really matters is how long the cutover takes. It is the cutover that will potentially involve some downtime.

Setup for 11*g* to 10*g* GoldenGate Replication

Sometimes you may be asked to set up reverse replication so that you can fail back to the older system in the event of some sort of application problem. We don't get this request often, but often enough that we want to tell you about it. This is just a high-level overview of the process. The detailed steps are similar to what you did in the 10*g* to 11*g* steps.

GoldenGate setup includes the following:

1. Create extract and pump parameter files and obey files on the 11*g* system.

> **TIP & TECHNIQUE**
> *We usually set up everything ahead of time in dirprm2 and diroby2 directories. This allows us to just move diroby to diroby1 and dirprm to dirprm1 and then move in the new files for reverse replication.*

2. Create replicat parameter files on the 10*g* system. You can use the parameter file in the "Sync Target with Source" section as an example.

3. Follow the steps in the "GoldenGate Cutover Procedure" section during cutover.

GoldenGate Cutover Procedure

GoldenGate cutover includes the following:

1. Discontinue all user activity on the source.

2. Stop all GoldenGate processes on both the source and target.

3. Configure GoldenGate DDL replication.
   - On 11*g* systems, run @ddl_enable.sql.
   - On 10*g* systems, run @ddl_disable.sql.

4. Manage trigger replication.

   - On 10*g* systems, run
     ```
     SQL> revoke execute on ggadmin.UpdateSequence to ggadmin;
     SQL> grant execute on ggadmin.ReplicateSequence to ggadmin;
     ```
   - On 11*g* systems, it is not necessary to grant or revoke permissions. In fact, the owner of the object always has permissions.

5. Manage triggers.
    - On 10*g* systems, disable triggers.
    - On 11*g* systems, enable triggers.
6. Manage table-level supplemental logging on the 11*g* database. Run obey scripts.
7. Verify consistency of the source and target databases.
8. Point application servers to the 11*g* database.
9. Optional: Disable user accounts on the 10*g* database.
10. Perform GoldenGate switchover.
    a. Stop all extract, pump, and replicat processes.
    b. Remove all processes and trails from the GoldenGate system.
    c. Delete extracts, trails, and replicats.
    d. Reset GoldenGate configuration:
        i. Move dirprm to dirprm1.
        ii. Move dirprm2 to dirprm.
        iii. Move diroby to diroby1.
        iv. Move diroby2 to diroby.
        v. Move dirdsc to dirdsc1.
        vi. Make the directory dirdsc.
        vii. Move dirrpt to dirrpt1.
        viii. Make the directory dirrpt.
        ix. Move all dirdat/gxx to dirdat/old/gxx.
    e. Set up GoldenGate for 11*g* to 10*g* replication. Run all setup scripts for extract, pump, and replicat.
    f. Restart replication from 11*g* to 10*g*:
        i. Start all extract processes.
        ii. Flush all sequences.
        iii. Start all pump processes.
    g. Validate GoldenGate operations.

11. Monitor GoldenGate.

12. Once a test of 11*g* has been completed, enable replicat on 10*g* systems.

GoldenGate Cleanup (Optional)

If GoldenGate will no longer be used, you can use the following steps to clean up the GoldenGate configuration and set the Oracle database back to a pre-GoldenGate state:

1. Validate that GoldenGate is no longer needed.

2. Stop all extract, pump, and replicat processes.

3. Delete extract, pump, and replicat processes.

4. Remove DDL replication:

   ```
   SQL>  @ddl_disable
   SQL>  @ddl_remove
   SQL>  @marker_remove
   ```

5. Remove sequence replication:

   ```
   SQL> @remove_seq
   ```

6. Remove supplemental log data.

   - If 10*g*:

     ```
     GGSCI> delete trandata <schema>.*
     ```

   - If 11*g*:

     ```
     GGSCI> delete schematrandata <schema>
     ```

7. Remove the ggadmin user from the database.

8. Drop the GoldenGate tablespace from the database, including the contents and datafile.

9. Remove all GoldenGate files.

The following steps are optional and not necessarily recommended for production systems. These steps should be completed to reset the options that were previously set for GoldenGate replication. Set these options to the exact same level that they were set to before GoldenGate replication.

1. Disable supplemental log data if applicable.

   a. Check the level:

      ```
      SQL> SELECT supplemental_log_data_min FROM v$database;
      ```

b. Lower the level:

```
SQL> ALTER DATABASE DROP SUPPLEMENTAL LOG DATA;
```

2. Disable force logging if applicable.

a. Check force logging:

```
SQL> SELECT force_loggging FROM v$database;
```

b. Change force logging:

```
SQL> ALTER DATABASE no force logging;
```

3. Validate all changes.

Summary

This chapter covered many steps that are used to migrate a database from one system to another using Oracle GoldenGate. The steps might vary depending on the version of Oracle databases and the version of Oracle GoldenGate. In addition, some of the steps are similar even if you are migrating to an Oracle database from a non-Oracle database. You will see many of the same steps later in this book in Chapter 12 which covers migrating from MS SQL Server to Oracle.

Migrating with GoldenGate is truly the only method that can be used to perform a near-zero downtime migration. This is important for very large databases where the amount of downtime you can handle is small.

NOTE
Remember, how long it takes to do the migration is not nearly as important as how long it takes to do the cutover. The cutover is where any downtime would be incurred.

Using Oracle GoldenGate for data migration is an efficient way to do a data migration that can incur minimal downtime during cutover. Oracle has been doing an awesome job enhancing and improving GoldenGate since acquiring it in 2009.

NOTE
You can find up-to-date information from the International GoldenGate Oracle Users Group at www.iggoug.org.

CHAPTER
9

Cross-Platform
Transportable Tablespace
Migration Utilities

A
s we demonstrated in Chapter 6, one of the most flexible and effective methods for transporting databases in piecemeal fashion between different OS platforms—especially when the platforms are of different endianness—is the Transportable Tablespace (TTS) feature set. But no matter which TTS method is selected, all of them still have one serious drawback: the need to bring the set of tablespaces to be transported from the source database's OS platform into READ ONLY mode for an extended period of time—what we have termed the *window of inopportunity*—until all datafiles for those tablespaces have been migrated to the destination OS platform. Starting with Oracle Database Release 11.2.0.3, it may be possible to leverage the features of Cross-Platform Transportable Tablespaces (XTTS) to transport tablespace sets between the source and destination platforms. Unlike the earlier TTS techniques, however, XTTS *requires* that the desired tablespace sets on the source database *remain* in READ WRITE mode until the final migration occurs. XTTS therefore offers a distinct advantage over other TTS techniques because *until the very last migration step, no application downtime is required on the source database.*

NOTE
Like any other Oracle Database feature, XTTS is constantly being improved, especially since Oracle Database Release 12.1.0.2 was made generally available in July 2014. For the most up-to-date information on this topic, please see My Oracle Support (MOS) Note 1389592.1, Reduce Transportable Tablespace Downtime Using Cross Platform Incremental Backup.

XTTS Migration Phases

Every XTTS operation involves four distinct phases, as outlined next. This chapter describes each of these phases in detail.

Phase One: Migration Preparations   During this phase, the source and destination OS platforms and databases are prepared for XTTS migration operations. This involves creating the necessary database objects on both databases as well as copying the required XTTS PL/SQL and SQL scripts to each platform.

Phase Two: Initial Migration   The datafiles of the selected tablespace sets are transported between the source and destination platforms and placed into their final location on the destination database's file system. Depending upon the

Oracle database release at the destination, XTTS will leverage either RMAN or
DBMS_FILE_TRANSFER to transport the datafiles between OS platforms:

- If the destination database is currently *earlier* than version 11.2.0.4,
  then RMAN *must* be used to convert the tablespace set's datafiles to the
  appropriate format at the destination, and there are several restrictions on
  tablespace content.

- If the destination database is version 11.2.0.4 or later, then either RMAN
  or the DBMS_FILE_TRANSFER utility can be leveraged for conversion and
  transport, and there are fewer restrictions on tablespace content.

We'll explore the intricacies of both methods in the coming sections, but keep
in mind that both XTTS methods require careful planning to be used expediently
and effectively.

Phase Three: Incremental Synchronization After initial datafile image copies have
been captured and transferred between source and destination databases, this phase
captures any incremental changes to the selected tablespaces' datafiles since the last
capture. Because the datafiles of the desired tablespace set on the source database
remain in READ WRITE mode, you can repeat this phase innumerable times until
you decide that it is finally time to complete the migration.

Phase Four: Final Synchronization and Migration To complete the transfer of all
datafiles in the tablespace set, this final phase requires bringing the selected
tablespaces into READ ONLY mode on the source database to forestall any other
transactions against them until one final incremental backup of those datafiles is
completed. But if the datafiles have been recursively synchronized during prior
Phase Three XTTS operation(s), the "window of inopportunity" will be quite short.
During this phase the tablespaces are at last plugged into the destination database
and—just like any other TTS operation—they will remain in READ ONLY mode until
you decide to open them in READ WRITE mode to complete the XTTS process.

XTTS Migration Scenario

The following XTTS migration scenario demonstrates how to best leverage these
new XTTS techniques to transport two tablespaces—AP_DATA and AP_IDX—from
a source 10.2.0.5 database to a destination 11.2.0.4 database, both of which use
the Oracle Linux x86-64 OS. We will also compare and contrast both available
transport techniques during the second phase of the XTTS migration.

Phase One: Migration Preparations

XTTS operations have the same basic restrictions as do any other Transportable Tablespace operation:

- All database objects to be transported must be self-contained within the same tablespace set.

- The character sets of the source and destination databases must be strict supersets of each other.

For an XTTS operation to be successful, the following additional prerequisites must be satisfied:

- The COMPATIBLE initialization parameter of the source database must already be set to *at least* 10.2.0, and the destination database's COMPATIBLE initialization parameter setting must be *greater than or equal to* that of the source database.

- The source database must be in ARCHIVELOG mode.

- The default RMAN channel setting on the source database cannot specify the COMPRESSED directive as one of the CONFIGURE DEVICE TYPE DISK channel attributes.

- On the source database, all tablespaces that are going to be transported must be online and cannot contain any offline datafiles. (While a READ ONLY tablespace *can* be moved via XTTS, tablespaces that are already in READ ONLY mode do not benefit from XTTS methods. Note that this is not a *disadvantage* of XTTS; rather, it highlights the distinct *advantage* that XTTS has over traditional TTS and TDB methods. In fact, XTTS may even replace those methods because of its flexibility, and it may become the only method you need to employ to transport data between different OS platforms.)

- The Oracle software owner (in this example, oracle) runs all XTTS steps. Because XTTS uses OS authentication to connect to source and destination databases, that OS user account must be part of the OS group dba.

There are a few minor but crucial preparation steps that XTTS requires, as shown in Checklist 9-1.

Step	Operation	Description	Done?
1	Identify tablespace sets	Identify which tablespace set(s) will be migrated from source to destination databases.	
2	Identify source and destination database versions and desired migration method(s)	Determine which migration method(s) are possible between the source and destination OS platforms.	
3	Download XTTS scripts and modules	See MOS Note 1389592.1 for the link to `rman_xttconvert_1.4.zip`.	
4	Create supporting database objects/staging areas on source and destination platforms	■ If the `DBMS_FILE_TRANSFER` method is selected, create the required directory objects and database link. ■ If the RMAN method is selected, create *staging areas* at the destination.	
5	Decompress and install XTTS scripts	Save `rman_xttconvert_1.4.zip` contents to the staging directory on the source and destination database platforms.	
6	Configure XTTS properties and environment variables	Set up an `xtt.properties` file and establish a `TMPDIR` directory.	

CHECKLIST 9-1 *Preparing for Migration (XTTS)*

Identify Tablespace Sets

XTTS must still adhere to the same basic restrictions as any of the other TTS operations that we have already described in Chapter 6. See the section named "Verify Transportability of Selected Tablespace Set" in that chapter for a deeper discussion of how to identify whether the tablespaces about to be transported are truly transportable based on those guidelines.

Identify Source and Destination Database Versions and Desired Migration Method(s)

This is the most crucial preparation step because if the destination database is Oracle Database Release 11.2.0.3 or earlier, it will be necessary to prepare the destination environment by constructing an 11.2.0.4 database home on the destination OS platform and then creating an Oracle 11.2.0.4 database instance so that the XTTS operation can proceed.

Download XTTS Scripts and Modules

You can download the source code needed for all XTTS operations as a ZIP file from a link in the Appendix of MOS Note 1389592.1. You will need to decompress this source code and then deploy it to an OS directory on both the source and destination platforms.

Create Supporting Database Objects/Staging Areas on Source and Destination Platforms

As shown in Listing 9-1, create the directory objects on the source database.

Listing 9-1   *Source Database Objects*

```
-----
-- Prepare the source database
-----

$> mkdir /home/oracle/XTTS
$> mkdir /home/oracle/XTTSFILES

CREATE OR REPLACE DIRECTORY ora10g_dbf
    AS '/u02/app/oracle/oradata/ora10g';
GRANT READ, WRITE ON DIRECTORY ora10g_dbf TO PUBLIC;

CREATE OR REPLACE DIRECTORY xttsfiles
    AS '/home/oracle/XTTSFILES';
GRANT READ, WRITE ON DIRECTORY xttsfiles TO PUBLIC;
```

If the destination database's version is at least 11.2.0.4, then you need to create the directory objects plus a database link that points back to the source database, as shown in Listing 9-2.

Listing 9-2   *Destination Database Objects*

```
-----
-- Prepare the destination database
-----
$> mkdir /home/oracle/XTTS
$> mkdir /home/oracle/XTTSFILES
```

```
DROP DATABASE LINK ora10g;
CREATE DATABASE LINK ora10g
    CONNECT TO system IDENTIFIED BY oracle_4U
    USING 'ORA10G';

CREATE OR REPLACE DIRECTORY ora11g_dbf
    AS '+DATA/ORA11G/DATAFILE';
GRANT READ, WRITE ON DIRECTORY ora11g_dbf TO PUBLIC;

CREATE OR REPLACE DIRECTORY xttsfiles
    AS '/home/oracle/XTTSFILES';
GRANT READ, WRITE ON DIRECTORY xttsfiles TO PUBLIC;
```

Decompress and Install XTTS Scripts

Now that there is a home directory for XTTS objects, it is time to decompress the previously downloaded ZIP file into that directory. Perform the same procedure on both the source and destination OS platforms, as shown in Listing 9-3.

Listing 9-3   *Decompressing and Installing XTTS Scripts*

```
-----
-- Do this on source and destination platforms
-----
$> unzip -d /home/oracle/XTTS rman_xttconvert_1.4.zip
```

Table 9-1 describes each unzipped script or object and its purpose.

Script/Object	Purpose
xttdriver.pl	PERL "driver" script that executes appropriate XTTS operations, depending on the source and destination database releases.
xtt.properties	Sets XTTS properties for the source and destination databases. See Listing 9.4 for a complete listing of these properties.
xttcnvrtbkupdest.sql	Handles conversion of incremental backups (if necessary).
xttdbopen.sql	Completes the transition of the destination database's state from MOUNT to OPEN.
xttstartupnomount.sql	Opens the destination database in NOMOUNT mode during XTTS operations.
xttprep.tmpl	PL/SQL object used to construct statements for copying and conversion of datafiles from source to destination.

TABLE 9-1.   *XTTS Scripts and Objects*

Configure XTTS Properties and Environment Variables

Two more configuration tasks are required to complete Phase One:

■ By default, all output from XTTS operations are written to the directory specified by the `TMPDIR` environment variable, so be sure to set this to the same directory defined previously for all XTTS objects:

```
$> export TMPDIR=/home/oracle/XTTS
```

■ The `xtt.properties` file contains settings that control how XTTS operations are performed. The settings for source and destination databases differ depending on which XTTS transport method—RMAN or `DBMS_FILE_TRANSFER`—will be used during the XTTS process.

Listing 9-4 shows the contents of this file for the XTTS demonstrations, while Table 9-2 describes what each directive in this parameter file controls.

Listing 9-4   *xtt.properties Contents*

```
#####
# xtt.properties
# Parameters for Cross-Platform Transportable Tablespace (XTTS) demonstrations
#####
# Tablespace(s) for XTTS transport:
tablespaces=AP_DATA,AP_IDX
# Source database parameters:
platformid=2
srcdir=ORA10G_DBF
srclink=ORA10G
dfcopydir=/home/oracle/XTTSFILES
backupformat=/home/oracle/XTTSFILES
# Destination database parameters:
dstdir=ORA11G_DBF
stageondest=/home/oracle/XTTSFILES
storageondest=+DATA
backupondest=+FRA
asm_home=/u01/app/oracle/product/11.2.0/grid
asm_sid=+ASM
parallel=4
rollparallel=2
```

Phase Two: Initial Migration, Method A: RMAN

Depending on the release of the *destination* database, XTTS will leverage either RMAN or `DBMS_FILE_TRANSFER` to perform the initial migration of the datafiles for the selected tablespace set(s). The first transport method leverages RMAN on the source platform to create datafile copies of all the datafiles in each tablespace set. If any endian conversion is necessary, this method also uses RMAN `CONVERT` commands on the destination platform to convert those datafiles to their appropriate endianness.

Parameter	Purpose
tablespaces	A list of which tablespaces are to be transported between source and destination platforms. Note that all tablespaces listed must be part of a tablespace set.
platformid	Enumerated constant for the OS platform (corresponds to the value in $VTRANSPORTABLE_PLATFORM.PLATFORM_ID).
srcdir	The source database's directory *object*.
dstdir	The destination database's directory *object*.
srclink	The source database's database *link* to the destination database.
dfcopydir	The source system directory in which datafile copies are created during XTTS transport operations that leverage RMAN.
backupformat	The source system directory in which INCREMENTAL LEVEL 1 backup sets are created during XTTS transport operations.
stageondest	The destination system directory in which datafile copies are placed during XTTS transport operations.
storageondest	The destination system directory in which converted datafile copies are placed after XTTS conversion operations are completed.
backupondest	The destination system directory in which INCREMENTAL LEVEL 1 backup sets are placed during XTTS incremental roll-forward operations.
cnvinst_home	The incremental convert database home on the destination (only necessary when the existing destination database is earlier than 11.2.0.4).
cnvinst_sid	The incremental convert database instance on the destination (only necessary when the existing destination database is earlier than 11.2.0.4).
asm_home	The Automatic Storage Management (ASM)/Grid Infrastructure home directory of the destination OS platform.
asm_sid	The name of the ASM instance on the destination OS platform.
parallel	The degree of parallelism to use when allocating RMAN channels for both TARGET and AUXILIARY instances for the copying of and conversion of datafiles. Defaults to a total of eight (8) channels if left unspecified.
rollparallel	The degree of parallelism to use when allocating RMAN channels for *roll-forward* operations—that is, when INCREMENTAL LEVEL 1 backup sets are applied to the destination database. Defaults to none (0) if left unspecified.

TABLE 9-2. *xtts.properties Parameters and Settings*

However, there are some potentially serious disadvantages to the RMAN method:

- Staging areas for the RMAN backup files must be set up on both source and destination platforms. Obviously, this requires considerable additional amounts of disk space on both platforms and may not be viable for all conversions.

- If the destination database release is earlier than Oracle 11.2.0.4, a separate *database home* must be created on the destination platform and an Oracle 11.2.0.4 *database instance* must be created so that the incremental backups shipped in the next phase from the source database can be converted on the destination database.

- Although ASM storage is certainly not a requirement for XTTS, it is important to remember that if the destination database is using ASM for its database files, the Grid Infrastructure ASM software version must be upgraded to at least 11.2.0.4 as well so that the ASM instance is running at that level. (Note that the source and destination databases can use *either* ASM storage or non-ASM storage for the staging directories and the final locations of all database files.)

Checklist 9-2A describes the steps necessary to transport these tablespaces between the source and destination platforms, both of which use the Oracle Linux x86-64 OS.

Step	Operation	Description	Done?
1	Prepare tablespace sets for transport	■ Check that all selected tablespaces on the source database are ready for XTTS migration. ■ Stage image copies of all selected tablespaces' datafiles on the source platform. ■ If required, build an RMAN command script for eventual datafile conversion on the destination database.	
2	Push datafile copies from source platform to destination platform	Use OS commands to *push* all datafile copies from the source platform to the destination platform.	
3	Perform endian conversion at destination	If necessary, convert the tablespaces' datafiles to the endian format on the destination OS platform.	

CHECKLIST 9-2A *Initial Migration Using RMAN*

Prepare Tablespace Sets for Transport

When you invoke the xttdriver.pl PERL script with the –p (prepare) option, it first verifies that all the tablespaces listed in xtt.properties are in READ WRITE mode and that all datafiles are online. It also creates all necessary datafile image copies of the tablespaces' datafiles that are about to be transported to the source platform's staging area as defined by the dfcopy parameter in xtt.properties. Finally, if endian conversion is necessary, running xttdriver.pl –p creates an RMAN script that will perform that eventual conversion on the destination platform. The results of running xttdriver.pl –p are shown in Listing 9-5.

Listing 9-5   *Invoking xttdriver.pl -p*

```
$> /home/oracle/XTTS/xttdriver.pl -p

$> ./xttdriver.pl -p
Prepare source for Tablespaces:
                'AP_DATA'  /home/oracle/XTTSFILES
xttpreparesrc.sql for 'AP_DATA' started at Wed Jul 30 19:13:46 2014
xttpreparesrc.sql for  ended at Wed Jul 30 19:13:46 2014
Prepare source for Tablespaces:
                'AP_IDX'  /home/oracle/XTTSFILES
xttpreparesrc.sql for 'AP_IDX' started at Wed Jul 30 19:13:52 2014
xttpreparesrc.sql for  ended at Wed Jul 30 19:13:52 2014
Prepare source for Tablespaces:
                ''  /home/oracle/XTTSFILES
xttpreparesrc.sql for '' started at Wed Jul 30 19:13:57 2014
xttpreparesrc.sql for  ended at Wed Jul 30 19:13:57 2014
Prepare source for Tablespaces:
                ''  /home/oracle/XTTSFILES
xttpreparesrc.sql for '' started at Wed Jul 30 19:13:58 2014
xttpreparesrc.sql for  ended at Wed Jul 30 19:13:58 2014

>> Contents of xttplan.txt:

AP_DATA::::2883487
6
AP_IDX::::2883501
7
```

Transport Datafile Copies from Source Platform to Destination Platform

Next, transfer the datafile image copies from the source platform's staging area to the destination platform's staging area using the appropriate OS commands. In a Linux environment, for example, using the scp (Secure Copy) command is strongly recommended to ensure the security of the datafile copies being transferred, as shown in Listing 9-6.

TIP & TECHNIQUE

Note that the RMAN CONVERT script can be copied to the destination staging platform simultaneously while copying the datafile copies.

Listing 9-6 *Transporting Datafile Copies Using scp*

```
$> scp AP*.tf oracle@oel01:/home/oracle/XTTSFILES
oracle@oel01's password: ******
AP_DATA_6.tf         100%  100MB  50.0MB/s   00:02
AP_IDX_7.tf          100%  100MB  50.0MB/s   00:02
```

Perform Endian Conversion at Destination

Once the image copies have been transferred, you can execute the RMAN CONVERT script created during the first step in this phase on the destination platform, as Listing 9-7 demonstrates. Remember that it is only necessary to run the CONVERT script if endian conversion is required; otherwise, you can safely skip this step.

Listing 9-7 *Converting Datafile Copies Using RMAN*

```
host 'echo ts::AP_DATA';
  convert from platform 'Linux 64-bit for AMD'
  datafile
   '/home/oracle/XTTSFILES/AP_DATA_6.tf'
  format '+DATA/%N_%f.xtf'
 parallelism 4;
host 'echo ts::AP_IDX';
  convert from platform 'Linux 64-bit for AMD'
  datafile
   '/home/oracle/XTTSFILES/AP_IDX_7.tf'
  format '+DATA/%N_%f.xtf'
 parallelism 4;
```

Phase Two: Initial Migration, Method B: DBMS_FILE_TRANSFER

If the source database is at least Oracle Database Release 10.2.0.1 and your destination database is at least Oracle Database Release 11.2.0.4, then it's not necessary to use RMAN at all to perform the initial migration—even if the source database is a different endianness than the destination database. Starting with Release 11.2.0.4, the DBMS_FILE_TRANSFER utility automatically and transparently converts the datafiles on the destination database to the required endian format. Checklist 9-2B shows the steps required to perform the initial migration using this method.

Step	Operation	Description	Done?
1	Prepare tablespace sets for transport	■ Check that all selected tablespaces on the source database are ready for XTTS migration. ■ Prepare the `getfile.sql` script and `xttnewdatafiles.txt` parameter file. ■ Copy the script and parameter file to the destination platform.	
2	Pull transport datafiles from source platform to destination platform	Invoke `DBMS_FILE_TRANSFER` to *pull* all datafiles and Data Pump dump set from the source platform to the destination platform.	

CHECKLIST 9-2B *Initial Migration Using DBMS_FILE_TRANSFER*

Prepare Tablespace Sets for Transport

When the `xttdriver.pl` PERL script is invoked with the –S (source) option, it first verifies that all the tablespaces listed in `xtt.properties` are in READ WRITE mode and that all datafiles are online. It also creates two files that are used in the next step in this phase that you must copy to the destination platform using an appropriate secure file copy utility like `scp`:

■ `getfile.sql` comprises the `DBMS_FILE_TRANSFER` commands that will be invoked on the destination database to pull the appropriate datafiles from the source database, as well as perform any necessary endian conversion.

■ `xttnewdatafiles.txt` contains a list of the datafiles that will be pulled from the source platform to the destination platform.

The results of running `xttdriver.pl` –S are shown in Listing 9-8.

Listing 9-8 *Invoking xttdriver.pl –S on Source Platform*

```
$> /home/oracle/XTTS/xttdriver.pl -S

Prepare source for Tablespaces:
                'AP_DATA'  /home/oracle/XTTS
xttpreparesrc.sql for 'AP_DATA' started at Thu Jul 24 20:43:28 2014
xttpreparesrc.sql for  ended at Thu Jul 24 20:43:28 2014
```

```
Prepare source for Tablespaces:
                'AP_IDX'   /home/oracle/XTTS
xttpreparesrc.sql for 'AP_IDX' started at Thu Jul 24 20:43:28 2014
xttpreparesrc.sql for  ended at Thu Jul 24 20:43:29 2014
Prepare source for Tablespaces:
                ''  /home/oracle/XTTS
xttpreparesrc.sql for '' started at Thu Jul 24 20:43:29 2014
xttpreparesrc.sql for  ended at Thu Jul 24 20:43:29 2014

$> scp /home/oracle/XTTSFILES/xttnewdatafiles.txt oracle@ora10g:/home/oracle/XTTS
$> scp /home/oracle/XTTSFILES/getfile.sql oracle@ora10g:/home/oracle/XTTS

>> Contents of getfile.sql:
BEGIN
DBMS_FILE_TRANSFER.GET_FILE(
source_directory_object    => 'ORA10G_DBF',
source_file_name           => 'ap_data.dbf',
source_database            => 'OEL01',
destination_directory_object => 'ORA11G_DBF',
destination_file_name      => 'ap_data.dbf');
END;
/

BEGIN
DBMS_FILE_TRANSFER.GET_FILE(
source_directory_object    => 'ORA10G_DBF',
source_file_name           => 'ap_idx.dbf',
source_database            => 'OEL01',
destination_directory_object => 'ORA11G_DBF',
destination_file_name      => 'ap_idx.dbf');
END;
/

quit

>> Contents of xttnewdatafiles.txt:
::AP_DATA
6,DESTDIR:/ap_data.dbf
::AP_IDX
7,DESTDIR:/ap_idx.dbf
```

Pull Transport Datafiles from Source Platform to Destination Platform

To complete this phase, simply execute the xttsdriver.pl script with the -G (getfile) option. Since the destination database must be at least release 11.2.0.4, there is no need to run an RMAN CONVERT script to convert the datafiles to the destination platform's endian format because, as of 11.2.0.4, DBMS_FILE_CONVERT automatically performs the endian conversion if necessary. The script invocation, the results of its execution, and output from the asmcmd ls -l command show that this step was invoked successfully, as Listing 9-9 illustrates.

Listing 9-9 *Invoking xttdriver.pl –G on Destination Platform*

```
$> /home/oracle/XTTS/xttdriver.pl -G
>> Results:
sh: line 5: warning: here-document at line 0 delimited by end-of-file (wanted 'EOF)
sh: line 5: warning: here-document at line 0 delimited by end-of-file (wanted 'EOF')

>> Results from asmcmd ls -l:
Type       Redund  Striped  Time             Sys  Name
DATAFILE   MIRROR  COARSE   JUL 24 20:00:00  Y    EXAMPLE.265.853791377
DATAFILE   MIRROR  COARSE   JUL 24 21:00:00  Y    FILE_TRANSFER.267.853796481
DATAFILE   MIRROR  COARSE   JUL 24 21:00:00  Y    FILE_TRANSFER.268.853796483
DATAFILE   MIRROR  COARSE   JUL 24 21:00:00  Y    SYSAUX.257.853791277
DATAFILE   MIRROR  COARSE   JUL 24 20:00:00  Y    SYSTEM.256.853791277
DATAFILE   MIRROR  COARSE   JUL 24 20:00:00  Y    UNDOTBS1.258.853791277
DATAFILE   MIRROR  COARSE   JUL 24 20:00:00  Y    USERS.259.853791277
                                            N    ap_data.dbf => +DATA/ORA11G/DATAFILE/
FILE_TRANSFER.267.853796481
                                            N    ap_idx.dbf => +DATA/ORA11G/DATAFILE/
FILE_TRANSFER.268.853796483
```

Phase Three: Incremental Synchronization

Regardless of which method you used in Phase Two to transport the selected tablespaces' datafiles to the destination platform, this phase accomplishes the following:

- Captures INCREMENTAL LEVEL 1 backup sets for the selected tablespaces on the source database

- Transfers these backup sets to the destination platform

- Applies these backup sets to the selected tablespaces' datafiles

As previously mentioned, you can repeat this phase innumerable times until you decide that a sufficient "window of inopportunity" has presented itself and that it is finally time to complete the XTTS operation in Phase Four. Checklist 9-3 shows the steps for this iterative phase.

Step	Operation	Description	Done?
1	Create incremental backups via RMAN	Build INCREMENTAL LEVEL 1 backups for XTTS tablespaces on the source database and create parameter files for later synchronization steps.	

CHECKLIST 9-3 *Synchronizing Iteratively via Incremental Backups*

Step	Operation	Description	Done?
2	Push incremental backups from source platform to destination platform	Invoke OS commands to *push* all incremental backups from the source platform to the destination platform.	
3	Convert and apply incremental backups to destination database	If necessary, convert the incremental backups to the endian format on the destination OS platform. Apply the converted incremental backups to the destination database.	
4	Capture FROM_SCN for next incremental backup	Determine and record the starting SCN for the next INCREMENTAL LEVEL 1 backup.	

CHECKLIST 9-3 *Synchronizing Iteratively via Incremental Backups* (Continued)

Create Incremental Backups via RMAN

Phase Three's first step uses the −i option of xttdriver.pl to create INCREMENTAL LEVEL 1 backup sets for all database blocks that have changed in the tablespace sets that are being transported, as illustrated in Listing 9-10. It also creates two parameter files for use in later steps of this phase:

- incrbkups.txt contains a list of the INCREMENTAL LEVEL 1 backup sets that should be transferred to the destination platform.

- tsbkupmap.txt contains a list of the incremental backup files that will be pushed over from the source platform to the destination platform.

Listing 9-10 *Invoking xttdriver.pl −i on Source Platform*

```
$> /home/oracle/XTTS/xttdriver.pl -i
Prepare newscn for Tablespaces: 'AP_DATA'
Prepare newscn for Tablespaces: 'AP_IDX'

rman target /  cmdfile /home/oracle/XTTS/rmanincr.cmd

Recovery Manager: Release 10.2.0.1.0 - Production on Fri Jul 25 16:03:27 2014

Copyright (c) 1982, 2005, Oracle.  All rights reserved.

connected to target database: ORA10G (DBID=4168941045)

RMAN> set nocfau;
2> host 'echo ts::AP_DATA';
```

```
 3> backup incremental from scn 2498191
 4>   tag tts_incr_update tablespace 'AP_DATA' format
 5>  '/home/oracle/XTTSFILES/%U';
 6> set nocfau;
 7> host 'echo ts::AP_IDX';
 8> backup incremental from scn 2498202
 9>   tag tts_incr_update tablespace 'AP_IDX' format
10>  '/home/oracle/XTTSFILES/%U';
11>
executing command: SET NOCFAU
using target database control file instead of recovery catalog

ts::AP_DATA
host command complete

Starting backup at 25-JUL-14
allocated channel: ORA_DISK_1
channel ORA_DISK_1: sid=158 devtype=DISK
channel ORA_DISK_1: starting full datafile backupset
channel ORA_DISK_1: specifying datafile(s) in backupset
input datafile fno=00006 name=/u02/app/oracle/oradata/ora10g/ap_data.dbf
channel ORA_DISK_1: starting piece 1 at 25-JUL-14
channel ORA_DISK_1: finished piece 1 at 25-JUL-14
piece handle=/home/oracle/XTTSFILES/0qpe9q6g_1_1 tag=TTS_INCR_UPDATE comment=NONE
channel ORA_DISK_1: backup set complete, elapsed time: 00:00:01
Finished backup at 25-JUL-14

executing command: SET NOCFAU

ts::AP_IDX
host command complete

Starting backup at 25-JUL-14
using channel ORA_DISK_1
channel ORA_DISK_1: starting full datafile backupset
channel ORA_DISK_1: specifying datafile(s) in backupset
input datafile fno=00007 name=/u02/app/oracle/oradata/ora10g/ap_idx.dbf
channel ORA_DISK_1: starting piece 1 at 25-JUL-14
channel ORA_DISK_1: finished piece 1 at 25-JUL-14
piece handle=/home/oracle/XTTSFILES/0rpe9q6i_1_1 tag=TTS_INCR_UPDATE comment=NONE
channel ORA_DISK_1: backup set complete, elapsed time: 00:00:01
Finished backup at 25-JUL-14

Recovery Manager complete.
```

TIP & TECHNIQUE

We found that jotting down the SCN of each
INCREMENTAL LEVEL 1 backup that is created
during this phase makes it easy to track the progress
of each iteration to ensure that no unexpected gaps
occur when preparing for the final synchronization
processing in Phase Four.

Push Incremental Backups from Source Platform to Destination Platform

In this step you use `scp` to copy the `tsbkupmap.txt` file; you also use the list of `INCREMENTAL LEVEL 1` backup sets stored in `incrbackups.txt` to copy those files via `scp` to the destination platform, as shown in Listing 9-11.

Listing 9-11   *Pushing Incremental Backups to Destination via scp*

```
$> scp tsbkupmap.txt oracle@oel01:/home/oracle/XTTS
oracle@oel01's password:
tsbkupmap.txt        100%    47     0.1KB/s    00:00

$> scp 'cat incrbackups.txt' oracle@oel01:/home/oracle/XTTSFILES

oracle@oel01's password:
0rpe9q6i_1_1         100%   808KB 808.0KB/s    00:00
0qpe9q6g_1_1         100%   208KB 208.0KB/s    00:00
```

NOTE
XTTS does support using the identical NFS storage location for the directory identified by the `backupformat` parameter for the source system and the directory identified by the `stageondest` parameter for the destination system. If this is the case, then you can skip this complete step because all `INCREMENTAL LEVEL 1` backups have already been made available for the destination system as well.

Convert and Apply Incremental Backups to Destination Database

On the destination system, invoking the `xttdriver.pl` script with the `-r` (roll forward) option uses the contents of the previously created parameter files `xttplan.txt` and `tsbkupmap.txt` to apply the `INCREMENTAL LEVEL 1` backups, thus rolling forward the datafiles incrementally. Listing 9-12 shows an example of this technique.

Listing 9-12   *Invoking xttdriver.pl –r on Destination Platform*

```
$> /home/oracle/XTTS/xttdriver.pl -r
Start rollforward
asmcmd rm +FRA/xtts_incr_backup_1406323245_7239_25  /u01/app/oracle/product/11.2.0/
grid .. +ASM
asmcmd rm +FRA/xtts_incr_backup_1406323245_7238_417  /u01/app/oracle/product/11.2.0/
grid .. +ASM
```

```
ASMCMD-8002: entry 'xtts_incr_backup_1406323245_7239_25' does not exist in directory
'+FRA/'
ASMCMD-8002: entry 'xtts_incr_backup_1406323245_7238_417' does not exist in directory
'+FRA/'
ASMCMD:
ASMCMD:
End of rollforward phase
```

Capture FROM_SCN for Next Incremental Backup

So that the next iteration of the INCREMENTAL LEVEL 1 backup operation starts at the proper point in time, running the xttdriver.pl script with the -s (SCN) option on the source system writes those SCNs into the xttplan.txt parameter file. Listing 9-13 demonstrates the first iteration of this step.

Listing 9-13   *Invoking xttdriver.pl –s on Destination Platform*

```
$> /home/oracle/XTTS/xttdriver.pl -s
Prepare newscn for Tablespaces: 'AP_DATA'
Prepare newscn for Tablespaces: 'AP_IDX'
Prepare newscn for Tablespaces: ''
Prepare newscn for Tablespaces: ''
New /home/oracle/XTTSFILES/xttplan.txt with FROM SCN's generated

>> Contents of xttplan.txt:
AP_DATA::::2498191
6
AP_IDX::::2498202
7
```

At this point, you can continue to *repeat* the steps in Checklist 9-3—*capturing* INCREMENTAL LEVEL 1 backups for the specified tablespaces on the source database, *transferring* them to the destination platform, and *applying* them on the destination database—until an appropriate "window of inopportunity" arrives...at which point it is time to move on to Phase Four and complete the XTTS migration.

Phase Four: Final Synchronization and Migration

Once an appropriate "window of inopportunity" has at last arrived, you must place the selected tablespaces into READ ONLY mode to perform a final synchronization. This will cause an extremely brief, but necessary, disruption to any application workloads that are attempting to apply DML while accessing the selected tablespaces on the source database. Here's a brief summary of the process performed during this final phase:

■ Since the tablespaces are in READ ONLY mode, no further transactions can occur, so when you perform one final INCREMENTAL LEVEL 1 backup of the tablespaces' datafiles on the source database, these tablespaces are synchronized between source and destination.

- Once you have transferred the datafiles to the destination platform and applied them one last time on the destination database, open the tablespaces in READ WRITE mode on the destination database, thus completing the synchronization phase.

- You can either leave the source database's tablespaces in READ ONLY mode, so that you can switch application activity to the destination database, or you can return them to READ WRITE mode.

- Finally, it is important to remember to redirect any applications that had been pointing to the source database to point to the new destination database instead—most likely by creating and starting the appropriate database services on the new destination platform.

Checklist 9-4 lists the final operations to complete an XTTS migration.

Step	Operation	Description	Done?
1	Switch tablespaces to READ ONLY mode at destination	Issue ALTER TABLESPACE <*tablespace name*> READ ONLY; for selected tablespace(s) on the source database.	
2	Create incremental backups via RMAN	Build INCREMENTAL LEVEL 1 backups for XTTS tablespaces on the source database and create parameter files for later synchronization steps.	
3	Push incremental backups from source platform to destination platform	Use OS commands to *push* all incremental backups from the source platform to the destination platform.	
4	Convert and apply incremental backups to destination database	If necessary, convert the incremental backups to the endian format on the destination OS platform. Apply converted incremental backups to the destination database.	
5	Import source tablespace metadata via Data Pump Import	Generate and execute Data Pump Import commands to import the source database tablespaces' metadata into the destination database.	

Step	Operation	Description	Done?
6	Switch transported tablespaces to READ WRITE mode at destination	Issue ALTER TABLESPACE <tablespace name> READ WRITE; for each tablespace that has been incorporated into the destination database.	
7	Revert tablespaces to READ WRITE mode at source	If desired, issue ALTER TABLESPACE <tablespace name> READ WRITE; for each tablespace transported from the source platform.	
8	Redirect applications to destination database	Create and start appropriate database services and/or network connectivity on the new destination database.	
9	Clean up staging directories	Remove unneeded files from the source and destination systems.	

CHECKLIST 9-4   *Final Synchronization and Migration*

Note that Steps 2, 3, and 4 in Checklist 9-4 correspond exactly to Steps 1, 2, and 3, respectively, in Checklist 9-3. Therefore, those steps won't be covered again in this section. Please refer to the Phase 3 coverage of those steps after you complete the following step of switching the tablespaces to READ ONLY mode at the destination. Then, return here to complete the remaining steps in Phase Four.

Switch Tablespaces to READ ONLY Mode at Destination

First, switch the selected tablespaces to READ ONLY mode on the source database via the SQL*Plus commands in Listing 9-14. However, note that this "window of inopportunity" will likely be quite short because it is only required while a final set of INCREMENTAL LEVEL 1 backups are taken for those tablespaces.

Listing 9-14   *Switching Transportable Tablespaces to READ ONLY Mode*

```
SQL> ALTER TABLESPACE ap_data READ ONLY;
Tablespace altered.

SQL> ALTER TABLESPACE ap_idx READ ONLY;
Tablespace altered.
```

NOTE
Since this is the final iteration of INCREMENTAL LEVEL 1 backup processing, there is no need to run the xttdriver.pl -s (SCN) step on the source system this time.

Import Source Tablespace Metadata via Data Pump Import

Now that the final INCREMENTAL LEVEL 1 backup set for the selected tablespaces has been generated, shipped, and applied on the destination database, you can import their metadata using Data Pump Import directly across a network connection to the source database. Running the xttdriver.pl script with the -e (export) option from the destination database will store all required Data Pump Import commands in a file named xttplugin.txt. The default commands written into that file are shown in Listing 9-15.

Listing 9-15 *Invoking xttdriver.pl –e on Destination Platform*

```
$> /home/oracle/XTTS/xttdriver.pl -e
>> Contents of xttplugin.txt:
impdp directory=<DATA_PUMP_DIR> logfile=<tts_imp.log> \
network_link=<ttslink> transport_full_check=no \
transport_tablespaces=
```

This release of XTTS is unable to format xttplugin.txt appropriately, so it needed to be edited before it could be executed. We have found that if the list of transportable tablespace datafiles is exceedingly long, it is better to create a Data Pump Import parameter file to invoke the metadata import instead, as shown in Listing 9-16.

Listing 9-16 *Invoking Data Pump Import on Destination Platform*

```
$> impdp system/<pwd> parfile=xttplugin.prm

>> Contents of xttplugin.prm:

DIRECTORY=XTTSFILES
LOGFILE=XTTSFILES:tts_imp.log
NETWORK_LINK=ora11g
TRANSPORT_FULL_CHECK=no
TRANSPORT_TABLESPACES=AP_DATA,AP_IDX
TRANSPORT_DATAFILES='+DATA/ORA11G/DATAFILE/ap_data.dbf','+DATA/ORA11G/DATAFILE/ap_idx.dbf'
```

Switch Transported Tablespaces to READ WRITE Mode at Destination

If you want to bring the tablespaces that were just imported into the destination database into READ WRITE mode, you can use the SQL*Plus commands in Listing 9-17.

Listing 9-17   *Switching Transported Tablespaces to READ WRITE Mode*

```
SQL> ALTER TABLESPACE ap_data READ WRITE;
Tablespace altered.

SQL> ALTER TABLESPACE ap_idx READ WRITE;
Tablespace altered.
```

Revert Tablespaces to READ WRITE Mode at Source

Finally, you can use these same SQL*Plus commands to return the newly migrated tablespaces into READ WRITE mode on the source database, if desired.

Redirect Applications to Destination Database

Now that all XTTS operations have been completed successfully, you can redirect all referencing applications to the destination database.

Clean Up Staging Files and Directories

Finally, if you used the RMAN method during Phase Two of the XTTS operation, you can remove the contents of the directories shown in Table 9-3 until the next XTTS operation is required.

Directory	Purpose
dfcopydir	The source system directory in which datafile copies were created during XTTS transport operations that leverage RMAN
backupformat	The source system directory in which INCREMENTAL LEVEL 1 backup sets were created during XTTS transport operations
stageondest	The destination system directory in which datafile copies were placed during XTTS transport operations
backupondest	The destination system directory in which INCREMENTAL LEVEL 1 backup sets were placed during XTTS incremental roll-forward operations

TABLE 9-3.   *XTTS RMAN Staging Directories*

Summary

Here's a brief summary of the key concepts we have discussed in this chapter:

- Although XTTS features are not quite as simple to leverage as those of TTS and TDB, when applications can tolerate only an extremely tight "window of inopportunity" during which tablespace migration can occur without DML access, XTTS is more likely to satisfy those requirements because the tablespaces selected for transport must remain in `READ WRITE` mode until just before the final migration occurs.

- Since the Oracle 12c R1 version of `DBMS_FILE_TRANSFER` has been back-ported to Oracle Database Release 11.2.0.4, it's now possible to convert database files transparently to a different endian format without having to rely on RMAN's `CONVERT` commands, as was required in earlier releases.

CHAPTER
10

Migrating to New Storage Platforms Using ASM

U sing Oracle Automatic Storage Management (ASM) for a data migration probably isn't the first option that comes to mind, but in many cases, a storage migration can be accomplished online with little or no downtime using ASM. ASM includes the capability to add disks to and remove disks from disk groups dynamically. This process enables you to move or swap out storage while the Oracle databases are still up and running, with no interruption in service.

TIP & TECHNIQUE

If you are migrating storage only, you should consider this method.

ASM can be used for storage migrations only. You cannot perform any transformations or upgrades of Oracle databases using ASM migration. This type of migration is very specific and only serves one purpose.

ASM Overview

Automatic Storage Management was introduced in Oracle Database 10g R1 as a new way to manage database storage. It is Oracle's built-in storage solution for Oracle databases. Oracle has enhanced ASM in Oracle Database 11g and Oracle Database 12c with new features and functionality. ASM has now become the recommended and most popular technology for storing Oracle databases.

Oracle introduced ASM to fill the gap between a high-overhead cluster file system and hard-to-manage raw devices. In addition, it enabled Oracle's philosophy of Stripe and Mirror Everywhere (SAME). ASM is a storage system that has been designed from the ground up to manage and maintain Oracle datafiles. Starting with Oracle 11g R2, Oracle added the ASM Dynamic Volume Manager (ADVM) and ASM Cluster File System (ACFS) to provide general-purpose file system support. Starting with release 12.x of the Oracle Database Appliance (ODA) software, ACFS is the preferred storage of choice for database files.

ASM provides storage for Oracle datafiles by providing a container called a *disk group*, which behaves much like a logical volume. Similar to a logical volume, a disk group is composed of one or more physical disks or LUNs that are striped and/ or mirrored. The disk group is made up of one or more disks. The disk group is the location where Oracle datafiles are stored. Within the disk group, data is striped at the Oracle datafile level, not at the block level. This ensures that the datafiles are balanced across all of the disks in the disk group.

One of the most exciting features of ASM is that when a disk is added to ASM, rather than just adding that new storage into the pool for future use, all of the disks in the disk group are re-striped. This provides the ability to add and remove disks. Although re-striping makes the disk add/remove process take longer, it provides for enhanced performance by allowing all new disk drives to be used equally. This is unlike a normal volume manager that just adds new storage to the end of the disk pool and does not provide the ability to remove disks.

Starting with Oracle 11*g* R2, the OCR and Voting Disk for Oracle Clusterware are now stored in ASM. This is accomplished by adding an Oracle Local Registry (OLR), which can be used to bootstrap the Clusterware and identifies the location of the ASM. In Oracle 12*c*, the ASM services can be centralized on systems other than those providing the database services, which adds a whole new level of performance and cost savings. Storing the OCR and Voting Disk in ASM makes migrating to new storage even easier, as you will see later in this chapter.

ASM Configuration

You can view the ASM storage configuration by using any of these methods: `crsctl`, `srvctl`, OEM Cloud Control 12*c*, SQL statements, or `asmcmd`. Starting with Oracle version 11.2, ASM is included as part of the Grid Infrastructure and is no longer part of an Oracle Home. Following are examples of using each of the previously mentioned methods to see which disk groups are available and whether ASM is up and running.

crsctl

You can use the `crsctl` command (in the Grid Infrastructure home) to view and administer the Clusterware. Use the command `crsctl status resource -t` as shown in the following example:

```
[grid@oel04 ~]$ crsctl status resource -t
--------------------------------------------------------------------------------
Name           Target  State       Server              State details
--------------------------------------------------------------------------------
Local Resources
--------------------------------------------------------------------------------
ora.DATA.dg
               ONLINE  ONLINE      oel04               STABLE
ora.LISTENER.lsnr
               ONLINE  ONLINE      oel04               STABLE
ora.RECO.dg
               ONLINE  ONLINE      oel04               STABLE
ora.asm
               ONLINE  ONLINE      oel04               Started,STABLE
ora.ons
               OFFLINE OFFLINE     oel04               STABLE
--------------------------------------------------------------------------------
Cluster Resources
--------------------------------------------------------------------------------
ora.cssd
      1        ONLINE  ONLINE      oel04               STABLE
ora.diskmon
      1        OFFLINE OFFLINE                         STABLE
ora.evmd
      1        ONLINE  ONLINE      oel04               STABLE
--------------------------------------------------------------------------------
```

srvctl

Another command that you can use within the Grid Infrastructure home or database home is `srvctl`, which is used to administer objects controlled by the Clusterware. There are many commands to show the state and configuration of ASM, such as `srvctl status asm`, `srvctl status diskgroup -g <diskgroup>`, and `srvctl config asm`. These commands are shown here:

```
[grid@oel04 ~]$ srvctl status asm
ASM is running on oel04
[grid@oel04 ~]$ srvctl status diskgroup -diskgroup DATA
Disk Group DATA is running on oel04
[grid@oel04 ~]$ srvctl config asm
ASM home: <CRS home>
Password file: +DATA/orapwasm
ASM listener: LISTENER
Spfile: +DATA/ASM/ASMPARAMETERFILE/registry.253.855759185
ASM diskgroup discovery string:
```

> **TIP & TECHNIQUE**
> *The `srvctl` command is the recommended method of administering Oracle Clusterware and ASM.*

OEM Cloud Control 12*c*

Oracle Enterprise Manager Cloud Control 12*c* provides a wealth of information on the state and configuration of ASM and the ASM disk groups. The main ASM screen, shown in Figure 10-1, provides an overview of ASM.

From the main screen you can open the Disk Groups page by selecting Disk Groups from the Automatic Storage Management drop-down menu. On the Disk Groups page you see the disk groups as well as the number of member disks, as shown in Figure 10-2.

You can click an individual disk group to see the disk group along with all of the member disks, as shown in Figure 10-3.

This screen will become important to the migration process later in this chapter. Many ASM tasks are much easier to complete via OEM Cloud Control 12*c*.

SQL Statements

In addition to using the graphical OEM Cloud Control 12*c* and the OS commands, you can also view attributes of ASM via SQL*Plus. A number of SQL statements relate to ASM and ASM disk groups, such as ALTER DISKGROUP, CREATE DISKGROUP,

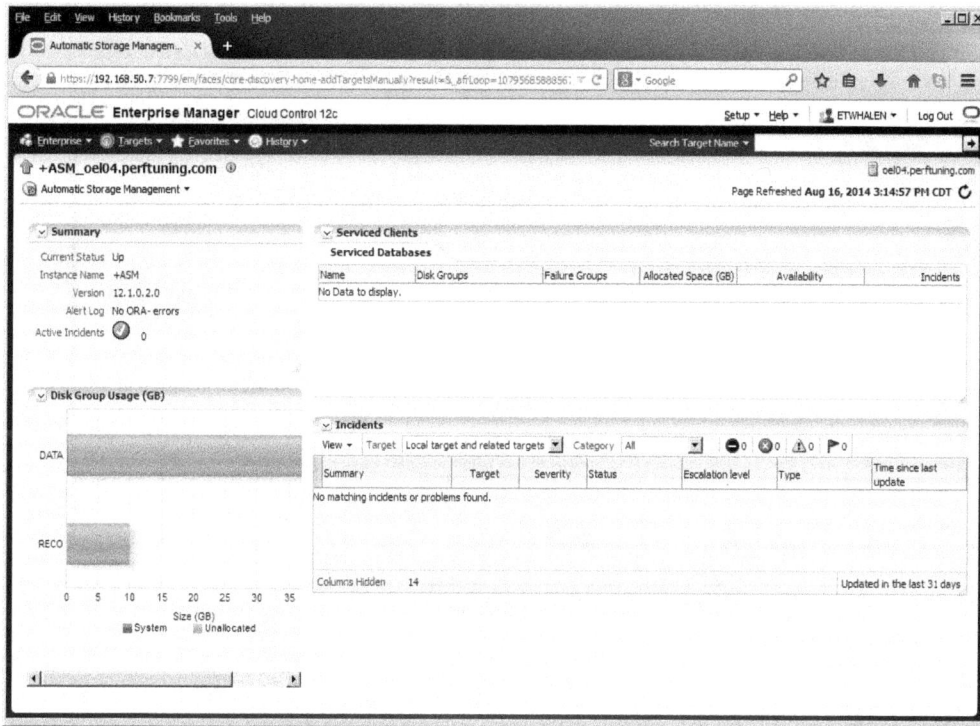

FIGURE 10-1. *OEM Cloud Control 12c ASM main screen*

and so forth. In addition, several internal tables can be used to view the attributes and status of ASM and disk groups, such as v$asm_diskgroups, etc.

```
SQL> select name, state, type, total_mb, free_mb, database_compatibility from v$asm_diskgroup;
NAME    STATE      TYPE    TOTAL_MB   FREE_MB    DATABASE_COMPATIBILITY
------  ---------  ------  ---------- ---------- ------------------------
RECO    MOUNTED    EXTERN  10228      10172      10.1.0.0.0
DATA    MOUNTED    EXTERN  40912      40829      10.1.0.0.0
```

NOTE
SQL statements that make modifications to ASM must be run using the SYSASM privilege rather than SYSDBA.

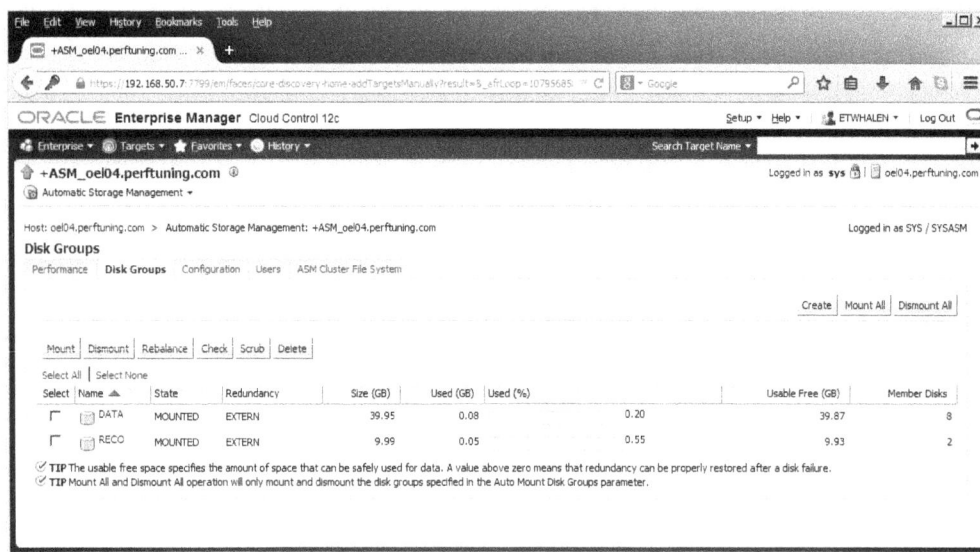

FIGURE 10-2. *OEM Cloud Control 12c Disk Groups page*

asmcmd

Starting with Oracle Database 11*g* R2, there is little you can do with SQL statements that you cannot do with `asmcmd`. The `asmcmd` script provides a shell into ASM, enabling you to run commands to view the status and configuration of ASM.

Some of the `asmcmd` commands are shown in this example:

```
[grid@oel04 ~]$ asmcmd
ASMCMD> ls
DATA/
RECO/
ASMCMD> lsdg
State     Type     Rebal  Sector  Block       AU  Total_MB  Free_MB  Req_mir_free_MB
Usable_file_MB  Offline_disks  Voting_files  Name
MOUNTED   EXTERN   N         512    4096  1048576     40912    40829                0
40829                0               N  DATA/
MOUNTED   EXTERN   N         512    4096  1048576     10228    10172                0
10172                0               N  RECO/
```

All of these commands can be very useful, as you will see later in this chapter.

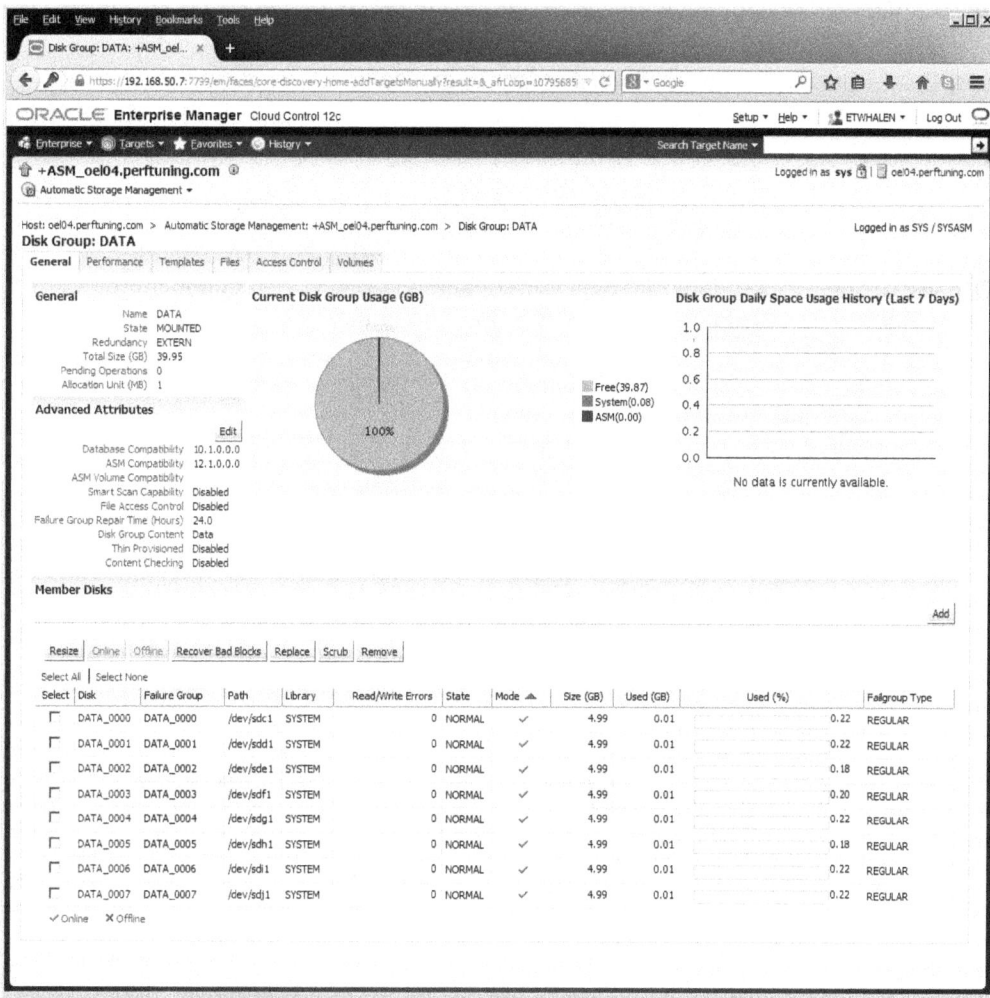

FIGURE 10-3. *OEM Cloud Control 12c DATA disk group*

Storage System Overview

There are several types of storage systems on the market today. The most popular of these are storage area network (SAN) and network-attached storage (NAS) storage systems. SAN systems are based on a dedicated storage network that is typically associated with the Fibre Channel network storage hardware. NAS systems use standard Ethernet hardware and software as a transport layer for communication between the host and the storage system. Whether using NAS or SAN, ASM provides the capability to add and remove ASM disks from an ASM disk group as needed. This process does not require any downtime or loss of service.

SAN Storage

SAN storage is probably the most popular type of storage used with Oracle databases today. SAN storage consists of a storage server that is attached to a SAN switch and subsequently attached to host bus adapters (HBAs) that reside in the database servers. SAN systems are typically configured to be highly redundant. This is accomplished by including two or more HBAs, two or more SAN switches, and a SAN storage system with built-in redundancy.

Storage presented by a SAN storage system might consist of one or more entire disk drives, or it might simply consist of a small piece of many physical disk drives pieced together and presented to the server as a logical unit number (LUN). A LUN, also known as a logical disk drive, appears to the server as a physical disk drive. Once the LUN is presented to the server, it can be partitioned using OS tools or presented to ASM as an entire disk.

As mentioned earlier, once the SAN storage has been presented to the system and is visible as a disk, then this disk can be added to the ASM disk group and used as part of the ASM storage system. This disk can be used for any number of disk groups and will simplify your Oracle database storage needs.

NAS Storage

NAS storage is different from SAN storage in two ways. First, NAS storage uses existing network hardware such as TCP/IP over Ethernet. Second, NAS storage is usually presented as either iSCSI or NFS. When using iSCSI, the storage presented to Oracle looks like disk drives as in the SAN storage previously discussed. When NAS storage is presented as NFS storage, other considerations must be taken into account, since you can't simply assign an NFS mount point as a disk to ASM. In either case, the storage is still presented to ASM as disks in order to create an ASM disk group.

Starting in Oracle Database version 11g R1, there are several new features for Oracle databases on NFS storage. ASM files for NFS allows you to create an empty file on an NFS volume and use that for ASM storage. This supports many of the features that we expect from ASM, such as the ability to dynamically add and remove disk drives from the ASM disk group.

Another new feature, called Oracle Direct NFS (dNFS), allows the Oracle database server to access NFS files directly, rather than go through the database host NFS subsystem. This reduces overhead and improves performance when using NAS storage.

Migration Process Using ASM

The migration process with ASM is fairly straightforward. As a reminder, an ASM migration only moves Oracle datafiles from one ASM disk(s) to another. No transformations can be made to the database itself during this migration.

TIP & TECHNIQUE

It is perfectly acceptable to perform a storage migration while the database is up and running. There will be no loss of access to storage. You might see some temporary performance degradation. Even though this is a very safe method of migration, it is always a good idea to back up all databases before doing any type of migration.

To successfully perform a migration using ASM, simply follow these steps (described in detail in the following sections):

1. Add new storage to the system and then:

   a. Add the storage.

   b. Verify that the storage is functioning properly.

2. Add the new storage to the desired ASM disk group(s), using any of the tools that were described previously.

3. Validate that the new storage is functioning properly.

4. Remove the old disks from the ASM disk group(s), using any of the tools described previously.

5. Validate that the old storage is no longer being accessed.

6. Remove the old storage from the system.

Once this is completed the migration is over.

Add New Storage to the System

Adding new storage to the system is a task for your system administrator to perform. Whether or not the system administrator can add storage dynamically depends on your operating system. In most modern operating systems, storage can be added and made visible to the OS without having to restart the system. There is usually some sort of refresh process that must be completed for the new storage to be visible.

The following example uses Oracle Linux 6.5. The system used for this example currently has ten 5GB disk drives configured in ASM. To view the physical disks, you can use the cat /proc/partitions command as shown here:

```
[root@oel04 ~]# cat /proc/partitions
major minor  #blocks   name

   8        0  16777216 sda
   8        1    512000 sda1
   8        2  16264192 sda2
   8       16  16777216 sdb
   8       17  16771828 sdb1
   8       32   5242880 sdc
   8       33   5237158 sdc1
   8       48   5242880 sdd
   8       49   5237158 sdd1
   8       80   5242880 sdf
   8       81   5237158 sdf1
   8       96   5242880 sdg
   8       97   5237158 sdg1
   8      112   5242880 sdh
   8      113   5237158 sdh1
   8      128   5242880 sdi
   8      129   5237158 sdi1
   8       64   5242880 sde
   8       65   5237158 sde1
   8      144   5242880 sdj
   8      145   5237158 sdj1
   8      160   5242880 sdk
   8      161   5237158 sdk1
   8      176   5242880 sdl
   8      177   5237158 sdl1
 252        0   8052736 dm-0
 252        1   8208384 dm-1
 252        2  16769024 dm-2
   8      192  16777216 sdm
   8      208  16777216 sdn
```

The disk partitions used for the DATA disk group are /dev/sdc1 through /dev/sdj1, and the disk partitions used for the FRA disk group are /dev/sdk1 and /dev/sdl1. In this example the eight 5GB disk drives used for DATA are going to be migrated to four 16GB disk drives, and the two 5GB disk drives used for FRA will be migrated to one 16GB drive.

TIP & TECHNIQUE
You can create a disk group with one disk drive if it is configured for external redundancy and protected via RAID on the hardware system itself.

Once the new disk drives have been added, it is necessary for the System Administrator to perform a scan of the SCSI bus to allow the OS to see the new drives. This is done by echoing a series of dashes to the file /sys/class/scsi_host/<host#>/scan, where # in <host#> is the controller number.

First list the host#'s:

```
[root@oel04 ~]# ls /sys/class/scsi_host
host0   host1   host2   host3
```

You can see that there are four hosts. It's okay to scan all four:

```
[root@oel04 ~]# echo "- - -" > /sys/class/scsi_host/host0/scan
[root@oel04 ~]# echo "- - -" > /sys/class/scsi_host/host1/scan
[root@oel04 ~]# echo "- - -" > /sys/class/scsi_host/host2/scan
[root@oel04 ~]# echo "- - -" > /sys/class/scsi_host/host3/scan
[root@oel04 ~]# cat /proc/partitions
major minor  #blocks  name

   8         0   16777216 sda
   8         1     512000 sda1
   8         2   16264192 sda2
   8        16   16777216 sdb
   8        17   16771828 sdb1
   8        32    5242880 sdc
   8        33    5237158 sdc1
   8        48    5242880 sdd
   8        49    5237158 sdd1
   8        80    5242880 sdf
   8        81    5237158 sdf1
   8        96    5242880 sdg
   8        97    5237158 sdg1
   8       112    5242880 sdh
   8       113    5237158 sdh1
   8       128    5242880 sdi
   8       129    5237158 sdi1
   8        64    5242880 sde
   8        65    5237158 sde1
   8       144    5242880 sdj
   8       145    5237158 sdj1
   8       160    5242880 sdk
   8       161    5237158 sdk1
   8       176    5242880 sdl
   8       177    5237158 sdl1
 252         0    8052736 dm-0
 252         1    8208384 dm-1
 252         2   16769024 dm-2
   8       192   16777216 sdm
   8       208   16777216 sdn
   8       224   16777216 sdo
   8       240   16777216 sdp
  65         0   16777216 sdq
```

You now see the five new 16GB disk drives that have been added. The final step is to partition the disks with a single partition.

TIP & TECHNIQUE

The reason that we like to partition the disk drive is for the sole purpose of identifying to system administrators that the disk drive is being used. Without a partition, it can be difficult to identify which disk drives are being used and which are not being used. The partition is a red flag to indicate that a disk drive is being used.

Use `fdisk` to create the single partition:

```
[root@oel04 ~]# fdisk /dev/sdm
Device contains neither a valid DOS partition table, nor Sun, SGI or OSF disklabel
Building a new DOS disklabel with disk identifier 0xd389fd89.
Changes will remain in memory only, until you decide to write them.
After that, of course, the previous content won't be recoverable.

Warning: invalid flag 0x0000 of partition table 4 will be corrected by w(rite)

WARNING: DOS-compatible mode is deprecated. It's strongly recommended to
         switch off the mode (command 'c') and change display units to
         sectors (command 'u').

Command (m for help): n
Command action
   e   extended
   p   primary partition (1-4)
p
Partition number (1-4): 1
First cylinder (1-2088, default 1):
Using default value 1
Last cylinder, +cylinders or +size{K,M,G} (1-2088, default 2088):
Using default value 2088

Command (m for help): w
The partition table has been altered!

Calling ioctl() to re-read partition table.
Syncing disks.
```

Repeat this process for all of the newly added drives. Once you are done, you will see them within `cat /proc/partitions`:

```
   8     192   16777216 sdm
   8     193   16771828 sdm1
   8     208   16777216 sdn
   8     209   16771828 sdn1
   8     224   16777216 sdo
```

```
8     225    16771828 sdo1
8     240    16777216 sdp
8     241    16771828 sdp1
65      0    16777216 sdq
65      1    16771828 sdq1
```

Once the new disk drives have been added to the operating system and partitioned, you are ready to move on to the next step, which is to add the disks to the ASM disk group(s).

Add Storage to the ASM Disk Group(s)

Before we demonstrate how to add storage to your ASM disk group, we will show you how to prepare a SQL script that you can use to watch the progress of your addition of disk drives to your disk group. In this case the SQL script is called diskgroup_info.sql and we've placed it in the /tmp directory on our Linux server. We will be running it as the grid user. Here are the contents of the SQL script:

```
column disk_group_name format a20;
column disk_file_path format a20;
column disk_file_name format a20;

SELECT
    NVL(a.name, '[CANDIDATE]')                    disk_group_name
--  , decode(a.type,'EXTERN','EXTERNAL',a.type)   disk_group_type
--  , a.compatibility                             asm_comp
--  , a.database_compatibility                    db_comp
  , b.path                                        disk_file_path
  , b.name                                        disk_file_name
--  , b.preferred_read                            pread
--  , b.voting_file                               vote
--  , b.failgroup                                 disk_file_fail_group
--  , b.failgroup_type                            fail_type
--  , b.mount_status                              mt_stat
--  , b.mode_status                               mode_stat
--  , b.state                                     state
  , b.total_mb                                    total_mb
--  , a.required_mirror_free_mb                   mirror_free_mb
  , (b.total_mb - b.free_mb)                      used_mb
  , CASE b.total_mb
      WHEN 0 THEN 0
      ELSE ROUND((1- (b.free_mb / b.total_mb))*100, 2)
    END pct_used
FROM
    v$asm_diskgroup a RIGHT OUTER JOIN v$asm_disk b USING (group_number)
WHERE
    a.name not like '%CAND%'
ORDER BY
    a.name, b.failgroup, b.path;
```

TIP & TECHNIQUE
If we were using redundancy groups or other advanced features, we would uncomment some of the lines. As is, we understand the configuration of the ASM disk groups and want a compact set of information. However, the complete query is provided for you.

Here is the output of the SQL script:

```
SQL> @/tmp/diskgroup_info

DISK_GROUP_NAME  DISK_FILE_PATH   DISK_FILE_NAME   TOTAL_MB  USED_MB   PCT_USED
---------------  ---------------  ---------------  --------  --------- --------
DATA             /dev/sdc1        DATA_0000        5114      3548      69.38
DATA             /dev/sdd1        DATA_0001        5114      3555      69.52
DATA             /dev/sde1        DATA_0002        5114      3547      69.36
DATA             /dev/sdf1        DATA_0003        5114      3554      69.5
DATA             /dev/sdg1        DATA_0004        5114      3551      69.44
DATA             /dev/sdh1        DATA_0005        5114      3548      69.38
DATA             /dev/sdi1        DATA_0006        5114      3550      69.42
DATA             /dev/sdj1        DATA_0007        5114      3555      69.52
RECO             /dev/sdk1        RECO_0000        5114      118       2.31
RECO             /dev/sdl1        RECO_0001        5114      122       2.39

10 rows selected.
```

The goal now is to add four 16GB disks to the DATA disk group. Since the disks will all be re-striped, it is more efficient to add all of the new disks at one time. In newer versions it is possible to postpone the re-striping. This could save time, however, you are not migrated until it is completed.

TIP & TECHNIQUE
Although this is a safe process and has been well tested, you should never perform such an operation without having first backed up your database.

There are a number of methods that can be used to add the disks, including OEM Cloud Control 12c or SQL statements. For this example let's use SQL statements.

TIP & TECHNIQUE
For the sake of documentation and consistency, we put the SQL into a SQL script.

The following is the contents of /tmp/add_disks.sql:

```
ALTER DISKGROUP DATA ADD DISK '/dev/sdm1' DISK '/dev/sdn1' DISK '/dev/sdo1' DISK
'/dev/sdp1';
```

Once the script is run, you can occasionally run /tmp/diskgroup_info.sql to watch the progress, as shown here:

```
SQL> @/tmp/add_disks

Diskgroup altered.

SQL> @/tmp/diskgroup_info

DISK_GROUP_NAME  DISK_FILE_PATH  DISK_FILE_NAME  TOTAL_MB  USED_MB  PCT_USED
---------------  --------------  --------------  --------  -------  --------
DATA             /dev/sdc1       DATA_0000          5114     3540     69.22
DATA             /dev/sdd1       DATA_0001          5114     3540     69.22
DATA             /dev/sde1       DATA_0002          5114     3540     69.22
DATA             /dev/sdf1       DATA_0003          5114     3539     69.20
DATA             /dev/sdg1       DATA_0004          5114     3538     69.18
DATA             /dev/sdh1       DATA_0005          5114     3540     69.22
DATA             /dev/sdi1       DATA_0006          5114     3537     69.16
DATA             /dev/sdj1       DATA_0007          5114     3542     69.26
DATA             /dev/sdm1       DATA_0008         16378       26       .16
DATA             /dev/sdn1       DATA_0009         16378       26       .16
DATA             /dev/sdo1       DATA_0010         16378       26       .16
DATA             /dev/sdp1       DATA_0011         16378       26       .16
RECO             /dev/sdk1       RECO_0000          5114      118      2.31
RECO             /dev/sdl1       RECO_0001          5114      122      2.39

14 rows selected.
```

The new disks are larger than the original disks, so more data will be added to them because Oracle ASM uses a proportional fill strategy. Eventually, the reconfiguration will be complete.

```
DISK_GROUP_NAME  DISK_FILE_PATH  DISK_FILE_NAME  TOTAL_MB  USED_MB  PCT_USED
---------------  --------------  --------------  --------  -------  --------
DATA             /dev/sdc1       DATA_0000          5114     1822     35.63
DATA             /dev/sdd1       DATA_0001          5114     1822     35.63
DATA             /dev/sde1       DATA_0002          5114     1823     35.65
DATA             /dev/sdf1       DATA_0003          5114     1822     35.63
DATA             /dev/sdg1       DATA_0004          5114     1823     35.65
DATA             /dev/sdh1       DATA_0005          5114     1822     35.63
DATA             /dev/sdi1       DATA_0006          5114     1822     35.63
DATA             /dev/sdj1       DATA_0007          5114     1823     35.65
DATA             /dev/sdm1       DATA_0008         16378     3460     21.13
DATA             /dev/sdn1       DATA_0009         16378     3460     21.13
DATA             /dev/sdo1       DATA_0010         16378     3461     21.13
DATA             /dev/sdp1       DATA_0011         16378     3460     21.13
RECO             /dev/sdk1       RECO_0000          5114      118      2.31
RECO             /dev/sdl1       RECO_0001          5114      122      2.39

14 rows selected.
```

The same process must be completed for the `RECO` disk group:

```
RECO          /dev/sdk1          RECO_0000          5114          118          2.31
RECO          /dev/sdl1          RECO_0001          5114          122          2.39
RECO          /dev/sdq1          RECO_0002          16378           3          .02
```

In this case, since `RECO` had not yet been used, the rebalance doesn't have much to balance. We are now ready to move on to the next stage, which is to remove the old disks.

Remove Old Disks from ASM Disk Group(s)

Once you have added all of the disks that you need to add, you will have a combination of old disks and new disks. The next step is to remove the old, unneeded disks from the disk group. As is true when adding disks, it is more efficient to remove as many disks at a time as you feel comfortable removing simultaneously. Be careful that you still have sufficient space.

As with the addition of disks, the removal of disks from a disk group can be done either with OEM Cloud Control 12*c* or with SQL statements. With the disk removal process, the disk name is used rather than the path. So, to remove the eight 5GB disks from our disk group, we use the following command:

```
ALTER DISKGROUP DATA
  DROP DISK DATA_0000
       DISK DATA_0001
       DISK DATA_0002
       DISK DATA_0003
       DISK DATA_0004
       DISK DATA_0005
       DISK DATA_0006
       DISK DATA_0007
       DISK DATA_0008
```

The output is shown in this example:

```
SQL> @/tmp/drop_disks

Diskgroup altered.

SQL> @/tmp/diskgroup_info
```

DISK_GROUP_NAME	DISK_FILE_PATH	DISK_FILE_NAME	STATE	TOTAL_MB	USED_MB	PCT_USED
DATA	/dev/sdc1	DATA_0000	DROPPING	5114	1327	25.95
DATA	/dev/sdd1	DATA_0001	DROPPING	5114	1328	25.97
DATA	/dev/sde1	DATA_0002	DROPPING	5114	1327	25.95
DATA	/dev/sdf1	DATA_0003	DROPPING	5114	1331	26.03
DATA	/dev/sdg1	DATA_0004	DROPPING	5114	1327	25.95
DATA	/dev/sdh1	DATA_0005	DROPPING	5114	1330	26.01
DATA	/dev/sdi1	DATA_0006	DROPPING	5114	1328	25.97
DATA	/dev/sdj1	DATA_0007	DROPPING	5114	1330	26.01

```
DATA            /dev/sdm1        DATA_0008        DROPPING 16378       4249        25.94
DATA            /dev/sdn1        DATA_0009        NORMAL   16378       4520        27.6
DATA            /dev/sdo1        DATA_0010        NORMAL   16378       4521        27.6
DATA            /dev/sdp1        DATA_0011        NORMAL   16378       4522        27.61
RECO            /dev/sdk1        RECO_0000        NORMAL    5114         52         1.02
RECO            /dev/sdl1        RECO_0001        NORMAL    5114         51         1
RECO            /dev/sdq1        RECO_0002        NORMAL   16378        140         .85

15 rows selected.
```

Notice that we have added back in the state column, which reflects the dropping status. This process should be repeated for the RECO disk group. You can use the diskgroup_info SQL script to validate. Eventually, all of the old disks will have been removed from the ASM disk group, as shown here:

```
DISK_GROUP_NAME  DISK_FILE_PATH   DISK_FILE_NAME   STATE     TOTAL_MB    USED_MB    PCT_USED
---------------- ---------------- ---------------- --------  ----------  ---------  --------
DATA             /dev/sdn1        DATA_0009        NORMAL    16378       9471       57.83
DATA             /dev/sdo1        DATA_0010        NORMAL    16378       9470       57.82
DATA             /dev/sdp1        DATA_0011        NORMAL    16378       9472       57.83
RECO             /dev/sdq1        RECO_0002        NORMAL    16378        237        1.45
```

After a quick validation, the only remaining task is to remove the disks from the system.

Validate

At this point it is always a good idea to validate the configuration and make sure that no other applications or OS processes are using the disks that you want to now remove.

TIP & TECHNIQUE
This step is important to ensure that you don't remove anything that you shouldn't.

Remove Old Storage from the System

Removing the old storage is a very delicate operation. It can adversely affect the operating system and potentially risk the stability of the system. It is usually good enough to remove the storage from the back-end SAN or NAS system and allow the OS to rescan when it is a convenient time to reboot the system. Some operating systems support dynamic removal of disk drives.

TIP & TECHNIQUE
My Oracle Support (MOS) Note 367445.1 provides a script to check the imbalance of disks in a diskgroup. Running this periodically can provide information on how well the diskgroups are balanced and if there is an issue.

Best Practices, Tips, and Techniques

The following list summarizes the best practices, tips, and techniques presented in this chapter, along with a few more.

Back Up Your Database   Do not attempt to migrate storage or add/remove storage without having an up-to-date backup.

Add/Remove Max Drives   Because the rebalance process moves data from the old drives and stripes across all of the drives in the new disk group at one time, it is more efficient to move as many disks at a time as you are comfortable moving simultaneously.

Any Migration Method Is Good   Whether you use SQL scripts or OEM Cloud Control 12c for ASM migration, the effect is the same. It doesn't matter which method you choose.

Document   Good documentation will improve the repeatability of tasks. It might be years before you do this type of migration again. Good documentation will make it easier the next time you do this.

Script SQL   Scripting SQL statements not only provides for repeatability but provides automatic documentation.

Monitor   Monitor the status of the migration using SQL statements or OEM.

Use SYSASM   To make changes to ASM via SQL statements or ASMCMD, you must log on as SYSASM, not as SYSDBA.

Install the Grid Infrastructure Using a Dedicated Grid OS User Account   Use a separate grid user for Clusterware/ASM installation, for separation of duties.

Partition Disks   Always create a single partition when adding drives to ASM or to logical volumes. This sends a signal to system admins that the drive is being used. ASM supports nonpartitioned disks.

Summary

If you simply need to move from one storage system to another and you are using ASM, you can migrate using the ASM migration method. It does not allow for any changes to the database or structure of the database—only to the storage system—but it avoids downtime and is easy to do. Although this might seem like a strange way to migrate a database, using this method is not uncommon when storage is your only concern.

PART

IV

Optimized Upgrades/ Migration

CHAPTER
11

Database Upgrade
Assistant

The Database Upgrade Assistant (DBUA) has been an integral part of Oracle upgrades for many years. This tool, which has been enhanced over the years, provides a guided method of assessing, planning, and implementing Oracle database upgrades. You take the DBUA from the version of Oracle Database that you are upgrading to and run it on the database that you are upgrading. This means that it is necessary to install the target database software on the system to be upgraded. Optionally, you can download the Oracle Database Pre-Upgrade Utility from My Oracle Support (https://support.oracle.com). It is provided as part of Doc ID 884522.1.

> **NOTE**
> *When using the DBUA to upgrade to an Oracle 12c database, this process upgrades to a traditional non-container database. Using container databases (CDBs) and pluggable databases (PDBs) is recommended with Oracle 12c databases. The DBUA currently does not provide an option for that.*

The DBUA is a graphical tool that guides you though the database upgrade process. You can either run this tool as part of the upgrade process or run it beforehand to provide information on the upcoming upgrade. The DBUA is used for upgrading a database. Since the Grid Infrastructure doesn't really have a database, the DBUA does not assist with that. Instead, the Grid Infrastructure is upgraded via the installation of the new version and is upgraded appropriately.

This chapter provides examples of the DBUA performing an upgrade from Oracle Database Version 11.2.0.4 to Oracle Database Version 12.1.0.2. Currently, the DBUA upgrades and 11g database to a traditional (non-container) database. This database can then be plugged into a CDB as a PDB if desired. Pluggable databases are recommended and is the future of Oracle databases.

Upgrade vs. Migration

What is the difference between an upgrade and a migration? Most of the methods that have been described so far are intended to move your database's data from one system to another. That is known as a migration. Some of the methods allowed for the version of the database to change. In a few chapters you will even see how to move from a non-Oracle database to an Oracle database.

A migration involves moving the data or database to a new platform. An upgrade involves transforming the database to a new version. A transformation involves enhancing the data itself. In this book there are migration chapters, upgrade chapters, and migration with upgrade/transformation chapters. In this chapter, where we are talking about an upgrade, all objects are upgraded, including the data dictionary.

The DBUA and associated tools are designed for upgrading a database. This is also known as an in-place upgrade. The database software and database are upgraded to a newer version, but the same physical data is maintained. This is particularly useful for very large databases. However, since the database is not copied, this will involve some downtime while the upgrade is being performed. In addition, if something goes wrong, the database might need to be restored.

TIP & TECHNIQUE
Before attempting any database upgrade, make sure that the database has been completely backed up and that the backup has been validated. This backup is your only chance of returning to services if the upgrade has an issue.

Upgrading the Grid Infrastructure

The Grid Infrastructure is entirely upgraded via the Oracle Upgrade process. Even though there are some databases embedded in the Grid Infrastructure, DBUA is not used to upgrade them. However, before you can proceed with upgrading the database using the DBUA, you must first upgrade the Grid Infrastructure and ASM. You do so by running the installer from the version that you want to upgrade to. The process will upgrade the Grid Infrastructure and ASM.

TIP & TECHNIQUE
It is not uncommon to upgrade the Grid Infrastructure and ASM during a different maintenance window than the one in which the database is upgraded. Running an older version of a database on a newer version of the Grid Infrastructure/ASM is always supported. You should, however, check with the Clusterware Compatibility document Doc ID 337737.1 on the My Oracle Support website.

Upgrading GI and Database at Separate Times

Whether you upgrade both the Grid Infrastructure/ASM and the database during the same maintenance window or upgrade them weeks or months apart does not change the upgrade process. However, from a personnel standpoint, you have two large tasks that take a lot of concentration. By splitting them up, you can ensure that you are fresh for each task and able to better focus on the task at hand. This will also reduce risk.

In addition, if you are migrating to Oracle Database 12c, separating the tasks gives you the opportunity to create the container database and some practice pluggable databases before the actual real upgrade, thus providing a degree of confidence.

To start the Grid Infrastructure and ASM upgrade process, download and unzip the Grid Infrastructure installation media. You can obtain it from either the Oracle website or the My Oracle Support website. This example shows how to upgrade from Oracle 11g version 11.2.0.4 to Oracle 12c version 12.1.0.2.

NOTE
Starting in Oracle 11.2.0.1, the Grid Infrastructure Oracle Home is now created as part of a separate installation. The process presented here is valid as of Oracle 11.2.0.2.

Next, invoke the **runInstaller** program to open the Oracle Grid Infrastructure Installer. You are met with the Select Installation Option screen, shown in Figure 11-1. The default selection should be Upgrade Oracle Grid Infrastructure Or Oracle Automatic Storage Management. If it is not, then the Installer has not detected an existing Grid Infrastructure or ASM and you cannot proceed with the installation until it can be detected properly.

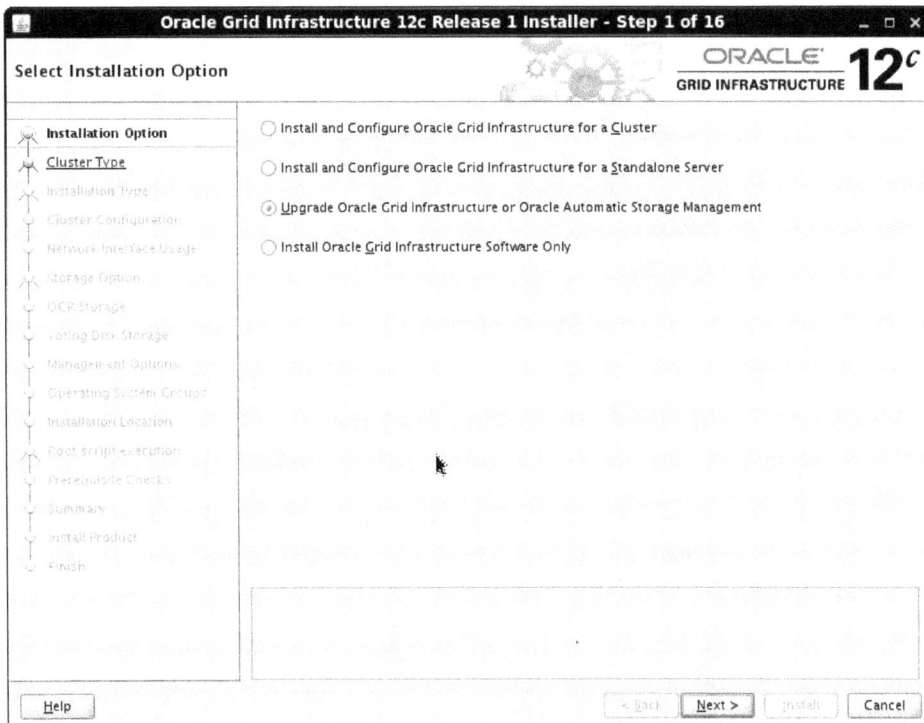

FIGURE 11-1. *Select Installation Option screen*

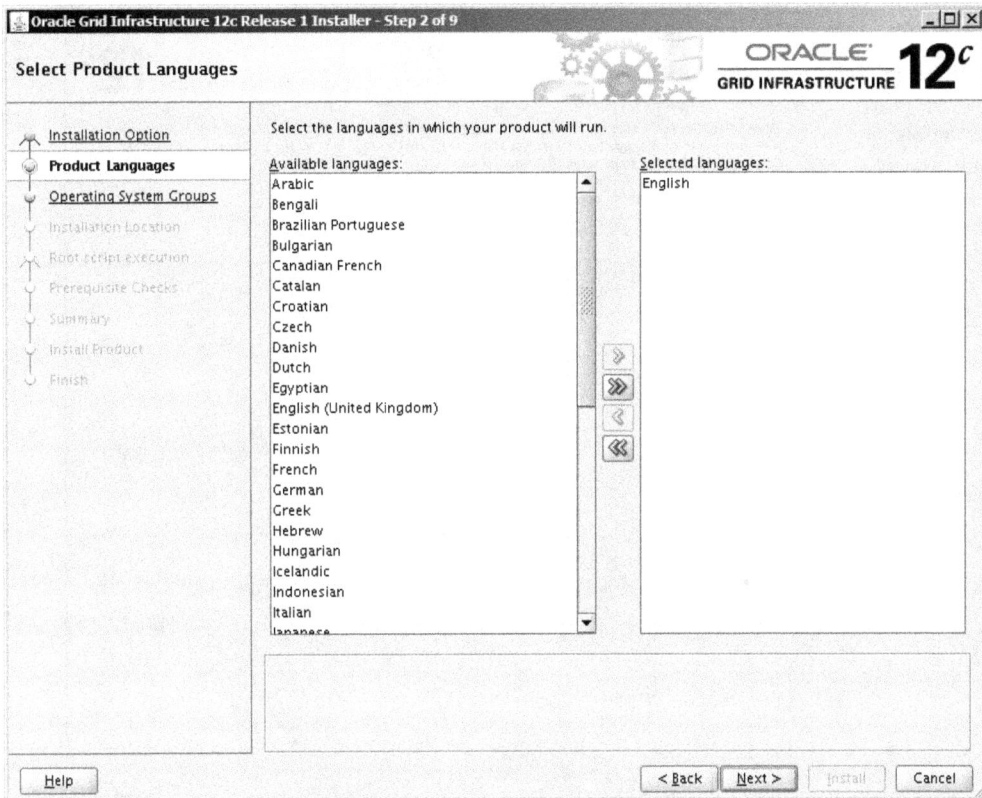

FIGURE 11-2. *Select Product Languages screen*

After confirming the default selection to upgrade, click the Next button to move to the Select Product Languages screen, shown in Figure 11-2. This is the language that is used for messages from the database.

After you select the language, click Next to move to the Specify Management Options screen, shown in Figure 11-3. If you have an Oracle Enterprise Manager Cloud Control 12c system, you can register it here. This step is optional. You can always register later. Using OEM Cloud Control to manage and monitor your Grid Infrastructure is recommended. Click Next to continue.

TIP & TECHNIQUE
We always recommend that you register with OEM Cloud Control 12c after the database has been installed and configured.

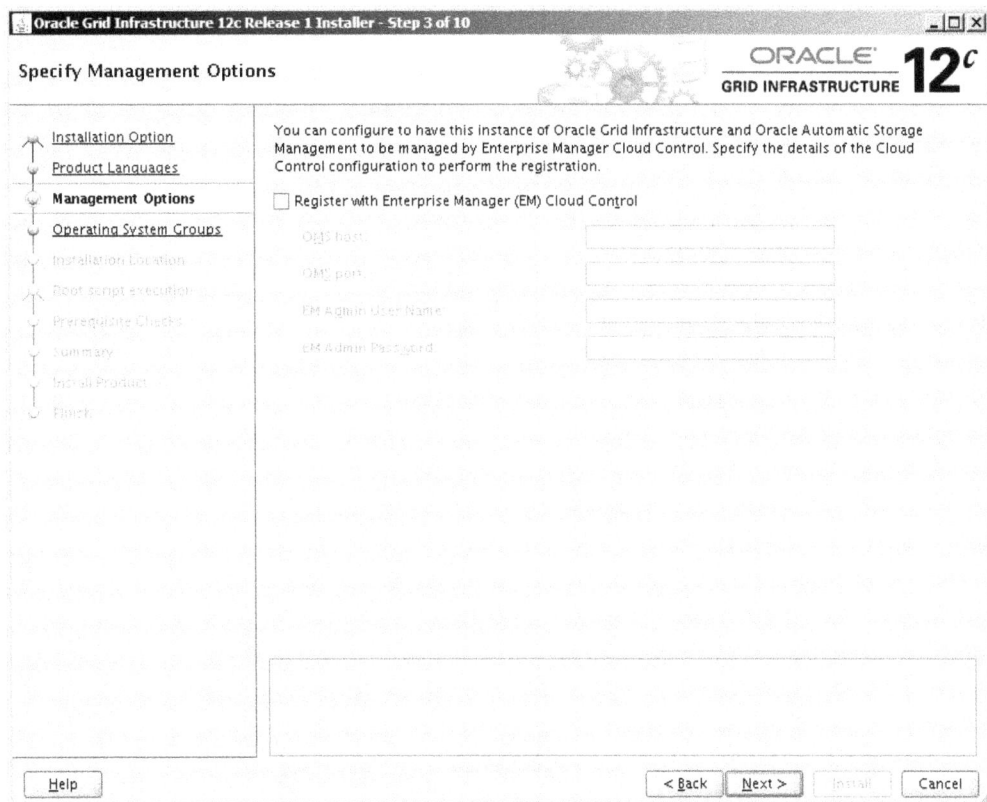

FIGURE 11-3. *Specify Management Options screen*

The Privileged Operating Systems Groups screen, shown in Figure 11-4, is where you set up the group privileges for ASM. The Grid Infrastructure has its own privileged groups that are managed by either `root` or the `grid` user that you have chosen.

TIP & TECHNIQUE
It is now considered best practice to create the Grid Infrastructure under a non-Oracle group such as "grid." Using the Oracle account is supported if your organization is small and one person is responsible for the operating systems, Grid Infrastructure/ASM, and Database.

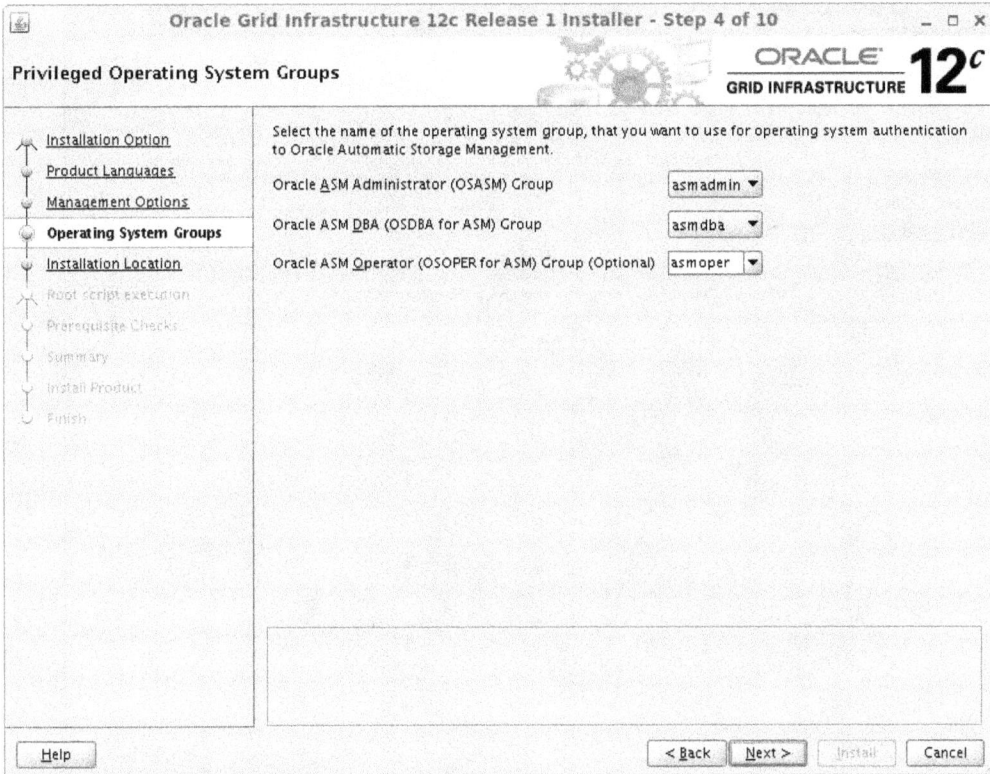

FIGURE 11-4. *Privileged Operating Systems Groups screen*

After you select the privileged operating system groups, click Next to move to the Specify Installation Location screen. The default location is /u01/app/12.1.0/grid for a new Grid Infrastructure installation. For an upgrade, it will put the location in an area similar to the existing Oracle Home. In this case, /u01/app/grid/product/12.2.0/grid, but we prefer to add that fourth digit of the version number so that we can specify the exact release. So, our directory is /u01/app/grid/product/12.1.0.2/grid, as shown in Figure 11-5.

NOTE
The Oracle Home installation location for the Grid Infrastructure is not under the Oracle Base directory.

Click Next to continue.

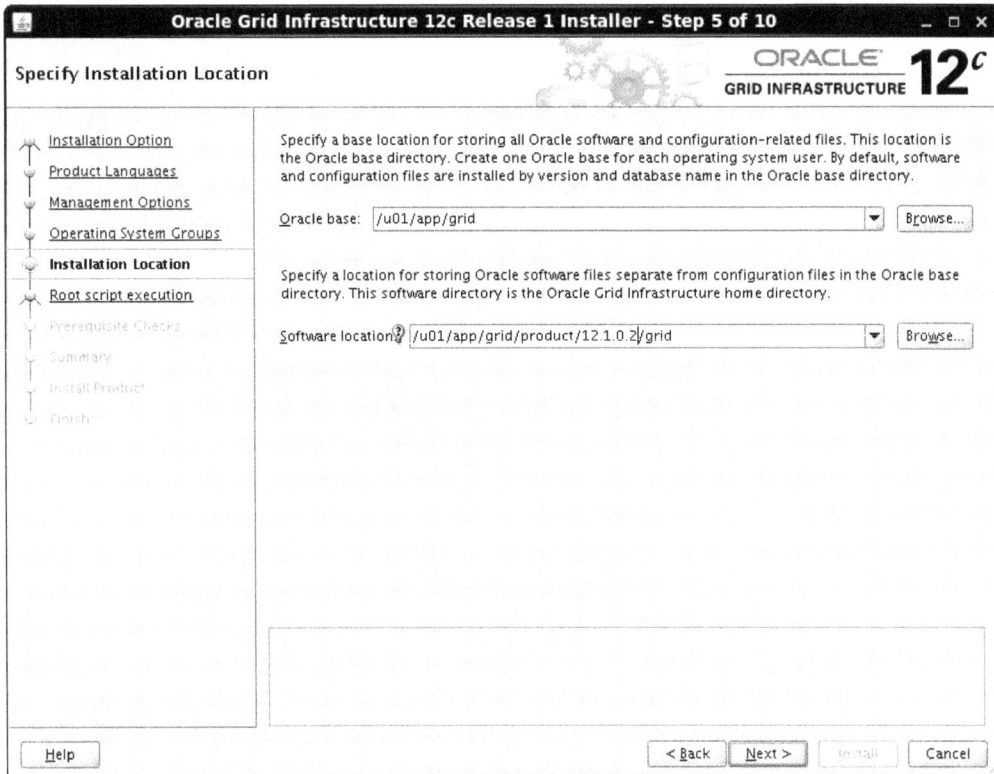

FIGURE 11-5. *Specify Installation Location screen*

The next screen allows you to set up automatic execution of the `root.sh` script after the installation has completed. You can either skip this screen and run `root.sh` later, enter the root password, or specify sudo for the grid user as shown here in Figure 11-6. Click Next when you are done.

Next, the Perform Prerequisites Checks screen indicates that automatic checks are being run to ensure that the target environment meets the minimum installation

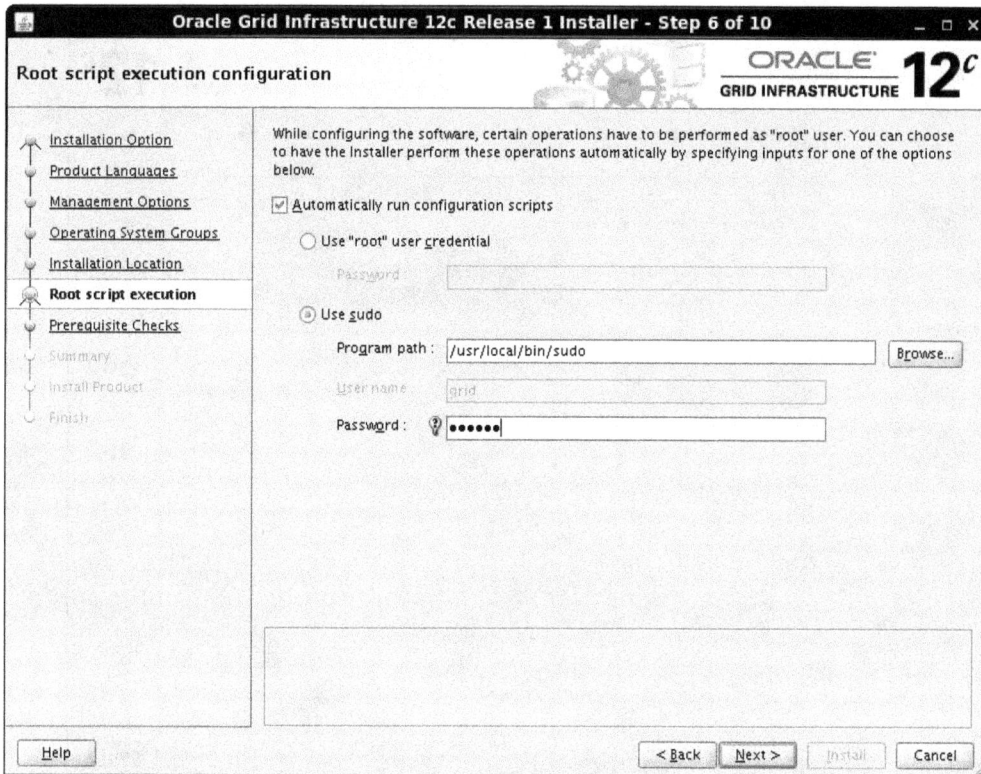

FIGURE 11-6.   *Root Script Execution Configuration screen*

and configuration requirements, as shown in Figure 11-7. Once the checks have completed, you will see the results of those checks on the same screen, as shown in Figure 11-8. Here you can ignore the problem (if you know it is okay) or if the problem is fixable, click the Fix & Check Again button.

If you click Fix & Check Again, you will see the Fixup Script pop-up box, as shown in Figure 11-9. Run the specified script as root and click OK. Then click the Next button.

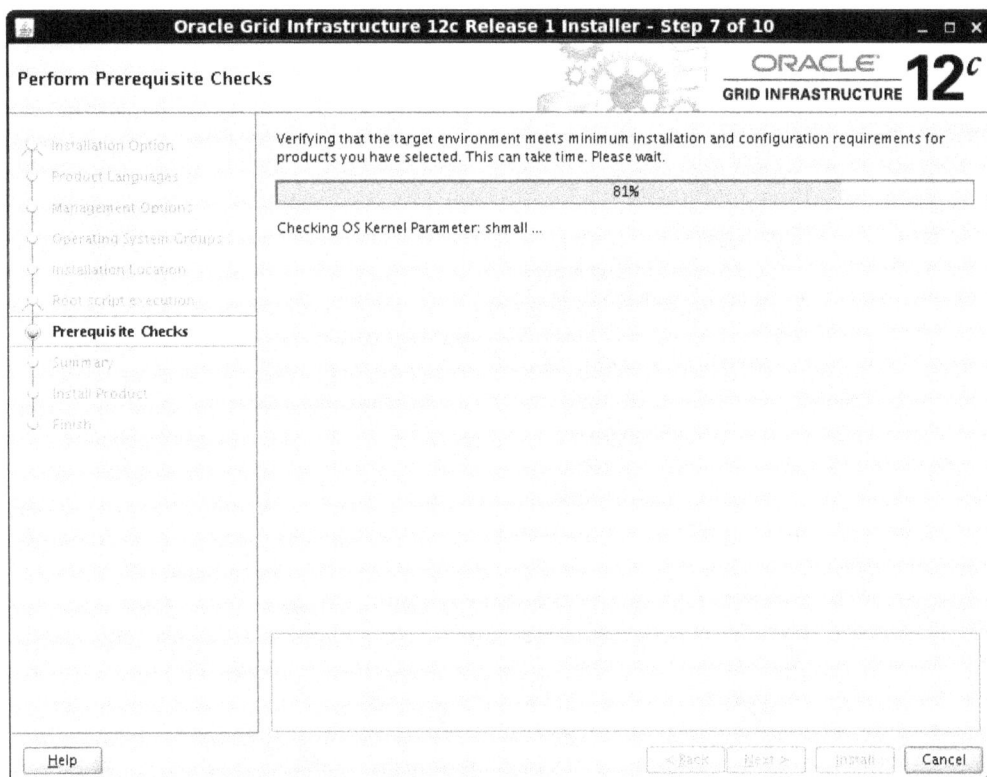

FIGURE 11-7. *Initial Perform Prerequisite Checks screen*

This will bring you to the Summary screen, shown in Figure 11-10. Click Install to proceed with the Grid Infrastructure/ASM upgrade.

You can watch the progress of the installation on the Install Product screen, as shown in Figure 11-11. This example is a stand-alone system, but in a RAC cluster both nodes would be installed. The upgrade of the OCR and ASM instance is done via the `root.sh` script. Since we specified credentials for `root.sh` in this example,

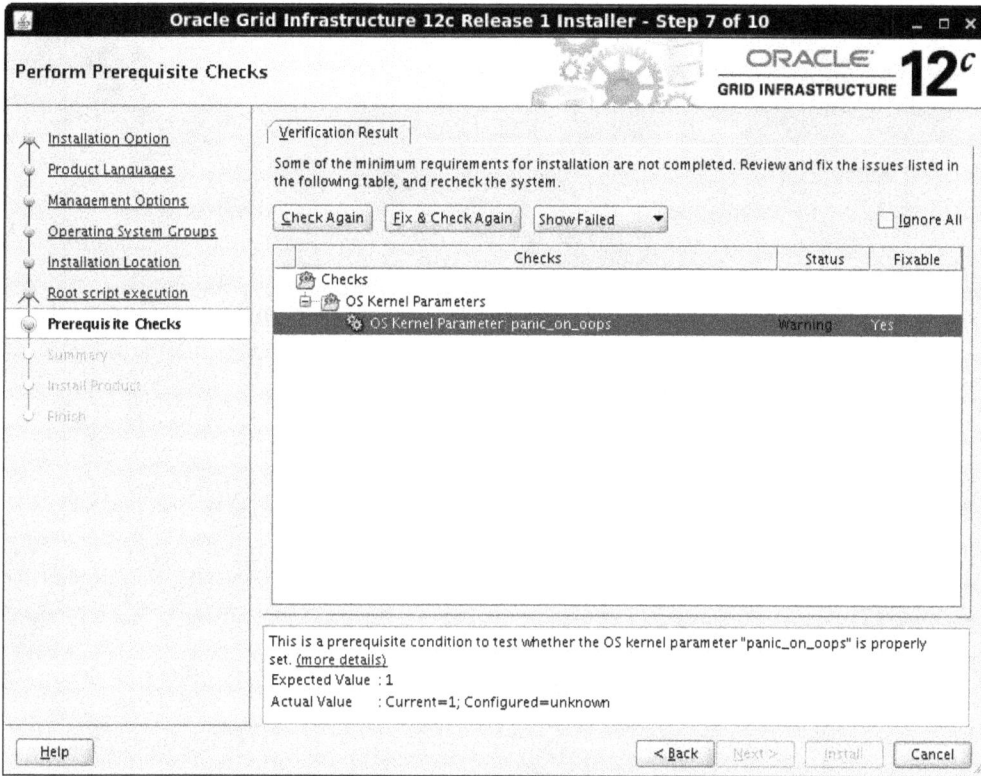

FIGURE 11-8. *Perform Prerequisite Checks results screen*

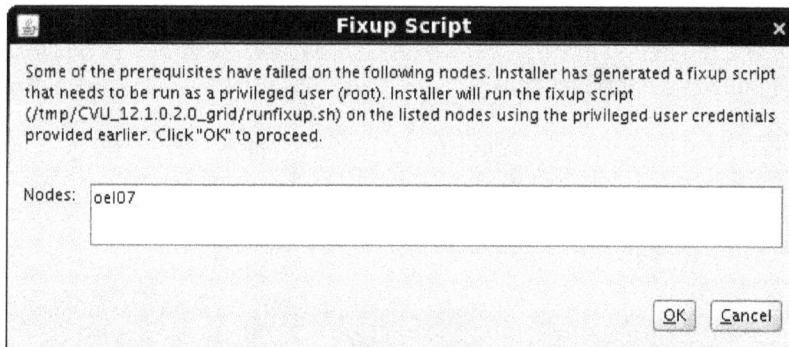

FIGURE 11-9. *Fixup Script pop-up box*

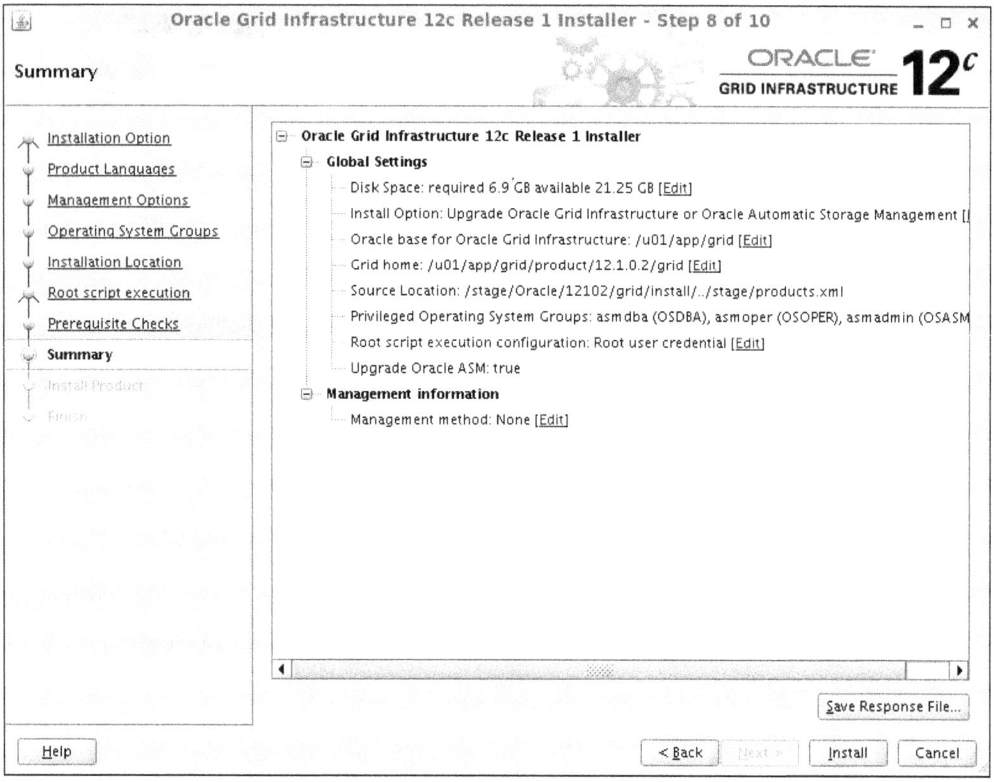

FIGURE 11-10. *Summary screen*

we will not be prompted for them; rather, a pop-up will ask if we want the Installer to run them. If you did not set that up, you would be prompted via a pop-up box to run root.sh, and then the installation would proceed. This installation process will take several minutes.

Once the installation has completed, you will see the Finish screen, shown in Figure 11-12, which tells you that the upgrade process has completed. You have finished the Grid Infrastructure/ASM upgrade. As mentioned earlier, in a RAC cluster, this can be done dynamically in a rolling fashion.

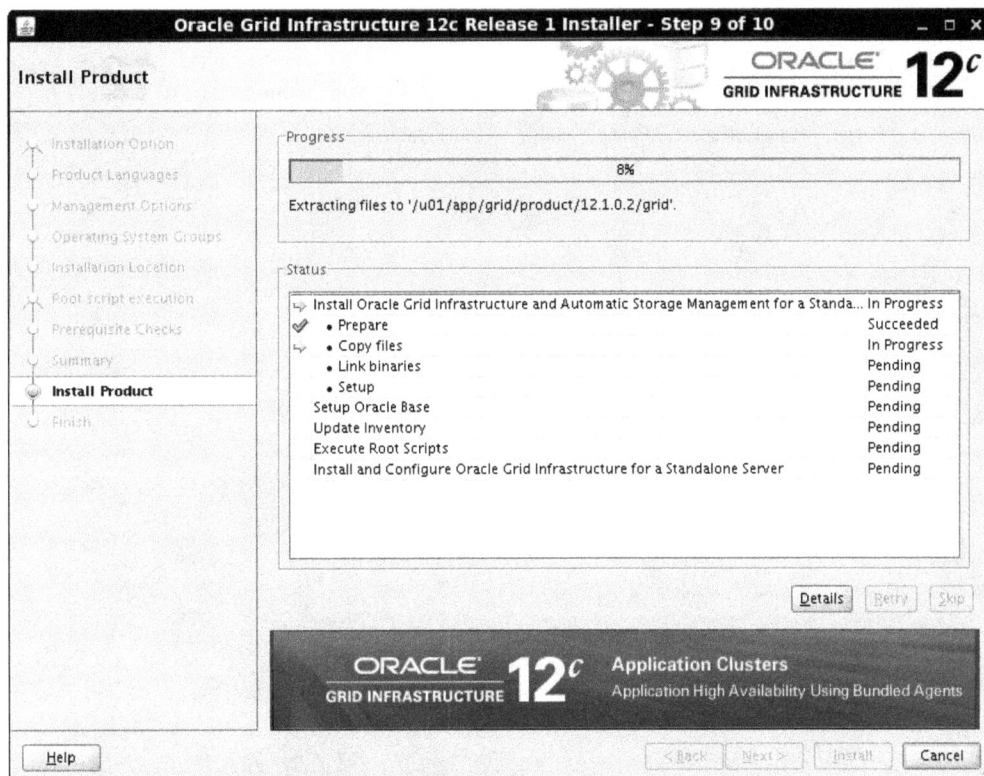

FIGURE 11-11.   *Install Product screen*

TIP & TECHNIQUE

It is a good idea to check to make sure the cluster processes are running before proceeding. We prefer to use the `crsctl status resource -t` *to see if all of the services are up and running on all nodes.*

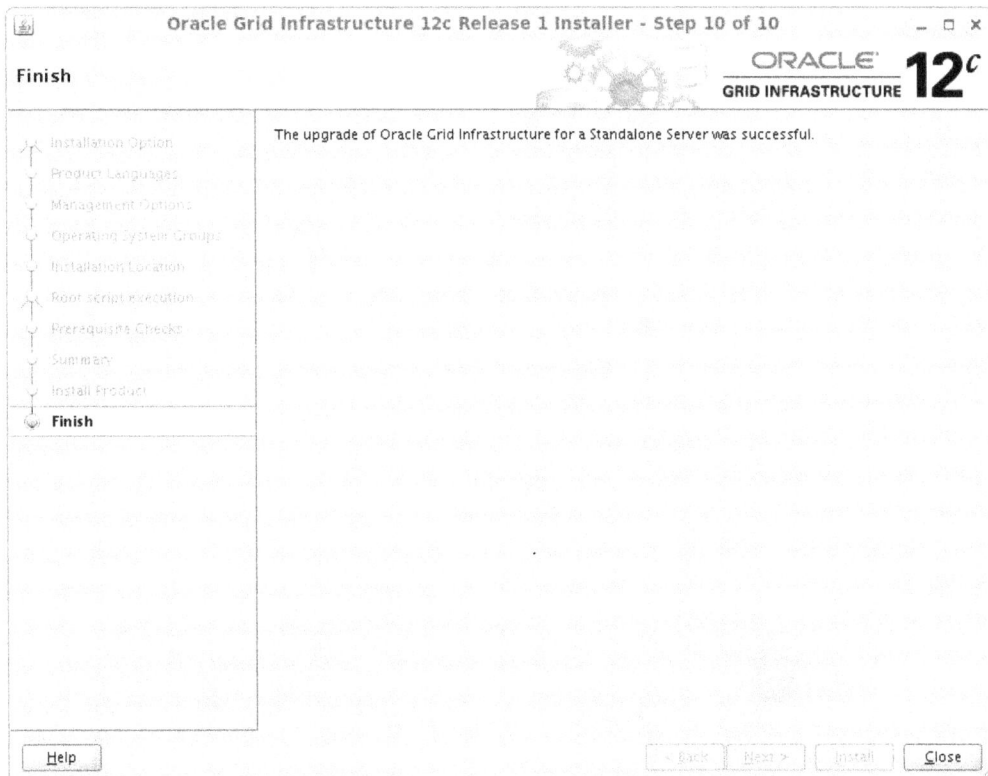

FIGURE 11-12. *Finish screen*

Installing the New Database Software

Before you can use the DBUA, you must install it. Just as you did with the Grid Infrastructure/ASM, you must unzip and install the software using the Oracle Installer. At this point we would recommend doing the software-only installation. The steps for installing the Oracle software will not be shown here.

TIP & TECHNIQUE

We prefer to use the full release number in the Oracle Home path. So, rather than the default of /u01/app/oracle/product/12.1.0/dbhome_1, we will use the directory /u01/app/oracle/product/12.1.0.2/ dbhome_1. After you have installed the Oracle software (version 12.1.0.2), you will have access to the DBUA.

Using the Database Upgrade Assistant to Plan an Upgrade

Before you even attempt to run the DBUA, it is useful to run the pre-upgrade scripts in order to analyze your database. You can find these scripts in the rdbms/admin directory in the new software installation directory. These scripts are `preupgrd.sql` and `utluppkg.sql`.

> **NOTE**
> *preupgrd.sql will run utluppkg.sql. You will only run preupgrd.sql.*

Running preupgrd.sql

You should run the pre-upgrade script as part of your planning process, well in advance of any upgrade, so that you have an idea of what needs to be done to prepare for the upgrade. So, how do you do this? One method is to install the Oracle software on a test system of the same architecture and copy the script to your current system. If you have a quality assurance (QA) or user acceptance testing (UAT) system, you can test and pre-check that system rather than the production system if you have the same exact database installed.

Running the Pre-Upgrade Script

Once you have copied the pre-check script, or have installed the new Oracle software, you can run them. The pre-check script provides valuable information as to what needs to be done prior to the upgrade.

Run Script

So, once you are ready and have copied or installed the new Oracle Home, run the `preupgrd.sql` script as sysdba, as shown here:

```
[oracle@oel07 admin]$ sqlplus / as sysdba @preupgrd

SQL*Plus: Release 11.2.0.4.0 Production on Sun Sep 7 08:31:51 2014

Copyright (c) 1982, 2013, Oracle.  All rights reserved.

Connected to:
Oracle Database 11g Enterprise Edition Release 11.2.0.4.0 - 64bit Production
With the Partitioning, Automatic Storage Management, OLAP, Data Mining
and Real Application Testing options


Loading Pre-Upgrade Package...
```

```
*****************************************************************************
Executing Pre-Upgrade Checks in TESTDB...
*****************************************************************************


            ************************************************************


                    ====>> ERRORS FOUND for TESTDB <<====

    The following are *** ERROR LEVEL CONDITIONS *** that must be addressed
                    prior to attempting your upgrade.
             Failure to do so will result in a failed upgrade.

            You MUST resolve the above errors prior to upgrade


            ************************************************************


            ************************************************************


                    ====>> PRE-UPGRADE RESULTS for TESTDB <<====

ACTIONS REQUIRED:

1. Review results of the pre-upgrade checks:
 /u01/app/oracle/cfgtoollogs/testdb/preupgrade/preupgrade.log

2. Execute in the SOURCE environment BEFORE upgrade:
 /u01/app/oracle/cfgtoollogs/testdb/preupgrade/preupgrade_fixups.sql

3. Execute in the NEW environment AFTER upgrade:
 /u01/app/oracle/cfgtoollogs/testdb/preupgrade/postupgrade_fixups.sql

            ************************************************************


*****************************************************************************
Pre-Upgrade Checks in TESTDB Completed.
*****************************************************************************


*****************************************************************************
*****************************************************************************
```

The result of this are three files, a log file, a pre-upgrade fixup SQL script, and a post-upgrade SQL script. The output of the log file is shown here:

```
[oracle@oel07 admin]$ cat /u01/app/oracle/cfgtoollogs/testdb/preupgrade/preupgrade.log
Oracle Database Pre-Upgrade Information Tool 09-07-2014 08:32:07
Script Version: 12.1.0.2.0 Build: 006
******************************************************************
   Database Name:  TESTDB
  Container Name:  Not Applicable in Pre-12.1 database
    Container ID:  Not Applicable in Pre-12.1 database
         Version:  11.2.0.4.0
      Compatible:  11.2.0.4.0
       Blocksize:  8192
        Platform:  Linux x86 64-bit
   Timezone file:  V14
******************************************************************
```

```
                        [Update parameters]
        [Update Oracle Database 11.2.0.4.0 init.ora or spfile]

--> If Target Oracle is 32-bit, refer here for Update Parameters:
WARNING: --> "processes" needs to be increased to at least 300

--> If Target Oracle is 64-bit, refer here for Update Parameters:
WARNING: --> "processes" needs to be increased to at least 300
************************************************************************
************************************************************************
                        [Renamed Parameters]
                 [No Renamed Parameters in use]
************************************************************************
************************************************************************
                   [Obsolete/Deprecated Parameters]
            [No Obsolete or Desupported Parameters in use]
************************************************************************
                          [Component List]
************************************************************************
--> Oracle Catalog Views                  [upgrade]  VALID
--> Oracle Packages and Types             [upgrade]  VALID
--> JServer JAVA Virtual Machine          [upgrade]  VALID
--> Oracle XDK for Java                   [upgrade]  VALID
--> Oracle Workspace Manager              [upgrade]  VALID
--> OLAP Analytic Workspace               [upgrade]  VALID
--> Oracle Enterprise Manager Repository  [upgrade]  VALID
--> Oracle Text                           [upgrade]  VALID
--> Oracle XML Database                   [upgrade]  VALID
--> Oracle Java Packages                  [upgrade]  VALID
--> Oracle Multimedia                     [upgrade]  VALID
--> Oracle Spatial                        [upgrade]  VALID
--> Expression Filter                     [upgrade]  VALID
--> Rule Manager                          [upgrade]  VALID
--> Oracle Application Express            [upgrade]  VALID
--> Oracle OLAP API                       [upgrade]  VALID
************************************************************************
                          [Tablespaces]
************************************************************************
--> SYSTEM tablespace is adequate for the upgrade.
     minimum required size: 1248 MB
--> SYSAUX tablespace is adequate for the upgrade.
     minimum required size: 1429 MB
--> UNDOTBS1 tablespace is adequate for the upgrade.
     minimum required size: 400 MB
--> TEMP tablespace is adequate for the upgrade.
     minimum required size: 60 MB

                    [No adjustments recommended]

************************************************************************
************************************************************************
                       [Pre-Upgrade Checks]
************************************************************************
WARNING: --> Process Count may be too low

    Database has a maximum process count of 150 which is lower than the
```

```
    default value of 300 for this release.
    You should update your processes value prior to the upgrade
    to a value of at least 300.
    For example:
       ALTER SYSTEM SET PROCESSES=300 SCOPE=SPFILE
    or update your init.ora file.

WARNING: --> Enterprise Manager Database Control repository found in the database

    In Oracle Database 12c, Database Control is removed during
    the upgrade. To save time during the Upgrade, this action
    can be done prior to upgrading using the following steps after
    copying rdbms/admin/emremove.sql from the new Oracle home
  - Stop EM Database Control:
   $> emctl stop dbconsole

  - Connect to the Database using the SYS account AS SYSDBA:

    SET ECHO ON;
    SET SERVEROUTPUT ON;
    @emremove.sql
      Without the set echo and serveroutput commands you will not
      be able to follow the progress of the script.

INFORMATION: --> OLAP Catalog(AMD) exists in database

    Starting with Oracle Database 12c, OLAP Catalog component is desupported.
    If you are not using the OLAP Catalog component and want
    to remove it, then execute the
    ORACLE_HOME/olap/admin/catnoamd.sql script before or
    after the upgrade.

INFORMATION: --> Older Timezone in use

    Database is using a time zone file older than version 18.
    After the upgrade, it is recommended that DBMS_DST package
    be used to upgrade the 11.2.0.4.0 database time zone version
    to the latest version which comes with the new release.
    Please refer to My Oracle Support note number 977512.1 for details.

INFORMATION: --> There are existing Oracle components that will NOT be
    upgraded by the database upgrade script.  Typically, such components
    have their own upgrade scripts, are deprecated, or obsolete.
    Those components are:  OLAP Catalog,OWB

INFORMATION: --> Oracle Application Express (APEX) can be
    manually upgraded prior to database upgrade

    APEX is currently at version 3.2.1.00.12 and will need to be
    upgraded to APEX version 4.2.5 in the new release.
    Note 1: To reduce database upgrade time, APEX can be manually
            upgraded outside of and prior to database upgrade.
    Note 2: See MOS Note 1088970.1 for information on APEX
            installation upgrades.
```

```
**************************************************************************
                    [Pre-Upgrade Recommendations]
**************************************************************************


                ******************************************
                ********* Dictionary Statistics *********
                ******************************************

Please gather dictionary statistics 24 hours prior to
upgrading the database.
To gather dictionary statistics execute the following command
while connected as SYSDBA:
    EXECUTE dbms_stats.gather_dictionary_stats;

^^^ MANUAL ACTION SUGGESTED ^^^


**************************************************************************
                    [Post-Upgrade Recommendations]
**************************************************************************


                ******************************************
                ******** Fixed Object Statistics ********
                ******************************************

Please create stats on fixed objects two weeks
after the upgrade using the command:
    EXECUTE DBMS_STATS.GATHER_FIXED_OBJECTS_STATS;

^^^ MANUAL ACTION SUGGESTED ^^^

**************************************************************************
                ************ Summary ************

0 ERRORS exist in your database.
2 WARNINGS that Oracle suggests are addressed to improve database performance.
4 INFORMATIONAL messages that should be reviewed prior to your upgrade.

After your database is upgraded and open in normal mode you must run
rdbms/admin/catuppst.sql which executes several required tasks and completes
the upgrade process.

You should follow that with the execution of rdbms/admin/utlrp.sql, and a
comparison of invalid objects before and after the upgrade using
rdbms/admin/utluiobj.sql

If needed you may want to upgrade your timezone data using the process
described in My Oracle Support note 1509653.1
                **************************************
```

The output of the `preupgrd.sql` script provides really valuable information on how to prepare your database for the upcoming upgrade. As you will see in the next section, the DBUA provides the exact same feedback. In fact, we believe it runs the same script. However, when you run the DBUA, it is probably late in the upgrade cycle, so you really want to run the `preupgrd.sql` script a significant time in advance.

Fix Issues

The output of the `preupgrd.sql` script has listed two WARNING items: the `PROCESSES` setting needs to be increased to at least 300 and the Enterprise Manager Database Control repository needs to be removed. The following addresses these two issues:

```
SQL> alter system set PROCESSES=300 scope=spfile;
SQL>   SET ECHO ON;
SQL>   SET SERVEROUTPUT ON;
SQL>   @/emremove.sql
```

NOTE
This can also be accomplished via `emca -deconfig dbconsoledb -repos drop`*.*

There are also several optional items that can be resolved. We decided to go ahead and remove the OLAP catalog before proceeding with the upgrade:

```
SQL>   @?/olap/admin/catnoamd.sql
```

The recycle bin needs to be purged and/or disabled prior to upgrade. We will do both by purging and setting the recycle bin off as shown in the following example:

```
SQL> EXECUTE dbms_preup.purge_recyclebin_fixup;
SQL> alter system set recyclebin=off scope=spfile;
```

Once we have completed these items, we will restart the database and run the prerequisite checks again.

TIP & TECHNIQUE
If you choose to upgrade Oracle Application Express (APEX) during the DBUA database upgrade, the upgrade will take longer. You can upgrade APEX prior to running the DBUA. This is recommended.

Running the Database Upgrade Utility Scripts

We recommend running the DBUA in two phases. The first phase, covered in this section, analyzes the database, does prerequisite checks, and provides you with options on how to proceed with the upgrade. At that point you might have to stop and perform some fixes in your database to avoid an extended upgrade period. The second phase, covered in the next section, performs the actual upgrade.

Invoke the DBUA from the `$ORACLE_HOME/bin` directory of the newly installed Oracle database software (version 12.1.0.2) by running the following command:

```
/u01/app/oracle/product/12.1.0.2/dbhome_1/bin/dbua
```

The first DBUA screen, shown in Figure 11-13, allows you to select the operation: either upgrade Oracle Database or move a database to a new home directory of the same release.

Once you have installed Oracle Database 12.1.0.2, you can run the DBUA from the `$ORACLE_HOME`/bin directory. Select Upgrade Oracle Database and click Next to proceed to the next screen.

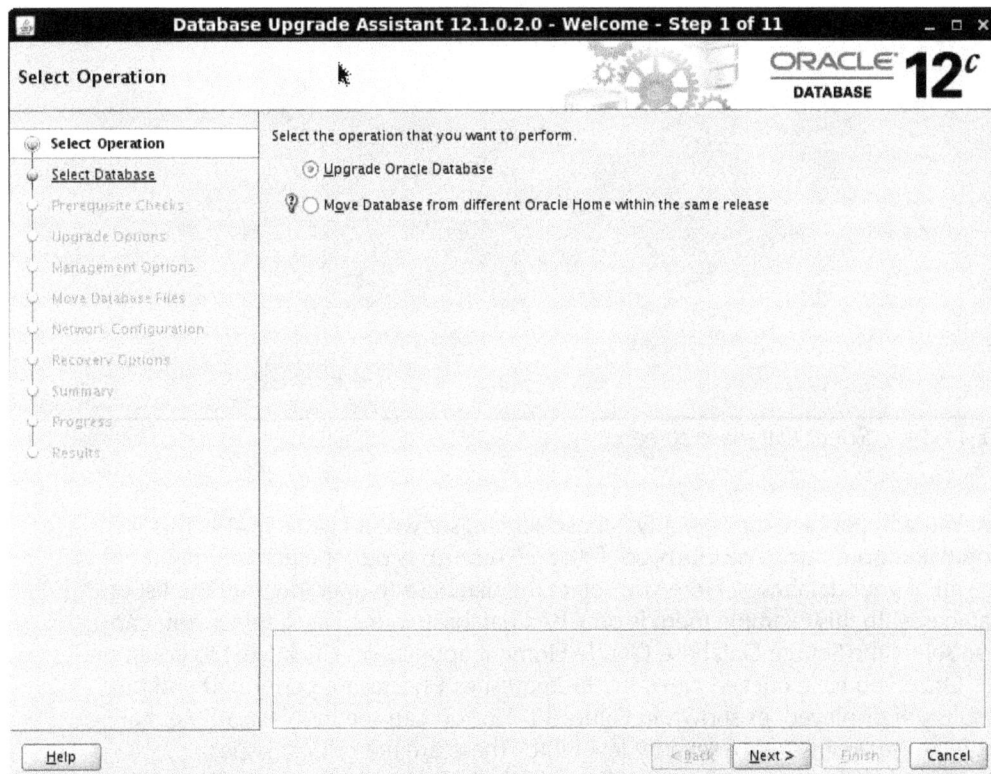

FIGURE 11-13. *Select Operation screen*

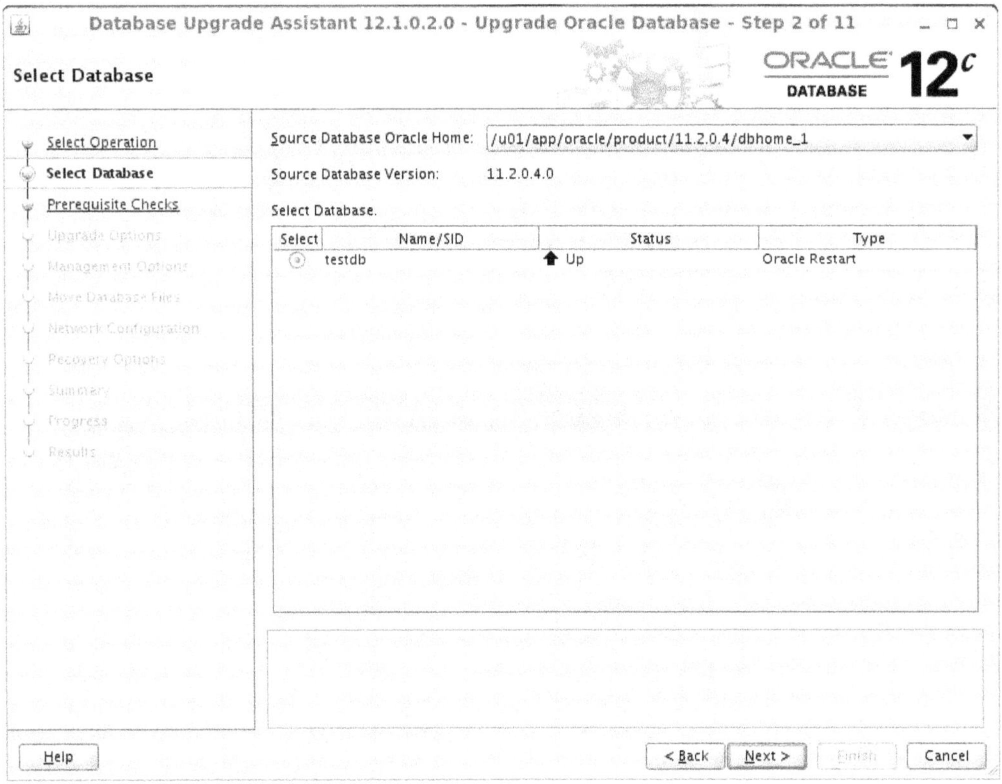

FIGURE 11-14. *Select Database screen*

You will now see the Select Database screen, shown in Figure 11-14. This is populated from /etc/oratab, so if /etc/oratab is out of date, you might not see all of your databases. Here you select the database to upgrade from the list of databases. In this example there is only one database in the list to select. You can also select the Source Database Oracle Home if applicable. Click Next to continue.

Once you have clicked Next, the Prerequisites Checks are performed and the results are displayed, as shown in Figure 11-15. You can see in this example that there are several issues of severity level Info. These are not critical issues.

You can select any of the items listed in the Validation column and then click the More Details link in the bottom window to see more information on the

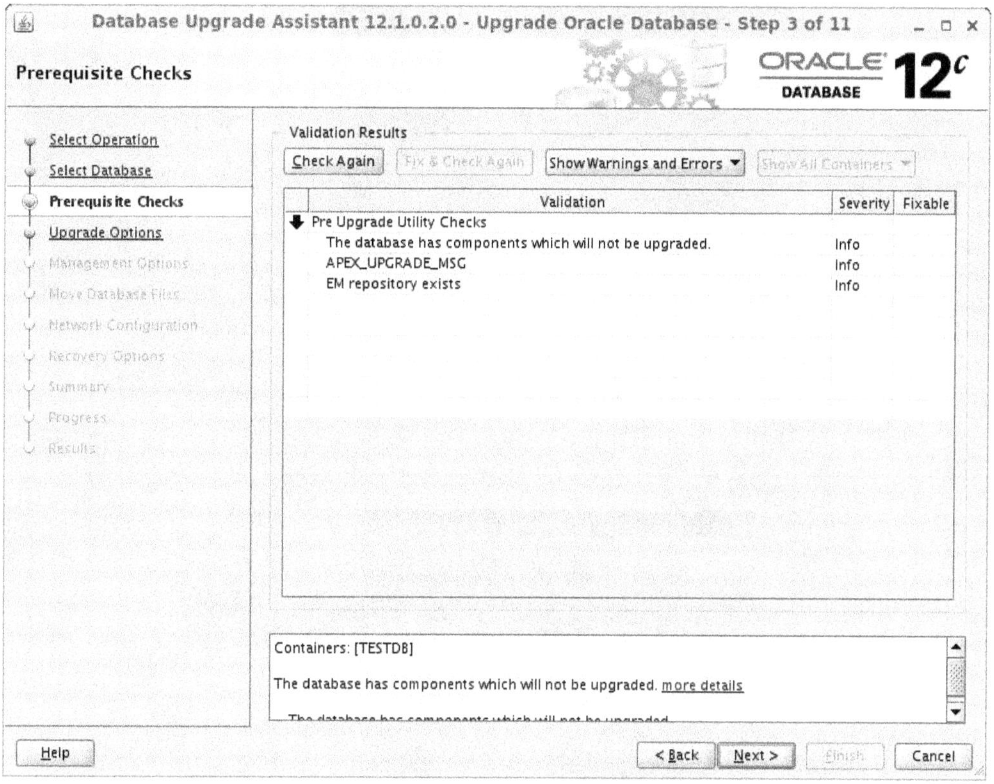

FIGURE 11-15.   *Prerequisite Checks screen*

particular issue in a pop-up window. Examples of this are shown in Figures 11-16, 11-17, and 11-18.

At this point in the upgrade you will most likely want to stop, assess the results of the prerequisites checks, and make any changes that are appropriate to your configuration. In the example shown here there are several items to be fixed.

If you ran the `preupgrd.sql` script prior to running the DBUA and have already addressed the issues contained in that output, you should have no upgrade issues at this point and can proceed immediately to the upgrade.

FIGURE 11-16. *Validation Details screen, first example*

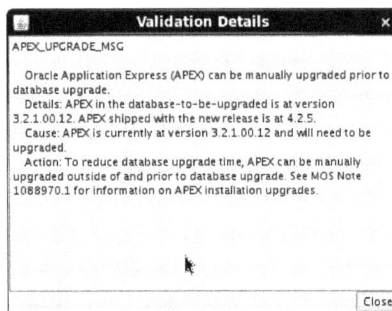

FIGURE 11-17. *Validation Details screen, second example*

FIGURE 11-18. *Validation Details screen, third example*

Using the Database Upgrade Assistant to Perform an Upgrade

Once you have taken care of the prerequisites that you chose not to do as part of the DBUA process itself, you can restart the DBUA and proceed to the Upgrade Options screen, as shown in Figure 11-19. Here you can choose what additional steps you want to perform as part of the upgrade.

In addition to the default chosen option to recompile invalid objects, we will choose the Upgrade Timezone Data option for purposes of this example. We will not choose to gather statistics because the process takes too much time. The second tab gives you the option to specify custom SQL scripts. You can also set user tablespaces to READ ONLY during the upgrade so that they can still be accessed.

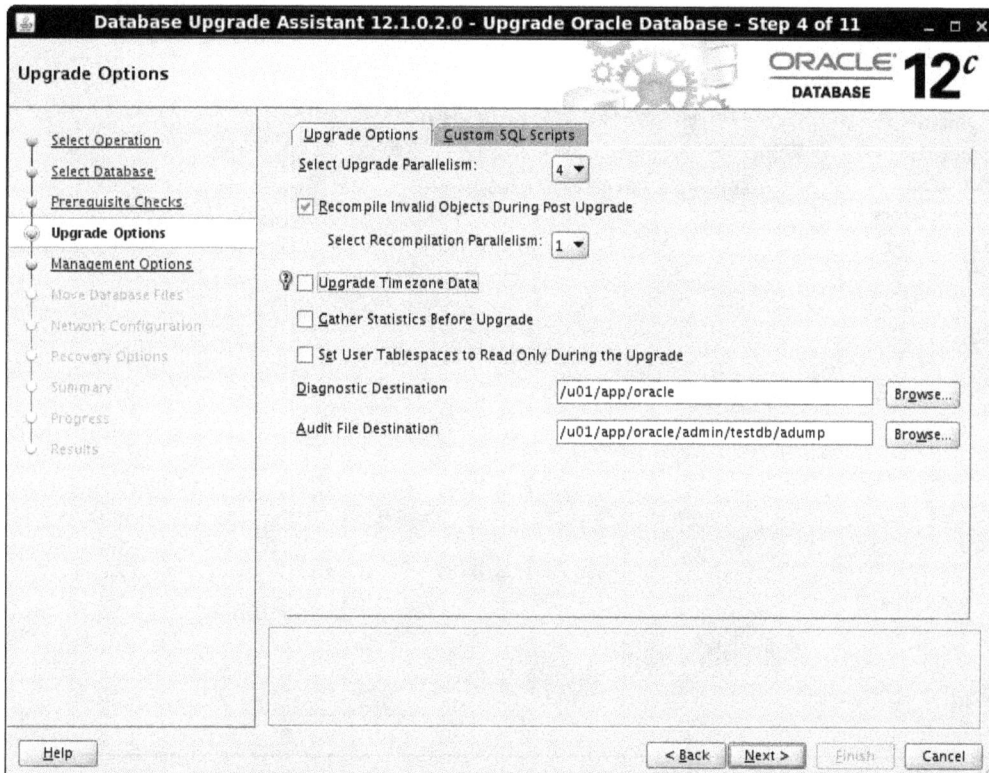

FIGURE 11-19.   *Upgrade Options screen*

TIP & TECHNIQUE

If you are worried about execution plans that might be problematic after the upgrade, you can save SQL Tuning Sets from Oracle Enterprise Manager or from SQL statements. If you ever needed to use an old plan, they are saved in the tuning set. Using SQL Plan Baselines you can import the saved plans and force them to be used.

Clicking Next takes you to the Management Options screen. As shown in Figure 11-20, we have unchecked the Configure Enterprise Manager (EM) Database

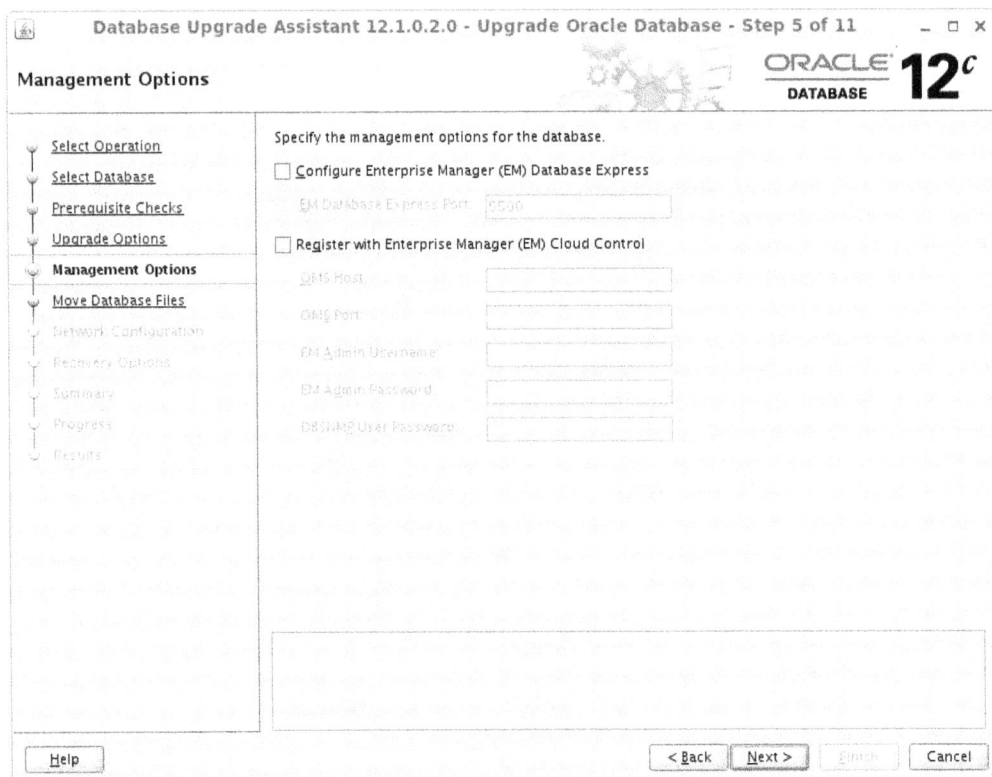

FIGURE 11-20. *Management Options screen*

Express box since we will be using OEM Database 12*c* Cloud Control. Click Next to continue.

On the Move Database Files screen you can specify whether or not you want to move the database files during the upgrade. If you decide to move the files, you can specify whether to go to or from ASM, move disk groups, or leave everything the same. As shown in Figure 11-21, we have chosen not to move database files. Click Next to proceed.

On the Network Configuration screen, shown in Figure 11-22, you can select the Oracle listener for the upgrade or even create a new listener. Remember, the

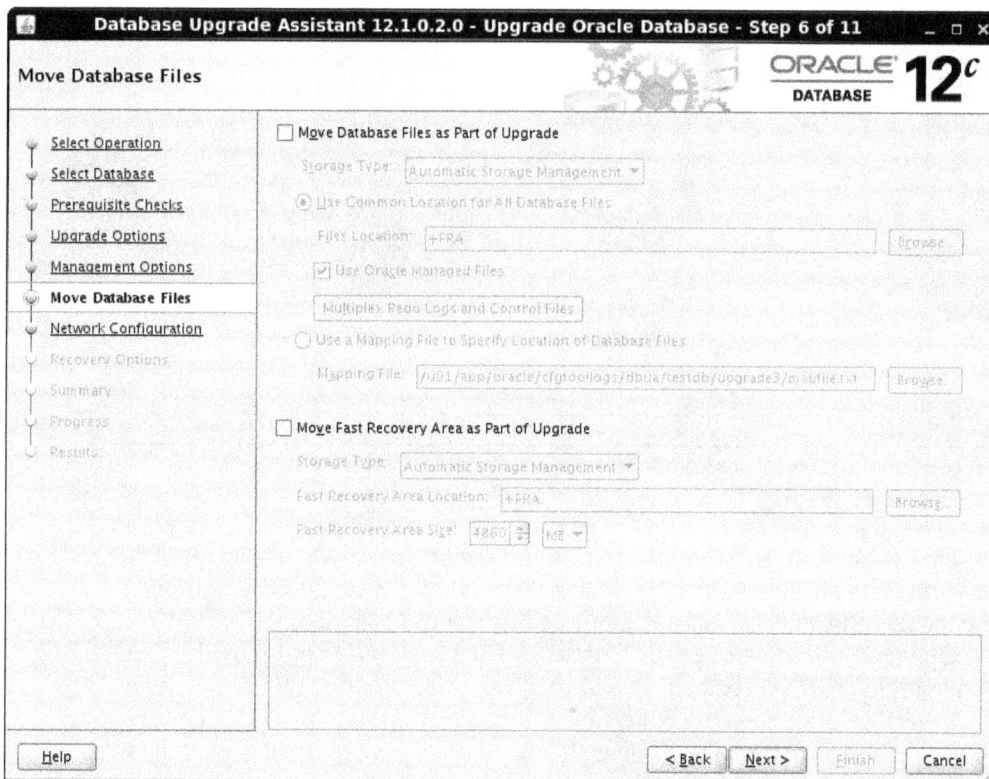

FIGURE 11-21. *Move Database Files screen*

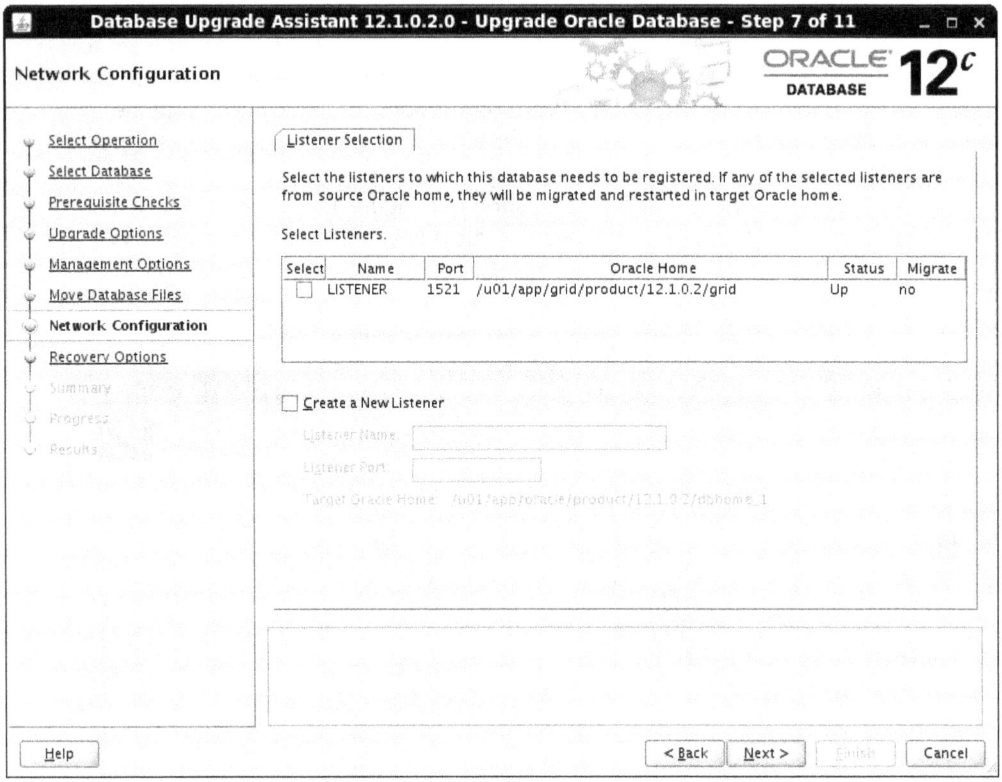

FIGURE 11-22. *Network Configuration screen*

Oracle listener resides in the Grid Infrastructure directory if you're using RAC or ASM. You can always reconfigure the Listener later if desired and needed. We are leaving the listener as is in this example. Click Next to continue.

One really nice feature of the Oracle 12.1.0.2 DBUA is that it provides you the option to do an RMAN backup as part of the upgrade process. This is shown on the Recovery Options screen in Figure 11-23. You can create a new RMAN Offline Backup or use Flashback Database with a guaranteed restore point or skip. If you are using storage with snapshot technology, that is also a good option. Depending on the size of the database, the RMAN backup could take a long time.

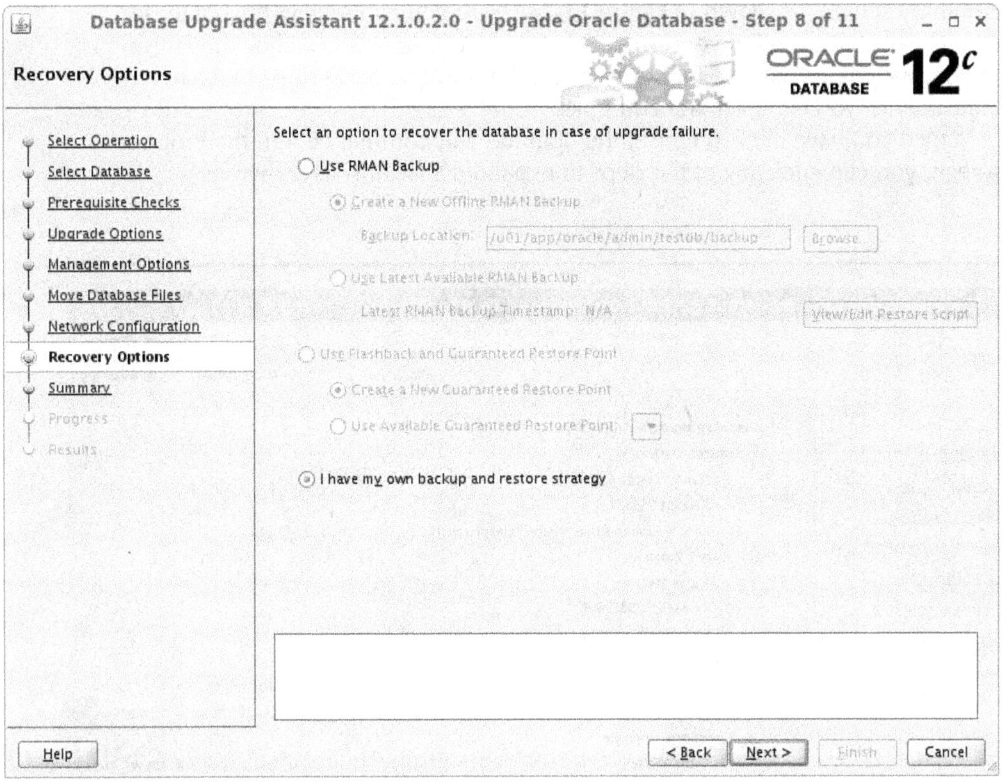

FIGURE 11-23.   *Recovery Options screen*

We are skipping the backup in this example; however, you should make sure that you have a back-out plan.

> **TIP & TECHNIQUE**
> *There is an inherent risk to an in-place upgrade. If something goes wrong, you must be able to return to the previous state. When doing a zero or near-zero downtime migration using GoldenGate, we often reverse replication so that our old system is available for failback. In an in-place upgrade, this option is not available. Having a backup and restore strategy in place is critical before starting the upgrade.*

Upon clicking Next in the Recovery Options screen, you are taken to the Summary screen, as shown in Figure 11-24. Here you can review the database upgrade summary and, if you are satisfied with your selections, click the Finish button, which prompts the DBUA to begin the backup. If you need to make any adjustments, you can click the Edit links.

Once you have clicked Finish, the upgrade will commence. On the Progress screen, you can click any of the steps to expand the details, as shown in

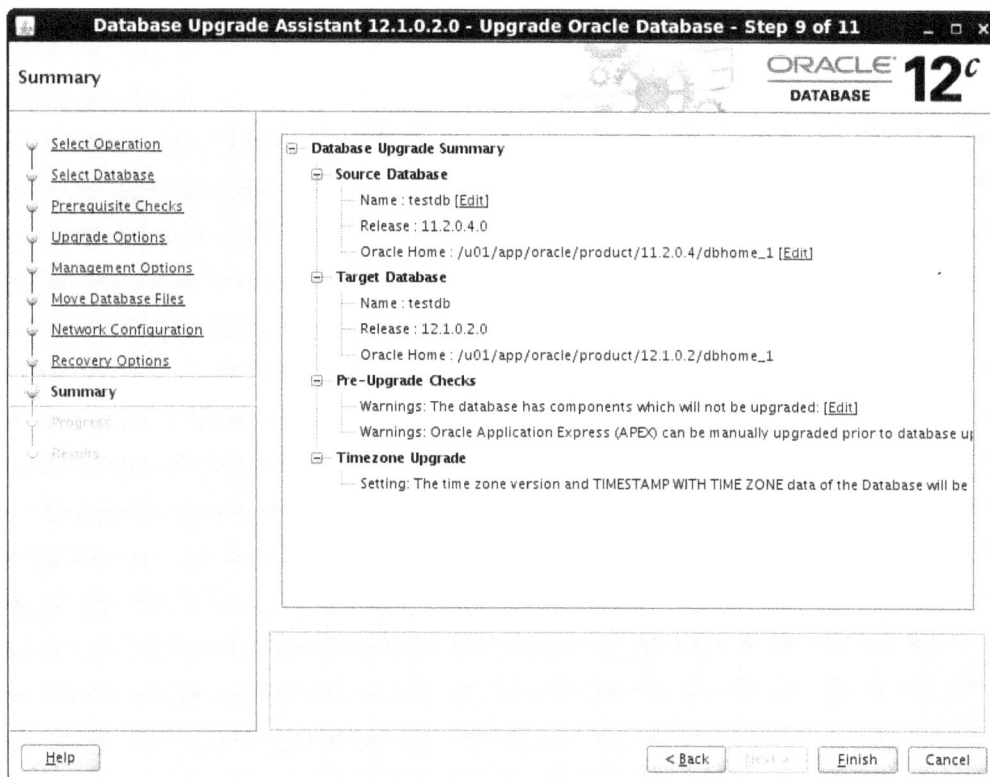

FIGURE 11-24. *Summary screen*

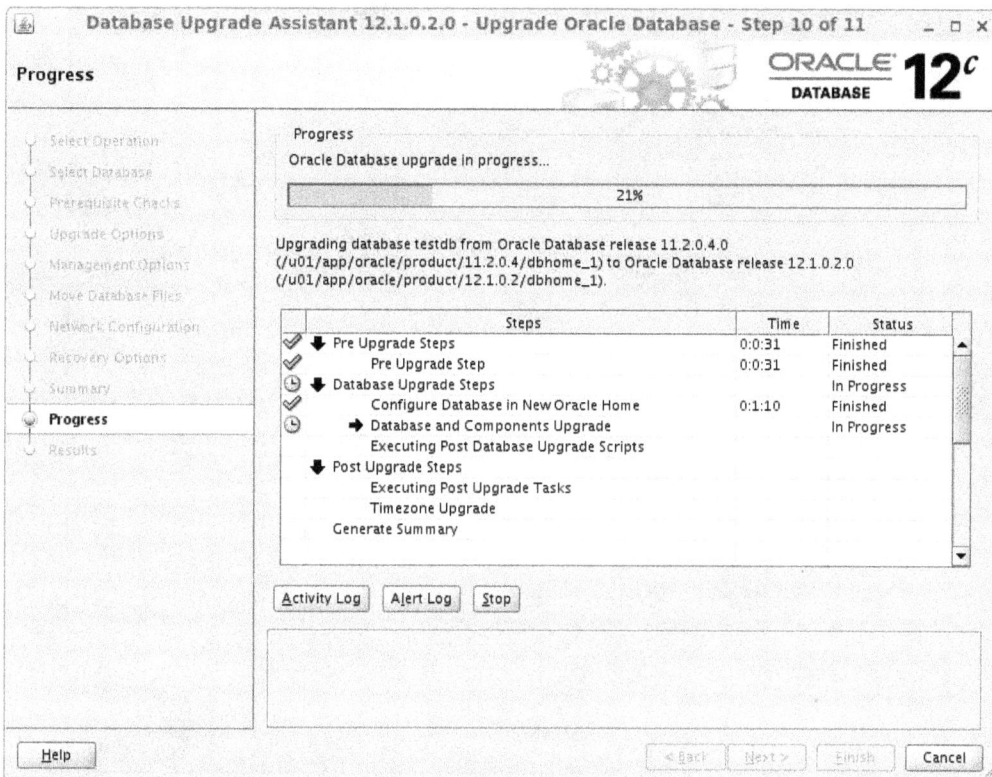

FIGURE 11-25.   *Progress screen*

Figure 11-25. Depending on the type of system that you have, this upgrade could take some time. You can expand and scroll down and watch the progress as the upgrade runs. Timings for each step are displayed in the Time column.

Once the upgrade has completed, you will see the completed Progress screen, as shown in Figure 11-26. This completes the upgrade from an 11.2.0.4 database to a 12.1.0.2 database using the Database Upgrade Assistant.

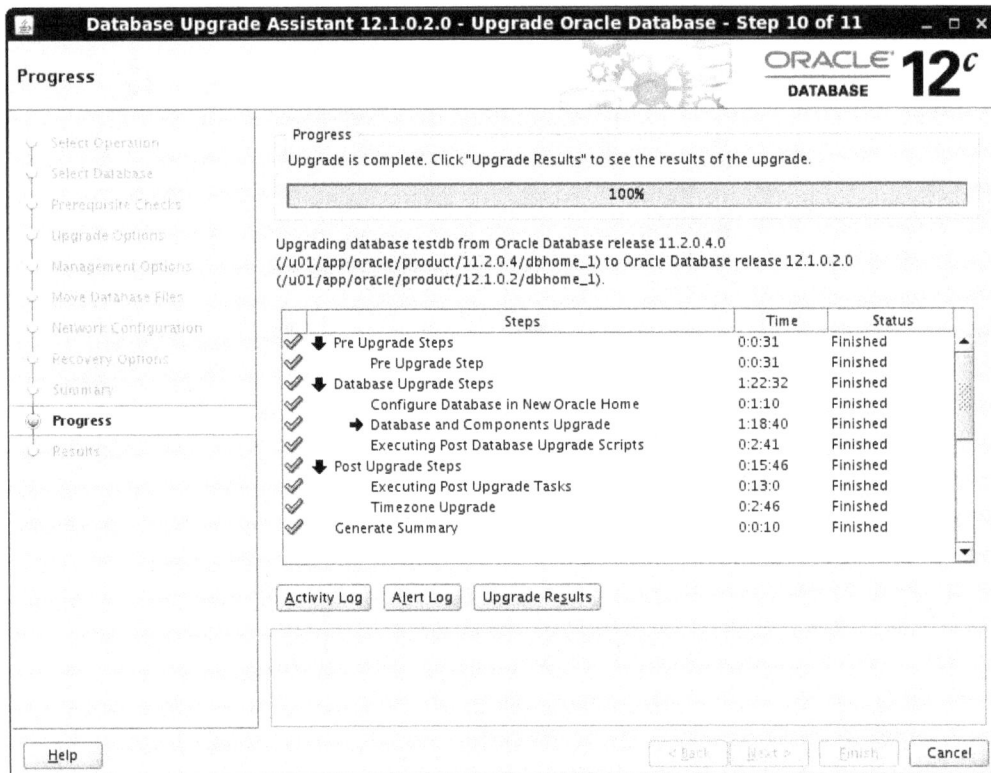

FIGURE 11-26. *Completed Progress screen*

Notice, however, that the only active button at the bottom of the screen is Cancel. To finish the upgrade, click the Upgrade Results button. You will see the Results screen, shown in Figure 11-27, where the Cancel button has changed to Close.

If you are not satisfied with the upgrade results, you can click the Restore Settings Only button to revert the Oracle Home. If you performed a backup, that option is available to you to use as well. If you are satisfied with the upgrade, click the Close button and you can proceed to use your newly upgraded database.

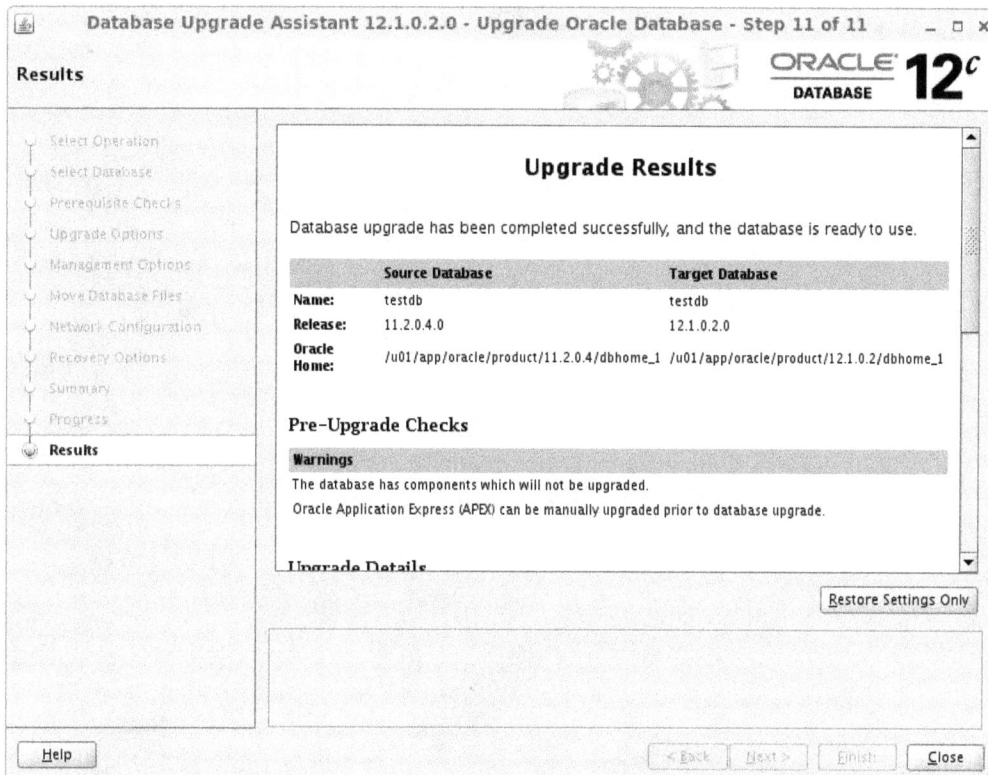

FIGURE 11-27. *Results screen*

Summary

This chapter has described how to perform an in-place upgrade using the DBUA. To upgrade a database that uses the Grid Infrastructure/ASM, that component must be upgraded first, as shown in this chapter. Then the DBUA can be used to upgrade the database itself.

The upgrade methodology just covered illustrates how to upgrade an existing pre-12c database to a traditional Oracle database in 12c—what is now termed a non-container database. Note that if the source database is at least at version 11.2.0.3, it is also possible to simultaneously migrate and upgrade a pre-12c database to a 12c PDB using Oracle 12c Data Pump's new Full Transportable Export (FTE) utility. Chapter 13 will explore FTE and several other methods to complete migration of a pre-12c Oracle database to a PDB.

CHAPTER
12

Migrating from Microsoft
SQL Server to Oracle

As we saw back in Chapter 8, Oracle GoldenGate provides a method of migrating from one Oracle system to another Oracle system with little or no downtime. In addition to enabling you to migrate from an Oracle database to another Oracle database, GoldenGate enables you to perform cross-platform migrations from any supported GoldenGate platform to any other GoldenGate platform. In this chapter, you will see how to migrate from Microsoft SQL Server to Oracle using GoldenGate. The process is essentially the same general process described in Chapter 8, so some material is repeated here, but there are also a few major differences.

TIP & TECHNIQUE

Using GoldenGate allows you to complete the migration from SQL Server to Oracle with very little downtime.

Because SQL Server and Oracle have many basic differences, a direct initial copy of data is not possible, so a different process must be used. However, the same general steps of starting replication, migrating the data, and then synchronizing are similar.

Introduction to Oracle GoldenGate

As mentioned in Chapter 8, GoldenGate Software was founded in 1995 and was acquired by Oracle in 2009. GoldenGate is a leading heterogeneous replication technology that is used for many different purposes, including data migration.

Uses of Oracle GoldenGate

One of the strengths of GoldenGate is that, as a heterogeneous replication technology, the source and target database technologies may be different. That includes different database vendors and products, operating systems, and even different endianess. (See the Oracle website or My Oracle Support for supported platforms.) GoldenGate can be used in a number of different configurations including unidirectional (one source, one target), bidirectional (source replicates to target and target replicates back to source), mesh (multiple systems replicating to each other), broadcast (one source, multiple targets), and consolidation (multiple sources, one target). GoldenGate can either be end-to-end or cascade. In this chapter, we will specifically be discussing using GoldenGate to replicate between SQL Server and Oracle in a unidirectional fashion (or bidirectional for zero downtime migrations).

How Does GoldenGate Work?

GoldenGate replication works by capturing log information from the source platform and mining (extracting and filtering) that information. In this case, we are talking about the SQL Server transaction log. The mined log information is transformed into INSERT, UPDATE, and DELETE statements, which are then applied on the target database.

> **NOTE**
> *Depending on the target type, some statements might not be supported; for example, some targets might only support INSERT.*

Which method you should use to read the transaction log will vary based on your own individual configuration and requirements. The available log reading options will vary based on the database that you are running and your version of Oracle GoldenGate. GoldenGate can be used for replication between SQL Server and SQL Server or between SQL Server and any other supported database. For a complete list of supported databases (and other, non-database targets), go to the Oracle website and check out the Downloads | MiddleWare | GoldenGate section.

> **NOTE**
> *For the latest updates, you should always check the My Oracle Support website under the Patches section.*

GoldenGate Components

GoldenGate consists of three different processes that control various parts of overall replication:

- **Manager**   The controlling process.

- **Extract**   The process that reads data from a data source and writes it to the GoldenGate trail file.

- **Replicat**   The process that reads trail file data and writes it to the target database. (The word *replicate* is shortened to *replicat* in GoldenGate because of the original eight-character legacy.)

As described next, each of these processes work together to move data from one system/database to another.

Manager Process

The manager process is the controlling process of the GoldenGate system. The manager process is also responsible for starting the collector process, which does not show up in GoldenGate but can be seen in the OS processes. The collector process is the process that receives data from the pump process (see the next section). It is possible, and sometimes necessary, to create multiple manager processes.

Extract Process

The extract process is responsible for taking data from a data source (such as the Oracle redo log files) and writing that data into the GoldenGate trail file. The GoldenGate trail file is a platform-independent, GoldenGate-specific file that contains transactional information from the source. The extract can source its data from many different sources, such as database log files or other trail files.

Best practice is to set up a GoldenGate system with two extracts. The first extracts data from the source database and writes the trail file locally. The second extract is used to take that trail file as its source and write it to the target system. This second extract is known as the *pump process*. By writing the first trail file locally, there is little chance of interrupting log mining in the event of a network error.

It is only possible to support about 250 extract and/or replicat processes per manager. Because SQL Server is often created with multiple databases, this might be an issue. If you have more than 250 processes, simply create a second manager to support those processes. As previously stated, it is possible to have multiple manager processes.

> **NOTE**
> *The manager process is registered as a Windows Service on the SQL Server side. The MGRSVRNAME parameter is placed in the GLOBALS file to name the Windows Service.*

Replicat Process

The replicat process takes trail file data and writes it into the target database, in this case Oracle. This is done via INSERT, UPDATE, and DELETE statements. If there is a performance problem with GoldenGate, it is usually found on the replicat side because of the serial nature of the replicat process. GoldenGate version 12 introduced more parallelism into the replicat process. As with the extracts, no more than 250 extract and/or manager processes per manager are feasible.

So, how do these processes work together? That information is provided in the next section.

GoldenGate Workflow

GoldenGate works by taking transaction log information from the source system, converting it into INSERT, UPDATE, and DELETE statements, and applying those statements on the target system. As you have seen earlier, in addition to the manager process, there are two types of processes, extracts and replicats, and typically there are two extracts—one to extract data from the log into a local trail file, and one to copy that data remotely to the remote trail file. Regardless of whether this is an Oracle database or a SQL Server database, the trail files are the same.

The reason to use the second extract (aka pump) is to isolate the reading of the database log from the network. By having the extract process local, there is less chance of log reads being delayed due to the inability to write to a remote file.

Planning a SQL Server Migration with GoldenGate

GoldenGate can replicate many object types and table types but not all. Therefore, you must do a little planning and pre-replication work to determine if the desired tables are supported. The best way to determine this is to run the GoldenGate check script. This script is available for multiple platforms and is downloadable from the Oracle Support website; see MOS Note 1298562.1, *Oracle GoldenGate database Complete Database Profile check script (All Schemas)*, for an example.

NOTE
GoldenGate cannot replicate all objects. Running the GoldenGate check script or profile script is recommended during the planning phase to determine which, if any, objects cannot be replicated so that you can make other arrangements.

If the check script identifies objects that are not supported with GoldenGate, those objects must be migrated separately, either at cutover or at an earlier point if the data is static. The tables that you will be replicating will be included in the instructions that follow.

In addition to planning the migration, you must also plan to have enough storage for GoldenGate trail files. The size of the trail files will depend on how busy the database is and how long you want to retain the trail files. It is important that you plan this ahead of time and be prepared.

Oracle GoldenGate for SQL Server Database Profile Script

At the time of writing, the My Oracle Support document for the GoldenGate check script for SQL Server is Doc ID 1315720.1. This provides information on prerequisites for Oracle GoldenGate for SQL Server as well as a download of the script itself. As mentioned in that document, GoldenGate for SQL Server supports the following versions:

- SQL Server 2005

- SQL Server 2008

- SQL Server 2012

NOTE
Previous versions are not supported.

The most important thing that the check script does is report items that will cause problems with GoldenGate replication. This is why you must run this script during the planning phase, so that you can address those problems. In addition to the normal items that you might have seen with Oracle-to-Oracle replication, such as tables with no primary key, there might be additional items of concern such as:

- Unsupported schema names

- Unsupported table names

- Unsupported column names

- Unsupported data types

- Tables with identity columns

As you can see, it is important to run this script during the planning phase and determine what to do with these items.

In addition to addressing items from the check script, you must also decide how you want to handle multiple databases in SQL Server. They can be migrated into a single Oracle database as schemas, migrated into separate Oracle databases, or migrated into Oracle Database 12c pluggable databases (PDBs).

Migrating a Database with GoldenGate

At the highest level, a minimal downtime migration using GoldenGate involves the following main steps:

1. Set up GoldenGate and enable replication from SQL Server to Oracle Database 11g.

2. Configure and validate the database.

3. Enable replication by starting the extract and pump processes on the SQL Server databases and/or tables that are to be migrated.

4. Perform the Initial Data Migration using one of several methods (or your own) using a variety of methods.

5. Sync the database by enabling the replicat process (at the proper place).

6. Monitor until cutover.

7. Perform pre-cutover validation.

8. Perform the cutover.

9. (Optional) GoldenGate Cleanup.

This is the high-level overview. Let's look at the detailed steps involved in performing a zero or near-zero downtime migration using GoldenGate. This narrative outlines the general steps for performing a migration/upgrade from SQL Server to Oracle 11*g* using GoldenGate version 11.2.

TIP & TECHNIQUE
When migrating from one system to another, you might be asked by management to enable reverse replication, so that the old system can be used as a failback in case any application failures occur. In this example, only SQL Server to Oracle will be shown (unidirectional).

Set Up GoldenGate on MS SQL Server and Oracle 11*g*

Before you can configure and enable GoldenGate to replicate from the SQL Server system to the 11*g* system, GoldenGate must be installed on the source and target systems.

NOTE
GoldenGate software can be downloaded from the Oracle Software Delivery Cloud at http://edelivery .oracle.com. The latest version is usually found at http://support.oracle.com. You must have a My Oracle Support (MOS) account to download the latest version from support.

1. To set up GoldenGate for SQL Server, install the GoldenGate software on both the source and target:

    a. Create a directory to be used for GoldenGate. Depending on your system this could be D:\GGHOME, E:\GGHOME, etc.

    b. Unzip the GG distribution files into that directory.

    c. Change the directory to the install directory and invoke ggsci.

2. To set up GoldenGate for Oracle, install the GoldenGate software on both the source and target.

NOTE
The version of Oracle GoldenGate on MS SQL Server might not be the exact same as the version of Oracle GoldenGate for Oracle database. That's okay as long as they are within the same major release.

   a. Create a directory to be used for GoldenGate.

   b. Unzip and untar (Linux or Unix) the GG distribution files.

   c. Set the environment variable for GGHOME to point to that directory.

   d. Set the environment variable for LD_LIBRARY_PATH for the 11*g* database (Oracle side only).

   e. Add an alias for $GGHOME to point to the goldengate home directory.

   f. Change the directory to the install directory and invoke ggsci:

```
$ cd $GGHOME or cd d:\GG
$ ggsci
```

TIP & TECHNIQUE
For Linux or Unix, create an alias to cd to $GGHOME and enable ggsci. For example,
alias ggsci="cd $GGHOME; ./ggsci"

   g. Create subdirs. This creates the subdirectories that you need for GoldenGate.

```
GGSCI> create subdirs
```

   h. Manually create subdirectories for dirdsc and diroby. These are optional for the discard directory and for the obey files.

   i. Link dirdat to a large file system for trail files. This is so that the trail files don't fill up your regular file systems.

3. On the SQL Server system, create the manager process:

```
C:\GG>  INSTALL ADDSERVICE
```

4. Create a GoldenGate Administrator account (ggadmin) on the target database.

   a. Create a unique tablespace for the ggadmin user (ggadmin):

   ```
   SQL> create tablespace ggadmin;
   ```

   b. Create the ggadmin user:

   ```
   SQL> create user ggadmin identified by "ggadmin" default
   tablespace ggadmin temporary tablespace temp;
   ```

   c. Grant DBA privilege to the ggadmin user. This is the easiest way to handle the ggadmin user; however, if you need to be more restrictive, the GoldenGate documentation specifies the necessary permissions.

   ```
   SQL> grant dba to ggadmin;
   ```

   d. Grant an unlimited quota on the ggadmin to ggadmin:

   ```
   SQL> alter user ggadmin quota unlimited on ggadmin;
   ```

5. If desired, create encryption keys for both ggadmin users. Refer to steps 4–8 of the "Set Up GoldenGate" section in Chapter 8 for instructions on creating encryption keys.

Configure and Validate the Database

Now that GoldenGate is configured, you need to configure and validate the database to make sure that it is ready to run GoldenGate. To prepare the source database (SQL Server):

1. Verify that the SQL Server database is running in full-recovery mode.

2. Create an ODBC Data Source.

3. Invoke ggsci.exe.

4. Log in to the SQL Server database:

   ```
   GGSCI (MSSQL) > DBLOGIN SOURCEDB <DB_NAME>
   ```

5. Add Trandata:

   ```
   GGSCI (MSSQL) > ADD TRANDATA <SCHEMA>.<TABLE>
   ```

Enable Replication from SQL Server to Oracle 11*g*

The first step of the actual migration (assuming the databases are in place and operational) is to configure and enable GoldenGate to replicate from the SQL Server system to the 11*g* system.

1. Prepare the source database (SQL Server):

   a. Edit DefGen parameters:

      ```
      GGSCI (MSSQL) > EDIT PARAMS DEFGEN

      defsfile c:\gg\dirdef\<name>.def
      sourcedb <DB_NAME>
      table <SCHEMA>.<TABLE>;
      ```

   b. Run DefGen:

      ```
      C:\GG> defgen paramfile c:\gg\dirprm\defgen.prm
      ```

   c. Copy a DefGen file to the target system.

   d. Create and start the manager process:

      ```
      GGSCI (MSSQL) > EDIT PARAM MGR
      ```

   e. Add the following to the manager parameter file:

      ```
      PORT 7809
      DYNAMICPORTLIST 7850-7860
      LAGINFOMINUTES 0
      LAGREPORTMINUTES 10
      LAGCRITICALMINUTES 60
      GGSCI (MSSQL) > START MANAGER
      ```

2. Prepare the target database (Oracle).

TIP & TECHNIQUE
*There are additional steps necessary to perform
reverse replication. They will not be covered here.*

On any database that is 11.2.0.4 or newer, set the following parameter:

```
SQL> ALTER SYSTEM SET ENABLE_GOLDENGATE_REPLICATION = TRUE
SCOPE=BOTH SID='*';
```

TIP & TECHNIQUE
*A checkpoint table (option) can be beneficial in
both Oracle and SQL Server. This allows GoldenGate
to restart and is a little more reliable than the
checkpoint file.*

3. Enable checkpoint tables on both the source and target.

   a. Run ggsci on the source and target systems:

   ```
   SQL Server
   GGSCI (MSSQL) > DBLOGIN SOURCEDB <DB_NAME>
   GGSCI (MSSQL) > add checkpointtable ggadmin.checkpoint
   Oracle
       GGSCI> dblogin userid ggadmin , password ggadmin
       GGSCI> add checkpointtable ggadmin.checkpoint
   ```

   b. Add the following to the GLOBALS file:

   ```
   CHECKPOINTTABLE ggadmin.checkpoint
   ```

4. Create the manager parameter file on the Oracle system. The manager parameter file mgr.prm is shown here:

   ```
   PORT 7809
   DYNAMICPORTLIST 7850-7860
   LAGINFOMINUTES 0
   LAGREPORTMINUTES 10
   LAGCRITICALMINUTES 60
   ```

TIP & TECHNIQUE

*The ports listed in the manager parameter file
(mgr.prm) must be opened in every firewall that
you have between the source and target systems.*

5. Create the extract parameter file. Exclude unsupported and problematic tables. A sample is shown here:

   ```
   Extract parameter file mssqlext1.prm
   EXTRACT MSSQLEXT1
   SOURCEDB <DB_NAME>
   TRANLOGOPTIONS MANAGESECONDARYTRUNCATIONPOINT
   RMTHOST ORADB, MGRPORT 7809
   EXTTRAIL C:\GG\DIRDAT\la
   TABLE <SCHEMA>.<TABLE>;
   ```

6. Create the pump parameter file. This parameter file is shown here:

   ```
   Pump trail file pump1.prm
   EXTRACT PUMP1
   SOURCEDB <DB_NAME>
   TRANLOGOPTIONS MANAGESECONDARYTRUNCATIONPOINT
   PASSTHRU
   RMTHOST ORADB, MGRPORT 7809
   ```

```
STATOPTIONS REPORTFETCH
REPORTCOUNT EVERY 10 MINUTES, RATE
RMTTRAIL /u01/app/oracle/gg/dirdat/ms
TABLE <SCHEMA>.<TABLE>;
```

7. Add extract and pump.

NOTE
These steps should be scripted in the diroby directory as add_ext01.oby, add_pump01.oby, and so on.

    a. Create the add_ext01.oby obey file:

```
add extract mssqlext1, tranlog, begin now
add exttrail C:\GG\DIRDAT\la, extract MSSQLEXT1, megabytes 200
```

    b. Create the add_pump.oby obey file:

```
add extract pump1, exttrailsource C:\GG\DIRDAT\la, extract
MSSQLEXT1, extseqno 0, extrba 0
add rmttrail /u01/app/oracle/gg/dirdat/ms, extract pump1,
megabytes 200
```

8. Start the extract on the source.

9. Set up the manager parameter file on the target and start it.

10. Start the pump process on the source. It is at this point that you must check the target to make sure that trail files are getting written there.

TIP & TECHNIQUE
If trail files aren't showing up on the target system, the reason is probably either that the manager isn't running or you have a firewall problem.

Perform the Initial Migration from MS SQL Server to Oracle

This is where things get interesting. When migrating from SQL Server to Oracle, you cannot simply use Export/Import, Data Pump, RMAN, and so forth, as covered earlier in this book. There are fewer options. These options include, but are not limited to:

■ GoldenGate initial replication with the SOURCEISTABLE option

■ Microsoft SQL Server Integration Services

■ Oracle SQL Developer

There are other options to choose from as well, such as writing a program to migrate data or dumping SQL Server data to a file that can be used by the SQL*Loader program. Which method you should use depends on the size of the database, the performance of the systems, the performance requirements, and other factors.

TIP & TECHNIQUE

The initial migration is the critical part of moving from SQL Server to Oracle. Performing this task accurately is critical. This is typically a custom program or can be done with tools such as SQL Developer.

At this point you must decide which method to use for your Initial Migration and how you want to proceed. Because there is no one clear-cut method that is recommended from the SQL Server to Oracle migration, and because your skill set will vary, we will leave it up to you. If you are very familiar with SQL Server Integration Services, that might be the best choice for you. If you are very familiar with SQL Developer, that might be the best choice. There are many other tools that might help, such as Oracle Enterprise Manager Cloud Control 12c. Depending on your skills, this might be the hard part or the easy part.

Sync Target with Source

Once you have configured and started the extract and pump processes in GoldenGate, and completed the initial migration, it is necessary to bring the source and target databases in sync and keep them that way. This is done with GoldenGate.

1. Enable the SUPPRESSTRIGGERS option on the target.

2. Set up the manager and replicat processes on the target. The replicat parameter file is shown here:

```
REPLICAT REP01
SETENV (ORACLE_HOME=/app/oracle/product/11.2.0.4/dbhome_1)
SETENV (NLS_LANG="AMERICAN_AMERICA.AL32UTF8")
USERID ggadmin, PASSWORD ggadmin
SOURCEDEFS /u01/app/oracle/gg/dirdef/emp.def
REPORTCOUNT EVERY 10 MINUTES, RATE
DISCARDFILE /app/oracle/goldengate/dirdsc/rep01.dsc, APPEND,
MEGABYTES 100
DISCARDROLLOVER ON SUNDAY
GROUPTRANSOPS 2000
DBOPTIONS SUPPRESSTRIGGERS

MAP <SCHEMA>.<TABLE>, TARGET <ORACLE_SCHEMA>.<ORACLE_TABLE>;
```

3. Add the replicat to the target using the following syntax. This should be scripted in an obey file.

```
dblogin userid ggadmin password ggadmin
add replicat rep01, exttrail /app/oracle/goldengate/dirdat/ra ,
extseqno 0, extrba 0
```

4. Start the manager and target. This should already have been done. Check the target and make sure it is running without error.

```
GGSCI> start mgr
GGSCI> start replicat rep01
```

Monitor Until Cutover

At this point, GoldenGate should be up and running. After a while, the source and target will become in sync. You will usually want to synchronize several days before going live so that you have time to prepare for the cutover. And you can monitor GoldenGate with the `info all` command in GGSCI. The lag shown is the amount of time that the target is behind the source. Fix issues as they arise.

TIP & TECHNIQUE
We often tell people that when using GoldenGate for migration, it doesn't matter how long the migration takes; what really matters is how long the cutover takes. It is the cutover that will potentially involve some downtime.

Perform Pre-Cutover Validation

You should always validate the source and target before beginning the cutover. This can be as simple as row counts or something more sophisticated such as using Oracle GoldenGate Veridata. Your process will vary based on your needs.

GoldenGate Cutover Procedure

GoldenGate cutover includes the following:

1. Discontinue all user activity on the source.

2. Stop all GoldenGate processes on both the source and target.

3. Verify consistency of the source and target databases.

4. Point application servers to the Oracle database.

5. Disable applications and the database on the SQL Server system.

GoldenGate Cleanup (Optional)

If GoldenGate will no longer be used, you can use the following steps to clean up the GoldenGate configuration and set the Oracle database back to a pre-GoldenGate state:

1. Validate that GoldenGate is no longer needed.

2. Stop all extract, pump, and replicat processes.

3. Delete extract, pump, and replicat processes.

4. Remove the ggadmin user from the database.

5. Drop the GoldenGate tablespace from the database, including the contents and datafile.

6. Remove all GoldenGate files.

Summary

This chapter covered many steps that are used to migrate a database from a SQL Server database to an Oracle database using Oracle GoldenGate. Migrating with GoldenGate is truly the only method that can be used to perform a near zero-downtime migration. This is important for very large databases where the amount of downtime you can handle is small.

NOTE
Remember, how long it takes to do the migration is not nearly as important as how long it takes to do the cutover. The cutover is where any downtime would be incurred.

Using Oracle GoldenGate for data migration is an efficient way to do a data migration that can incur minimal downtime during cutover. Oracle has been doing an awesome job enhancing and improving GoldenGate since acquiring it in 2009.

NOTE
You can find up-to-date information from the International GoldenGate Oracle Users Group at www.iggoug.org.

CHAPTER
13

Moving to Oracle
Database 12c

There is an old saying among science fiction fans that enjoy the universe of *Star Trek*: The even-numbered movies are the best. We've found that there is a similar sentiment among Oracle DBAs regarding releases of Oracle Database: Even-numbered releases usually comprise the most significant and ground-breaking feature sets. The latest release of the database, Oracle Database 12*c* R1, certainly proves to be consistent with this sentiment because it is quite literally a sea change in terms of the way the RDBMS works. While the formal Oracle documentation and sales materials maintain that the "*c*" in this release stands for the first *cloud*-ready version of the Oracle database, we contend that several of its new feature sets point toward two other candidates: *consolidation* and *container*.

This chapter provides a brief primer of the paradigm shift that Oracle Database 12*c* provides for database application consolidation with its new multitenant features. We'll then dive a bit deeper into this new database architecture to demonstrate how it makes short work of cloning, migrating, and upgrading databases with minimal impact to application workloads. We'll finish our exploration with a brief discussion of the new multitenant features available in Oracle Database 12c Release 12.1.0.2.

Oracle Database 12*c*: A Brave New World

As the hardware platforms that host Oracle databases have grown ever more powerful—the raw computing power in terms of the number of CPU cores available, the relatively huge increase in the amount of available DRAM for database memory components, and the ready availability of either inline or near-line flash storage—it finally makes excellent sense to consolidate databases with compatible workloads onto a single computing platform. It's still certainly true that, depending on the database's application workload, some Oracle database background processes will always be more active than others, especially Log Writer (`LGWR`), which writes out the contents of the log buffer to disk at least every three seconds; however, other background processes are much less active. (Recall that Oracle technical documents often refer to Database Writer, `DBWn`, as a "lazy writer.") Thus, it's perfectly acceptable to consider *consolidating* two active Oracle databases—say, one that is hosting a moderate OLTP application workload during peak hours, and another that is hosting a moderate decision support system (DSS) workload during off-peak hours—onto the same physical hardware platform.

Another situation that's not uncommon in many organizations is the existence of "passive" databases that are only started up at infrequent intervals to handle a particular cyclical application workload, but are then shut down immediately after the workload cycle is complete. Consolidating these databases onto a common platform also makes excellent sense.

Another implicit advantage of consolidating databases onto the same hardware platform is the elimination of the hardware platform itself as a potential variable when an Oracle DBA needs to determine the real root cause of an application workload's variance in performance. Every seasoned Oracle DBA has likely encountered the maddening situation in which the final root cause of poor performance turns out to be a different I/O subsystem RAID configuration, a lower amount of server memory, fewer CPU resources, or—in the case of Microsoft Windows versus Linux or UNIX— even the OS itself. If the development, testing, and production databases had been hosted on the identical hardware platform, however, these sets of potential variance would have been eliminated from the start. One stumbling block to consolidating databases in this situation is that, in the absence of robust resource management software, it's difficult to prevent one or more "rival" database instances—those that are hosting workloads that are less crucial than others—from overwhelming those hosting the more crucial database instances; unfortunately, that task will be relegated to the OS platform itself, which is often the least-informed referee to make that decision.

Finally, if their organization has gone through the trouble to purchase and implement an *engineered system* like an Oracle Exadata X5-2, Oracle DBAs and their management are under significant pressure to wring out the last possible ounce of capacity from that platform to obtain maximum advantage from the costs of that capital expenditure. Database consolidation is likely to be one of the most cost-effective methods to accomplish the organization's financial goal.

Container and Pluggable Databases: A Primer

Fortunately, Oracle 12c R1 offers a completely revamped database architecture that Oracle DBAs can leverage for database consolidation: the *container database (CDB)*. This new architecture at last introduces the concept of *multitenancy* to Oracle Database. (Be sure to see the upcoming sidebar for a deeper discussion of the relative novelty of multitenancy for other RDBMSs.) As its name indicates, a CDB is simply a *container*, and it contains one or more *pluggable databases (PDBs)*. Each CDB is still an Oracle database, with at least one database instance—more than one, of course, if it is a Real Application Clusters (RAC) database. Each database instance has its own *Shared Global Area (SGA)* and *Program Global Area (PGA)*, but these memory areas and all of the crucial database background processes like LGWR, DBW0, CKPT, PMON, and SMON are now shared between all PDBs.

As we have already mentioned, sharing these background processes offers the possibility of extremely efficient process management because in many cases these background processes are doing very little work except when they need to handle an occasional application workload "spike." For example, consider a typical Oracle 11g R2 database—in Oracle 12c R1 terms, a *non-CDB* database that's using the pre-12c

R1 architecture—that is responsible for handling "hybrid" application workloads for both OLTP and DSS/DW applications:

- When several hundred OLTP users are concurrently connected and their sessions perform intense OLTP activity usually consisting of very short duration and very tiny logical units of work, LGWR tends to be the busiest background process.

- When just a few users suddenly issue a complex DSS or DW query, LGWR will most likely be the least busy background process; instead, the users' server processes will most likely become the busiest processes as they request physical reads against the I/O subsystem to obtain all required database blocks to the database buffer cache.

- Once CKPT detects enough free buffer waits because the OLTP process has produced many dirty buffers in the database's buffer cache that need to be written to disk to fit all the required new buffers for the queries that were issued, the DBW0 background process will likely become the busiest process as it writes dirtied buffers back to their respective database blocks on disk.

While it's certainly possible that this hybrid database may experience periods where both types of workloads collide, it's also quite unlikely that *all* Oracle databases in any given IT environment are experiencing *identical* CPU and memory demands *simultaneously*. Oracle 12*c* R1's new multitenant architecture takes advantage of this situation, now enabling an Oracle DBA to *plug* several databases as PDBs into a single CDB, thus allowing them to leverage the same memory and CPU architecture simultaneously. Since all PDBs leverage the same background processes within their CDB's database instance, this also eliminates multiple individual copies of the crucial background processes like DBW0, LGWR, and CKPT. The CDB/PDB architecture also overcomes the need to constantly "over-provision" memory and CPU resources for a handful of Oracle database instances to accommodate each instance's peak resource demands, as Figure 13-1 shows.

NOTE
Exploring the depths of the new Oracle Database 12c R1 CDB and PDB architecture and its extensive features would require a book of its own. Since this book is all about migration, transformation, and upgrade of Oracle databases, our scope will focus primarily on the techniques that an Oracle DBA can leverage to quickly migrate a pre-12c database to the 12c environment. We will especially concentrate on the most effective and appropriate methods to transform a non-CDB database into a PDB.

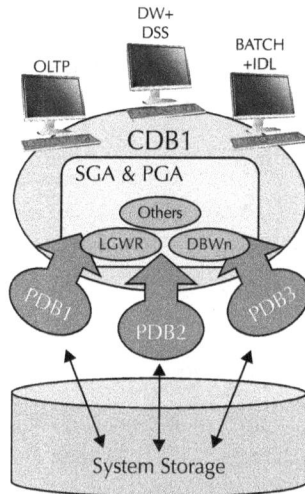

CDBs and PDBs also share common memory and background processes:

- *All* PDBs share same SGA and PGA
- *All* PDBs share same background processes
  - OLTP: Intense random reads and writes (DBWn and LGWR)
  - DW/DSS: Intense sequential reads and/or logical I/O
  - Batch and Data Loading: Intense sequential physical reads and physical writes

FIGURE 13-1. *CDB and PDBs share memory and background processes.*

Oracle 12c R1 and Multitenant: So … What's the Big Deal?

SQL Server and Sybase DBAs are almost certain to react to Oracle Database 12c's new multitenant features with a wry smile because these RDBMSs have offered this feature for several years. However, we have also noticed that these databases have added their own versions of these familiar features—for example, the capability to partition tables—over the years as well.

One crucial point to remember about CDBs and PDBs: If a single CDB hosts only one PDB, then there is no additional charge; however, as soon as a CDB contains more than one PDB, the licensing costs may increase dramatically, depending on the organization's Oracle Database licensing agreement. This may or may not jibe with how other RDBMSs handle this conundrum, but it's a key decision point for Oracle DBAs when deciding upon the relative advantages of deploying multiple PDBs within a CDB versus the additional costs involved.

We believe that the biggest advantage of the new multitenant architecture boils down quite simply to *database availability*, because even if a PDB is temporarily unavailable for application access while it is being cloned, unplugged, or replugged, *all other pluggable databases within that CDB continue to service application workloads without any interruptions*.

CDBs and their PDBs certainly share memory and background processes, but the sharing doesn't stop there; in fact, it extends deep into the architecture of how Oracle 12c R1 either shares or isolates database files and database objects—including users, privileges, and roles—as we will discuss in the following sections.

Common vs. Local Database Files

First, each CDB (also known as the *root* container named CDB$ROOT) owns the control files, online redo logs, archived redo logs, and Recovery Manager (RMAN) backup sets and image copies necessary for database recovery of the *entire* CDB, as shown in Figure 13-2.

- ■ The redo log entries for transactions generated within each PDB are therefore commingled within each online redo log and archived redo log.

- ■ Each CDB and its PDBs *must* use the same character set, and each PDB shares the specific database feature set(s) of its parent CDB as well.

- ■ Initialization parameter settings are retained within a single SPFILE for each CDB. An initialization parameter that can be modified at a PDB level will report a value of TRUE for the new ISPDB_MODIFIABLE column of V$PARAMETER.

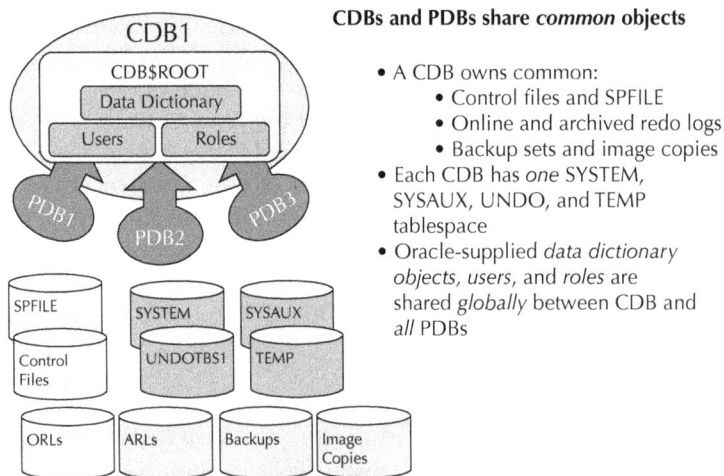

FIGURE 13-2. *CDB and PDB database file ownership*

Listing 13-1 shows a sample of which initialization parameters in the `cdb121` container could be modified at the PDB level.

Listing 13-1 *Sample CDB and PDB Initialization Parameter Settings*

```
SET PAGESIZE 20000
SET LINESIZE 80
COL con_id  FORMAT 999          HEADING "Con|ID"
COL name    FORMAT A40          HEADING "Parameter Name"
COL value   FORMAT A30          HEADING "Parameter Value"
TTITLE "PDB Initialization Parameters|(from GV$PARAMETER)"
SELECT
      con_id
     ,name
     ,value
  FROM gv$parameter
 WHERE ispdb_modifiable = 'TRUE'
 ORDER BY con_id, name;
TTITLE OFF


                    PDB Initialization Parameters
                        (from GV$PARAMETER)


 Con
  ID Parameter Name                         Parameter Value
---- --------------------------------------- ----------------------------
   1 O7_DICTIONARY_ACCESSIBILITY            FALSE
   1 asm_diskstring
   1 cell_offload_compaction                ADAPTIVE
   1 cell_offload_decryption                TRUE
   1 cell_offload_parameters
   1 cell_offload_plan_display              AUTO
   1 cell_offload_processing                TRUE
   1 cell_offloadgroup_name
   1 commit_logging
   1 commit_wait
   1 commit_write
   1 create_stored_outlines
   1 cursor_bind_capture_destination        memory+disk
   1 cursor_sharing                         EXACT
   1 db_create_file_dest
   1 db_create_online_log_dest_1
   1 db_create_online_log_dest_2
   1 db_create_online_log_dest_3
   1 db_create_online_log_dest_4
   1 db_create_online_log_dest_5
   1 db_file_multiblock_read_count          128
   1 db_index_compression_inheritance       NONE
   1 db_securefile                          PREFERRED
   1 db_unrecoverable_scn_tracking          TRUE
   1 ddl_lock_timeout                       0
   1 deferred_segment_creation              TRUE
   1 dst_upgrade_insert_conv                TRUE
```

```
     1 enable_ddl_logging                   FALSE
     1 fixed_date
     1 global_names                         FALSE
     1 heat_map                             OFF
     1 java_jit_enabled                     TRUE
     1 listener_networks
     1 log_archive_dest_1
     . . .
     << many lines omitted for sake of brevity >>
     . . .
     1 result_cache_mode                    MANUAL
     1 result_cache_remote_expiration       0
     1 resumable_timeout                    0
     1 sessions                             472
     1 skip_unusable_indexes                TRUE
     1 smtp_out_server
     1 sort_area_retained_size              0
     1 sort_area_size                       65536
     1 spatial_vector_acceleration          FALSE
     1 sql_trace                            FALSE
     1 sqltune_category                     DEFAULT
     1 star_transformation_enabled          FALSE
     1 statistics_level                     TYPICAL
     1 temp_undo_enabled                    FALSE
     1 timed_os_statistics                  0
     1 timed_statistics                     TRUE
     1 workarea_size_policy                 AUTO
     1 xml_db_events                        enable

171 rows selected.
```

Common vs. Local Tablespaces and Datafiles

As we explore a CDB's tablespaces and their datafiles, however, the dichotomy between CDB and PDB becomes immediately apparent. As Figure 13-3 illustrates, tablespaces are classified as either *common* or *local*.

- Recall that the online redo logs are shared between all PDBs in a CDB. Likewise, UNDO segments and extents are also shared centrally between all PDBs in a CDB, and they are stored in UNDO tablespaces—one per each CDB database *instance*.

- Each CDB owns a *common* SYSTEM and a *common* SYSAUX permanent tablespace. The data dictionary objects for the CDB are contained within this root SYSTEM tablespace. As we will demonstrate, this dramatically reduces the usually painful process of database upgrades because now only this set of common data dictionary objects needs to be updated, instead of having to upgrade the data dictionary one database at a time as is still required for any Oracle 12c non-CDB database.

■ Each CDB has its own common default temporary tablespace (TEMP) that can be shared among other PDBs. But if its application workloads require it, a PDB is also permitted to have its own local TEMP tablespace as well—for example, to permit the existence of *global temporary tables* that are useful only to the OLTP application within that PDB, or to support high volumes of sorting, aggregation, or hash joins outside of PGA memory for a DSS application workload.

■ Each PDB has its own SYSTEM and SYSAUX tablespace as well. But instead of comprising a complete database data dictionary, as would a non-CDB, these tablespaces contain only the database objects that are *local* to that PDB. For example, the data dictionary metadata for the HR user account and all objects it owns within pluggable database PDB1 will be housed within that PDB's SYSTEM tablespace.

As we will demonstrate later in this chapter, this dichotomy is at the heart of a pluggable database's "pluggable-ness" because all common database objects are retained within a single PDB, so the PDB can facilitate their use specific to their application workload type, their recoverability requirements, and even their *purpose* within an IT organization—that is, *production* versus *test* versus *development* environments.

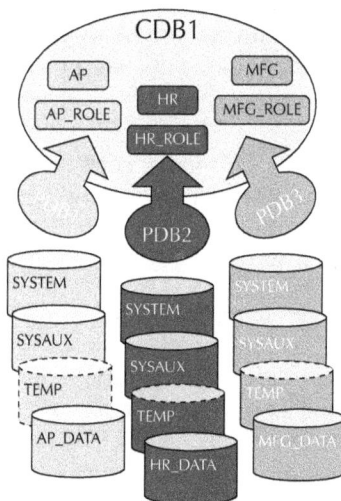

FIGURE 13-3. *CDB and PDBs: common vs. local tablespaces, objects, users, and roles*

Playing Well with Others: Avoiding Database Resource Contention Between Rival PDBs

While a deep discussion is beyond the scope of this chapter, be aware that Oracle Database 12c R1 significantly extends the capabilities of its venerable *Database Resource Manager (DBRM)* to the PDB level within the context of its CDB. For example, a PDB can be granted one or more *shares* of the total available CPU and I/O resources, with crucial database instances receiving more shares than noncrucial instances; as more PDBs are opened within the CDB, resource shares are automatically redistributed across all active PDBs (and vice versa). It's also possible to limit the maximum CPU and I/O resources that any one PDB can consume on a percentage basis. Finally, DBRM can apply most of its considerable *intra-database* resource management features to limit resources to particular Resource Consumer Groups (RCGs) within individual PDBs.

Common vs. Local Users and Objects

The distinction between non-CDBs, CDBs, and PDBs also demands some new ways of distinguishing users, database objects, and the permissions to access those objects. Database objects that are common to the CDB are called *common* objects, while objects that are owned within the jurisdiction of a single PDB are called *local* objects. Probably the most important distinction between a non-CDB and a CDB lies within where Oracle stores metadata structures and the metadata itself.

The metadata for *shared objects* exists only within the Oracle-supplied schemas (for example, SYSTEM and SYSMAN) of the CDB, and shared objects are classified as either object-linked or metadata-linked:

- *Object-linked* objects reside only within the CDB, and as such they're shared between all PDBs within that CDB. For example, all data for the Automatic Workload Repository (AWR) is retained in CDB$ROOT, and each PDB maintains an object link to that data.

- The definitions for *metadata-linked* objects are retained in CDB$ROOT, but the actual data for a metadata-linked object is retained privately within each PDB. For example, table AP.INVOICES resides within PDB1, so its metadata is stored within PDB1's SYSTEM tablespace; however, the data dictionary object for table metadata, TAB$, is actually retained within CDB$ROOT, and PDB1 uses a metadata link to point to the data definition for TAB$.

Database user accounts also acknowledge the dichotomy between common and local:

- The so-called "system" users—SYS, SYSTEM, SYSMAN, OUTLN, and DBSNMP— can be considered as the *system-supplied* common users, so their objects are retained in the common SYSTEM tablespace of the root CDB.

- It's also possible to create additional *common* users that are common to all containers within a CDB. And if they are granted the system privileges to do so, common users may also even have the ability to plug PDBs into the CDB or unplug PDBs from the CDB.

- A *local* user, on the other hand, owns schemas only within the jurisdiction of the local user's PDB. These local schemas and their corresponding objects are essentially invisible to other local users in other PDBs. This means that the only way for a local user in one PDB to access the schema objects of another local user in a different PDB is via a *database link*.

These Aren't Your Grandfather's Database Links!

If you are a seasoned Oracle DBA, you may be a bit apprehensive about using a database link to establish communication between PDBs within a CDB. However, these aren't the same type of database links that we have employed in pre-12c database releases; instead, all intra-CDB database links are essentially handled as *inter-process communication (IPC)* calls. Oracle 12c is simply leveraging the SQL database link objects to implement these cross-PDB linkages; because all PDBs have access to the same SGA, the database links don't involve any network traffic.

CDB Security: Local vs. Common Privileges and Roles

Privileges and roles can be defined as either local to a single PDB or common, meaning they are shared across multiple PDBs within a CDB:

- System and object privileges can be granted *commonly* so that they are accessible within all PDBs within the CDB; however, the scope of privileges granted *locally* to a user account is limited to just that PDB. Local privileges are granted via the CONTAINER=CURRENT directive, while common privileges are granted via the CONTAINER=ALL directive.

■ System and object privileges can also be granted collectively via roles. *Local* roles encompass privileges granted locally to a PDB, and these roles cannot be used beyond the PDB in which they have been granted. Common users can also create *common* roles: For example, the standard Oracle-supplied security roles—CONNECT, RESOURCE, SCHEDULER_ADMIN, and SELECT_ CATALOG_ROLE—are common roles that can be granted to a local or common user within a PDB.

CDB Data Dictionary and Dynamic Views

Finally, the viewpoints of data dictionary views and dynamic views become quite important. There is a definite and necessary distinction between the metadata stored *locally* within each PDB's SYSTEM tablespace versus the metadata stored with the root CDB's SYSTEM tablespace:

■ Several new *dynamic* (that is, V$ and GV$) views describe the intrinsic components of CDBs and PDBs. Listing 13-2 shows an example query and its corresponding results against the new V$PDBS view.

Listing 13-2   *Querying V$PDBS Dynamic View*

```
SQL> select name, open_mode from v$pdbs;

NAME                            OPEN_MODE
------------------------------- ----------
PDB$SEED                        READ ONLY
PROD_AP                         READ WRITE
```

■ The well-known DBA_* data dictionary views are still available at the PDB level. For example, querying DBA_OBJECTS will return only those objects that are *local* to the PDB as well as any *common* objects stored in the root CDB; however, *none* of the local objects stored in *any other* PDB will be returned.

■ A new series of data dictionary views also exists at the CDB level as well. Prefixed with CDB_*, each of these views incorporates the CON_ID (container ID) column that uniquely identifies whether a database object belongs to only the CDB or to a PDB within that CDB. Listing 13-3 shows a sample query against the CDB_DATAFILES view and the corresponding output; note that the root CDB is assigned the container ID of 1 and all other PDBs are assigned a different value for CON_ID.

NOTE
*As of Oracle Database Release 12.1.0.1.2, the total
number of PDBs is currently fixed at 253, which
includes the standard seed database (PDB$SEED)
and 252 additional PDBs.*

Listing 13-3 *Querying CDB_DATAFILES Data Dictionary View*

```
SET PAGESIZE 20000
SET LINESIZE 120
COL con_id           FORMAT 999     HEADING "Con|ID"
COL file_id          FORMAT 999     HEADING "File|#"
COL tablespace_name FORMAT A12      HEADING "Tablespace"
COL file_name        FORMAT A60     HEADING "File Name"
TTITLE "Database Files|(from CDB_DATA_FILE)"
SELECT
      con_id
     ,file_id
     ,tablespace_name
     ,file_name
  FROM cdb_data_files
 ORDER BY con_id, file_id;
TTITLE OFF

                              Database Files
                            (from CDB_DATA_FILES)

Con File
 ID   # Tablespace   File Name
---- ---- ----------- --------------------------------------------------------
   1    1 SYSTEM      /u01/app/oracle/oradata/cdb121/system01.dbf
   1    3 SYSAUX      /u01/app/oracle/oradata/cdb121/sysaux01.dbf
   1    4 UNDOTBS1    /u01/app/oracle/oradata/cdb121/undotbs01.dbf
   1    6 USERS       /u01/app/oracle/oradata/cdb121/users01.dbf
   2    5 SYSTEM      /u01/app/oracle/oradata/cdb121/pdbseed/system01.dbf
   2    7 SYSAUX      /u01/app/oracle/oradata/cdb121/pdbseed/sysaux01.dbf
   3   22 SYSTEM      /u01/app/oracle/oradata/cdb121/prod_ap/system01.dbf
   3   23 SYSAUX      /u01/app/oracle/oradata/cdb121/prod_ap/sysaux01.dbf
   3   24 AP_DATA     /u01/app/oracle/oradata/cdb121/prod_ap/ap_data.dbf
   3   25 AP_IDX      /u01/app/oracle/oradata/cdb121/prod_ap/ap_idx.dbf
   3   26 USERS       /u01/app/oracle/oradata/cdb121/prod_ap/users.dbf
```

These concepts—CDB versus PDB, local versus common—can appear a bit
daunting at first, but it is also what we believe is one of the key advantages of the
Oracle 12c multitenant database environment: It is extremely easy to upgrade a CDB
and all of its PDBs from one version to the next highest version because the database
upgrade *only affects the shared objects* residing within CDB$ROOT without affecting
any of the objects stored locally within its PDBs. As we will discuss later in this

chapter, upgrading a single PDB from release 12.1.0.1 to release 12.1.0.2 is as simple as unplugging that PDB from its original CDB, replugging it into a CDB that has been upgraded to the next release, and then upgrading just that PDB to 12.1.0.2.

NOTE
Once a pre-12c non-CDB has been upgraded to a 12c PDB, there is no simple method to downgrade it back to its prior status.

Directly Upgrading a Pre-12*c* Database to a 12*c* CDB

As with earlier Oracle Database releases, it is definitely possible to upgrade an existing pre-12*c* R1 Oracle database directly to a non-CDB database at release 12.1.0.1 or higher, either via Oracle 12*c*'s Database Upgrade Assistant (DBUA) or via purely manual methods. See Chapter 11 for detailed checklists and complete examples of how to accomplish this. However, if the additional features of CDBs and PDBs appear to be an attractive alternative, it is also possible to directly upgrade an existing pre-12*c* R1 database to a CDB.

Creating an Empty Container Database

Before you can create a PDB, a CDB must already exist to provide the required container database infrastructure. Fortunately, Oracle 12*c* R1 offers the upgraded Database Configuration Assistant (DBCA) that makes short work of creating an empty CDB. Figure 13-4 shows the Welcome screen that DBCA displays when creating any new Oracle 12.1.0.2 database.

After you choose the option to create a database and click Next, the next screen (see Figure 13-5) offers you the chance to create a new database quickly via a basic set of choices or to use advanced configuration options to construct the database. You will use the advanced dialog options in this example, so once you have selected the Advanced Mode checkbox, simply click Next to proceed to the next screen to

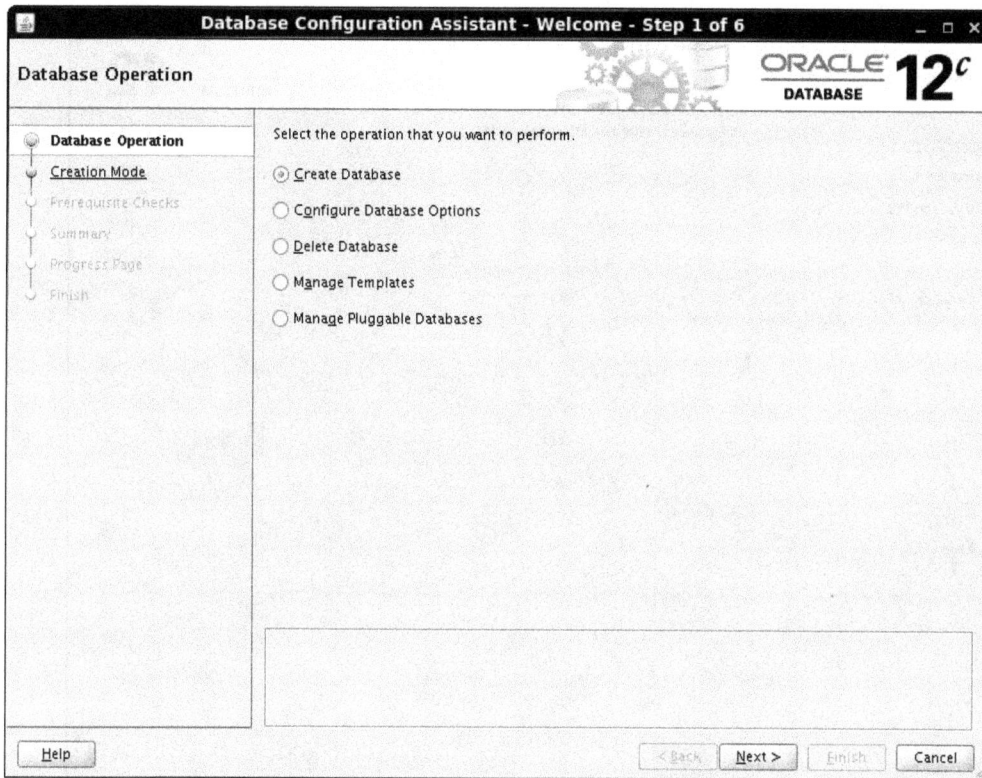

FIGURE 13-4. *DBCA Welcome Screen*

choose the type of database to create. As Figure 13-6 shows, you will choose the default *General Purpose or Transaction Processing* database template for your new database and then click Next.

The next screen (see Figure 13-7) asks for your decision on how to name your new database. In this example you've specified both the Global Database Name and the Oracle SID as cdb122. This screen also offers the choice to create the new

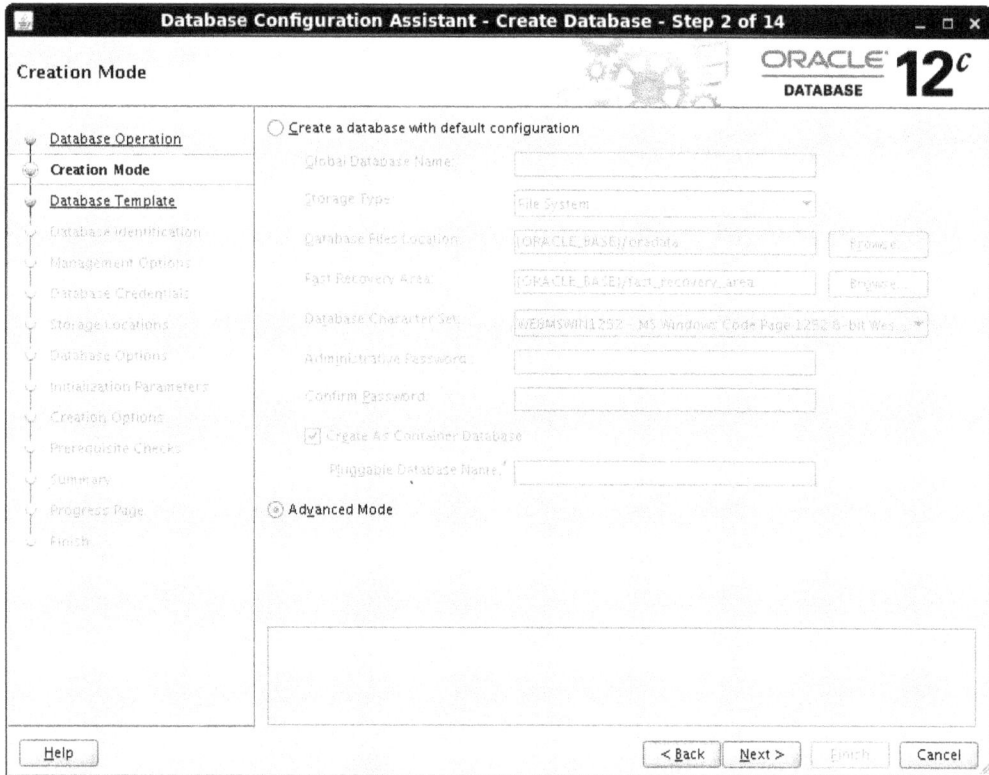

FIGURE 13-5. *Choosing basic vs. advanced database creation options*

database as either a non-CDB or a CDB. Note that in this example you will choose to create an "empty" CDB—that is, without any PDB yet—but it's also possible to create an initial PDB that has been cloned from the empty PDB$SEED seed database. Once you've specified the desired options, click Next.

The Management Options screen shown in Figure 13-8 displays the choices available for configuring Oracle Enterprise Manager (EM) Database Express (the new, lightweight replacement for EM Database Control) and for registering your new

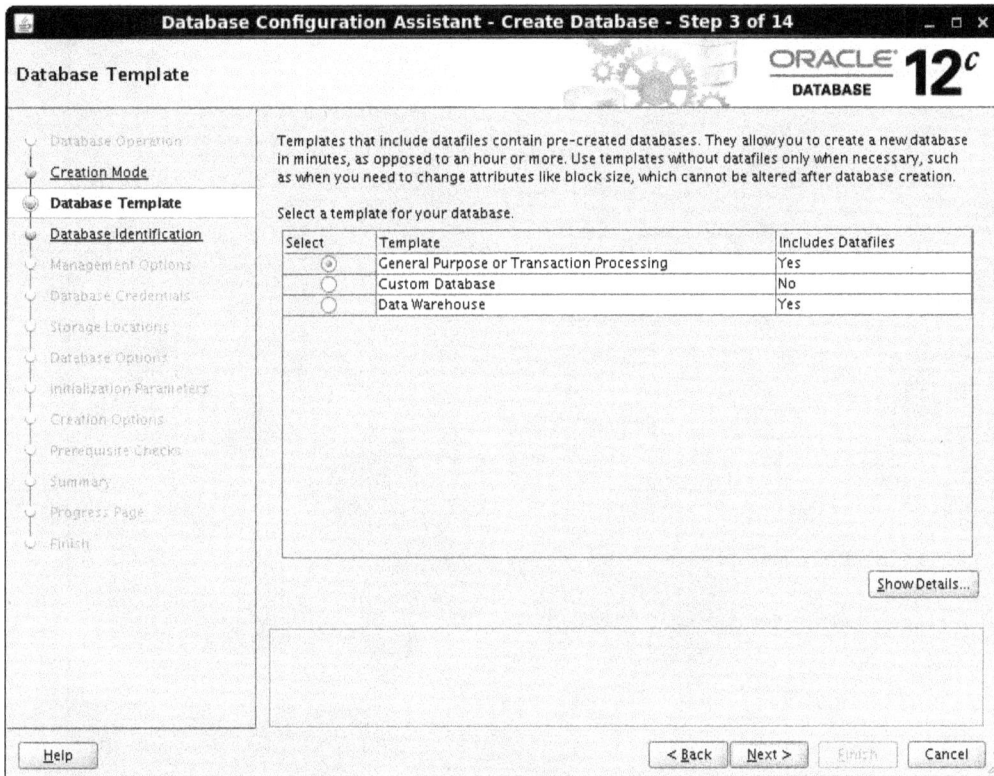

FIGURE 13-6. *Choosing database type*

CDB with Oracle EM Cloud Control immediately after its successful creation. In this example you'll choose to configure Oracle Enterprise Manager Cloud Control and assign the default communication port of 5500, and then click Next to proceed.

Now it's time for you to choose a sufficiently robust password for the SYS and SYSTEM Oracle database user accounts for your new CDB (see Figure 13-9). In this example you'll choose to use the same password for both accounts and click Next to proceed.

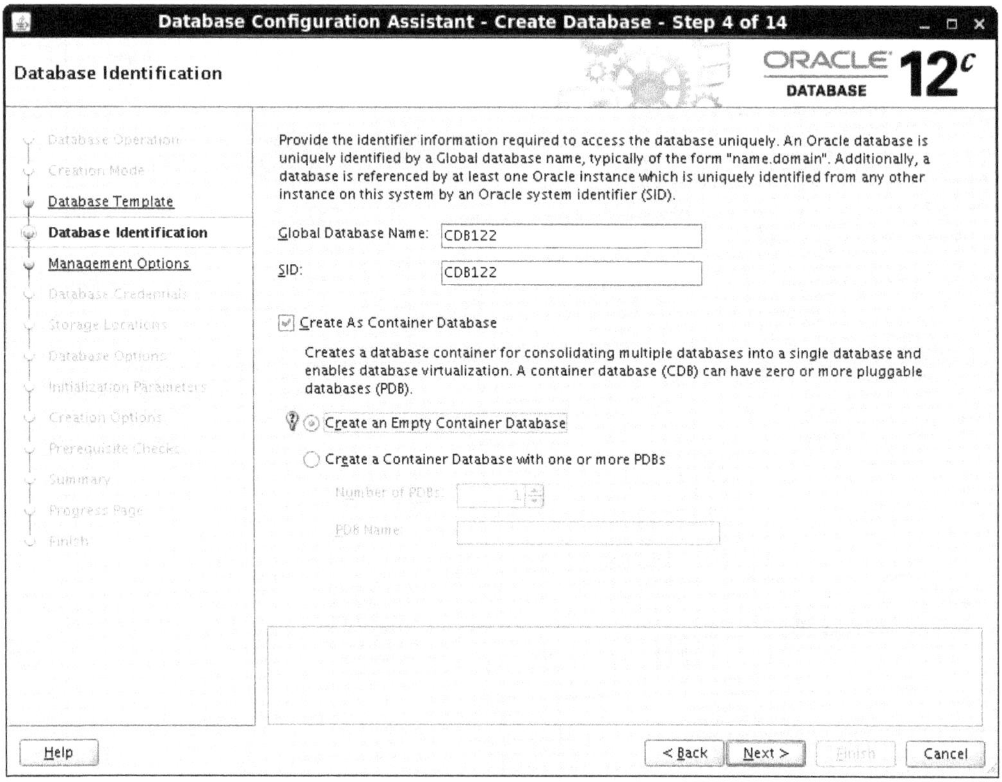

FIGURE 13-7. *Choosing non-CDB vs. CDB database creation options*

You will now decide how to establish application connectivity to your new CDB. Note that you can choose to use either an existing Listener (the default) or to choose to create a new Listener for your new CDB (see Figure 13-10). Note that it's possible to specify a different listener than the default database listener that's usually part of the Grid Infrastructure home. This allows some flexibility in case Grid Infrastructure and Automatic Storage Management (ASM) haven't yet been upgraded to Oracle 12*c* R1. Of course, once Grid Infrastructure has been upgraded to 12*c* R1,

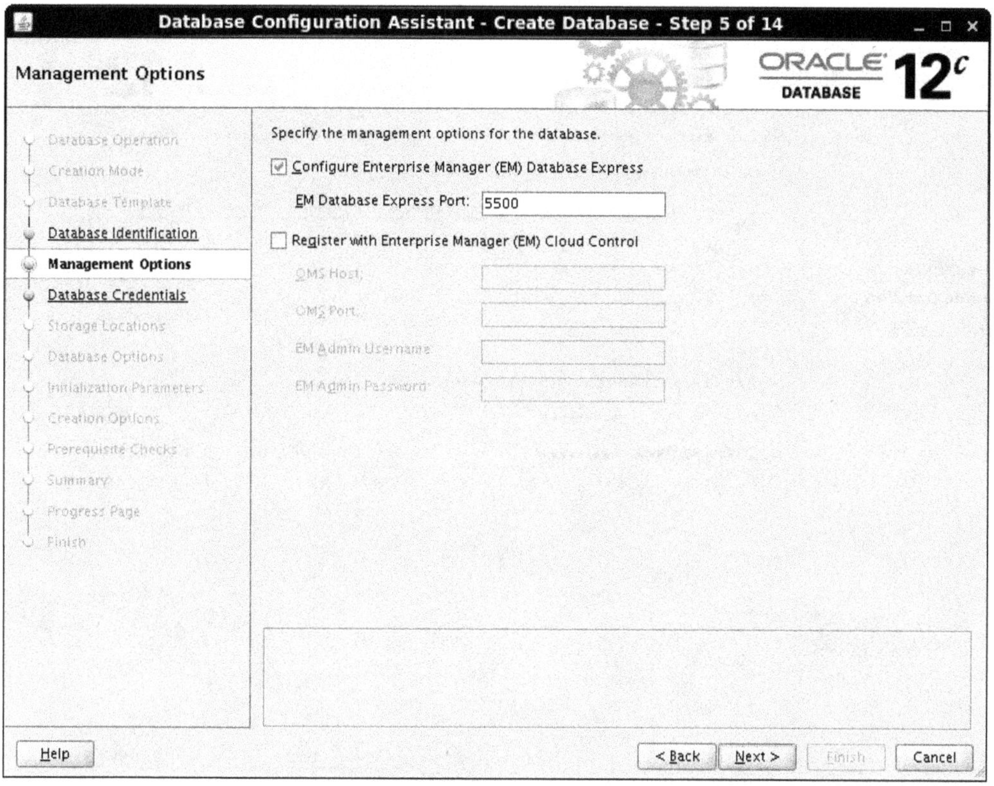

FIGURE 13-8. *Configuring Enterprise Manager options*

it is advisable (but not necessary) to switch to that listener. Once you have made your decision, click Next to proceed.

Next, it's time to decide where the CDB's database files will reside, as shown on the Storage Locations screen (see Figure 13-11). To simplify the illustration of how Oracle places database files within CDBs and PDBs, you will choose to use the traditional OS file system (EXT4); however, note that ASM is an equally robust solution for your new CDB. In this example, you will also choose to configure the

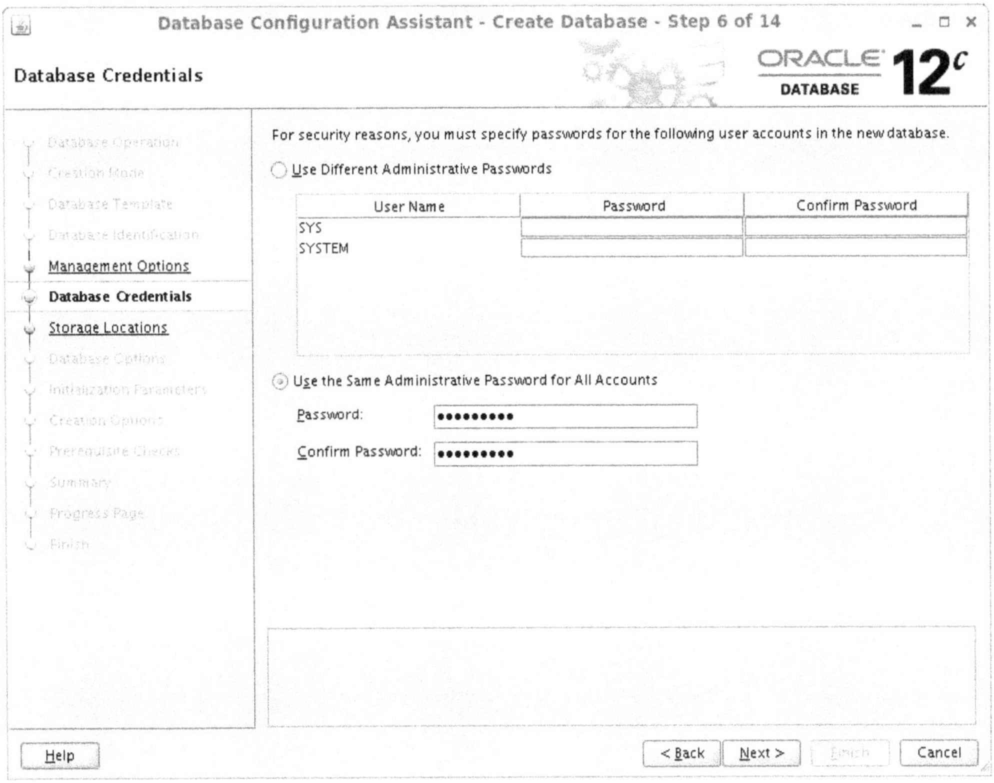

FIGURE 13-9. *Specifying database passwords*

Fast Recovery Area location and allocate 4.5GB of disk space for its creation. Once you've specified your decisions, click Next to continue.

The final configuration screens before running the prerequisite checks are summarized here:

- **Database Options**   The optional configuration of Oracle Database Vault and Oracle Label Security features (see Figure 13-12) are offered here. (Note that these options can be installed at a later time, and that both options may require additional licensing costs.) In this example, you'll choose to ignore both options and click Next to continue.

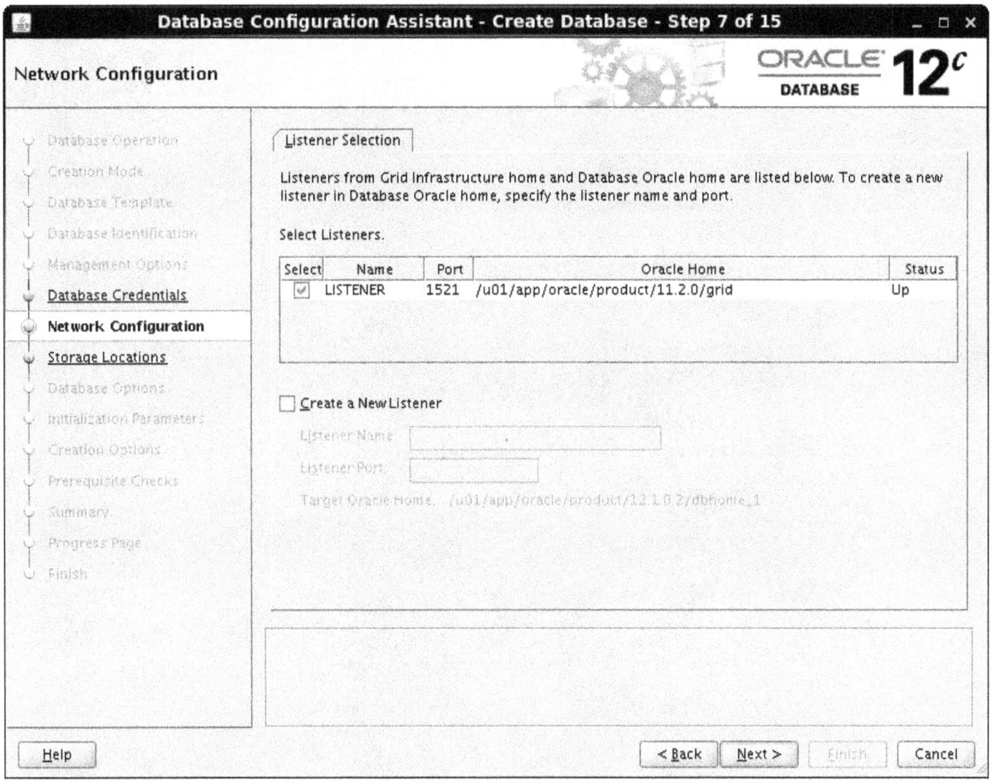

FIGURE 13-10. *Choosing a listener*

- ■ **Initialization Parameters (Memory tab)** This screen (see Figure 13-13) is where you'll specify memory management options for your new CDB. Selecting the Custom Settings radio button enables you to choose between Automatic Memory Management (AMM) and Automatic Shared Memory Management (ASMM) options, as well as how much memory should be allocated to the CDB's SGA and PGA.

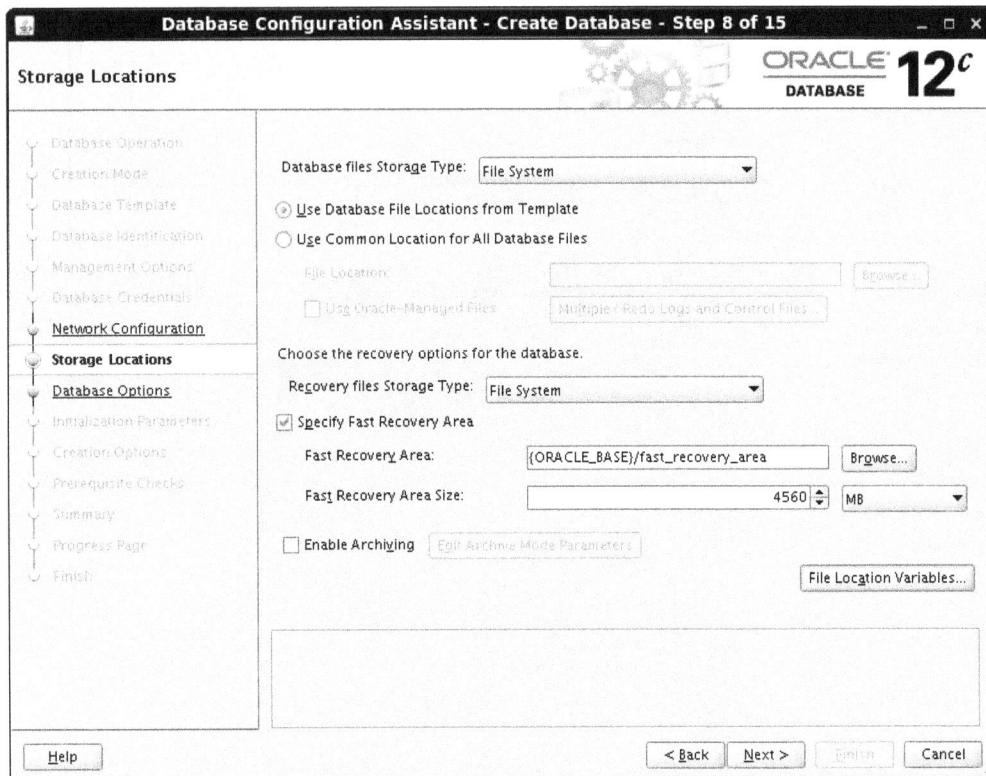

FIGURE 13-11. *Choosing database file destinations*

TIP & TECHNIQUE

Remember that if this database will reside on a platform that supports Linux Huge Page Memory, it's absolutely crucial to disable AMM before Huge Pages is activated. See My Oracle Support (MOS) Note 749851.1, HugePages and Oracle Database 11g Automatic Memory Management (AMM) on Linux, for complete information about this incompatibility.

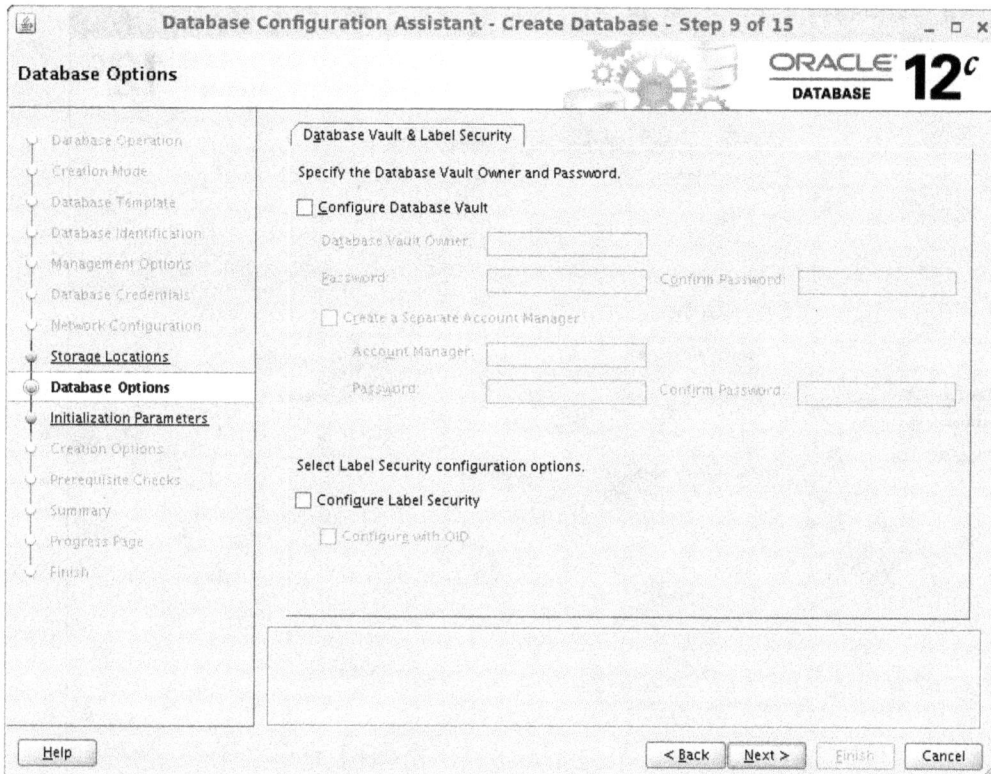

FIGURE 13-12. *Specifying Database Vault and Label Security options*

■ **Initialization Parameters (Character Sets tab)**   This tab allows you to specify which database character set and national language character set should be used (see Figure 13-14). Note that if you want to follow Oracle's recommendation to use the Unicode character set, you must choose that option specifically, as is shown in the figure.

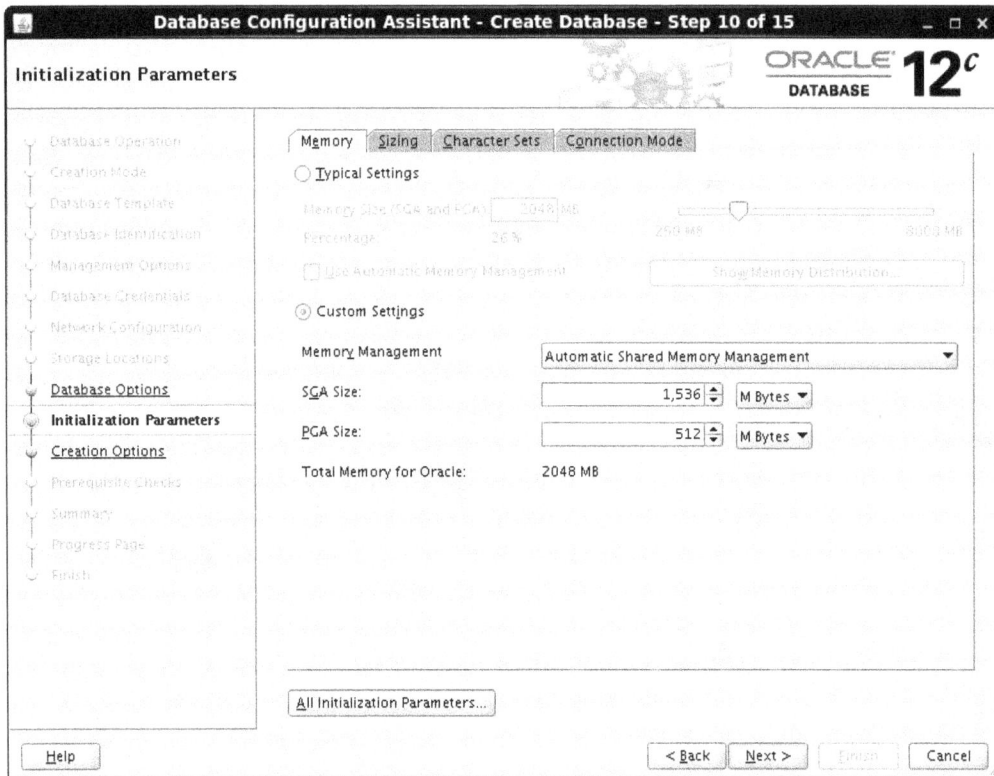

FIGURE 13-13. *Choosing AMM or ASMM features*

Once you've finished specifying these options, click Next to proceed. Figure 13-15 shows the final confirmation of the options for database creation. Once you click Next, DBCA will verify that all prerequisites for a successful CDB creation have been satisfied and if any are missing, it will display a screen informing you of the actions you have to take to correct those issues. If all prerequisites have

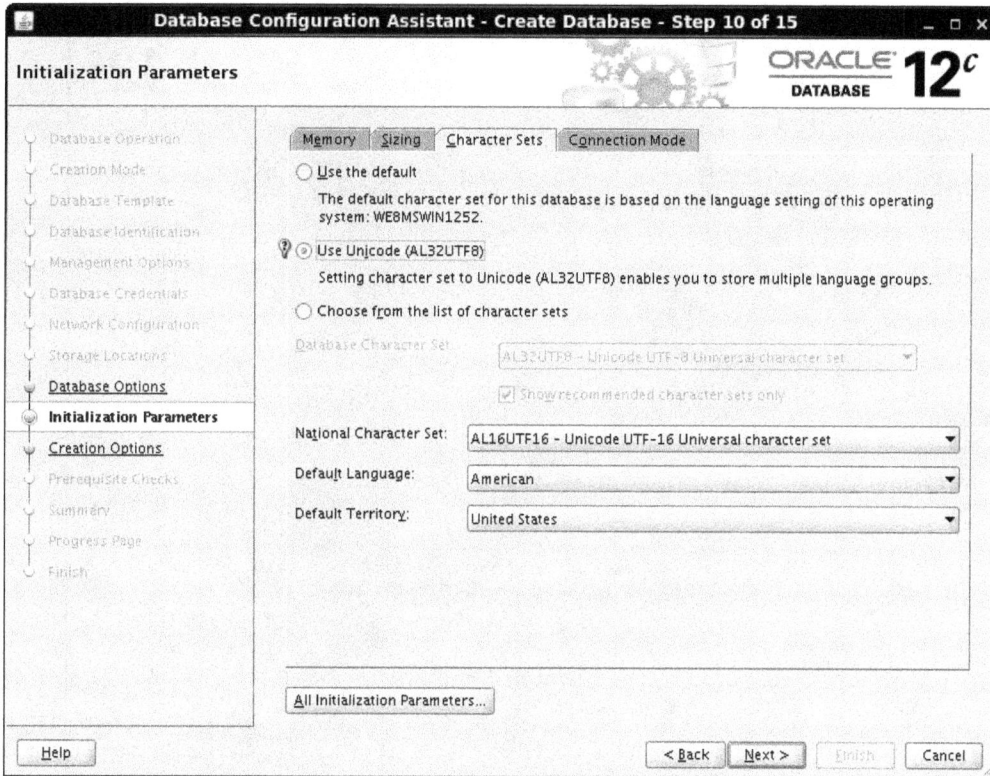

FIGURE 13-14. *Selecting database and national character sets*

been satisfied, you will have a final chance to review all configuration options before you proceed to create your CDB (see Figure 13-16).

Once you have clicked the Finish button, the actual creation of the CDB begins and the progress screen shown in see Figure 13-17 is displayed.

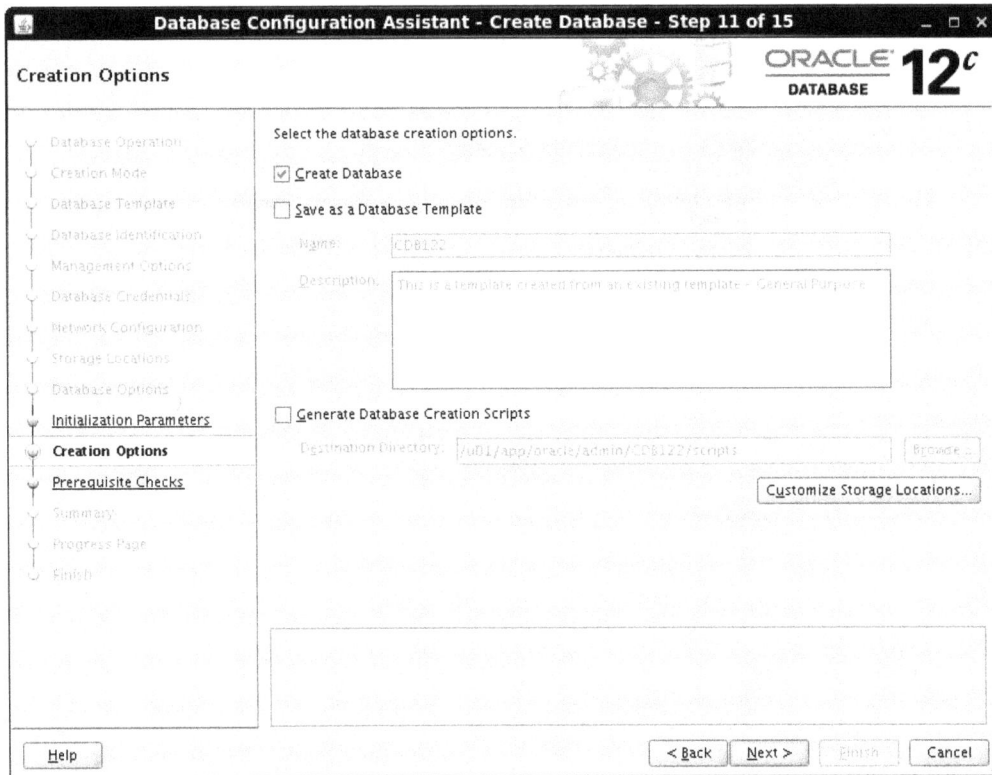

FIGURE 13-15. *Final confirmation of database creation options*

Finally, DBCA will show you a confirmation of the successful creation of your new CDB (see Figure 13-18). Note that at this point you can also choose to manage the passwords of any locked or expired user accounts from this screen by clicking the Password Management button; otherwise, click the Close button to end the DBCA session.

Now that you have successfully created your first CDB, you can decide which method is most appropriate to build and populate its corresponding PDBs. We discuss your options for PDB creation in an upcoming section.

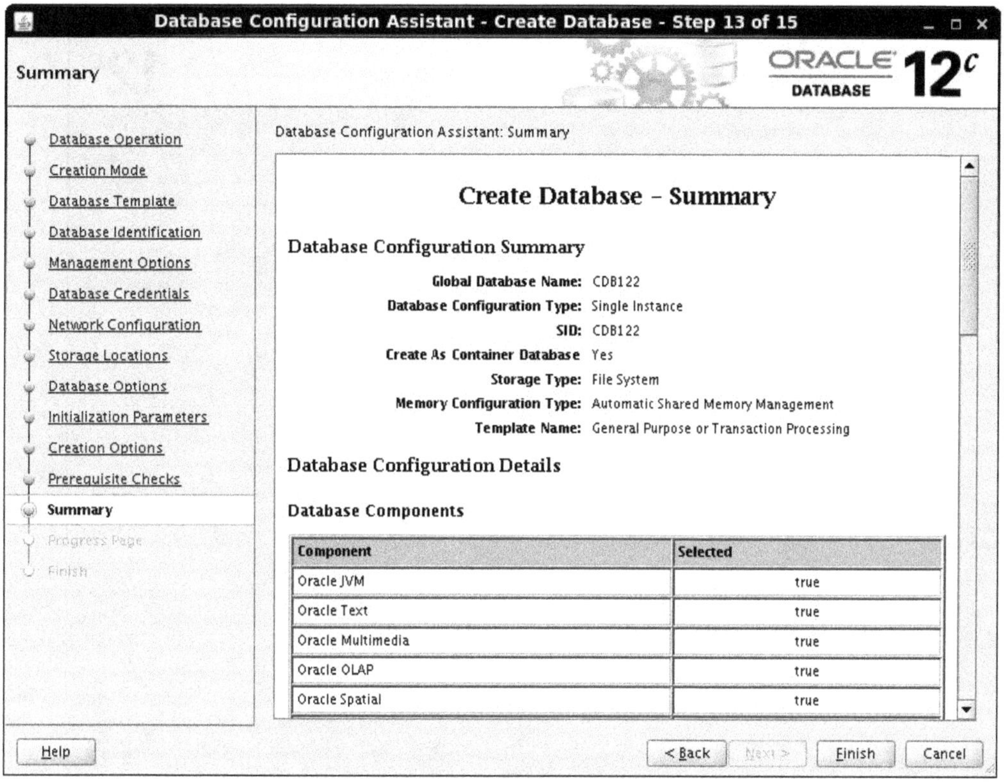

FIGURE 13-16. *Summary of selected database options*

"Upgrating" a Pre-12c Database to a 12c PDB: Mixed-Mode Methods

While it does take some time to transition to the new multitenant database environment of CDBs and PDBs, fortunately, creating a PDB once its CDB has been created is quite easy. In fact, it often only takes a matter of minutes (if not seconds!) to create an empty PDB that can serve as a container for the data stored within a pre-12c database. The end result is that it's often possible to "upgrade"—almost

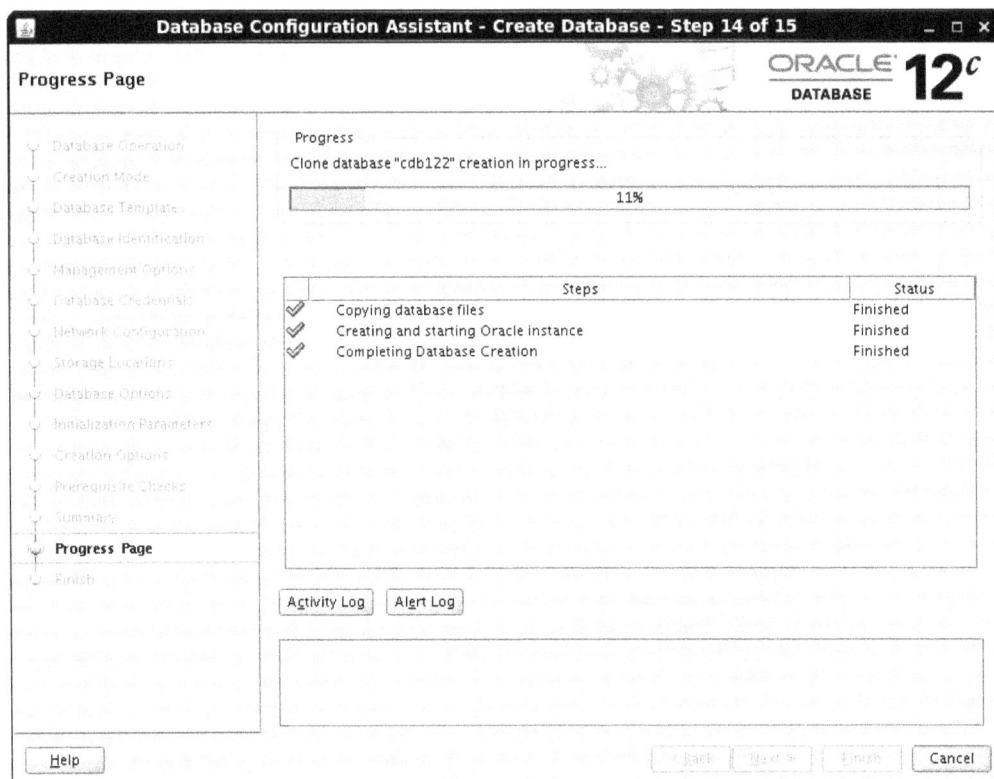

FIGURE 13-17. *Database creation progress report*

simultaneously *upgrade* and *migrate*—a pre-12*c* Oracle database to a 12*c* database using one or more of the methods we will discuss in the following sections.

Once a CDB is available to provide container capabilities for PDBs, Oracle 12*c* R1 offers three primary methodologies to transfer data from a non-CDB to a 12*c* PDB; of course, the appropriate choice of data transferal method will depend on the "window of inopportunity" (introduced in Chapter 3) that the source database's application workload(s) can tolerate.

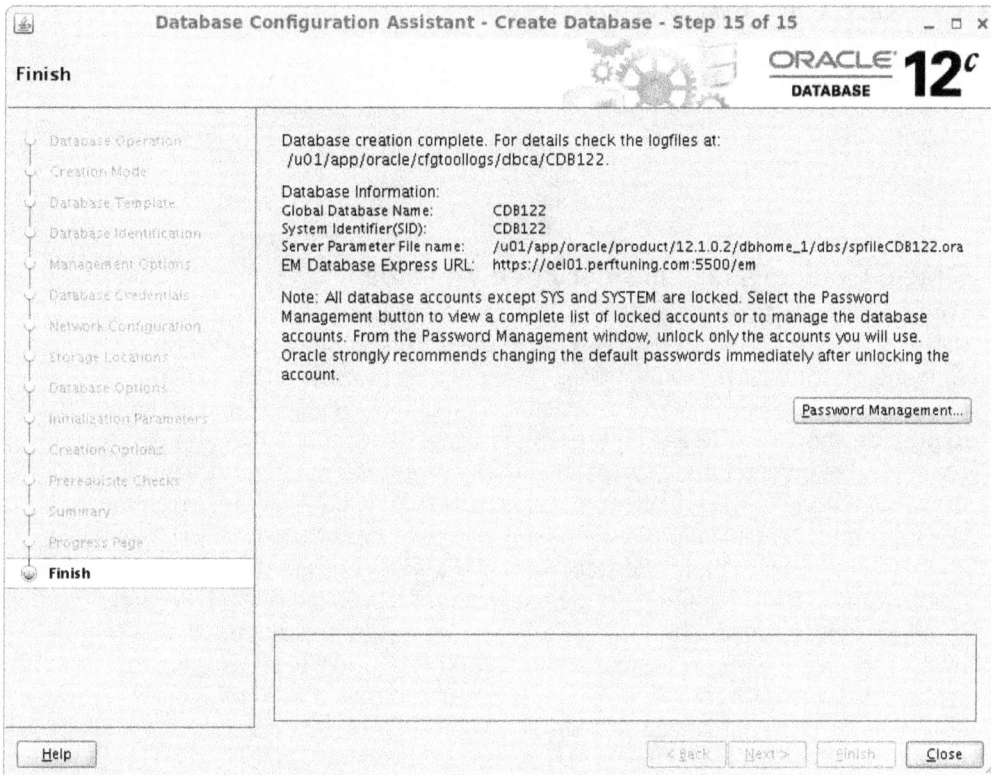

FIGURE 13-18. *Successful database creation summary*

Upgrading via Oracle GoldenGate

For an extremely short window of inopportunity, Oracle GoldenGate may be one of the best possible alternatives. GoldenGate offers an extensive array of data extraction, transformation, and data loading tools for heterogeneous database environments, but it is also an excellent mechanism to transfer data synchronously when application downtime must be kept to a bare minimum.

NOTE
See Chapter 8 for a detailed discussion on how to implement Oracle GoldenGate in various scenarios for migrating data from one database environment to another with virtually no downtime in most circumstances.

Oracle GoldenGate: Consider Price vs. Value

We have often heard our clients and colleagues complain about "sticker shock" when they have asked their Oracle sales representative to price out GoldenGate for their IT organizations … and we do indeed feel their pain. However, we have also heard anecdotal evidence that Oracle is often willing to provide short-term licensing for GoldenGate, especially when a large conversion effort is required to upgrade an organization's database systems to newly purchased hardware platforms like Oracle's Exadata Database Machine. We suggest that organizations remember the phrase "*Everything* is negotiable!" and repeat it often to their sales representatives when considering whether GoldenGate is a viable option. In the final analysis, the value of the DBA and developer effort saved when using GoldenGate to seamlessly convert a mission-critical database—and also keep the destination database's data *synchronized with that of its original source database*—may significantly outweigh the costs of even a short-term GoldenGate license.

Conversion via Cross-Platform Transportable Tablespace

If an application workload has a relatively narrow window of inopportunity during which it can accommodate at least a few moments of read-only access, then the Cross-Platform Transportable Tablespace (XTTS) migration method is probably the most appropriate choice for migrating the pre-12c database's tablespace sets. XTTS makes it possible to transfer INCREMENTAL LEVEL 0 image copies of the tablespace sets directly to the destination database and keep them synchronized between source and destination via periodic INCREMENTAL LEVEL 1 backup sets while those tablespaces are still open in READ WRITE mode. Only when the Oracle DBA makes the decision to finally synchronize source and destination one last time will those tablespaces need to be opened in READ ONLY mode.

NOTE
See Chapter 9 for detailed checklists and extensive examples of how the XTTS migration method can be employed to perform conversions.

Conversion via Transportable Tablespace Sets, Cross-Platform Transport, or Full Transportable Export

If the database's application workload can tolerate a reasonable window of inopportunity during which read-only access to its data is perfectly acceptable, then one of the conversion methods, described in the following sections, may be appropriate.

Transportable Tablespace Sets

If all application data to be migrated is contained within tightly defined tablespace sets, then the Transportable Tablespace Set (TTS) migration method is likely to work well. This is especially true when the application data is confined to only one or two schemas and can be migrated *en masse* to a single PDB.

NOTE
See Chapter 5 for detailed checklists and practical examples of using TTS to transfer tablespace sets.

Cross-Platform Transport via Backup Sets

If both the source and destination databases are at least Oracle release 12.1, then Oracle 12c R1's new *Cross-Platform Transport (CPT)* features may be an excellent option for transporting one or more self-contained tablespace sets between either non-CDBs or PDBs. CPT uses RMAN *backup sets* to capture tablespace sets at the source database, DBMS_FILE_TRANSFER to transfer and convert the tablespaces at the destination database, and Data Pump Export and Import to capture and load the tablespace sets' object metadata. Figure 13-19 shows an example of how CPT can be used to accomplish tablespace transport. (We will demonstrate how to use CPT to migrate data from a 12.1.0.1 non-CDB to a 12.1.0.2 PDB in the upcoming sections on PDB cloning.)

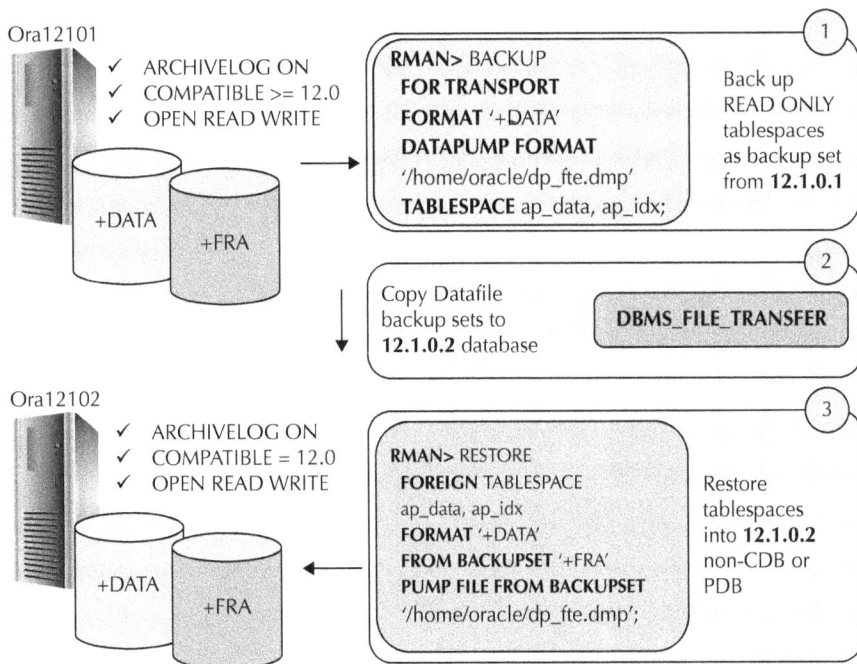

FIGURE 13-19. *Cross-Platform Transport via backup sets*

Data Pump Full Transportable Export

As long as the source database is at least Oracle release 11.2.0.3, Oracle 12*c* R1 provides the new Data Pump *Full Transportable Export (FTE)* to quickly accommodate the transfer of all relevant database objects—including those stored in the source database's data dictionary—to either a non-CDB or PDB. Figure 13-20 is an illustrated overview of how FTE can be leveraged to migrate data from a pre-12*c* R1 database directly into an existing non-CDB or PDB. (We will demonstrate how to leverage FTE to migrate a self-contained 11.2.0.4 non-CDB to a 12.1.0.1 PDB in the upcoming sections on PDB cloning.)

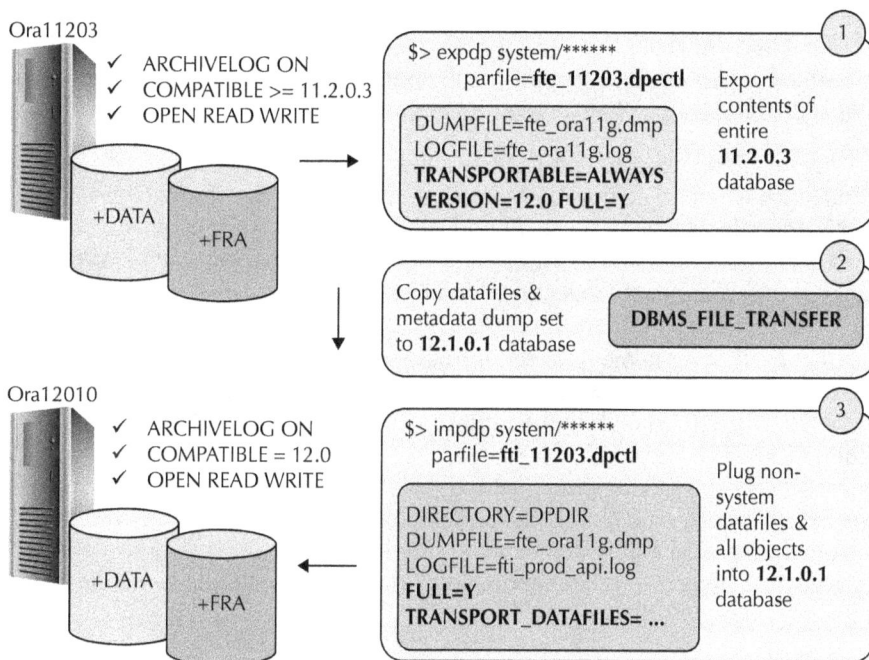

FIGURE 13-20. *Data Pump Full Transportable Export*

PDB Cloning Methods

The distinct advantages of multitenant CDBs become immediately apparent when we look at how easy it is to clone a pluggable database. Oracle 12.1.0.2 offers four distinct methods, each of which we will illustrate in the following sections:

- **Cloning a new empty PDB from PDB$SEED**   This method is especially effective when the goal is to migrate one or more tablespace sets from either a pre-12c or 12c non-CDB Oracle database using TTS or XTTS methods.

- **Cloning a new PDB from an existing PDB**   Once a PDB has already been created, this method works well when the migration goal is to create an exact copy of that source PDB.

■ **Unplugging and replugging an existing PDB**   When the goal is to migrate a PDB from one CDB environment to another, or even upgrade a PDB to the *next* release of Database 12c—for example, from 12.1.0.1 to 12.1.0.2—this method is likely the most appropriate option because it takes advantage of the shared metadata between the CDB and PDBs.

■ **Plugging in an existing non-CDB as a new PDB**   Finally, this method is effective when a 12c non-CDB database needs to be transformed into a 12c PDB. However, because all non-CDB's metadata must essentially be stripped out of the PDB during its transformation, this method typically requires a somewhat longer window of inopportunity.

Note that each of these methods requires the source non-CDB or PDB database's tablespaces to tolerate a window of inopportunity during which they are available only in READ ONLY mode while the tablespaces' datafiles are copied to the destination CDB.

Table 13-1 lists the four different methods available for specifying exactly where datafiles should be placed within either an OS file system or within an ASM disk group. Note that the order in which they are listed is also the order of precedence that Oracle 12c R1 will use to determine the ultimate location to place the datafiles within the destination PDB.

Parameter	Description	Version First Available
CREATE_FILE_DEST	■ Issued *only* "inline" as part of CREATE PLUGGABLE DATABASE command	12.1.0.2
	■ Sets a default location for all Oracle Managed Files (OMF) in this new PDB, regardless of the default location specified by DB_CREATE_FILE_DEST in CDB$ROOT	
	■ Most useful for shared storage environments	
FILE_NAME_CONVERT	■ Issued *only* "inline" as part of CREATE PLUGGABLE DATABASE command	12.1.0.1
	■ Most useful when PDB files are not yet at their ultimate destination but will be moved or copied during PDB creation	

Parameter	Description	Version First Available
DB_CREATE_FILE_DEST	■ If set at the CDB$ROOT level, becomes the default location for *all* PDBs *within* that CDB ■ If set at individual PDB level, defines the default location for *just* that PDB ■ Can be issued as part of CREATE PLUGGABLE DATABASE command	12.1.0.1
PDB_FILE_NAME_CONVERT	■ Issued as part of CREATE PLUGGABLE DATABASE command for a PDB, or as part of ENABLE PLUGGABLE DATABASE clause when creating a CDB ■ Unlike other parameters, maps *pairs* of source and destination tablespace name *replacement patterns*	12.1.0.1

TABLE 13-1.   *Directives Determining Placement of PDB Tablespaces in Destination PDB*

Scenario 1: Cloning a New Empty PDB from PDB$SEED and Transferring Data Into It

When the window of inopportunity for an application workload to access the source database's underlying data is relatively large, the source database's release is at least version 10.2.0.1, and all data is contained within one or more tablespace sets, then migration via either the TTS method or the XTTS method is probably most appropriate. This cloning method leverages an existing PDB "seed" database—appropriately named PDB$SEED—to create a new empty PDB into which the source database's data can then be transferred. Once a CDB has been opened in READ WRITE mode, PDB$SEED is *always* open in READ ONLY mode. Since the SYSTEM and SYSAUX tablespaces of PDB$SEED are the only tablespaces required to create a new empty PDB, this cloning operation takes no longer than the time required to clone the datafiles for these two tablespaces—usually a matter of seconds—and then the appropriate migration method can be employed. Checklist 13-1 lists the steps necessary to perform these cloning and data transfer operations.

Step	Operation	Description	Done?
1	Clone a New Empty PDB from PDB$SEED	Create a new empty PDB by cloning it from the PDB$SEED PDB	
2	Transfer Data into New PDB	Transfer data from the source database into the new PDB using the most appropriate migration method	

CHECKLIST 13-1 *Cloning a New Empty PDB from PDB$SEED and Transferring Data Into It*

Clone a New Empty PDB from PDB$SEED

The example in Listing 13-4 illustrates how to create an initially empty PDB named `prod_ap` within the `cdb121` CDB that can then immediately accept migrated data.

Listing 13-4 *Creating a New Empty prod_ap PDB*

```
SQL> CREATE PLUGGABLE DATABASE prod_ap
     ADMIN USER ap_admin
     IDENTIFIED BY oracle_4U
     ROLES=(CONNECT)
     FILE_NAME_CONVERT =
     ('/u01/app/oracle/oradata/cdb121/pdbseed'
     ,'/u01/app/oracle/oradata/cdb121/prod_ap';

Pluggable database created.

SQL> ALTER PLUGGABLE DATABASE prod_ap OPEN;

Pluggable database altered.
```

Here are the end results of cloning the empty `prod_ap` PDB using this method:

■ Two new tablespaces—`SYSTEM` and `SYSAUX`—owned *locally* by the `prod_ap` PDB are automatically cloned from those present in `PDB$SEED` and placed within the directory specified by the `FILE_NAME_CONVERT` directive.

■ Any of the `cdb121` CDB's existing *common* users are immediately available to `prod_ap`, as well as a new *local* user (in the previous example, `AP_ADMIN`) that is automatically granted the `PDB_DBA` role. Note that this user account can be granted any of the required privileges for PDB administration—even the ability to shut down and reopen the PDB—so it can essentially function as an intra-PDB database administration account.

■ A new default database service named `prod_ap` is also automatically created for communication directly to the new PDB via the existing listener(s).

Because the PDB$SEED database is always open in READ ONLY mode, cloning from this empty PDB usually takes no more than a few minutes, as this portion of the cdb121 CDB's alert log in Listing 13-5 shows.

Listing 13-5 *CDB121 Alert Log Entries Showing Creation of prod_ap PDB*

```
. . .
CREATE PLUGGABLE DATABASE prod_ap
    ADMIN USER ap_admin
    IDENTIFIED BY *      ROLES=(CONNECT)
    FILE_NAME_CONVERT =
    ('/u01/app/oracle/oradata/cdb121/pdbseed'
    ,'/u01/app/oracle/oradata/cdb121/prod_ap')
Fri Sep 12 20:21:13 2014
Pluggable Database PROD_AP with pdb id - 3 is created as UNUSABLE.
If any errors are encountered before the pdb is marked as NEW,
then the pdb must be dropped
****************************************************************
Deleting old file#5 from file$
Deleting old file#7 from file$
Adding new file#22 to file$(old file#5)
Adding new file#23 to file$(old file#7)
Successfully created internal service prod_ap at open
ALTER SYSTEM: Flushing buffer cache inst=0 container=3 local
****************************************************************
Post plug operations are now complete.
Pluggable database PROD_AP with pdb id - 3 is now marked as NEW.
****************************************************************
Completed: CREATE PLUGGABLE DATABASE prod_ap
    ADMIN USER ap_admin
    IDENTIFIED BY *      ROLES=(CONNECT)
    FILE_NAME_CONVERT =
    ('/u01/app/oracle/oradata/cdb121/pdbseed'
    ,'/u01/app/oracle/oradata/cdb121/prod_ap')
Fri Sep 12 21:49:08 2014
alter pluggable database prod_ap open
Fri Sep 12 21:49:08 2014
Pluggable database PROD_AP dictionary check beginning
Pluggable Database PROD_AP Dictionary check complete
Fri Sep 12 21:49:10 2014
Opening pdb PROD_AP (3) with no Resource Manager plan active
XDB installed.
XDB initialized.
Pluggable database PROD_AP opened read write
Completed: alter pluggable database prod_ap open
. . .
```

Transfer Data into New PDB

Now that the new prod_ap PDB exists, we will leverage the features of Data Pump FTE to transfer all data from a non-CDB into the new PDB.

Verify TTS Self-Containment   Just as with a TTS operation, the first step is to verify that all desired tablespaces are self-contained within tablespace sets, as shown in Listing 13-6.

Listing 13-6   *Verifying Self-Contained Tablespace Sets*

```
EXEC DBMS_TTS.TRANSPORT_SET_CHECK('AP_DATA,AP_IDX,USERS',TRUE,TRUE);

PL/SQL procedure successful.

SELECT * FROM transport_set_violations;

No rows returned
```

Prepare TTS for Transport and Metadata Capture   Next, all "non-system" tablespaces about to be transported are brought into READ ONLY mode, as shown in Listing 13-7.

Listing 13-7   *Bringing Transportable Tablespaces into READ ONLY State*

```
SQL> ALTER TABLESPACE ap_data READ ONLY;

Tablespace altered.

SQL> ALTER TABLESPACE ap_idx READ ONLY;

Tablespace altered.

SQL> ALTER TABLESPACE users READ ONLY;

Tablespace altered.
```

Perform TTS Metadata Capture   As Listing 13-8 shows, Data Pump Export is invoked to capture all TTS metadata as well as all database objects that have been stored within the database's data dictionary (for example, packages and stored procedures). Listing 13-9 shows the Data Pump Export parameter file, and Listing 13-10 displays abbreviated results of the Data Pump Export process.

Listing 13-8   *Exporting Tablespace Metadata into prod_ap*

```
$> expdp system/oracle_4U parfile=/home/oracle/fte_ora11g.dpectl
```

Listing 13-9   *Contents of fte_ora11g.dpectl Parameter File*

```
DIRECTORY=DATA_PUMP_DIR
DUMPFILE=fte_ora11g.dmp
LOGFILE=fte_ora11g.log
FULL=Y
TRANSPORTABLE=ALWAYS
VERSION=12.0
```

Listing 13-10 *Results of FTE Export*

```
Export: Release 11.2.0.4.0 - Production on Fri Sep 12 22:23:34 2014

Copyright (c) 1982, 2011, Oracle and/or its affiliates.  All rights reserved.

Connected to: Oracle Database 11g Enterprise Edition Release 11.2.0.4.0 - 64bit Pro-
duction
With the Partitioning, Automatic Storage Management, OLAP, Data Mining
and Real Application Testing options
Starting "SYSTEM"."SYS_EXPORT_FULL_01":  system/******** parfile=/home/oracle/fte_or-
a11g.dpectl
Estimate in progress using BLOCKS method...
Processing object type DATABASE_EXPORT/PLUGTS_FULL/FULL/PLUGTS_TABLESPACE
Processing object type DATABASE_EXPORT/PLUGTS_FULL/PLUGTS_BLK
Processing object type DATABASE_EXPORT/EARLY_OPTIONS/VIEWS_AS_TABLES/TABLE_DATA
Processing object type DATABASE_EXPORT/NORMAL_OPTIONS/TABLE_DATA
Processing object type DATABASE_EXPORT/NORMAL_OPTIONS/VIEWS_AS_TABLES/TABLE_DATA
Processing object type DATABASE_EXPORT/SCHEMA/TABLE/TABLE_DATA
Total estimation using BLOCKS method: 64.93 MB
Processing object type DATABASE_EXPORT/PRE_SYSTEM_IMPCALLOUT/MARKER
. . .
<< many lines omitted for sake of brevity >>
. . .
. . exported "SYSTEM"."REPCAT$_TEMPLATE_SITES"            0 KB       0 rows
. . exported "SYSTEM"."REPCAT$_TEMPLATE_TARGETS"          0 KB       0 rows
. . exported "SYSTEM"."REPCAT$_USER_AUTHORIZATIONS"       0 KB       0 rows
. . exported "SYSTEM"."REPCAT$_USER_PARM_VALUES"          0 KB       0 rows
. . exported "SYSTEM"."SQLPLUS_PRODUCT_PROFILE"           0 KB       0 rows
Master table "SYSTEM"."SYS_EXPORT_FULL_01" successfully loaded/unloaded
******************************************************************************
Dump file set for SYSTEM.SYS_EXPORT_FULL_01 is:
  /u01/app/oracle/admin/ora11g/dpdump/fte_ora11g.dmp
******************************************************************************
Datafiles required for transportable tablespace AP_DATA:
  +DATA/ora11g/datafile/ap_data.258.858108115
Datafiles required for transportable tablespace AP_IDX:
  +DATA/ora11g/datafile/ap_idx.257.858108117
Datafiles required for transportable tablespace USERS:
  +DATA/ora11g/datafile/users.263.858105481
Job "SYSTEM"."SYS_EXPORT_FULL_01" successfully completed at Fri Sep 12 22:29:49 2014
elapsed 0 00:06:14
```

Set Up the Destination PDB   At the destination PDB (`prod_ap`), Listing 13-11 shows the creation of a database link to the source non-CDB (`ora11g`) as well as a directory object that corresponds to the eventual destination for all of the non-CDB's database files that are about to be transferred.

Listing 13-11   *Creating Database Objects on prod_ap for Data Transfer*

```
DROP DATABASE LINK ora11g;
CREATE DATABASE LINK ora11g
   CONNECT TO system IDENTIFIED BY "oracle_4U"
   USING 'ora11g';

CREATE OR REPLACE DIRECTORY prod_ap
   AS '/u01/app/oracle/oradata/cdb121/prod_ap';
```

Transfer Datafiles to PDB   Listing 13-12 demonstrates how to use DBMS_FILE_
TRANSFER to migrate the non-CDB's datafiles directly to the appropriate directory
for the prod_ap PDB.

Listing 13-12   *Transferring Database Files to prod_ap Datafile Directory*

```
BEGIN
    DBMS_FILE_TRANSFER.GET_FILE(
        source_directory_object => 'ORA11G_DBF'
        ,source_file_name => 'USERS.263.858105481'
        ,destination_directory_object => 'PROD_AP'
        ,destination_file_name => 'users.dbf'
        ,source_database => 'ORA11G'
    );
    DBMS_FILE_TRANSFER.GET_FILE(
        source_directory_object => 'ORA11G_DBF'
        ,source_file_name => 'AP_DATA.258.858108115'
        ,destination_directory_object => 'PROD_AP'
        ,destination_file_name => 'ap_data.dbf'
        ,source_database => 'ORA11G'
    );
    DBMS_FILE_TRANSFER.GET_FILE(
        source_directory_object => 'ORA11G_DBF'
        ,source_file_name => 'AP_IDX.257.858108117'
        ,destination_directory_object => 'PROD_AP'
        ,destination_file_name => 'ap_idx.dbf'
        ,source_database => 'ORA11G'
    );
END;
/
```

Import Data into PDB   One interesting wrinkle with using FTE with a PDB is that
it's necessary to create a separate directory object for the PDB to access the appropriate
files and metadata, as Listing 13-13 shows.

Listing 13-13   *Creating Directory Object for PDB Access to Data Pump Directory*

```
CREATE OR REPLACE DIRECTORY dpdir
    AS '/u01/app/oracle/admin/cdb121/dpdump';
GRANT READ ON DIRECTORY dpdir TO PUBLIC;
GRANT WRITE ON DIRECTORY dpdir TO PUBLIC;
```

Finally, it's time to import the metadata into the prod_ap PDB. Listing 13-14
shows how Data Pump Import is invoked to complete the transfer of all TTS metadata
as well as all database objects that have been stored within the database's data
dictionary (for example, packages and stored procedures). Listing 13-15 shows the
Data Pump Export parameter file, and Listing 13-16 displays abbreviated results of
the Data Pump Import process.

Listing 13-14 *Importing Tablespace Metadata into prod_ap*

```
$> impdp system/oracle_4U@prod_ap parfile=/home/oracle/fti_prod_ap.dpictl
```

Listing 13-15 *Contents of fti_prod_ap.dpictl Parameter File*

```
DIRECTORY=DATA_PUMP_DIR
DUMPFILE=fte_ora11g.dmp
LOGFILE=fti_prod_api.log
FULL=Y
TRANSPORT_DATAFILES='/u01/app/oracle/oradata/cdb121/prod_ap/users.dbf',
'/u01/app/oracle/oradata/cdb121/prod_ap/ap_data.dbf',
'/u01/app/oracle/oradata/cdb121/prod_ap/ap_idx.dbf'
```

Listing 13-16 *Results of FTE Import*

```
Import: Release 12.1.0.1.0 - Production on Fri Sep 12 23:23:46 2014

Copyright (c) 1982, 2013, Oracle and/or its affiliates.  All rights reserved.

Connected to: Oracle Database 12c Enterprise Edition Release 12.1.0.1.0 - 64bit
Production
With the Partitioning, OLAP, Advanced Analytics and Real Application Testing options
Master table "SYSTEM"."SYS_IMPORT_FULL_01" successfully loaded/unloaded
Source timezone version is +00:00 and target timezone version is -07:00.
Starting "SYSTEM"."SYS_IMPORT_FULL_01":  system/********@prod_ap parfile=/home/oracle/
fti_prod_ap.dpictl
Processing object type DATABASE_EXPORT/PRE_SYSTEM_IMPCALLOUT/MARKER
Processing object type DATABASE_EXPORT/PRE_INSTANCE_IMPCALLOUT/MARKER
Processing object type DATABASE_EXPORT/PLUGTS_FULL/PLUGTS_BLK
Processing object type DATABASE_EXPORT/TABLESPACE
ORA-39083: Object type TABLESPACE:"UNDOTBS1" failed to create with error:
ORA-02236: invalid file name
Failing sql is:
CREATE UNDO TABLESPACE "UNDOTBS1" DATAFILE SIZE 26214400 AUTOEXTEND ON NEXT 5242880
MAXSIZE 32767M BLOCKSIZE 8192 EXTENT MANAGEMENT LOCAL AUTOALLOCATE
ORA-39083: Object type TABLESPACE:"TEMP" failed to create with error:
ORA-02236: invalid file name
Failing sql is:
CREATE TEMPORARY TABLESPACE "TEMP" TEMPFILE SIZE 30408704 AUTOEXTEND ON NEXT 655360
MAXSIZE 32767M EXTENT MANAGEMENT LOCAL UNIFORM SIZE 1048576
Processing object type DATABASE_EXPORT/PROFILE
Processing object type DATABASE_EXPORT/SYS_USER/USER
Processing object type DATABASE_EXPORT/SCHEMA/USER
ORA-31684: Object type USER:"OUTLN" already exists
. . .
<< many lines omitted for sake of brevity >>
. . .
```

Scenario 2: Cloning a New PDB from an Existing PDB

Oracle 12*c* R1 also makes it extremely simple to clone an existing PDB to a new PDB. An excellent business case for this scenario is the need to create a new QA or staging database from a current production database:

- If the source production database is already housed within a separate PDB, then this technique makes extremely short work of creating an exact copy of the production environment because all that really needs to be done in this situation is to copy the source PDB's local tablespaces, users, and roles to a new target PDB.

- This means the duplicated PDB can be plugged into the *same* CDB as its production source so that application workloads can be tested within the *identical* database infrastructure.

- It is also possible to plug the newly cloned PDB into a completely *different* CDB—for example, another CDB that's hosting the physical standby database for the source PDB—to alleviate any potential contention for resources on the original platform.

Again, it's important to remember that during the cloning of the selected source PDB, all *other* PDBs within both the source and destination CDBs remain open and thus remain *completely accessible* for executing application workloads.

Checklist 13-2 lists the steps necessary to perform this cloning operation.

Step	Operation	Description	Done?
1	Determine destination directory for new PDB	Determine where the new PDB tablespaces' datafiles should reside on the destination platform.	
2	Quiesce source PDB	Bring the source PDB into READ ONLY mode to guarantee transactional consistency before and after data transference.	
3	Clone new PDB	Copy the source PDB's contents to a new PDB at the destination CDB.	
4	Reactivate source PDB	Return the source PDB to READ WRITE mode.	

CHECKLIST 13-2   *Cloning a New PDB from an Existing PDB*

To demonstrate the simplicity of this technique, we will clone the `prod_ap` PDB to a new PDB, `qa_ap`, within the `cdb121` CDB.

Step 1: Determine Destination Directory for New PDB

Once the location for the new PDB's files has been determined, that new location must be specified using one of the clauses and methods previously described in Table 13-1.

Step 2: Quiesce Source PDB

The source PDB for the cloning operation—`prod_ap`—must first be quiesced so that its tablespaces can be quickly copied to the new target PDB. The quiesce operation is accomplished by connecting to the `CDB$ROOT` container, shutting down the `prod_ap` PDB, and then reopening it in `READ ONLY` mode, as Listing 13-17 shows.

Listing 13-17   *Quiescing a Pluggable Database*

```
SQL> ALTER SESSION SET CONTAINER=cdb$root;

SQL> ALTER PLUGGABLE DATABASE prod_ap CLOSE IMMEDIATE;

Pluggable database altered.

SQL> ALTER PLUGGABLE DATABASE prod_ap OPEN READ ONLY;

Pluggable database altered.
```

Step 3: Clone New PDB

Now that the source PDB is in the proper state for cloning, we can immediately create the new `qa_ap` PDB. Since the source PDB's tablespaces are simply copied to the specified destination for the new PDB, the key limiting factor for this operation is the relative size of the source database's files. Listing 13-18 shows the commands issued to create the new PDB, while Listing 13-19 displays the corresponding information from the CDB's alert log.

Listing 13-18   *Cloning a Quiesced Pluggable Database*

```
SQL> CREATE PLUGGABLE DATABASE qa_ap FROM prod_ap
     FILE_NAME_CONVERT=(
       '/u01/app/oracle/oradata/cdb121/prod_ap'
       '/u01/app/oracle/oradata/cdb121/qa_ap');

Pluggable database created.

SQL> ALTER PLUGGABLE DATABASE qa_ap OPEN;

Pluggable database altered.
```

Listing 13-19   *Results of Cloning Quiesced Pluggable Database*

```
. . .
ALTER PLUGGABLE DATABASE prod_ap CLOSE IMMEDIATE
Sun Sep 14 22:12:23 2014
ALTER SYSTEM: Flushing buffer cache inst=0 container=3 local
Pluggable database PROD_AP closed
Completed: ALTER PLUGGABLE DATABASE prod_ap CLOSE IMMEDIATE
ALTER PLUGGABLE DATABASE prod_ap OPEN READ ONLY
Opening pdb PROD_AP (3) with no Resource Manager plan active
Pluggable database PROD_AP opened read only
Completed: ALTER PLUGGABLE DATABASE prod_ap OPEN READ ONLY
CREATE PLUGGABLE DATABASE qa_ap FROM prod_ap
     FILE_NAME_CONVERT=(
       '/u01/app/oracle/oradata/cdb121/prod_ap'
      ,'/u01/app/oracle/oradata/cdb121/qa_ap')
Sun Sep 14 22:13:31 2014
****************************************************************
Pluggable Database QA_AP with pdb id - 4 is created as UNUSABLE.
If any errors are encountered before the pdb is marked as NEW,
then the pdb must be dropped
****************************************************************
Deleting old file#22 from file$
Deleting old file#23 from file$
Deleting old file#24 from file$
Deleting old file#25 from file$
Deleting old file#26 from file$
Adding new file#27 to file$(old file#22)
Adding new file#28 to file$(old file#23)
Adding new file#29 to file$(old file#24)
Adding new file#30 to file$(old file#25)
Adding new file#31 to file$(old file#26)
Successfully created internal service qa_ap at open
ALTER SYSTEM: Flushing buffer cache inst=0 container=4 local
****************************************************************
Post plug operations are now complete.
Pluggable database QA_AP with pdb id - 4 is now marked as NEW.
****************************************************************
Completed: CREATE PLUGGABLE DATABASE qa_ap FROM prod_ap
     FILE_NAME_CONVERT=(
       '/u01/app/oracle/oradata/cdb121/prod_ap'
      ,'/u01/app/oracle/oradata/cdb121/qa_ap')
alter pluggable database qa_ap open
Sun Sep 14 22:14:00 2014
Pluggable database QA_AP dictionary check beginning
Opening pdb QA_AP (4) with no Resource Manager plan active
Sun Sep 14 22:14:12 2014

XDB installed.

XDB initialized.
Pluggable database QA_AP opened read write
Completed: alter pluggable database qa_ap open
. . .
```

Step 4: Reactivate Source PDB

Once PDB cloning operations are complete, the source PDB can be put back immediately into READ WRITE mode and transaction activity can resume, as shown in Listing 13-20.

Listing 13-20   *Reactivating a Quiesced Pluggable Database*

```
SQL> ALTER PLUGGABLE DATABASE prod_ap CLOSE IMMEDIATE;

Pluggable database altered.

SQL> ALTER PLUGGABLE DATABASE prod_ap OPEN;

Pluggable database altered.
```

Scenario 3: Unplugging and Replugging an Existing PDB

When the migration goal is to create an exact copy of a source PDB within a different CDB, the methods we are about to describe work particularly well. In this situation, you simply quiesce and then *unplug* the source PDB from its current CDB, capture that PDB's metadata, transfer the PDB and its metadata to a new destination CDB, and then *replug* that PDB into its new CDB.

Checklist 13-3 summarizes the required steps to migrate an existing PDB between CDBs using these techniques.

Step	Operation	Description	Done?
1	Quiesce source PDB	Bring the source database into READ ONLY mode to guarantee transactional consistency before and after data transference.	
2	Unplug PDB from source CDB	Issue the ALTER PLUGGABLE DATABASE … UNPLUG command to unplug the source PDB from its current CDB.	
3	Drop unplugged PDB from source CDB	Issue the DROP PLUGGABLE DATABASE command to drop the source PDB.	

CHECKLIST 13-3   *Unplugging and Replugging a PDB*

Step	Operation	Description	Done?
4	Verify compatibility of unplugged PDB with its destination CDB	Run the `CHECK_PLUG_COMPATIBILITY` procedure of the `DBMS_PDB` package to verify the PDB's compatibility with the destination CDB.	
5	Replug PDB into destination CDB	Issue `CREATE PLUGGABLE DATABASE` command to replug source PDB into its new destination CDB.	
6	Reactivate replugged PDB	Issue `ALTER DATABASE OPEN;` to open the replugged PDB at its new CDB location.	

CHECKLIST 13-3 *Unplugging and Replugging a PDB* (Continued)

Step 1: Quiesce Source PDB

Just as in Scenario 2, the source PDB must first be quiesced so that its tablespaces and their metadata can be quickly copied to the new target PDB; this also guarantees transactional consistency until the PDB has been cloned to its new CDB. As Listing 13-21 shows, the CDB$ROOT user account must be used for all unplugging activity.

Listing 13-21 *Quiescing Source PDB*

```
SQL> CONNECT / AS SYSDBA;

Connected.

SQL> ALTER PLUGGABLE DATABASE qa_ap CLOSE IMMEDIATE;

Pluggable database altered.
```

Step 2: Unplug PDB from Source CDB

Next, the PDB is unplugged and all of its metadata is captured in XML format into a configuration file for later processing within its eventual target CDB, as shown in Listing 13-22.

Listing 13-22 *Unplugging Source PDB*

```
SQL> ALTER PLUGGABLE DATABASE qa_ap
     UNPLUG INTO '/home/oracle/qa_ap.xml';

Pluggable database altered.
```

The contents of this XML are actually quite simple and describe the makeup of the PDB within its current CDB, as Listing 13-23 shows.

Listing 13-23 *Unplugged PDB XML File*

```xml
<?xml version="1.0" encoding="UTF-8"?>
<PDB>
  <pdbname>QA_AP</pdbname>
  <cid>4</cid>
  <byteorder>1</byteorder>
  <vsn>202375168</vsn>
  <dbid>2578733401</dbid>
  <cdbid>3817595895</cdbid>
  <guid>03130008AA0C53AEE0531C32A8C0B301</guid>
  <uscnbas>5833902</uscnbas>
  <uscnwrp>0</uscnwrp>
  <rdba>4194824</rdba>
  <tablespace>
    <name>SYSTEM</name>
    <type>0</type>
    <tsn>0</tsn>
    <status>1</status>
    <issft>0</issft>
    <file>
      <path>/u01/app/oracle/oradata/cdb121/qa_ap/system01.dbf</path>
      <afn>27</afn>
      <rfn>1</rfn>
      <createscnbas>5790803</createscnbas>
      <createscnwrp>0</createscnwrp>
      <status>1</status>
      <fileblocks>53760</fileblocks>
      <blocksize>8192</blocksize>
      <vsn>202375168</vsn>
      <fdbid>2578733401</fdbid>
      <fcpsw>0</fcpsw>
      <fcpsb>5833900</fcpsb>
      <frlsw>0</frlsw>
      <frlsb>1720082</frlsb>
      <frlt>857383736</frlt>
    </file>
  </tablespace>
  . . .
  << many lines omitted for sake of brevity >>
  . . .
  <tablespace>
    <name>USERS</name>
    <type>0</type>
    <tsn>5</tsn>
    <status>1</status>
    <issft>0</issft>
    <file>
      <path>/u01/app/oracle/oradata/cdb121/qa_ap/users.dbf</path>
      <afn>31</afn>
      <rfn>4</rfn>
```

```
      <createscnbas>5790813</createscnbas>
      <createscnwrp>0</createscnwrp>
      <status>1</status>
      <fileblocks>640</fileblocks>
      <blocksize>8192</blocksize>
      <vsn>202375168</vsn>
      <fdbid>2578733401</fdbid>
      <fcpsw>0</fcpsw>
      <fcpsb>5833900</fcpsb>
      <frlsw>0</frlsw>
      <frlsb>1720082</frlsb>
      <frlt>857383736</frlt>
    </file>
  </tablespace>
  <optional>
    <csid>873</csid>
    <ncsid>2000</ncsid>
    <options>
      <option>APS=12.1.0.1.0</option>
      <option>CATALOG=12.1.0.1.0</option>
      <option>CATJAVA=12.1.0.1.0</option>
      <option>CATPROC=12.1.0.1.0</option>
      <option>CONTEXT=12.1.0.1.0</option>
      <option>DV=12.1.0.1.0</option>
      <option>JAVAVM=12.1.0.1.0</option>
      <option>OLS=12.1.0.1.0</option>
      <option>ORDIM=12.1.0.1.0</option>
      <option>OWM=12.1.0.1.0</option>
      <option>SDO=12.1.0.1.0</option>
      <option>XDB=12.1.0.1.0</option>
      <option>XML=12.1.0.1.0</option>
      <option>XOQ=12.1.0.1.0</option>
    </options>
    <olsoid>0</olsoid>
    <dv>0</dv>
    <ncdb2pdb>0</ncdb2pdb>
    <APEX>4.2.0.00.27:1</APEX>
    <parameters>
      <parameter>processes=300</parameter>
      <parameter>sga_target=1610612736</parameter>
      <parameter>db_block_size=8192</parameter>
      <parameter>compatible=12.1.0.0.0</parameter>
      <parameter>open_cursors=300</parameter>
      <parameter>pga_aggregate_target=536870912</parameter>
      <parameter>enable_pluggable_database=TRUE</parameter>
    </parameters>
    <tzvers>
      <tzver>primary version:18</tzver>
      <tzver>secondary version:0</tzver>
    </tzvers>
    <walletkey>0</walletkey>
  </optional>
</PDB>
```

NOTE
While it is certainly possible and even tempting to edit this XML file via your favorite editor, we strongly discourage it. If you feel the urge to edit it anyway, we strongly recommend making a backup copy of it first.

Step 3: Drop Unplugged PDB from Source CDB

Before the unplugged source PDB can be replugged into its new destination CDB, it must be dropped from its original source CDB, as shown in Listing 13-24.

Listing 13-24   *Dropping Source PDB*

```
SQL> DROP PLUGGABLE DATABASE qa_ap;

Pluggable database dropped.
```

Step 4: Verify Compatibility of Unplugged PDB with Its Destination CDB

Before attempting to plug in the now-unplugged source PDB, it's a recommended best practice to employ 12c R1 procedure DBMS_PDB.CHECK_PLUG_COMPATIBILITY to verify that the destination CDB can actually accept the PDB that's about to be replugged. Listing 13-25 shows the results of executing this procedure from the CDB$ROOT container of the destination CDB against the unplugged qa_ap PDB's XML file.

NOTE
For the sake of simplicity, we are using the original CDB (CDB121) as the destination CDB to demonstrate this replugging operation.

Listing 13-25   *Verifying Unplugged PDB for Compatibility with Destination CDB*

```
SQL> CONNECT / AS SYSDBA;

Connected.

SQL> ALTER SESSION SET CONTAINER=CDB$ROOT;

Session altered.

SQL> SET SERVEROUTPUT ON
SQL> DECLARE
  compatible CONSTANT VARCHAR2(3) :=
    CASE DBMS_PDB.CHECK_PLUG_COMPATIBILITY(
           pdb_descr_file => '/home/oracle/qa_ap.xml'
          ,pdb_name       => 'qa_ap')
        WHEN TRUE
```

```
            THEN 'is'
        ELSE 'is +NOT+'
    END;
BEGIN
    DBMS_OUTPUT.PUT_LINE(
        'This PDB or non-CDB ' || compatible
        || ' compatible with its destination CDB.'
    );
END;
/
```

This PDB or non-CDB is compatible with its destination CDB.
PL/SQL procedure successfully completed.

Step 5: Replug PDB into Destination CDB

Once the unplugged PDB has been successfully validated for its "pluggability," it is time to plug it into the destination CDB. As Listing 13-26 shows, this command must be executed from the CDB$ROOT user account of the destination CDB.

Listing 13-26   *Replugging PDB into Destination CDB*

```
SQL> CONNECT / AS SYSDBA;

Connected.

SQL> ALTER SESSION SET CONTAINER=CDB$ROOT;

Session altered.

SQL> CREATE PLUGGABLE DATABASE qa_ap
     USING 'qa_ap.xml' NOCOPY;

Pluggable database created.
```

Table 13-2 shows the three options for determining exactly where the replugged PDB's datafiles will be placed. (See Table 13-1 for a breakdown of the available filename conversion options.)

Parameter Value	Result
COPY	The default action. A new *copy* of all datafiles will be created in the location specified by the filename conversion options.
MOVE	The source datafiles will be *moved* to the location specified by the filename conversion options.
NOCOPY	The source datafiles will be *retained and reused* at their current location.

TABLE 13-2.   *Directives Determining Migration of PDB Datafiles to Destination PDB*

Step 6: Reactivate "Replugged" PDB

Once the cloning operation has been verified, the target PDB can be put back immediately into READ WRITE mode within its target CDB, and transaction activity can resume, as shown in Listing 13-27.

Listing 13-27 *Reactivating Replugged PDB*

```
SQL> ALTER PLUGGABLE DATABASE qa_ap OPEN;

Pluggable database opened.
```

Listing 13-28 highlights edited sections of CDB cdb121's alert log that show the results of these successful unplugging and replugging operations for the qa_ap PDB.

Listing 13-28 *CDB121 Alert Log Entries for Scenario 3*

```
. . .
alter pluggable database qa_ap close immediate
Mon Sep 15 15:15:51 2014
ALTER SYSTEM: Flushing buffer cache inst=0 container=4 local
Pluggable database QA_AP closed
Completed: alter pluggable database qa_ap close immediate
ALTER PLUGGABLE DATABASE qa_ap
  UNPLUG INTO '/home/oracle/qa_ap.xml'
Mon Sep 15 15:20:07 2014
ALTER SYSTEM: Flushing buffer cache inst=0 container=4 local
ALTER SYSTEM: Flushing buffer cache inst=0 container=4 local
Completed: ALTER PLUGGABLE DATABASE qa_ap
  UNPLUG INTO '/home/oracle/qa_ap.xml'
. . .
drop pluggable database qa_ap
Mon Sep 15 15:29:25 2014
Deleted file /u01/app/oracle/oradata/cdb121/qa_ap/pdbseed_temp01.dbf
Completed: drop pluggable database qa_ap
. . .
Mon Sep 15 15:42:56 2014
CREATE PLUGGABLE DATABASE qa_ap
    USING '/home/oracle/qa_ap.xml' NOCOPY
Mon Sep 15 15:42:56 2014
*****************************************************************
Pluggable Database QA_AP with pdb id - 4 is created as UNUSABLE.
If any errors are encountered before the pdb is marked as NEW,
then the pdb must be dropped
*****************************************************************
Deleting old file#27 from file$
Deleting old file#28 from file$
Deleting old file#29 from file$
Deleting old file#30 from file$
Deleting old file#31 from file$
Adding new file#32 to file$(old file#27)
Adding new file#33 to file$(old file#28)
Adding new file#34 to file$(old file#29)
```

```
Adding new file#35 to file$(old file#30)
Adding new file#36 to file$(old file#31)
Successfully created internal service qa_ap at open
ALTER SYSTEM: Flushing buffer cache inst=0 container=4 local
****************************************************************
Post plug operations are now complete.
Pluggable database QA_AP with pdb id - 4 is now marked as NEW.
****************************************************************
Completed: CREATE PLUGGABLE DATABASE qa_ap
     USING '/home/oracle/qa_ap.xml' NOCOPY
. . .
ALTER PLUGGABLE DATABASE qa_ap OPEN
Mon Sep 15 15:44:23 2014
Pluggable database QA_AP dictionary check beginning
Pluggable Database QA_AP Dictionary check complete
Opening pdb QA_AP (4) with no Resource Manager plan active
XDB installed.
XDB initialized.
Pluggable database QA_AP opened read write
Completed: ALTER PLUGGABLE DATABASE qa_ap OPEN
```

Upgrading PDBs to Next Database Release via Unplugging and Replugging

Be aware that it's also possible to unplug an existing PDB from its *current* CDB that is running under one Oracle release—say, 12.1.0.1—and then plug it back into a *different* CDB that's running at a higher release level—say, 12.1.0.2. This method also requires that the PDB being upgraded must first be opened in UPGRADE mode. It is also necessary to upgrade the PDB's metadata to the latest Oracle release by invoking the new catctl.pl Perl script. (Whenever a non-CDB, CDB, or PDB is upgraded, by the way, as of Oracle 12c R1 the invocation of catctl.pl is now a mandatory prerequisite of any manual database upgrade process.)

While the invocation of catctl.pl admittedly can take a considerable amount of time to complete, it's important to remember that *only the PDB being upgraded* is temporarily unavailable while the upgrade scripts proceed. This method therefore makes it extremely simple to perform database upgrades from one release to the next without requiring that an entire CDB remain offline while the upgrade completes.

Scenario 4: Plugging In an Existing Non-CDB as a New PDB

Whenever a non-CDB database must be transformed into a Oracle 12c PDB, this method usually provides an optimal path. However, the current database version of the non-CDB is the crucial determinant for this method's effectiveness:

■ If the non-CDB is *already* an Oracle 12c R1 database, then all that needs to be done is to quiesce the non-CDB, convert it to a PDB, and plug it into an existing CDB, as we will demonstrate in the workflow that follows.

■ On the other hand, if the non-CDB is *not* an Oracle 12c R1 database, then two other options for plugging it into an existing CDB are available:

   ■ *Upgrade* the existing pre-12c R1 database to a 12c R1 non-CDB, and then use the workflow that follows to plug it into an existing CDB as a new PDB.

   ■ *Clone* a new empty PDB from PDB$SEED as described in Scenario 1, and then *reload* the non-CDB's data into the new PDB. As we have already mentioned, reloading data into the empty PDB can be accomplished in several ways, including Oracle GoldenGate, TTS, CPT, and FTE.

Which of these methods is most appropriate, of course, depends primarily on the uptime requirements of the non-CDB, as well as its upgradeability based on whether it is a pre-12c or 12c non-CDB. In addition, this method tends to take considerably longer than the previous three methods because all extraneous metadata must be removed from the PDB after it has been plugged into its CDB.

Checklist 13-4 lists the steps necessary to transform an Oracle 12c non-CDB into a 12c PDB.

Step	Operation	Description	Done?
1	Quiesce source Non-CDB	Bring source non-CDB into READ ONLY mode to guarantee transactional consistency before and after data transference.	
2	Construct PDB metadata	Build corresponding metadata for the new PDB.	
3	Shut down source non-CDB	Close non-CDB database.	

CHECKLIST 13-4   *Transforming a Non-CDB into a PDB*

4	Plug in PDB	Use previously captured metadata to plug non-CDB into CDB as new PDB.	
5	Resolve extraneous metadata in new PDB	Execute `noncdb_to_pdb.sql` script to eliminate redundant metadata in new PDB.	
6	Open new PDB in `READ WRITE` mode	Bring new PDB into `READ WRITE` mode.	

CHECKLIST 13-4   *Transforming a Non-CDB into a PDB* (Continued)

Step 1: Quiesce Source Non-CDB

Before any data migration can occur, the *entire* source non-CDB must first be quiesced so that it is in a transactionally consistent state, as Listing 13-29 shows.

Listing 13-29   *Quiescing Source Non-CDB*

```
SQL> SHUTDOWN IMMEDIATE;
Database closed.
Database dismounted.
ORACLE instance shut down.

SQL> STARTUP MOUNT;
ORACLE instance started.
Total System Global Area 1610612736 bytes
Fixed Size                  2924928 bytes
Variable Size             486542976 bytes
Database Buffers          973078528 bytes
Redo Buffers               13848576 bytes
In-Memory Area            134217728 bytes
Database mounted.

SQL> ALTER DATABASE OPEN READ ONLY;
Database altered.
```

Step 2: Construct PDB Metadata

Via a call to the `DBMS_PDB.DESCRIBE` procedure, the non-CDB database's metadata is then captured in XML format into a configuration file for later use when it is plugged into its destination CDB, as Listing 13-30 shows.

Listing 13-30   *Constructing Non-CDB Metadata*

```
BEGIN
    DBMS_PDB.DESCRIBE (
        pdb_descr_file => '/home/oracle/ncdb122.xml'
    );
END;
/
```

The contents of this XML file are similar to what had been gathered in Scenario 3 when unplugging an existing PDB, as shown in Listing 13-31.

Listing 13-31   *Contents of Non-CDB Metadata XML File*

```xml
<?xml version="1.0" encoding="UTF-8"?>
<PDB>
  <xmlversion>1</xmlversion>
  <pdbname>NCDB122</pdbname>
  <cid>0</cid>
  <byteorder>1</byteorder>
  <vsn>202375680</vsn>
  <vsns>
    <vsnnum>12.1.0.2.0</vsnnum>
    <cdbcompt>12.1.0.2.0</cdbcompt>
    <pdbcompt>12.1.0.2.0</pdbcompt>
    <vsnlibnum>0.0.0.22</vsnlibnum>
    <vsnsql>22</vsnsql>
    <vsnbsv>8.0.0.0.0</vsnbsv>
  </vsns>
  <dbid>1241098598</dbid>
  <ncdb2pdb>1</ncdb2pdb>
  <cdbid>1241098598</cdbid>
  <guid>00EA1E6FCB5B1210E0531C32A8C0247D</guid>
  <uscnbas>2840615</uscnbas>
  <uscnwrp>0</uscnwrp>
  <rdba>4194824</rdba>
  <tablespace>
    <name>SYSTEM</name>
    <type>0</type>
    <tsn>0</tsn>
    <status>1</status>
    <issft>0</issft>
    <file>
      <path>/u01/app/oracle/oradata/NCDB122/system01.dbf</path>
      <afn>1</afn>
      <rfn>1</rfn>
      <createscnbas>7</createscnbas>
      <createscnwrp>0</createscnwrp>
      <status>1</status>
      <fileblocks>104960</fileblocks>
      <blocksize>8192</blocksize>
      <vsn>202375680</vsn>
      <fdbid>1241098598</fdbid>
      <fcpsw>0</fcpsw>
      <fcpsb>2840614</fcpsb>
      <frlsw>0</frlsw>
      <frlsb>1594143</frlsb>
      <frlt>855916519</frlt>
    </file>
  </tablespace>
  . . .
  << many lines omitted for sake of brevity >>
  . . .
```

```
<tablespace>
  <name>AP_IDX</name>
  <type>0</type>
  <tsn>8</tsn>
  <status>1</status>
  <issft>0</issft>
  <file>
    <path>/u01/app/oracle/oradata/NCDB122/ap_idx.dbf</path>
    <afn>7</afn>
    <rfn>7</rfn>
    <createscnbas>2173178</createscnbas>
    <createscnwrp>0</createscnwrp>
    <status>1</status>
    <fileblocks>25296</fileblocks>
    <blocksize>8192</blocksize>
    <vsn>202375680</vsn>
    <fdbid>1241098598</fdbid>
    <fcpsw>0</fcpsw>
    <fcpsb>2840614</fcpsb>
    <frlsw>0</frlsw>
    <frlsb>1594143</frlsb>
    <frlt>855916519</frlt>
  </file>
</tablespace>
<optional>
  <ncdb2pdb>1</ncdb2pdb>
  <csid>873</csid>
  <ncsid>2000</ncsid>
  <options>
    <option>APS=12.1.0.2.0</option>
    <option>CATALOG=12.1.0.2.0</option>
    <option>CATJAVA=12.1.0.2.0</option>
    <option>CATPROC=12.1.0.2.0</option>
    <option>CONTEXT=12.1.0.2.0</option>
    <option>DV=12.1.0.2.0</option>
    <option>JAVAVM=12.1.0.2.0</option>
    <option>OLS=12.1.0.2.0</option>
    <option>ORDIM=12.1.0.2.0</option>
    <option>OWM=12.1.0.2.0</option>
    <option>SDO=12.1.0.2.0</option>
    <option>XDB=12.1.0.2.0</option>
    <option>XML=12.1.0.2.0</option>
    <option>XOQ=12.1.0.2.0</option>
  </options>
  <olsoid>0</olsoid>
  <dv>0</dv>
  <APEX>4.2.5.00.08:1</APEX>
  <parameters>
    <parameter>processes=300</parameter>
    <parameter>sga_target=1610612736</parameter>
    <parameter>db_block_size=8192</parameter>
    <parameter>compatible='12.1.0.2.0'</parameter>
    <parameter>inmemory_size=134217728</parameter>
    <parameter>inmemory_query='ENABLE'</parameter>
    <parameter>open_cursors=300</parameter>
    <parameter>pga_aggregate_target=536870912</parameter>
  </parameters>
```

```
    <tzvers>
      <tzver>primary version:18</tzver>
      <tzver>secondary version:0</tzver>
    </tzvers>
    <walletkey>0</walletkey>
    <services>
      <service>SYS$BACKGROUND,</service>
      <service>SYS$USERS,</service>
      <service>NCDB122XDB,NCDB122XDB</service>
      <service>NCDB122,NCDB122</service>
    </services>
    <hasclob>1</hasclob>
    <hardvsnchk>0</hardvsnchk>
  </optional>
</PDB>
```

Step 3: Shut Down Source Non-CDB

The source non-CDB must now be shut down while it is migrated to its new PDB state, as Listing 13-32 demonstrates.

Listing 13-32 *Shutting Down Source Non-CDB*

```
SQL> SHUTDOWN IMMEDIATE;
Database closed.
Database dismounted.
ORACLE instance shut down.
```

Step 4: Plug In PDB

It's now time to plug the source non-CDB into its destination CDB, as illustrated in Listing 13-33.

Listing 13-33 *Plugging In Non-CDB as PDB into Destination CDB*

```
SQL> CONNECT / AS SYSDBA

SQL> ALTER SESSION SET CONTAINER = cdb$root;

Session altered.

Connected.

SQL> CREATE PLUGGABLE DATABASE dev_ap
     USING '/home/oracle/ncdb122.xml'
     COPY
     FILE_NAME_CONVERT = (
        '/u01/app/oracle/oradata/ncdb122'
       ,'/u01/app/oracle/oradata/cdb122/dev_ap'
     );

Pluggable database created.
```

Step 5: Resolve Extraneous Metadata in New PDB

Before the new PDB can be successfully opened, it's necessary to connect to the new PDB as SYSDBA and execute the noncdb_to_pdb.sql script in the target CDB's $ORACLE_HOME/rdbms/admin directory, as shown in Listing 13-34.

Listing 13-34 *Resolving Extraneous Metadata in New PDB*

```
SQL> ALTER SESSION SET CONTAINER = dev_ap;

Session altered.

SQL> @?/rdbms/admin/noncdb_to_pdb.sql;
```

> **NOTE**
> *Because this step needs to recompile all metadata and referencing objects in the PDB and its CDB, the execution time for this step will vary based on the computing power and memory of the CDB database's OS platform. It is not unusual for this process to execute as long as 15 to 20 minutes. The best advice is to remain patient and let the script do its job.*

Step 6: Open New PDB in READ WRITE Mode

Finally, the new PDB can be opened in READ WRITE mode, as Listing 13-35 shows; Listing 13-36 highlights the pertinent entries for Scenario 4 in the CDB's alert log.

Listing 13-35 *Opening New PDB*

```
SQL> ALTER PLUGGABLE DATABASE dev_ap READ WRITE;

Pluggable database opened.
```

Listing 13-36 *CDB122 Alert Log Entries for Scenario 4*

```
. . .
CREATE PLUGGABLE DATABASE dev_ap
    USING '/home/oracle/ncdb122.xml'
    COPY
    FILE_NAME_CONVERT = (
      '/u01/app/oracle/oradata/NCDB122'
     ,'/u01/app/oracle/oradata/cdb122/dev_ap'
    )
Tue Sep 16 08:24:45 2014
****************************************************************
Pluggable Database DEV_AP with pdb id - 3 is created as UNUSABLE.
```

```
If any errors are encountered before the pdb is marked as NEW,
then the pdb must be dropped
*******************************************************************
Database Characterset for DEV_AP is AL32UTF8
Deleting old file#1 from file$
Deleting old file#2 from file$
Deleting old file#3 from file$
Deleting old file#4 from file$
Deleting old file#5 from file$
Deleting old file#6 from file$
Deleting old file#7 from file$
Deleting old file#8 from file$
Deleting old file#9 from file$
Deleting old file#10 from file$
Deleting old file#11 from file$
Deleting old file#12 from file$
Deleting old file#13 from file$
Deleting old file#14 from file$
Deleting old file#15 from file$
Adding new file#13 to file$(old file#1)
Adding new file#16 to file$(old file#2)
Adding new file#14 to file$(old file#3)
Adding new file#15 to file$(old file#6)
Adding new file#17 to file$(old file#7)
Marking tablespace #2 invalid since it is not present in the describe file
Successfully created internal service dev_ap at open
ALTER SYSTEM: Flushing buffer cache inst=0 container=3 local
*******************************************************************
Post plug operations are now complete.
Pluggable database DEV_AP with pdb id - 3 is now marked as NEW.
*******************************************************************
Completed: CREATE PLUGGABLE DATABASE dev_ap
    USING '/home/oracle/ncdb122.xml'
    COPY
    FILE_NAME_CONVERT = (
       '/u01/app/oracle/oradata/NCDB122'
      ,'/u01/app/oracle/oradata/cdb122/dev_ap'
    )
Tue Sep 16 08:28:09 2014
alter pluggable database "DEV_AP" close IMMEDIATE instances = all
ORA-65020 signalled during: alter pluggable database "DEV_AP" close IMMEDIATE instanc-
es = all...
alter pluggable database "DEV_AP" open upgrade
Tue Sep 16 08:28:10 2014
Pluggable database DEV_AP dictionary check beginning
Tablespace 'UNDOTBS1' #2 found in data dictionary,
but not in the controlfile. Adding to controlfile.
Pluggable Database DEV_AP Dictionary check complete
Database Characterset for DEV_AP is AL32UTF8
Opening pdb DEV_AP (3) with no Resource Manager plan active
Tue Sep 16 08:28:15 2014
ALTER SYSTEM SET _system_trig_enabled=FALSE SCOPE=MEMORY;
Tue Sep 16 08:28:15 2014
ALTER SYSTEM SET enable_ddl_logging=FALSE SCOPE=MEMORY;
Resource Manager disabled during database migration: plan '' not set
Tue Sep 16 08:28:15 2014
ALTER SYSTEM SET resource_manager_plan= SCOPE=MEMORY;
```

```
Tue Sep 16 08:28:15 2014
ALTER SYSTEM SET recyclebin='OFF' DEFERRED SCOPE=MEMORY;
Pluggable database DEV_AP opened read write
Completed: alter pluggable database "DEV_AP" open upgrade
Tue Sep 16 08:28:45 2014
Thread 1 advanced to log sequence 41 (LGWR switch)
Current log# 2 seq# 41 mem# 0: /u01/app/oracle/oradata/cdb122/redo02.log
. . .
<< many lines omitted for sake of brevity >>
. . .
SERVER COMPONENT id=UTLRP_END: timestamp=2014-09-16 08:39:13 Container=DEV_AP Id=3
Tue Sep 16 08:39:38 2014
Resize operation completed for file# 4, old size 875520K, new size 880640K
alter pluggable database "DEV_AP" close
Tue Sep 16 08:39:57 2014
ALTER SYSTEM: Flushing buffer cache inst=0 container=3 local
Tue Sep 16 08:39:58 2014
Thread 1 cannot allocate new log, sequence 78
Checkpoint not complete
  Current log# 2 seq# 77 mem# 0: /u01/app/oracle/oradata/cdb122/redo02.log
Tue Sep 16 08:39:58 2014
Pluggable database DEV_AP closed
Completed: alter pluggable database "DEV_AP" close
alter pluggable database "DEV_AP" open upgrade
Database Characterset for DEV_AP is AL32UTF8
Opening pdb DEV_AP (3) with no Resource Manager plan active
Tue Sep 16 08:40:00 2014
ALTER SYSTEM SET _system_trig_enabled=FALSE SCOPE=MEMORY;
Tue Sep 16 08:40:00 2014
ALTER SYSTEM SET enable_ddl_logging=FALSE SCOPE=MEMORY;
Resource Manager disabled during database migration: plan '' not set
Tue Sep 16 08:40:00 2014
ALTER SYSTEM SET resource_manager_plan= SCOPE=MEMORY;
Tue Sep 16 08:40:00 2014
ALTER SYSTEM SET recyclebin='OFF' DEFERRED SCOPE=MEMORY;
Pluggable database DEV_AP opened read write
Completed: alter pluggable database "DEV_AP" open upgrade
Tue Sep 16 08:40:01 2014
Thread 1 cannot allocate new log, sequence 78
Private strand flush not complete
  Current log# 2 seq# 77 mem# 0: /u01/app/oracle/oradata/cdb122/redo02.log
alter pluggable database "DEV_AP" close
Tue Sep 16 08:40:02 2014
ALTER SYSTEM: Flushing buffer cache inst=0 container=3 local
Pluggable database DEV_AP closed
Completed: alter pluggable database "DEV_AP" close
Tue Sep 16 08:40:04 2014
Thread 1 advanced to log sequence 78 (LGWR switch)
  Current log# 3 seq# 78 mem# 0: /u01/app/oracle/oradata/cdb122/redo03.log
Tue Sep 16 08:46:51 2014
alter pluggable database dev_ap open read write
Tue Sep 16 08:46:51 2014
Database Characterset for DEV_AP is AL32UTF8
Opening pdb DEV_AP (3) with no Resource Manager plan active
Pluggable database DEV_AP opened read write
Completed: alter pluggable database dev_ap open read write
```

Oracle Database Release 12.1.0.2: New CDB and PDB Features

In late July 2014 Oracle released the latest version of Oracle Database, 12.1.0.2, which includes a plethora of new features for CDBs and PDBs. Here is a brief list of notable features that pertain to migrating and upgrading both non-CDBs and CDBs—many of which were not demonstrated in this chapter:

- **Improved state management on CDB restart**   Two new attributes— SAVE and DISCARD—make it possible to either *save* or *discard* the last state of a PDB before its CDB is closed. When the CDB is next reopened, Oracle will reinstate that prior state automatically without DBA intervention.

- **Selective tablespace availability**   The new USER_TABLESPACES attribute limits which *non-system tablespaces* should be left offline once a new PDB has been successfully cloned.

- **Specifying tablespace redo logging**   The new LOGGING attribute controls whether any future tablespaces are created in LOGGING or NOLOGGING mode within an existing PDB.

- **Metadata-only cloning**   The new NO DATA attribute captures only the *data dictionary definitions*—but no *application data*—during a PDB cloning operation.

- **Remote cloning**   It is now possible to clone a PDB or non-CDB on a *remote server* via a *database link*.

- **Cloning from snapshot copies**   The new SNAPSHOT COPY clause enables cloning a PDB *directly from snapshot copies* stored on supported file systems (e.g., ACFS or Direct NFS Client). This can potentially reduce the time to clone a PDB from several minutes to a matter of mere *seconds*.

As Oracle continues to refine the CDB and PDB feature set, additional functionality will certainly be made available in the future. We *strongly* recommend consulting the latest version of the Oracle 12c *Database New Features Guide* and the Oracle 12c *Database Administrator's Guide* for updated features made available since publication of this book.

TIP & TECHNIQUE

The features that were announced as part of Oracle Database Release 12.1.0.2—especially In-Memory Column Store, In-Memory Aggregation, Zone Maps, and Attribute Clustering—appear poised to offer significant increases in query performance with no change required to any SQL statement. It therefore seems wise to us to at least consider building your first Oracle 12c database using this latest version to take advantage of these latest features as well as the significant upgrades to CDB and PDB functionality.

Summary

Here's a brief summary of the key concepts we've covered in this chapter:

- The new multitenant features of Oracle Database 12c R1 make it possible to quickly migrate or clone a single PDB between different CDBs; meanwhile, all other PDBs within that CDB continue to service application workloads without any interruptions.

- There are four key methods for creating new PDBs and transporting current PDBs between existing CDBs; each has its advantages and disadvantages depending on the "window of inopportunity" that application workloads present.

- Most of the methods already discussed for transferring data between non-CDBs also work well with PDBs in a multitenant environment, including Full Transportable Export (FTE) and Cross-Platform Transport (CPT).

CHAPTER
14

Moving to Oracle
Engineered Systems

The first few years of the 21st century saw a shift toward *commodity computing* platforms—small, powerful, resilient servers usually clustered together using OS-based clusterware—to provide just the right amount of computing power on an as-needed basis to the most crucial database applications. But another sea change has shaken this model to its roots in the last few years: the rise of extremely large-scale computing platforms that the IT industry has collectively termed *engineered systems*.

Oracle entered this marketplace shortly after its purchase of Sun Microsystems in 2010 with the subsequent release of its Exadata Database Machine X2-2 and X2-8 engineered systems based on Sun's resilient and powerful server technology. This chapter will therefore discuss this sea change in Oracle's orientation towards database server technology, including its latest line of Exadata X5-2 and X5-8 Database Machine technology.

Engineered Systems: Not Our Father's Mainframe

We've often found that those of us who have been involved in IT for a few decades or more are quick to term engineered systems "the new mainframes." This is most likely because these systems' massive computing capacity and their tendency to centralize database applications onto a single platform reminds us of the good old days when IBM and Amdahl mainframes and DEC minicomputers ruled the computing domain. But there are some excellent reasons for this undeniable shift to centralized, powerful engineered systems.

Why Engineered Systems?

We have identified three broad business reasons for the expansion of engineered systems over the past decade—*capacity*, *centralization*, and *cost*—and there is a certain synergy between these reasons as well.

Capacity

Engineered systems offer incredible capacity in terms of raw *computing power* (CPUs), *direct-access memory* (DRAM), and—depending on the platform—*storage* (either spinning disks or flash memory, or sometimes both). As the upcoming survey of Oracle enterprise computing platforms illustrates, these systems often offer *hundreds* of CPU cores, DRAM in the *multi-terabyte* (TB) range, and—even without the use of readily available storage expansion units—storage capacity approaching *one petabyte*. And because these engineered systems have been specifically designed to handle massive data transfer traffic as well as tens of thousands of user connections per hour, they enable application workloads to scale out as well as scale up.

Centralization

Engineered systems also make it easier for overwhelmed Oracle DBAs to centralize databases on a single platform, and this makes it much simpler for a single DBA to manage the dramatic growth of individual databases over the past few decades. When we consider that every production database in essence needs at least one *QA* database to evaluate exactly how the *upcoming* release of the database application software will perform, and at least one *development* database to provide a "sandbox" for creating the *next* release of the database application, centralization of these databases enables us to eliminate—before we deploy the application to production—any potential variables that might contribute to unexpected variance in application performance.

Cost

The capability to host multiple individual Oracle databases on a single platform offers some incredibly attractive advantages from both capital expenditure (CAPEX) and operational expenditure (OPEX) perspectives. While the CAPEX for a full-rack Oracle Exadata Database Machine X5-2 may give even the most jaded C-level executive an initial case of extreme "sticker shock," IT organizations soon realize that the resulting OPEX savings from deploying an engineered system may compensate for the CAPEX almost immediately. For example, the Exadata Database Machine (DBM) has been architected so that the database server compute nodes communicate seamlessly with each other over 40 GbE InfiniBand as well as with their own self-contained pools of either high-speed or high-capacity storage devices.

That same resiliency and bandwidth the InfiniBand network brings to communication between compute nodes and storage cells in Exadata can be leveraged by Real Application Clusters (RAC) database instances as well. Therefore, there is virtually no need for either network administrators or storage administrators to become involved with any hardware or firmware tuning or fault diagnosis, thus freeing significant human capital for more valuable pursuits. It's even possible that the increased resiliency of an engineered system may reduce or eliminate the need for one or more RAC databases; the licensing costs thus saved may compensate for the initial higher CAPEX of an Exadata DBM.

A Brief Survey of Oracle Engineered Systems

Oracle released its first engineered system in September 2008. The Oracle Exadata Database Machine V1 was the product of a joint venture between Hewlett-Packard and Oracle. Oracle's acquisition of Sun Microsystems in 2010 signaled a shift in its Exadata strategy, and starting with the Exadata X2 line in 2011, all Exadata compute nodes and storage cells are based on Sun Server technology. Table 14-1 provides a brief survey of enterprise systems that have been designed specifically to run Oracle database software. This table is inclusive of all platforms that are either available or soon to be available as of March 2015.

Engineered System	Key Features	CPU Cores	Maximum DRAM Memory	Raw Physical Storage
Oracle SuperCluster M6-32	■ Between 16 and 32 12-core SPARC M6 processors	192–384	8TB–32TB	80TB (ZFS) 115TB (EHP) 432TB (EHC)
	■ Either:			
	■ 9 Exadata X5-2 storage cells, or			
	■ 1 ZFS ZS3-ES storage controller			
	■ Built-in support for Oracle Virtual Machine (OVM) virtual systems			
Oracle Exadata Database Machine X5-2 (full rack)	■ 8 Exadata compute nodes	288	2TB–6TB	179TB (HP) 672TB (HC)
	■ 14 Exadata storage cells			
	■ 89.6TB Smart Flash Cache			
	■ 112 NVMe high-performance solid-state drives or 168 high-capacity (7200 RPM) physical disks			
Oracle Exadata Database Machine X-8	■ 2 Exadata compute nodes	240	6TB	202TB (HP) 672TB (HC)
	■ 14 Exadata storage cells			
	■ 44.8TB Smart Flash Cache			
	■ 168 high-performance (10,000 RPM) or high-capacity (7200 RPM) physical disks			
Oracle Database Appliance	■ Oracle Enterprise Edition preinstalled	24	512GB–1.5TB	128TB
	■ Configurable as either two-node RAC Database, or RAC One Node database(s)			
	■ 2 Exadata X5-2 compute nodes			
	■ 2.4 TB SSD			
	■ 32 4TB 7200-RPM physical disks			
	■ Can be combined with Oracle ZFS Storage Appliance (ZFSSA) to obtain benefits of Hybrid Columnar Compression			

TABLE 14-1. *Oracle Engineered Systems: A Brief Survey (as of March 2015)*

Engineered System	Key Features	CPU Cores	Maximum DRAM Memory	Raw Physical Storage
Oracle ZFS Storage Appliance ZS4-4	■ Intelligent Storage Protocol provides close integration with storage cues from Oracle databases	120	3TB	3.5PB (HC)
	■ Offers benefits of Hybrid Columnar Compression			
	■ Oracle Snap Management Utility offers ability to take logical backups of Oracle databases as well as provide snap cloning of Oracle databases already backed up within it			
	■ Provides storage provisioning management for Oracle Enterprise Manager and Oracle VM Storage Connect			
Oracle Big Data Appliance (full rack)	■ 18 X5-2 compute/storage nodes	648	2.3TB–13.8TB	864TB (HC)
	■ Each node can be expanded from 128GB to 768GB DRAM			
	■ Cloudera Enterprise (Data Hub Edition) is preinstalled			
Virtual Compute Appliance	■ Between 2 and 25 X-2 compute nodes, each with 2–16 core CPUs	32–400	512GB–6.4TB	18TB
	■ 1 ZFS ZS3-ES storage controller			
	■ Built-in support for OVM virtual systems			
Oracle Zero Data Loss Recovery Appliance	■ Integrates with existing Oracle databases that require absolute guarantee against any data loss	64	512GB	144TB
	■ Uses real-time redo transport to quickly capture change data			
	■ Uses Delta Push and Delta Store technology to produce RMAN backups at blinding speed			
	■ Offers ability to offload tape backup requirements to platforms like Storage Tek Tape			
Oracle FS1-2 Flash Storage System	■ Designed specifically for Oracle database and application I/O	NA	64GB–384GB Cache	2.8TB–30.4TB (SSD)
	■ Offers both flash (SSD) and spinning disk (HDD) within same cabinet			7.2TB–96TB (HDD)
	■ Offers either high performance or high capacity flash storage			

TABLE 14-1.   *Oracle Engineered Systems: A Brief Survey (as of March 2015)* (Continued)

FIGURE 14-1. *Oracle SuperCluster M6-32*

Oracle SuperCluster M6-32

Released in September 2013, Oracle SuperCluster M6-32, shown in Figure 14-1, is an example of a massively parallel computing environment that's aimed at large-scale computing needs. It is designed specifically to support consolidation of Oracle databases and application servers onto a single, enterprise-ready platform. Its significant DRAM capacity is aimed at enabling both applications and databases to execute completely within memory.

Oracle Exadata Database Machine X5-2 and X-8

Any discussion of modern enterprise computing platforms would be incomplete without mentioning the Oracle Exadata Database Machine (DBM). The X5-2 and X4-8 models are the most recent additions to a product line that reaches back to the original V1 model—a 2008 joint venture between HP and Oracle—until Oracle's purchase of Sun Microsystems obviated the usage of Sun hardware and firmware for the X2 line. The latest iteration of Exadata—the X5 line—offers significant computing power and storage capacity. The X5-2 full rack model (see Figure 14-2) offers eight separate compute nodes, and the X4-8 model (see Figure 14-3) offers two compute nodes with larger amounts of physical memory per node. And when its InfiniBand HCA communication ports are enabled for active-active communication, any physical I/O that an Exadata DBM may need to perform will occur at storage network speeds of nearly 80 GbE, or roughly 10 gigabytes per second (GBps).

FIGURE 14-2. *Exadata X5-2 Database Machine: full rack configuration*

FIGURE 14-3. *Exadata X-8 Database Machine*

FIGURE 14-4. *Oracle Database Appliance*

Oracle Database Appliance and Oracle ZFS Storage Appliance

Though it's often overlooked, the Oracle Database Appliance (ODA) is a potential contender in the enterprise computing space without the acknowledged extreme cost outlay for an Oracle Exadata DBM. It offers two relatively powerful Exadata X4-2 servers plus 20 high-capacity disk drives to fully support a two-node RAC Enterprise Edition installation as soon as it is powered up (see Figure 14-4).

When the ODA is paired with the Oracle Zetabyte File System Storage Appliance (ZFSSA) (Figure 14-5), the true potential of this platform becomes immediately apparent because—just like its bigger cousin, the Exadata DBM platform—ZFSSA fully supports Hybrid Columnar Compression (HCC) features. The ODA/ZFSSA platform is thus a compact yet powerful enterprise computing system suitable for moderate online transaction processing (OLTP) and decision support system (DSS) application workloads that fully supports RAC high-availability features and can be viewed as a valuable transition point between "home-grown" computing platforms and full-scale enterprise computing platforms like the Exadata DBM.

Oracle Big Data Appliance

Oracle expanded its Exadata "footprint" into the universe of Big Data with its release of the Oracle Big Data Appliance (BDA), shown in Figure 14-6. Based on Exadata technology, the BDA platform is aimed at the NoSQL and Hadoop marketplace. The BDA has also been designed to take advantage of the latest Oracle database technology called *Big Data SQL* that permits data integration between NoSQL, Hadoop, and Oracle databases within the same SQL query statement. Introduced in July 2014 as part of Oracle Database 12.1.0.2, Big Data SQL makes it possible to incorporate, filter, and report against JSON data within the boundaries of a standard SQL query. It

FIGURE 14-5. *Oracle ZFS Storage Appliance*

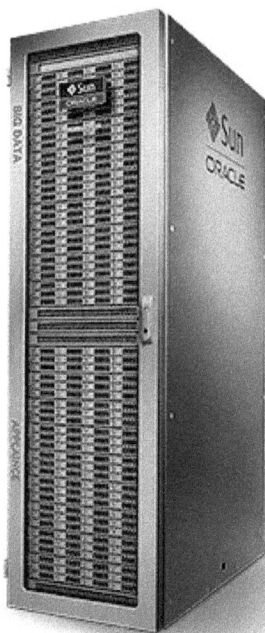

FIGURE 14-6. *Oracle Big Data Appliance*

is also possible to read directly from data stored within the Hadoop Distributed File System (HDFS) via the latest Oracle *Big Data Connectors* technology introduced as part of this database release. This dramatically improves the ability of the Oracle database to compete within the Big Data arena because existing Oracle database objects can be integrated with just about any NoSQL data source without having to offload data into other federated database structures.

Oracle Virtual Compute Appliance

Many IT organizations have already joined the steady trend toward *virtualization*— in other words, using virtualized "chunks" of memory, CPU, and even storage apportioned intelligently and then allocated from true physical devices—to provision hundreds or even thousands of application servers and Oracle databases. To support this trend, Oracle recently announced the release of its new Virtual Compute Appliance (VCA), shown in Figure 14-7, which leverages existing Exadata server technology and ZF3-ES storage devices to provide up to 400 physical CPU cores for virtualized computing needs.

FIGURE 14-7. *Virtual Compute Appliance*

Oracle Zero Data Loss Recovery Appliance

Released in October 2014, the Oracle Zero Data Loss Recovery Appliance is designed to provide extreme data protection—quite literally, zero data loss—for any Oracle database. This appliance uses Delta Push and Delta Store—technology that complements the already robust capabilities of Oracle RMAN—to insure that data is never lost and can be backed up within extremely short SLAs. It is also positioned as a platform against which tape backups can be taken without the added overhead that those backups often incur on primary database servers.

Oracle FS1-2 Flash Storage System

The Oracle FS1-2 Flash Storage System is the latest member of Oracle's enterprise computing family. Introduced at Oracle OpenWorld 2014, it offers both spinning disk (SATA-2 HDD) and flash (SSD) storage devices within a single cabinet for intelligent storage tiering. However, unlike SANs that already provide this capability, the FS1-2 has been designed specifically to provide the extreme I/O bandwidths needed specifically for both Oracle applications as well as Oracle databases.

Moving to Exadata DBM

Before migrating any Oracle database to an engineered system, it is crucial to understand the potential benefits that the engineered system's architecture promises for more efficient and rapid application workload execution. To illustrate the concerns that need to be addressed during migration from a non-engineered system platform, we will discuss the benefits and drawbacks of several methods available for database migration—either in whole or in part—to a destination Exadata DBM environment. While some of the issues we will raise will certainly pertain only to Exadata, it's important to remember that similar issues may arise during migration to any engineered system platform … as well as other completely different issues unique to that engineered system's architecture.

Exadata: Rules of Thumb

The Oracle Exadata DBM has been designed to provide maximum I/O throughput for complex queries typically found within data warehousing and analytic application workloads while also providing extremely low latency and high IOPS for OLTP applications. Oracle DBAs therefore must be aware of just a few simple rules of thumb and recommended best practices that cannot be ignored to ensure their application workloads will perform optimally within the Exadata hardware and software stack.

ASM, Wherever You Look

With ODA and Exadata software version 12.x, the default storage for Oracle databases is ACFS. It is primary for ODA and optional for Exadata. First and foremost, databases resident on Exadata DBMs *must* use Automatic Storage Management (ASM) to store all database files on this platform. It may also be necessary to implement HIGH (triple) redundancy instead of the default NORMAL (dual) redundancy for the datafiles of the tablespaces depending on the required resiliency and recoverability of the database objects stored within those tablespaces. It's important to remember that ASM triple redundancy has a considerable space penalty of nearly 70 percent of available physical disk space, resulting in only about 30 percent of available disk space for actual data storage. HIGH redundancy will thus likely require as much as 50 percent additional physical I/O to perform the required writes of the tertiary mirrored ASM allocation units. These factors must be taken into account when planning how much data can be migrated to Exadata storage, especially the potential for additional time it might take to perform initial data loads.

NOTE
We will discuss the advantages of the Oracle Database File System (DBFS) for non-database *files later in this chapter.*

TIP & TECHNIQUE
Starting with release 12.1.0.2 of the Oracle Exadata storage cell software, Exadata also supports the storage of Oracle database files within the ASM Cluster File System (ACFS). See My Oracle Support (MOS) Note 1929629.1, Oracle ACFS Support on Oracle Exadata Database Machine (Linux only), *for the most up-to-date information, including support for storing database files for earlier releases of Oracle databases on ACFS.*

The Rule of 4+8

Oracle has performed extensive heuristics against the Exadata DBM since its earliest incarnations; the results of these exhaustive tests have proven out the following best practices for best I/O performance:

- *The size of the initial Allocation Unit (AU) for all ASM disk groups should be 4MB.* While the default AU of 1MB is usually sufficient for other storage systems, Oracle's extensive testing has proven that the 4MB AU size is ideal for Exadata DBM storage cells. Another advantage of an initial 4MB AU is that when a datafile grows beyond 20,000 extents, the next 20,000 extents are automatically sized four times larger than the first 20,000 (16MB); when a datafile grows beyond 40,000 extents, all future extents are automatically sized 16 times larger than the initial 4MB AU (64MB). The initial AU size of 4MB therefore enables datafiles with large numbers of extents to take advantage of the maximum possible AU size (64MB) for an ASM file within an ASM disk group.

■ *The size of INITIAL and NEXT extents for all large tables should be a multiple of AU size.* Oracle has proven that a database object's data is most effectively accessed for physical I/O when its INITIAL extents are sized at no less than 8MB; larger sizes for an object's INITIAL and NEXT extents should always be an even multiple of the AU size.

These two rules of thumb are crucial to consider when planning to migrate a database to an Exadata DBM because both initial AU size and initial segment extent size can only be set when an ASM disk group or database object is first *created*. This means that even if a source database is already resident on storage that is leveraging ASM, those disk groups may not be directly migrated to Exadata if they have a different AU size. Likewise, any segment with extents that are not currently exact multiples of the disk group's AU size will likely suffer from poor I/O performance; this means the segment may need to be re-created during migration to Exadata to overcome this performance disadvantage.

Saying Goodbye to (Most) Indexes

Indexes are certainly beneficial for enforcing uniqueness (that is, PRIMARY KEY or UNIQUE KEY constraints) and are required for a foreign key reference between parent and child entities. But while an index may be beneficial for increasing selectivity of data that's often selected via equality searches, retrieving data in a particular sorted order, or joining together row sources on common column values, they are otherwise often deleterious to database performance, especially during addition of new rows to heavily indexed tables. Although it may sound counterintuitive, Oracle strongly suggests eliminating all but the most crucial indexes for tables stored within an Exadata DBM. This recommendation still holds true when a full table scan may have been anathema to the performance of complex queries in a non-Exadata environment because of the advantages of Exadata's Smart Scan technology (discussed in the next section).

As of Oracle Database 11*g* R1, an index that is not being used for enforcement of PRIMARY or UNIQUE KEY constraints or for the retrieval of a relatively small number of rows via OLTP query activities can be hidden from the Oracle query optimizer by making it invisible via the ALTER INDEX *<index_name>* INVISIBLE; SQL statement. This offers an Oracle DBA the ability to retain an index until she is thoroughly convinced that it offers no performance benefits whatsoever for queries; however, any DML that affects the index's underlying table will still be applied to the index while the index is marked invisible. And if the index actually turns out to be valuable for at least some queries, the Oracle DBA can simply reverse its invisibility by issuing an ALTER INDEX *<index_name>* VISIBLE; command for that index.

Smart Scan: Exadata's "Secret Sauce"

Smart Scan is at the heart of the Exadata DBM platform's extreme performance capabilities. The proprietary Smart Scan software—sometimes called the "secret sauce" of the Exadata environment—is present on every Exadata storage cell and leverages that platform's InfiniBand high-speed storage network to quickly identify exactly where an appropriate copy of the data required to answer a query is present within the storage network, regardless of whether it is on physical disk or already present in the extended database buffer cache known as the *Smart Flash Cache*. Since buffers in the Smart Flash Cache may only reside within the flash storage devices of each storage cell, retrieval of these data elements happens in a few hundred *microseconds* as compared to an average of 5–10 *milliseconds* when retrieved from a spinning disk.

The significant increase in Smart Scan's retrieval speed means that a database resident on an Exadata DBM can take full advantage of the fastest way to retrieve data from a data segment—via a full table scan instead of an indexed search. In addition, B-tree and bitmap fast full index scans can also leverage Smart Scan, so an index that has been retained because it has been proven beneficial for data retrieval may perform even more effectively through Smart Scan.

To Compress … or Not to Compress?

Exadata storage offers the advantages of Hybrid Columnar Compression (HCC) for data segments that can benefit from its extremely tight compression mechanisms. Even though Oracle claims that HCC typically yields data compression rates of 10X, in our experience this compression factor can vary dramatically depending upon several factors, including the number of columns within a table, the number of distinct values in a table's columns, and the number of NULL values present for each column.

The good news is that Oracle does provide the necessary intelligence to leverage HCC wisely in an Exadata environment. Starting with Oracle Database 11*g* R1, the DBMS_COMPRESSION package yields relatively accurate estimates of the expected compression ratios depending on the requested HCC compression level to be applied at a per-segment level. In addition, Oracle Database 12*c* R1 provides the *Automatic Data Optimization (ADO)* feature set that is extremely useful for determining exactly which tables and table partitions are most likely to benefit from higher compression levels. ADO makes these decisions based on *heat maps*—metadata about *when* a particular segment has been accessed last as well as exactly *how* the segment has been accessed (single block access, indexed lookup, full table scan, or DML).

Finally, you must remember that the most important reason for applying HCC compression is not necessarily to fit more data into a smaller physical space on spinning disks; rather, it is to increase the efficiency of physical reads when retrieving data from physical media becomes necessary. Because data compressed via HCC is automatically uncompressed on each Exadata DBM's storage cells before it is sent back to the database compute nodes for processing, the retrieval of compressed data is completely offloaded to the storage layer instead of the compute nodes, and therefore is almost negligible when compared to non-Exadata I/O subsystems.

TIP & TECHNIQUE

Oracle Database Release 12.1.0.2 offers several new features—especially the new In-Memory Column Store (IMCS)—*that complement the potentially immense benefits of Exadata HCC. Consult the latest version of the Oracle 12c* Database New Features Guide *for a more complete description of IMCS features and benefits.*

I/O Resource Manager

A unique feature of the Oracle Exadata DBM is its ability to track precisely which data is being utilized, how it is being accessed, and by which application workloads within the platform's storage cells. This tends to give an Exadata DBM a considerable advantage over other SANs because it is possible to implement specific *I/O Resource Manager (IORM)* directives that will apportion storage resources between separate I/O categories (e.g., OLTP vs. data warehouse), specific databases (e.g., a crucial production database vs. a Q/A or development database), and even a single intra-database Resource Consumer Group (e.g., OLTP application workload vs. reporting workload).

How IORM Works

IORM works in conjunction with the venerable Database Resource Manager (DBRM) feature set that has been available since Oracle8*i* Database. As shown in Figure 14-8, IORM plan directives are interpreted within each storage cell as I/O requests are received. Based on their relative importance specified within the storage cell's IORM plan directives, IORM will decide whether to immediately grant an I/O request or enqueue a request for later consideration.

IORM: Intra-Database, Inter-Database, and I/O Category Layer Directives

As Figure 14-9 illustrates, IORM plan directives can be specified within individual *categories* of I/O—for example, OLTP vs. DSS—and can also be specified for different *databases*—for example, PROD vs. QA. IORM then tags each I/O request with an I/O *category*, the *database name*, and the DBRM *Resource Consumer Group (RCG)* of the requesting session. These tags are then compared to IORM plan directives on each storage cell so that I/O resources can be apportioned intelligently. This tends to ensure that noncrucial application workloads that don't currently require large amounts of physical I/O are effectively throttled to the advantage of those application workloads that could most benefit from longer I/O run queue lengths or faster access to numerous shorter I/O run queue lengths.

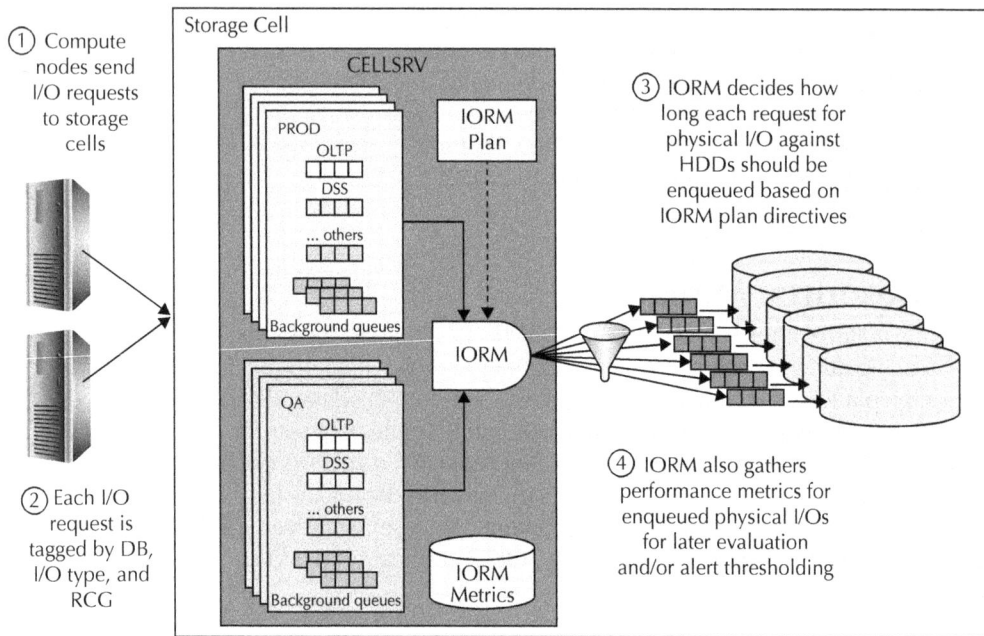

FIGURE 14-8. *IORM plan implementation*

Listing 14-1 shows the corresponding IORM plan that would need to be deployed to each storage cell in the Exadata DBM to enforce the IORM directives for the PROD and QA databases as well as the OLTP and DSS I/O categories shown in Figure 14-9.

Listing 14-1 *Sample Exadata I/O Resource Manager Plan*

```
ALTER IORMPLAN -
      objective=auto -
    ,catplan=(
               (name=oltp,   level=1, allocation=70)  -
             ,(name=dss,    level=1, allocation=30)  -
             ,(name=other,  level=2, allocation=80)  -
             ,(name=adhoc,  level=2, allocation=20)  -
             ) -
    ,dbplan=(
               (name=prod,   level=1, allocation=80,  limit=100) -
               (name=qa,     level=1, allocation=20,  limit=50) -
             ,(name=other,  level=2, allocation=100, limit=50)
             )
```

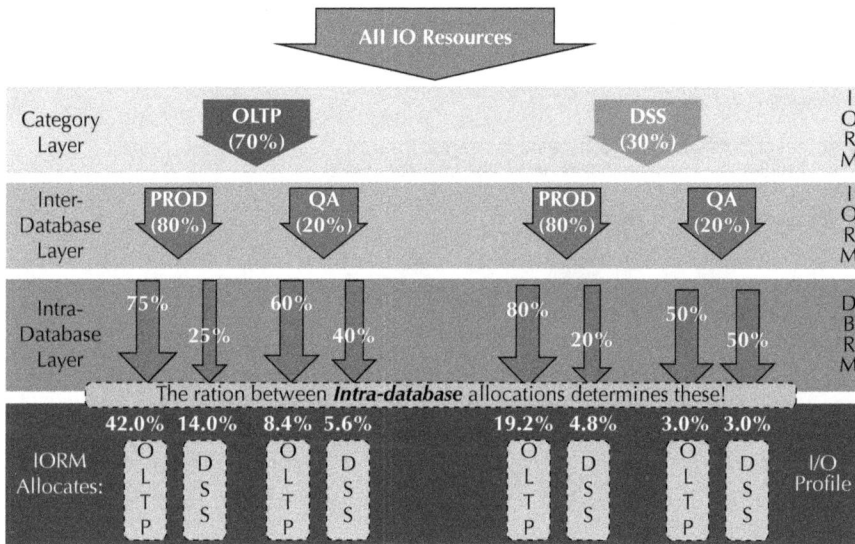

FIGURE 14-9. *IORM plan resource distribution*

Listing 14-2 shows the corresponding DBRM plans that would be deployed to the PROD and QA databases to duplicate the intra-database resource management plans shown in Figure 14-9.

Listing 14-2 *Sample Database Resource Manager Plan*

```
-----
-- Create new Resource Consumer Groups and map them directly
-- to the standard demonstration Services
-----
BEGIN
    DBMS_RESOURCE_MANAGER.CLEAR_PENDING_AREA();
    DBMS_RESOURCE_MANAGER.CREATE_PENDING_AREA();

    DBMS_RESOURCE_MANAGER.CREATE_CONSUMER_GROUP(
        consumer_group => 'OLTP'
        ,comment => 'On-Line Transaction Processing Applications'
        ,cpu_mth => 'ROUND-ROBIN'
    );
    DBMS_RESOURCE_MANAGER.CREATE_CONSUMER_GROUP(
        consumer_group => 'DSS'
        ,comment => 'Decision Support Applications'
        ,cpu_mth => 'ROUND-ROBIN'
    );

    -----
```

```
    -- Map each Service to a corresponding Resource Consumer Group
    -----
    DBMS_RESOURCE_MANAGER.SET_CONSUMER_GROUP_MAPPING(
         attribute => DBMS_RESOURCE_MANAGER.SERVICE_NAME
        ,value => 'OLTP'
        ,consumer_group => 'OLTP'
    );
    DBMS_RESOURCE_MANAGER.SET_CONSUMER_GROUP_MAPPING(
         attribute => DBMS_RESOURCE_MANAGER.SERVICE_NAME
        ,value => 'DSS'
        ,consumer_group => 'DSS'
    );

    DBMS_RESOURCE_MANAGER.VALIDATE_PENDING_AREA();
    DBMS_RESOURCE_MANAGER.SUBMIT_PENDING_AREA();
END;
/


-----
-- Build new RCG categories and assign RCGs to their appropriate
-- categories
-----
BEGIN
    DBMS_RESOURCE_MANAGER.CLEAR_PENDING_AREA();
    DBMS_RESOURCE_MANAGER.CREATE_PENDING_AREA();

    DBMS_RESOURCE_MANAGER.CREATE_CATEGORY(
         category => 'OLTP'
        ,comment => 'OLTP Operations'
    );
    DBMS_RESOURCE_MANAGER.CREATE_CATEGORY(
         category => 'DSS'
        ,comment => 'Decision Support Operations'
    );
    DBMS_RESOURCE_MANAGER.UPDATE_CONSUMER_GROUP(
         CONSUMER_GROUP => 'OLTP'
        ,NEW_CATEGORY => 'OLTP'
    );
    DBMS_RESOURCE_MANAGER.UPDATE_CONSUMER_GROUP(
         CONSUMER_GROUP => 'DSS'
        ,NEW_CATEGORY => 'DSS'
    );

    DBMS_RESOURCE_MANAGER.VALIDATE_PENDING_AREA();
    DBMS_RESOURCE_MANAGER.SUBMIT_PENDING_AREA();
END;
/


-----
-- Grant each Resource Consumer Group the ability to switch to any
-- other Resource Consumer Group
-----
BEGIN
    DBMS_RESOURCE_MANAGER.CLEAR_PENDING_AREA();
    DBMS_RESOURCE_MANAGER.CREATE_PENDING_AREA();

    DBMS_RESOURCE_MANAGER_PRIVS.GRANT_SWITCH_CONSUMER_GROUP(
```

```
        grantee_name => 'PUBLIC'
        ,consumer_group => 'OLTP'
        ,grant_option => FALSE
    );
    DBMS_RESOURCE_MANAGER_PRIVS.GRANT_SWITCH_CONSUMER_GROUP(
        grantee_name => 'PUBLIC'
        ,consumer_group => 'DSS'
        ,grant_option => FALSE
    );

    DBMS_RESOURCE_MANAGER.VALIDATE_PENDING_AREA();
    DBMS_RESOURCE_MANAGER.SUBMIT_PENDING_AREA();
END;
/


-----
-- Create resource plan for PROD database:
-----
BEGIN
    DBMS_RESOURCE_MANAGER.CLEAR_PENDING_AREA();
    DBMS_RESOURCE_MANAGER.CREATE_PENDING_AREA();

    DBMS_RESOURCE_MANAGER.CREATE_PLAN(
        plan => 'PEAKTIME'
        ,comment => 'Peak Time Service-Based Resource Plan'
    );

    DBMS_RESOURCE_MANAGER.CREATE_PLAN_DIRECTIVE(
        plan => 'PEAKTIME'
        ,group_or_subplan => 'OLTP'
        ,comment => 'Peak Time - OLTP Applications'
        ,mgmt_p1 => 75
        ,max_utilization_limit => 100
    );
    DBMS_RESOURCE_MANAGER.CREATE_PLAN_DIRECTIVE(
        plan => 'PEAKTIME'
        ,group_or_subplan => 'DSS'
        ,comment => 'Peak Time - DSS Applications'
        ,mgmt_p1 => 25
        ,max_utilization_limit => 50
    );
    DBMS_RESOURCE_MANAGER.CREATE_PLAN_DIRECTIVE(
        plan => 'PEAKTIME'
        ,group_or_subplan => 'OTHER_GROUPS'
        ,comment => 'Peak Time - Other'
        ,mgmt_p1 => 0
        ,max_utilization_limit => 25
    );

    DBMS_RESOURCE_MANAGER.VALIDATE_PENDING_AREA();
    DBMS_RESOURCE_MANAGER.SUBMIT_PENDING_AREA();
END;
/


-----
-- Create resource plan for QA database:
-----
```

```
BEGIN
    DBMS_RESOURCE_MANAGER.CLEAR_PENDING_AREA();
    DBMS_RESOURCE_MANAGER.CREATE_PENDING_AREA();

    DBMS_RESOURCE_MANAGER.CREATE_PLAN(
        plan => 'PEAKTIME'
        ,comment => 'Peak Time Service-Based Resource Plan'
    );

    DBMS_RESOURCE_MANAGER.CREATE_PLAN_DIRECTIVE(
        plan => 'PEAKTIME'
        ,group_or_subplan => 'OLTP'
        ,comment => 'Peak Time - OLTP Applications'
        ,mgmt_p1 => 60
        ,max_utilization_limit => 100
    );
    DBMS_RESOURCE_MANAGER.CREATE_PLAN_DIRECTIVE(
        plan => 'PEAKTIME'
        ,group_or_subplan => 'DSS'
        ,comment => 'Peak Time - DSS Applications'
        ,mgmt_p1 => 40
        ,max_utilization_limit => 75
    );
    DBMS_RESOURCE_MANAGER.CREATE_PLAN_DIRECTIVE(
        plan => 'PEAKTIME'
        ,group_or_subplan => 'OTHER_GROUPS'
        ,comment => 'Peak Time - Other'
        ,mgmt_p1 => 0
        ,max_utilization_limit => 25
    );

    DBMS_RESOURCE_MANAGER.VALIDATE_PENDING_AREA();
    DBMS_RESOURCE_MANAGER.SUBMIT_PENDING_AREA();
END;
/
```

Migrating Databases to an Exadata Environment

Designed with the sole purpose of running Oracle database application workloads, a strong point in favor of the Exadata DBM family is that transforming, migrating, and upgrading existing Oracle databases during their journey to take up residence on an Oracle engineered system is relatively simple. Just as with any migration effort, of course, the "window of inopportunity" for the application workloads that the databases support is still the driving factor for which migration method is most appropriate.

Logical Migration Methods

A database whose application workload requires an extremely short window of inopportunity will most likely benefit from one of the *logical* migration methods discussed in this section. Table 14-2 lists each method and its relative benefits and

Method	First Database Release	Window of Downtime	Benefits	Drawbacks
Logical standby database	10.2	Short	■ Relatively simple to set up ■ Real-time data synchronization ■ May permit heterogeneous database transformation	■ Requires Data Guard licensing ■ Requires making Logical Standby Database the new primary database
Oracle Streams	10.2	Short	■ Included with Oracle Enterprise Edition	Notoriously difficult to set up
Oracle GoldenGate	10.2	Short	■ Relatively simple to set up ■ Real-time data synchzronization ■ Permits transferal of data from non-Oracle databases as well	Requires GoldenGate licensing
Traditional Data Pump Export/ Import	10.2	Moderate	■ Included with Oracle Enterprise Edition ■ Relatively easy to set up ■ Permits transferal of data from non-Oracle databases as well	Requires transactions to be suspended on source database while data is transferred to destination database

TABLE 14-2.   *Moving to Engineered Systems: Logical Migration Methods*

drawbacks specific to Exadata DBM migration; in most cases, these same benefits and drawbacks will apply when migrating to any other Oracle engineered systems platform.

Logical Standby Database

Since a logical standby database captures online redo log entries, translates them into appropriate SQL statements, and then automatically applies them immediately via SQL Apply services, it is potentially an excellent tool for migration of a database from its source platform to an Exadata DBM. The logical standby database is first created as a physical standby on the destination platform, and it will continue to accept transactions from its primary database on the source platform until a switchover is performed, thus completing the migration.

NOTE
Chapter 4 illustrates how to leverage Oracle Data Guard capabilities to migrate a database between different OS platforms by implementing a logical standby database at the eventual destination platform.

Oracle Streams

For a reasonably tight window of inopportunity, Oracle Streams may be an appropriate option for logical database migration. It requires no additional licensing fees, and it essentially employs Oracle LogMiner technology to mine and capture transactions from the source database and then apply them to the target database. However, Oracle Streams is not simple to configure and is rather notorious for being difficult to tune for optimal throughput. Any apparent cost advantage that Streams appears to offer may be quickly consumed by higher human resource costs required for its initial configuration and to guarantee sufficient performance during the actual migration between non-Exadata and Exadata platforms.

> **NOTE**
> *Oracle has declared that Oracle Streams is deprecated as of Oracle Database Release 12.1.0.1 in favor of new Oracle GoldenGate technology that has been cleverly named* XStreamIn *and* XStreamOut.

Oracle GoldenGate

If an application workload truly does demand zero downtime during the migration of its corresponding database to an Exadata DBM environment, then Oracle GoldenGate is probably the most appropriate choice to handle the tight window of inopportunity that is demanded. GoldenGate's licensing costs may initially appear to be significant when compared to Oracle Streams, which is included in the cost of Oracle Enterprise Edition; on the other hand, GoldenGate offers extremely efficient replication methods that can be set up with relative simplicity. GoldenGate also provides powerful capabilities for filtering and transforming data even while the data is being migrated from a non-Exadata environment to its eventual target database on an Exadata platform.

> **NOTE**
> *Chapter 8 provides extensive examples on using Oracle GoldenGate features to migrate, transform, and synchronize data between source and destination databases.*

Traditional Data Pump Export/Import

If an application workload can tolerate a reasonably long window of inopportunity during which read-only access to its data is available, then Oracle Data Pump is likely to be the simplest method to transfer data between a non-Exadata source database and its Exadata destination database. Since Data Pump Export permits the specification of a particular timestamp or SCN at which read-consistent data collection should commence, it's even possible to capture a transactionally consistent version of all data that will be migrated from source to destination via Data Pump Import.

Finally, Data Pump Export and Import can be used in conjunction with other logical migration methodologies. For example, Oracle GoldenGate could be used to perform initial loading and migration of the database objects whose data tends to be the most volatile on the source database directly to their destination. Since Data Pump Export and Import can also handle data migration of specific partitioned data objects, Data Pump could be utilized to transfer data for those partitions whose data is nearly static or completely static in nature (for example, extremely historical data).

NOTE
Chapter 7 provides extensive examples of how to use the capabilities of Oracle Data Pump Export and Import to efficiently migrate data between the source and destination databases.

Physical Migration Methods

For databases that support application workloads with an extremely tight window of inopportunity, one of the aforementioned logical migration methods may be most appropriate when migrating to an engineered system. However, if there is sufficient time to perform a *physical* migration of all or part of an Oracle database, then one of the methods listed in Table 14-3 may be more appropriate. Table 14-3 lists the various methods that are available for migrating data into an Exadata DBM environment, as well as each method's relative benefits and drawbacks specific to Exadata DBM migration. As with the previously discussed logical migration methods, these same benefits and drawbacks will apply when migrating to other Oracle engineered systems platforms as well.

Physical Standby Database

If an entire database needs to be migrated to Exadata and the window of inopportunity to migrate is relatively short, one of the easiest and most efficient methods is to establish an Oracle Data Guard environment using the Exadata DBM as the destination OS platform and then create a physical standby copy of the source database there. During an appropriate off-peak time frame, migrating to Exadata only requires a simple switchover operation that establishes the original *physical standby* database as the new *primary* database on the Exadata DBM.

NOTE
Chapter 4 illustrates how to leverage Oracle Data Guard capabilities to migrate a database between different OS platforms by implementing a physical standby database at the eventual destination platform.

Method	First Database Release	Window of Downtime	Benefits	Drawbacks
Physical Standby Database	10.2	Short	■ Relatively simple to set up ■ May permit heterogeneous database transformation	Requires Data Guard licensing
RMAN Tablespace Migration	11.2	Moderate	■ Relatively simple to set up ■ Permits migration of non-ASM source database to ASM	■ Requires minimum database version of 11.2 ■ Requires source database platform to be little endian
Partition Exchange	11.2	Short	■ Relatively simple to set up ■ Permits migration of non-ASM source database to ASM	■ Requires minimum database version of 11.2 ■ Requires source database platform to be little endian
Transportable Database (TDB)	10.2	Moderate to long	■ Included with Oracle Enterprise Edition ■ Easiest method to move an entire source database to Exadata DBM	■ Requires minimum database version of 11.2 ■ Requires source database platform to be little endian ■ Requires *entire* source database to remain in READ ONLY mode while data is transferred to destination database
Transportable Tablespace Sets (TTS)	10.2	Moderate	■ Most flexible method for transferring data from source database to Exadata DBM ■ Permits endian conversion during transferal ■ Widest support of source database versions (minimum: 10.2)	■ Tablespace set referential integrity must be maintained ■ *Entire* source tablespace set must remain in READ ONLY mode while data is transferred to destination database
Cross-Platform Transportable Tablespace Sets (XTTS)	11.2.0.3	Short	■ Automates transfer of metadata and data via PERL scripts ■ Tablespaces *must* remain in READ WRITE mode, except during the execution of final transfer operations	■ Tablespace set referential integrity must be maintained ■ A short but controllable window of inopportunity is still required during final transfer operations
Data Pump Full Transportable Export (FTE)	12.1	Short	One-step creation of both transportable tablespace data and metadata	■ Tablespace set referential integrity must be maintained ■ *Entire* source tablespace set must remain in READ ONLY mode while data is transferred to destination database
Cross-Platform Transport (CPT)	12.1	Short	One-step creation of both transportable tablespace data and metadata	■ Tablespace set referential integrity must be maintained ■ *Entire* source tablespace set must remain in READ ONLY mode while data is transferred to destination database

TABLE 14-3. *Moving to Engineered Systems: Physical Migration Methods*

Method	First Database Release	Window of Downtime	Benefits		Drawbacks	
PDB to PDB cloning	12.1	Short	Simple, quick, efficient methods to:		■	Source and destination database releases must be 12*c*
			■	Create a new pluggable database (PDB) from an existing PDB	■	Source and destination CDBs must already exist
			■	Migrate an existing PDB to a different container database (CDB)		
			■	Upgrade an existing PDB from one database release to the next highest release		
Non-CDB to PDB cloning	12.1.0.2	Moderate	Simple, quick, efficient method(s) to create a new PDB from an existing non-CDB		■	Destination database release must be 12*c*
					■	Destination CDB must already exist
Programmatic methods	All	Short	Completely flexible depending on application downtime needs		■	Database links must be established before transferring data between source and destination databases
					■	Requires considerable skill to develop efficient, effective, accurate data transfer modules
					■	Time-consuming to test before production implementation

TABLE 14-3. *Moving to Engineered Systems: Physical Migration Methods* (Continued)

RMAN Tablespace Migration

If the source database is not already using ASM for its database files, then a slightly modified version of the non-ASM to ASM migration strategy using Oracle Recovery Manager (RMAN) may be an appropriate choice (as described in Chapter 5). Note that for this approach to work for a non-Exadata to Exadata DBM environment conversion, it will be necessary to make the source database's storage subsystem available for access by the Exadata DBM, and this can be accomplished via several methods already discussed in the ASM to ASM migration method previously. Otherwise, this migration strategy is virtually identical to the one identified near the end of Chapter 5.

> **NOTE**
> *See Chapter 5 for in-depth examples of how to leverage RMAN backups to migrate a database from non-ASM, non-Exadata storage to ASM-based storage on Exadata.*

Partition Exchange

As our colleague Oracle ACE Director Tim Gorman likes to say, "The fastest way to load data into a partitioned table…is by not loading the data at all." If the source database is a data warehouse, a data mart, or supports a decision support application workload, then leveraging partition exchange operations for the source database's partitioned tables and indexes is likely to be one of the fastest ways to migrate data between source and destination platforms because it employs metadata exchange to append the existing partitioned data without having to reload each partition's rows into the partitioned table.

This method involves the following steps:

1. Create a new "empty" database within the destination Exadata DBM database home, either via database creation scripts or Database Configuration Assistant (DBCA).

2. Capture the metadata for the tablespaces comprising the partitioned tables and indexes via Data Pump Export.

3. Migrate the tablespace sets that comprise just the older, infrequently used partitions of the partitioned tables and their indexes to Exadata by taking them into READ ONLY mode and then transporting them to the appropriate Exadata-based ASM disk groups.

4. Plug in these tablespaces' metadata to complete the data transfer, then bring the tablespaces into READ WRITE mode.

NOTE
Chapter 5 provides in-depth examples of how to leverage RMAN backups to migrate a database from non-ASM to ASM storage, and Chapter 6 illustrates how to leverage TTS features to migrate a tablespace set between different OS platforms.

Transportable Database

If the source database can tolerate a rather long window of inopportunity, then the features of Transportable Database (TDB) are definitely worth an investigation. However, it's important to remember that both source and destination databases must share the same endianness when using TDB for database migration, so any source database that is being migrated to Exadata must be running on a little-endian OS platform because the destination database on an Exadata DBM will always be little endian.

NOTE
Chapter 6 offers an excellent demonstration of how to leverage TDB features to migrate a complete database between different OS platforms.

Transportable Tablespace Sets

If the source database can only tolerate a short window of inopportunity, or if only certain tablespace sets need to be migrated from the source database to an Exadata DBM, then the features of Transportable Tablespace Sets (TTS) may be extremely appropriate. Since TTS fully supports endian conversion between source and destination databases of different endianness, it is one of the most flexible methods for migration. But like TDB, TTS requires that all tablespaces in the desired source tablespace set(s) must be brought into READ ONLY mode for the duration of the migration.

NOTE
Chapter 6 illustrates how to leverage TTS features to migrate self-contained tablespace sets between different OS platforms.

Cross-Platform Transportable Tablespace Sets

When an application workload requires an extremely short "window of inopportunity," then the Cross-Platform Transportable Tablespace Sets (XTTS) utility may be most appropriate to migrate one or more tablespaces from the source database to an Exadata DBM. XTTS supports transportation of tablespace sets between source and destination databases; just like TTS, it fully supports endian conversion between source and destination databases of different endianness. Since XTTS leverages RMAN to create incremental backups for initial transfer and later synchronization, the source database's tablespaces remain in READ WRITE mode until an appropriate off-peak time frame arrives, at which time those tablespaces are opened in READ ONLY mode while the final synchronization occurs.

NOTE
Chapter 9 provides extensive documentation and examples of how to use XTTS features to migrate a tablespace set between different OS platforms.

Data Pump Full Transportable Export

If the source database is at least Oracle Database release 11.2.0.3 and the destination database that's resident on Exadata is at least Oracle Database release 12.1.0.1, then Data Pump Full Transportable Export (FTE) may be an attractive option to complete the migration between source and destination platforms.

Cross-Platform Transport

If both the source and destination databases are at least Oracle Database release 12.1.0.1, then Cross-Platform Transport (CPT) may be an appropriate method to accomplish the database's migration from a non-Exadata source to an Exadata destination platform.

> **NOTE**
> Chapter 13 explains how to leverage Oracle Database 12c's new CPT and FTE features to migrate tablespace sets between different OS platforms.

PDB to PDB Cloning

If an Oracle 12c CDB already exists on the Exadata destination platform, then it is quite simple to unplug a PDB from its CDB on a non-Exadata source platform and then replug that unplugged PDB into the Exadata-based CDB.

Non-CDB to PDB Cloning

If an Oracle 12c CDB already exists on the Exadata destination platform, and the source database on a non-Exadata platform is at least upgraded to database 11.2.0.3, then it's also possible to transform the 11.2.0.3 non-CDB into a single 12c R1 PDB that can be plugged into the Exadata-resident CDB.

> **NOTE**
> Chapter 13 discusses the myriad methods for migrating and cloning PDBs via Oracle 12c's new CDB features.

Programmatic Methods

If none of the previously described methods and utilities provides sufficient flexibility or reduces the window of inopportunity to satisfy an application's service-level agreement, then it may be necessary to develop specialized SQL or PL/SQL application code to transform and/or migrate data between a source database and its destination database. This usually involves creating a database link to the appropriate source database from the destination database, and then writing custom code to load data into the destination database via either `INSERT INTO` <*destination table*>… `SELECT FROM` <*source table*>`@database_link` statements or `CREATE TABLE` <*destination table*> `AS SELECT FROM` <*source table*>`@source_database_link` statements.

An advantage of these two methods is that sufficient and appropriate degrees of parallelism can be invoked on the source and destination databases to speed data extraction and loading. And this methodology also works extremely well if only a few database objects need to be extracted, loaded, and perhaps even synchronized between source and destination databases. If the descriptions of the database objects match exactly between source and destination databases, consider using Data Pump Export and Import to capture and transport only the metadata for the desired database objects; alternatively, consider utilizing the myriad functions and procedures of the Oracle-supplied DBMS_METADATA package to extract and transport just the necessary metadata.

Handling External Data Efficiently for Exadata: Oracle Database File System

Most of the methods we have discussed so far in this chapter have focused on migrating data from a source database that doesn't currently reside on an engineered system to the Exadata DBM. But almost every IT organization is also required to process data feeds on a regular basis from so-called legacy systems that typically store their data in traditional OS files instead of an RDBMS. When it's time to scrub, normalize, and load that data into an Oracle database, Oracle provides the SQL*Loader utility to efficiently load huge volumes of data via direct path physical I/O. It's also possible to read legacy data from an *external table* via the SQL*Loader access method. An external table can then be joined to other RDBMS-resident tables for query purposes, or even used as a source for loading data into an RDBMS table via an INSERT INTO <destination_table> … SELECT … FROM <external_table> statement.

Fortunately, the Exadata DBM has been designed so that it can take particular advantage of the Database File System (DBFS), an Oracle-designed POSIX-compliant file system, to provide extreme processing bandwidth for both external tables and SQL*Loader direct path data loads. The standard Exadata DBM configuration reserves the innermost 29GB on all but the first two of its spinning disks within every Exadata storage cell for the +DBFS_DG ASM disk group. Disk group +DBFS_DG can then retain datafiles for one or more BIGFILE tablespaces within an Exadata-resident Oracle database. Once these tablespaces are configured for use within a DBFS file system, they are capable of storing OS files as SecureFile LOBs in 10MB "chunks" that can be read at incredible speed—as high as 5 GBps. This means that read-intensive queries and database load operations are freed of many of the physical I/O limitations that typically hamper other standard, general-purpose, OS-based file systems (for example, EXT4).

ASM Clustered File System Now Supported for Exadata

As of September 2014, Oracle announced that ASM Clustered File System (ACFS) is now fully supported for deployment on Exadata DBMs. To use this feature, it is necessary to upgrade Oracle Grid Infrastructure to release 12.1.0.2, so this means that the ASM disk groups that underlie the ACFS volumes must also be upgradeable to that release. While this is a welcome new feature set for ACFS, only limited details are available about its effectiveness and throughput capacity as compared to DBFS. See My Oracle Support (MOS) Note 1929629.1, *Oracle ACFS Support on Oracle Exadata Database Machine (Linux only)*, for the latest details on using ACFS in concert with Exadata. Also, be sure to check MOS Note 888828.1, *Exadata Database Machine and Exadata Storage Server Supported Versions*, for the latest updates on ACFS availability.

Oracle DBFS: A Practical Example

To illustrate the potential of DBFS, this example presents a use case that organizations encounter frequently, which is the need to quickly load data from an external source:

- A company's sales organization needs to deploy its sales force effectively for an upcoming product launch.

- The company's marketing department has captured approximately 1.25 million records containing detailed demographics data from statistical extracts of the United States 2010 census delimited in comma-separated values (CSV) format.

- The data in this eight-column table needs to be analyzed for population trends so that the sales force can be deployed most appropriately within different geographic locales in the United States.

Prerequisites

Listing 14-3 shows the initial setup for the Oracle software owner user account to permit its use of the *Filesystem in Userspace (FUSE)* technology. Then, Listing 14-4 shows the steps necessary to create a new `BIGFILE` tablespace in the `+DBFS_DG` ASM disk group and a new Oracle database user account (`dbfs`). Note that this user account has been granted basic database object creation privileges plus the ability to manage a DBFS file system through the grant of the `DBFS_ROLE` role.

Listing 14-3   *Modifying Oracle User Account*

```
[root@host01 ~]# usermod -a -G fuse oracle
[root@host01 ~]# echo user_allow_other > /etc/fuse.conf
[root@host01 ~]# chmod 644 /etc/fuse.conf
[root@host01 ~]# id oracle

uid=54321(oracle) gid=54321(oinstall)
groups=54321(oinstall),54322(dba),54324(asmdba),54326(oper),103(fuse)
```

Listing 14-4   *Building DBFS Infrastructure*

```
SQL> CONNECT / AS SYSDBA
Connected.

SQL> DROP TABLESPACE dbfs INCLUDING CONTENTS AND DATAFILES;

DROP TABLESPACE dbfs INCLUDING CONTENTS AND DATAFILES
*
ERROR at line 1:
ORA-00959: tablespace 'DBFS' does not exist

SQL> CREATE BIGFILE TABLESPACE dbfs
  DATAFILE '+DBFS_DG'
  SIZE 350M;

Tablespace created.

SQL> DROP USER dbfs CASCADE;

DROP USER dbfs CASCADE
      *
ERROR at line 1:
ORA-01918: user 'DBFS' does not exist

SQL> CREATE USER dbfs
  IDENTIFIED BY dbfs
  QUOTA UNLIMITED ON dbfs;

User created.

SQL> GRANT CREATE SESSION,   CREATE TABLE, \
        CREATE PROCEDURE, DBFS_ROLE TO dbfs;

Grant succeeded.
```

Creating and Mounting DBFS File System

Now that the infrastructure is in place, Listing 14-5 shows how to construct a new DBFS-based directory mount point at location /stage/dbfs_staging via procedure DBFS_CREATE_FILE_SYSTEM.

Listing 14-5 *Creating DBFS File System Mount Point*

```
$> mkdir /stage/dbfs_staging
$> chmod -R 775 /stage/dbfs_staging

SQL> connect dbfs/dbfs
Connected.
SQL> @?/rdbms/admin/dbfs_create_filesystem dbfs LEGACY
SQL> Rem
SQL> Rem $Header: rdbms/admin/dbfs_create_filesystem.sql /main/4 2010/06/01
11:01:01 nmukherj Exp $
SQL> Rem
SQL> Rem dbfs_create_filesystem.sql
SQL> Rem
SQL> Rem Copyright (c) 2009, 2010, Oracle and/or its affiliates.
SQL> Rem All rights reserved.
SQL> Rem
SQL> Rem    NAME
SQL> Rem         dbfs_create_filesystem.sql - DBFS create filesystem
SQL> Rem
SQL> Rem    DESCRIPTION
SQL> Rem        DBFS create filesystem script
SQL> Rem        Usage: sqlplus <dbfs_user> @dbfs_create_filesystem.sql
SQL> Rem             <tablespace_name> <filesystem_name>
SQL> Rem
SQL> Rem    NOTES
SQL> Rem
SQL> Rem    MODIFIED    (MM/DD/YY)
SQL> Rem    nmukherj   05/30/10 - changing default to non-partitioned SF segment
SQL> Rem    weizhang   03/11/10 - bug 9220947: tidy up
SQL> Rem    weizhang   04/06/09 - Created
SQL> Rem
SQL>
SQL> SET ECHO OFF
No errors.
--------
CREATE STORE:
begin dbms_dbfs_sfs.createFilesystem(store_name => 'FS_LEGACY', tbl_name =>
'T_LEGACY', tbl_tbs => 'dbfs', lob_tbs => 'dbfs', do_partition => false,
partition_key => 1, do_compress => false, compression => '', do_dedup => false,
do_encrypt => false); end;
--------
REGISTER STORE:
begin dbms_dbfs_content.registerStore(store_name=> 'FS_LEGACY', provider_name =>
'sample1', provider_package => 'dbms_dbfs_sfs'); end;
--------
MOUNT STORE:
begin dbms_dbfs_content.mountStore(store_name=>'FS_LEGACY',
store_mount=>'LEGACY'); end;
--------
CHMOD STORE:
declare m integer; begin m := dbms_fuse.fs_chmod('/LEGACY', 16895); end;
No errors.
```

Now the DBFS tablespace can be mounted under the DBFS file system mount point via a call to the DBFS_CLIENT utility, as shown in Listing 14-6. In this example, we have created a new directory named `legacy` beneath the `/stage/dbfs_staging` directory.

Listing 14-6   *Using DBFS_CLIENT to Mount Tablespace Within DBFS File System*

```
$> nohup $ORACLE_HOME/bin/dbfs_client DBFS@dbm \
        -o allow_other,direct_io /stage/dbfs_staging < passwd.txt &
[1] 5074
$> nohup: appending output to 'nohup.out'
```

TIP & TECHNIQUE

The most common error we see Oracle DBAs make when setting up DBFS is forgetting to add the Oracle software owner account to the `fuse` *group. When that assignment has been omitted, issuing the command string in Listing 14-6 will generate errors in the* `nohup.out` *file that report insufficient privileges to mount the DBFS file system.*

Issuing the Linux `MOUNT` command will show that the new DBFS file system has been mounted under the appropriate directory, as shown in Listing 14-7.

Listing 14-7   *Results of MOUNT Command*

```
$> mount
/dev/xvda2 on / type ext3 (rw)
proc on /proc type proc (rw)
sysfs on /sys type sysfs (rw)
devpts on /dev/pts type devpts (rw,gid=5,mode=620)
/dev/xvda1 on /boot type ext3 (rw)
tmpfs on /dev/shm type tmpfs (rw,size=4G)
/dev/xvdb1 on /u01 type ext3 (rw)
none on /proc/sys/fs/binfmt_misc type binfmt_misc (rw)
sunrpc on /var/lib/nfs/rpc_pipefs type rpc_pipefs (rw)
dbfs-DBFS@dbm:/ on /stage/dbfs_staging type fuse
(rw,nosuid,nodev,max_read=1048576,default_permissions,allow_other,user=oracle)

$> ls -la /stage/dbfs_staging/
total 4
drwxr-xr-x 3 root    root         0 Oct  9 13:54 .
drwxr-xr-x 8 oracle oinstall 4096 Oct  8 14:21 ..
drwxrwxrwx 3 root    root         0 Oct  9 13:49 legacy
$>
```

As Listing 14-8 shows, it's also possible to verify that the `legacy` directory is part of a DBFS file system by querying the `DBMS_DBFS_CONTENT` view.

Listing 14-8 *Querying the DBMS_DBFS_CONTENT View*

```
SET LINESIZE 65
COL store_name  FORMAT A12
COL store_mount FORMAT A20
COL created     FORMAT A30
TTITLE "DBFS File Stores (from DBMS_DBFS_CONTENT)"
SELECT store_name, store_mount, created
  FROM TABLE(dbms_dbfs_content.listMounts);
TTITLE OFF


           DBFS File Stores (from DBMS_DBFS_CONTENT)

STORE_NAME   STORE_MOUNT          CREATED
------------ -------------------- ------------------------------
FS_LEGACY    legacy               09-OCT-14 06.12.33.137105 PM
```

Querying Data via External Tables

To enable an Oracle database to leverage this DBFS file system, all that is needed is the creation of a new directory object that references the `/stage/dbfs_staging/legacy` directory. Once the OS file containing the U.S. census data has been copied to that directory, it can be accessed via external tables or SQL*Loader into that directory, as demonstrated in Listing 14-9.

Listing 14-9 *Configuring Access to OS Files in DBFS File System*

```
SQL> DROP DIRECTORY dbfs_staging;
     CREATE DIRECTORY dbfs_staging AS '/stage/dbfs_staging/legacy';
     GRANT READ, WRITE ON DIRECTORY dbfs_staging TO ap;

$> cp 'BaseTables1552004.csv' /stage/dbfs_staging/legacy
```

Listing 14-10 shows how to create a table of type `ORGANIZATION EXTERNAL` that uses the `ORACLE_LOADER` access method to describe the legacy census data stored in CSV format. Note that the descriptors immediately following the `ORGANIZATION EXTERNAL` declaration might appear vaguely familiar because the `ORACLE_LOADER` access method is based on the same file, record, and field descriptors that SQL*Loader uses to describe incoming data sources for loading into Oracle database tables.

Listing 14-10 *Creating External Table AP.XT_POPSTATS*

```
SQL> DROP TABLE ap.xt_popstats;

Table dropped.

SQL> CREATE TABLE ap.xt_popstats (
     geo_id          VARCHAR2(256)
```

```
        ,tab_nbr           VARCHAR2(50)
        ,tab_ord           VARCHAR2(20)
        ,line_nbr          VARCHAR2(32)
        ,stub              VARCHAR2(256)
        ,estimate          VARCHAR2(32)
        ,lower_bound       VARCHAR2(32)
        ,upper_bound       VARCHAR2(32)
)
ORGANIZATION EXTERNAL
(
  TYPE ORACLE_LOADER
  DEFAULT DIRECTORY dbfs_staging
  ACCESS PARAMETERS
  (
    RECORDS DELIMITED BY NEWLINE
    BADFILE dbfs_staging:'xt_popstats%a_%p.bad'
    LOGFILE dbfs_staging:'xt_popsstats%a_%p.log'
    READSIZE 1024000
    FIELDS TERMINATED BY ','
    OPTIONALLY ENCLOSED BY '"'
    MISSING FIELD VALUES ARE NULL
    (geo_id
    ,tab_nbr
    ,tab_ord
    ,line_nbr
    ,stub
    ,estimate
    ,lower_bound
    ,upper_bound
    )
  )
  LOCATION ('BaseTables1552004.csv')
)
PARALLEL
REJECT LIMIT UNLIMITED;

Table created.
```

Table `AP.XT_POPSTATS` can now be queried via SQL statements just as if it were a standard heap-organized table resident within the database. The statistics of the query's execution are also shown in Listing 14-11.

Listing 14-11 *Results of Querying AP.XT_POPSTATS External Table*

```
SQL> ALTER SYSTEM FLUSH BUFFER_CACHE;

System altered.

SQL> SET AUTOTRACE TRACEONLY

SQL> SELECT geo_id, tab_nbr, COUNT(estimate)
  FROM ap.xt_popstats
 GROUP BY geo_id, tab_nbr
 ORDER BY geo_id, tab_nbr
```

```
;

SQL> SQL>    2    3    4    5
84 rows selected.

Statistics
----------------------------------------------------------
        198  recursive calls
          0  db block gets
       1277  consistent gets
         49  physical reads
          0  redo size
       8013  bytes sent via SQL*Net to client
        574  bytes received via SQL*Net from client
          7  SQL*Net roundtrips to/from client
         14  sorts (memory)
          0  sorts (disk)
         84  rows processed

SQL> SET AUTOTRACE OFF
```

Importing Data via External Tables

External tables also make excellent sources of data for direct path, parallelized loading of heap-organized Oracle database tables. Listing 14-12 shows a simple example of this method: the creation of a new heap-organized table, AP.US_POPSTATS, and the corresponding INSERT INTO … SELECT FROM method to load only a selected subset of the data in AP.XT_POPSTATS directly into that new table. Note that the CREATE TABLE *<new table>* AS SELECT … (CTAS) method would also work in this situation.

Listing 14-12 *Creating and Populating New Heap-Organized Table from External Table Data*

```
CONN / AS SYSDBA

DROP TABLE ap.us_popstats;
CREATE TABLE ap.us_popstats (
    geo_id          VARCHAR2(256)
    ,criteria        VARCHAR2(256)
    ,value           VARCHAR2(32)
    ,min_value       VARCHAR2(32)
    ,max_value       VARCHAR2(32)
)
    TABLESPACE ap_data
    STORAGE (INITIAL 8M NEXT 8M)
    PARALLEL 4
;

SET AUTOTRACE TRACEONLY STATISTICS
INSERT /*+ APPEND NOLOGGING PARALLEL(2) */  INTO ap.us_popstats
VALUES(geo_id, criteria, value, min_value, max_value)
```

```
SELECT geo_id, stub, estimate, lower_bound, upper_bound
  FROM ap.xt_popstats
 WHERE SUBSTR(tab_ord,1,3) IN ('B01','B02','B98','B99')
   AND stub NOT LIKE '%total%'
 ORDER BY geo_id, stub
;
COMMIT;
SET AUTOTRACE OFF

55216 rows created.


Statistics
----------------------------------------------------------
        267  recursive calls
        473  db block gets
       2137  consistent gets
          0  physical reads
       7320  redo size
        818  bytes sent via SQL*Net to client
       1060  bytes received via SQL*Net from client
          3  SQL*Net roundtrips to/from client
         12  sorts (memory)
          0  sorts (disk)
      55216  rows processed
```

Importing Data into Exadata DBM-Resident Databases: Native SQL vs. SQL*Loader

The examples we have provided for loading data into Oracle databases that reside within an Exadata DBM using native SQL to access data within an external table are admittedly simplistic. But it's important to recognize that native SQL also offers the capability to join an external table to other heap-organized tables already resident within an Oracle database to provide access to additional data elements while loading a target table, or even for use in data filtering operations while gathering the data needed to load into the target table. It's even possible to gather optimizer statistics on external tables to provide the optimizer with enough metadata so that it can join or filter data intelligently against normal heap-organized tables.

SQL*Loader does offer the ability to build separate rows for multiple tables when parsing a single record in a legacy file. It can also take advantage of multiple degrees of parallelism when loading data, and it offers powerful column-based filtering as well. In our opinion, these features are outweighed by native SQL's capability to access data from other sources simultaneously during data loading. Best of all, using native SQL for data loading doesn't require learning the intricacies of SQL*Loader's powerful features.

Summary

Here's a quick summary of what we've covered in this chapter:

- Engineered systems like Oracle Exadata Database Machine X5-2 are at the forefront of the next wave of enterprise systems computing, and that wave appears to be destined to continue unabated for the foreseeable future.

- Virtualization is finally coming of age, and that's also driving engineered systems development and deployment as organizations struggle to find maximum reliability at the lowest TCO.

- Like it or not, Oracle DBAs are still tasked with moving data to engineered platforms, but the good news is that the tried-and-true tools we have already discussed are certainly employable in almost all migration, transformation, and upgrade scenarios.

CHAPTER
15

Migrating to Oracle
in the Cloud

A s we have seen in the previous chapters in this book, there are many ways to migrate from one database to another, even if they are not both Oracle databases. In this chapter we will look at a specific use case: moving to cloud computing. This is a little different from other types of migrations because of the type of system we are moving to, and might have some variations, but the methods will still be the same.

TIP & TECHNIQUE

Cloud computing is quickly becoming very popular. You should develop a thorough cloud computing strategy.

Cloud computing has become much more popular in the past few years and is becoming the database of choice for many applications, especially where management of the application requires specific, specialized skills. Cloud computing is still in its early stages, and even the term *cloud computing* is still evolving. The terminology used within this technology and administration stack is continuing to evolve as well.

Cloud Computing: What Is It?

Cloud computing is a term that cannot be defined easily because it has several variants and corresponding definitions. In the most generic sense of the term, cloud computing is a designation for a centralized computing model where the systems are virtual and accessed via the network (local or internet) while attempting to retain independence of the actual hosts/resource. For example, the system might be provided by Oracle but to your company they should not appear to be Oracle servers. Oracle defines cloud computing as "…a style of computing based on shared, elastic resources delivered to users in a self-service, metered manner using web technologies." The several variants of cloud computing include public clouds, private clouds, and hybrid clouds. These variants are distinguished primarily by where the cloud resides and who owns the equipment.

The definition of cloud computing typically depends on who you ask. Storage vendors consider virtualized storage to be cloud computing. Hardware vendors consider virtualization to be cloud computing. Oracle considers Database as a Service (DBaaS) to be cloud computing. Which is right? All of them. In this chapter we focus purely on cloud computing as it refers to an Oracle database, since that is what this book is all about. Furthermore, we focus simply on the Oracle public, private, and hybrid cloud products and services.

What Isn't Cloud Computing?

"Cloud computing" has become a marketing buzzword that most hardware and software companies associate with just about any product that allows sharing of resources. As with most buzzwords, it is quickly becoming overused. We already have public clouds, private clouds, and hybrid clouds, but you can expect marketing departments in the industry to come up with many more types of clouds for purposes of differentiating their products. So, do your research and make sure what the label says is what you really want.

Oracle itself offers a wide range of cloud computing options, which will be discussed later in this chapter. They vary from an instance on a database that is completely managed by the provider to an entire virtual machine that you have complete access to.

Public Cloud

The public cloud is simply one that offers some type of service (such as DBaaS, PaaS, SaaS) publicly to customers and is accessed by those customers via the Internet. There are many cloud vendors today, including Oracle, Microsoft's Azure, and Amazon's AWS.

TIP & TECHNIQUE

Be sure that you completely understand the cloud provider's service-level agreement (SLA) before you sign a contract.

Oracle offers several cloud database services. As of this writing, Oracle has three main offerings plus the Oracle Managed Cloud Services formerly known as Oracle On Demand services (also considered cloud):

- **Database Schema Service**   Gives you access to a database schema on an Oracle 11*g* database. This model provides limited access to the Oracle instance.

- **Database as a Service (DBaaS)**   Provides you with your own Oracle virtual machine with an 11*g* R2 or 12*c* database. This model allows you to have full access to root and SYSDBA.

- **Oracle Managed Cloud Services** AKA **Oracle On Demand**   Provides complete managed services for many of Oracle's CRM, sales, and business applications.

The public cloud has become more popular in the past few years, partly due to the ability to add resources on demand as needed.

Private Cloud

A private cloud differs from a public cloud in that the network that attaches the customers to the cloud systems is fully internal to the organization that owns it. This makes it more secure and easier to manage from both a technical and political standpoint. In addition, a private cloud can provide a higher level of security, because it runs behind the company's firewall.

TIP & TECHNIQUE
Private clouds are a great way to get started with cloud computing.

Public clouds and private clouds are configured and managed in much the same way, but a private cloud is typically managed by employees of the company that owns the cloud. However, that task is sometimes outsourced. If the cloud administration is outsourced, the equipment owner generally has considerably more input into the service definition and SLA than is generally available with a public cloud platform.

Hybrid Cloud

A hybrid cloud is one in which both public and private cloud resources are used by an organization, many times with related applications. A hybrid cloud model might be chosen for many reasons. In the context of Oracle, companies often want Oracle to manage a complex application such as Oracle Siebel CRM, allowing Oracle experts in Siebel CRM to manage that application while the in-house resources focus on custom business applications. The hybrid cloud often uses additional Oracle products, such as Oracle GoldenGate, to allow both external and internal cloud data to be synchronized. In this book we have covered how to use Oracle GoldenGate for data migration, but there are many other uses for it as well. GoldenGate is often used for specialized replication projects.

Oracle VM

Oracle VM is the product used to implement Oracle Database as a Servicer (DBaaS). DBaaS takes an Oracle VM virtual machine, installs the database and related infrastructure, and deploys it so that the customer can tailor the environment for their own use. The virtual machine can be used to host an Oracle 11*g* or 12*c* database as well as any applications that can run on the virtual machine itself.

The DBaaS product, introduced at Oracle OpenWorld 2014, includes access to the Oracle Cloud Management Pack for Oracle Enterprise Manager Cloud Control 12*c*.

This provides self-service virtualization as well as the ability to quickly and efficiently deploy Gold Images and/or Templates. In addition, Oracle officially announced support for OpenStack at Oracle OpenWorld 2014, with their own implementation.

Oracle Cloud Offerings

Oracle currently has a number of cloud solutions as described previously. They range from an instance on a server to a fully managed and monitored environment. Oracle offers something as simple as a virtual machine to do with as you want, up to a fully configured database. The Oracle On Demand solution provides application services, whereas the Oracle Cloud services provide database and virtual machine services.

Oracle Cloud (https://cloud.oracle.com/home) solutions include the following:

- Platform as a Service (PaaS)

- Infrastructure as a Service (IaaS)

- Software as a Service (SaaS)—applications

- Database as a Service (DBaaS)

- Data as a Service (DaaS)

- Private Cloud

- Managed Cloud

As you can see, the Oracle offerings are quite extensive. Not only do they include a number of cloud services but they are happy to offer services to help support your database migration.

Why Use Cloud Computing?

Why is cloud computing so appealing? There are many reasons, the first of which is ease of use. Instead of building servers and installing database software yourself, you can have all of this done for you. This offloads much of the work that you would have to do to set up computers, databases, and so forth. Cloud computing is still in its early stages but is quickly gaining in popularity. Oracle On Demand has been available for a relatively long period of time and is very popular among companies who do not want to invest in the skill set necessary to maintain complex products such as Siebel CRM or Oracle E-Business Suite.

One of the advantages of Oracle VM is its extensive set of prebuilt templates. These templates allow you to deploy complex environments within a very short amount of time. This includes applications such as E-Business Suite.

Cloud computing also provides the scalability to quickly and easily add additional resources without having to spend significant time provisioning systems, setting up new infrastructure, loading operating systems, and so on. Cloud computing allows for new systems to be deployed in a matter of minutes and, depending on how things are configured, using a self-serve model. In addition, for a fee cloud computing can offer a high level of redundancy and backup.

Considerations for Migrating to Cloud Computing

To be able to take full advantage of cloud computing, you need to be aware of several considerations. These include special considerations for security, support and SLAs, network performance and connectivity, application customization, costs, data access, and data migration. Let's look at these considerations next.

Cloud Security

One of the top concerns of using a public cloud or hybrid cloud is security. Protecting yourself from an "inside job" can be very difficult when it comes to security. We are all familiar with the case of U.S. National Security Agency (NSA) data being stolen by a contractor's employee who had been given security clearance. This type of security breach can be hard to protect yourself from because of the level of access that some employees require to do their job effectively.

TIP & TECHNIQUE
Don't forget to do a thorough security evaluation. Not all cloud providers can offer the same level of security.

In a private cloud, it is much easier to maintain a higher level of security because all of the systems are maintained inside of your own environment, behind a firewall. However, in some cases, a public cloud might offer a higher level of auditing and scrutiny because they are not running under the individual company's security umbrella. The security standards of a private cloud can conform to the internal security standards of your organization, rather than your organization having to conform to the security standards of the cloud provider.

Support and SLA

The level of support in a public or hybrid cloud environment is something that you need to consider carefully and plan for appropriately. Unlike what most of us are used to in the private organization environment, in a public or hybrid cloud the timeliness of the support you receive will be based on the SLA that you have signed. Don't expect an immediate response if your SLA contract doesn't include it.

Many of us are spoiled by the level of support we can get by walking down the hall and explaining the issue to the DBA or the system administrator (SA). If you are in the same building and know them personally, you can often get them to drop what they are doing and help you with your issue. In a public or hybrid cloud environment, if you are paying for a four-hour response time, don't expect anything faster.

In a private cloud, response time is not usually an issue. The DBAs and SAs are all part of your organization and are working as a team to provide the highest level of support that they can. They don't have to prioritize among different customers. They will often stay late and help … and won't charge you extra.

Network Performance and SLA

Because of criticality of the network in a public or hybrid cloud environment, network bandwidth is crucial. As with the level of support mentioned in the previous section, the network bandwidth that you receive will be exactly what you are paying for. As such, be careful when you are negotiating your contract to ensure that you are guaranteed the amount of bandwidth that you actually need to provide the access to your applications and database that is required for optimal performance.

Because of the nature of the architecture of a private cloud, you should always make sure that both the database servers and application servers reside in the same place. The latency and bandwidth requirements between the application servers and database servers is typically much higher than between the end users and application servers, so careful planning is required.

Application Customizations

Depending on the type of cloud services that you are contracting for, application customizations may or may not be supported. In a pure application-hosted environment, you might have to conform your business practices to those of the cloud provider, rather than customizing the application for your environment. This depends on the cloud provider and the applications that you wish to have hosted with them.

The Real Cost of Cloud Computing

In a private cloud environment, you are working as one company to provide a service to your customers. In public and hybrid cloud environments, you are the customer and you are paying for services. As such, the services you are provided are limited to those specified in your contract. Any service outside the contract is something that you must pay extra for. Beware of hidden costs that might arise from overages. These might include

- Extra charges for exceeding bandwidth
- Charges for disk space

- Charges for backups
- Charges for performing upgrades, customizations, or troubleshooting of nonstandard issues

You may often find that upgrading the Oracle database to the latest Critical Patch Update or Patch Set Update is a very expensive operation. Don't be afraid of cloud computing; just be aware of what you have contracted for and what hidden costs there might be. It is important that the DBAs and other administrators have access to the SLA of the contract.

Data Access

You might not think that data access is an issue, but with some cloud providers, depending on the type of contract that you have, you might not have direct access to your data at all times. If you are in a shared services environment where you have a database instance, or maybe even part of a database instance, you might not have direct access to your data.

This data access issue might seem hard to believe, but you really need to know what you are getting into before you sign up for a plan to make sure that your organization will be able to accomplish everything that it needs to accomplish. Even some of the Oracle cloud plans do not allow SQL*Plus access to your data.

For some customers, lack of direct access might be perfectly acceptable, whereas most other customers might not be able to function without this access. It really depends on the type of access that you need for your particular environment and application.

Data Migration

Data migration to the cloud may be exactly the same as data migration to any other system, or it might be different. It all depends on the type of cloud system that you are moving to. In a fully managed environment, you might not have very much control over the data migration. In an environment where you own the entire virtual machine, you will have full control over everything, including the data migration.

> **TIP & TECHNIQUE**
> *Careful planning is key to a successful cloud*
> *migration. Be sure to plan accordingly.*

Migrating to the cloud has a few special concerns, as discussed in the "Migration Options for Cloud Computing" section later in this chapter.

Oracle VM and Cloud Computing

As mentioned earlier in this chapter, "cloud computing" has many definitions. In terms of Oracle Cloud Services, there are two main offerings: Oracle On Demand, which gives you access to Oracle applications that are fully managed by Oracle, and Oracle Cloud Solutions, which is mainly based on virtual machines. These virtual machines are based on Oracle VM.

Oracle VM is based on Xen technology. Xen technology has been around since 2002 and has been improved constantly since then. Here is a brief timeline of the Xen Hypervisor.

The Xen virtualization product became available around the same time as VMware. Originating from the University of Cambridge Computer Laboratory, the first version of Xen was released in 2003. The leader of the project then went on to found XenSource. Unlike both VMware and Hyper-V, Xen is maintained by the open source community under the GNU General Public License. In 2007, XenSource was acquired by Citrix Systems.

Whereas VMware and Hyper-V only support the x86 architecture, Xen supports the x86, x86_64, Itanium, and PowerPC architectures.

To fully appreciate where the Xen kernel is at this point, let's look at a brief history of the Xen Hypervisor:

2002	Development begins on the Xen Hypervisor.
2003	The first release of Xen is made available.
2004	The second release of Xen is made available, and the first Xen developers' summit is held.
2005	XenSource is founded and version 3.0 is released.
2006	XenEnterprise is released. Linux begins adding enhancements for virtualization. VMware and Microsoft adopt paravirtualization as well. In addition, this year marks the launch of Amazon EC2 (Elastic Compute Cloud).
2007	Citrix acquires XenSource. Oracle announces Oracle VM, which is based on the Xen Hypervisor. The original version is Oracle VM 2.1.
2008	Xen begins showing up embedded in Flash memory in embedded systems.
2009	Oracle releases Oracle VM 2.2 based on Xen 3.4.
2011	Oracle VM 3.0 released, supporting up to 128 virtual CPUs per VM.
2012	Oracle VM 3.2 released.
2014	Oracle VM 3.3 released.

At the time of this writing, 3.3 is the latest version of Oracle VM. Oracle continues to support and enhance the Xen Hypervisor and has given no indication that this will not be the hypervisor for future versions of Oracle VM.

Benefits of Running Oracle Databases on Oracle VM

Unlike VMware, Oracle VM (Xen) will allocate specific CPU cores to a virtual machine. This difference allows Oracle databases to be licensed based on the cores allocated to the virtual machine. This provides a great advantage to running Oracle databases on Oracle VM versus VMware.

In addition, Oracle VM will not overallocate memory, which means you are always guaranteed to have available to the virtual machine the memory that you have allocated to it. That also guarantees that the virtual machine server will never swap out VM memory.

Oracle VM supports paravirtualization, in which the underlying operating system realizes that it is running on a virtual system and makes intelligent choices based on that knowledge. However, Oracle VM supports any OS that will run on the x86 platform as a fully virtualized guest. In addition, Oracle VM supports hardware virtualization acceleration.

Migration Options for Cloud Computing

The options for migrating to the cloud are the same as non-cloud migration options covered throughout this book. Whether you are moving to the cloud or moving to another system does not really matter. The considerations for moving to a cloud really are affected more by the infrastructure than by the cloud itself. For example, getting the data to the cloud will be more complicated than moving the data from one system to another within your data center. In a public cloud environment, you might have to deal with multiple firewalls, routers, and the significant distances between your organization's data center and that of your cloud provider.

> **TIP & TECHNIQUE**
> *Weigh all of your options before deciding how to migrate.*

Whether you are using a private connection to the public cloud provider or are going through the Internet makes a big difference. If you are moving data to a public cloud over the Internet rather than a VPN, it is much more important to encrypt the data. Security and encryption requirements should be discussed thoroughly by the migration team and documented during the planning phase.

These are all important considerations that must be taken into account.

Planning the Migration

As you have read over and over again in this book, planning the migration is critical. When moving to the cloud, planning is even more important. The planning phase should be done in conjunction with the planning of the cloud services contract, so that the entire process is coordinated. You should consider the following as part of the migration planning:

- Sizing

- Migrate or Transform (same or improved)

- Connectivity

- How the data is going to be moved

These are all important topics that must be included in the plan.

Sizing the Virtual Environment

Since a virtual environment might and probably will be shared, it is also important to size the environment carefully to ensure that it will be able to support the needed workload. Essentially, you can think of the virtual environment as a physical environment in terms of CPU and memory resources. The big difference in a virtual environment is that the resources can be modified. So, as part of the virtual sizing, you can consider that additional CPUs and memory can be added as needed. This might also be true of disk space as well.

Since you will potentially use much more disk space during the migration than you will under normal circumstances, research the possibility of leasing additional space for a short amount of time during the migration and then returning it once the migration has been completed. This is also true for a private cloud.

A good way of differentiating both private and public clouds from physical environments is that in a cloud you can take advantage of the resources that you need when you need them. When you no longer need those resources, you can release them back to the cloud. Don't underallocate your resources, but don't overallocate them either.

Some resources, such as disks, can be added to a Linux server without a reboot being required, but other resources, such as CPU and memory, will require an OS reboot in order to recognize the new resources. In an environment where scheduled downtime is scarce, you might need to overallocate some resources. Disk and network resources can both be added dynamically, as can a few other devices such as USB hardware.

Migrate or Transform

As with any type of migration, you will have to decide whether to keep the data in the same state or to transform the data. There is nothing magical about the cloud environment. It should be treated the same as any other environment. So, as with other types of migrations, the method will be determined in part by how much downtime during switchover is allowed (the "window of inopportunity") and whether any changes and improvements are being made to the database.

Probably the most important consideration during the planning process is how to move the data to the cloud during the initial migration. This is covered in the next section.

Connectivity

How you get to the cloud system depends on the level of connectivity that you have. In some cases you will be able to transfer the data across the internet. In other cases you might have to send tapes or disk drives containing encrypted data to the cloud provider. In either case, security is important. The use of a VPN or encrypted connection should be mandatory.

Moving the Data

Moving your data to the cloud is probably the biggest challenge that you will face. In a private cloud model, you will most likely have a high-performance network to deal with, but in a public or hybrid cloud model, you most likely will have a slower network. This can be an issue when moving terabytes of data.

So, what affects the speed of the data transfer? How long will it take to move your data to the cloud? These are questions that are important when moving to the cloud. The following are all factors that affect the performance of the data movement:

- **Speed of the network**   Remember, your connection is only as fast as the slowest component along the way.

- **Number of active network devices in the path**   Each router, firewall, and other network device along the path adds delay to the transmission of data.

- **Distance between source and target**   The longer the distance is, the longer it will take to transfer the data. The transfer of electrons across a wire is not infinite. The theoretical minimum time based on the speed of light for a transmission to go from New York to Los Angeles is 13 ms. Consider the round-trip time of 26 ms, and you can see how distance is an issue. Now add in all of the active network components in between and the effect of distance becomes clear.

So, what is the best way to get your data to the destination for migration? That depends on the method of migration, as presented earlier in the book, as well as the speed of data transfer and the amount of disk space.

In addition to network speed, you will also need to consider disk space. If the network is a prohibitive factor, you might need to copy all of your database data (backups, exports, and so forth) to the target database. This means getting a significant amount of disk space for the migration. Fortunately, this space can be given back to the cloud provider after the migration has completed.

Application Migration

In addition to migrating the database, it is also necessary to migrate your applications. This is something that will take some time and effort unless the applications are already running on the virtualization platform that you are moving to. In most cases that we are aware of, public cloud offerings are limited to the x86 platform and either Linux or Windows. In some cases there are exceptions. Of course, in a private cloud environment, you have many options.

If you are moving to a public cloud, you must be aware that you might need to make application changes to support the new OS that you are migrating to. This will have to be addressed during the planning stages as well as during the migration. Application changes can be quite extensive and quite time consuming.

Data Synchronization (Replication)

After successfully migrating to the cloud, most companies that we work with want to be able to access their data in one fashion or another. This can be done via regular syncs or via Oracle GoldenGate. GoldenGate is ideal to provide a constant stream of data from your cloud systems to your data warehouse, archive system, or other data stores. It is a very common practice to move data from the cloud to your company or from your company to the cloud. The GoldenGate data stream can be encrypted using FIPS-recognized standards and is very efficient.

Oracle GoldenGate for Data Migration

Oracle GoldenGate is perhaps our favorite Oracle option. Because of its flexibility and capability, it offers many opportunities to take advantage of it. Often when we are brought into a company to implement a specific GoldenGate project, we find many more areas where GoldenGate can be quite useful.

Oracle GoldenGate can be used for data migration, ETL, ELT, and reporting services, and now you can even use GoldenGate to replicate from an Oracle database to Hadoop. The potential is limitless.

Summary

This chapter provided information on what cloud computing is (or is represented to be) and the factors to consider when migrating to a cloud environment. As you have seen in this chapter, the cloud environment is not significantly different from your in-house environment except with respect to security and network performance. Most of the considerations for migration are the same as with any other migration.

PART
V

Best Practices and Tips

CHAPTER
16

In Summary: Recommendations, Reminders, and Best Practices

This book has covered quite a bit of ground, from recommendations on how to chart the right course for your database's migration, upgrade, and transformation all the way to a roadmap for leveraging the latest Oracle database technology like Exadata Database Machine and Oracle Cloud. This chapter provides a brief recap of the best practices we've discussed, along with some recommendations and reminders.

Planning a Smooth Migration

In Part I of this book we established that proper planning is the key to a successful migration. The planning should start well in advance of the migration itself and include all contingencies.

Migration Methodologies

Which method you should use for the migration will vary based on many factors. Determining the right method for you involves weighing your options; looking at your requirements, budget, and staffing; and careful planning. This book is all about those tasks. We have attempted to provide guidance in order to help you determine your own custom migration paths which might be one of the ones that we have described, something that is a combination of them, or something completely different. No two migrations are the same.

- Of the many migration methods, there is no right one or wrong one, just the one that is optimal for your environment. Everyone's migration is different.

- Plan the migration carefully.

- Consider resources, both internal and external.

- Allocate sufficient time to execute the migration plan.

Choosing the Right Migration Path

There are many ways to migrate an Oracle database. This book has attempted to show you the top methods. Which method, or hybrid of methods, that you should choose will vary depending on your requirements. How to choose the right migration plan has been discussed throughout this book. Here are some important points from Chapter 2:

- Determine the cutover/downtime requirements.

- Determine the database changes and improvements that are desired.

- Identify the source and target database versions (if upgrade is included).

- Identify the size of the database.

- Identify your budget.

- Identify the equipment and infrastructure availability.

These are all important factors that help you to determine your method. The choice of method is equally as important as the migration path.

Migration/Transformation/Upgrade Methodology

Choosing a method to perform the migration or upgrade is the first step in planning the task. It is important to look at your particular needs and requirements and decide on a method that fits your environment best, as discussed in Chapter 3.

- We set forth the principle of the *window of inopportunity*—the maximum time frame that an organization can tolerate having a database application be unavailable before the organization's business needs are compromised—as the key driver for any migration, transformation, or upgrade project.

- The key to a successful upgrade is to first determine the precise window of inopportunity for each affected application and then work toward satisfying that window with an appropriate migration/transformation/ upgrade approach.

- Don't be afraid to ask your user community if they really do need all the data to be present after the applications have been successfully migrated— you might be surprised at their answer!

- Like anything truly worth doing, preparing for the migration/transformation/ upgrade process is paramount, and the final deliverable is the migration plan. Don't neglect to build a checklist for every crucial milestone of the process.

- When it comes to testing the migration plan, consider that it may simply be blind luck that you've succeeded. Instead, execute at least three complete iterations of the plan before concluding you've worked out all the kinks and have the level of confidence to finally implement it in a production environment.

Cross-Platform Migration

One of the most common migration scenarios we encounter is the need to migrate an Oracle database between two completely different platforms (hardware or operating system). The following sections review some of the key strategies we have found to be successful to accomplish that goal.

Data Guard

As you saw in Chapter 4, Data Guard can be a very effective way to migrate an Oracle database under very special circumstances. These circumstances exist when no changes whatsoever need to be made between the source and target databases. Versions, schemas … everything must be the same except for the hardware.

- Data Guard is a great way to migrate a database, but only if your scenario meets the requirements.

- Don't settle for this easy migration method if you really need to improve your database (as covered in several chapters throughout the book). A migration is a good time to make improvements to the database.

Migration Using Recovery Manager

We built a compelling case in Chapter 5 for using RMAN as your primary mechanism for backing up, restoring, and recovering your Oracle databases:

- RMAN's ability to encrypt backups of your database via Transparent Data Encryption (TDE) make it an excellent candidate for guarding against inadvertent data theft. (Recall that an unencrypted backup of a datafile can be read "in the clear" with just about any editor.)

- Oracle Database 10g's enhancements to RMAN make it simple to take an `INCREMENTAL LEVEL 0` image copy backup of all datafiles only once, retain those backups in the Fast Recovery Area, and then use daily `INCREMENTAL LEVEL 1` backups to recover those image copies forward forever to meet your database's Recovery Point Objective (RPO).

- These same backup and recovery features make RMAN an excellent choice for migrating a database from one platform to another, or even between non-ASM and ASM file systems. We laid out several scenarios for quickly transferring an Oracle database all at once or gradually using RMAN, making this technique a flexible option for database migrations.

Cross-Platform Tablespace Migration Utilities

As discussed in Chapter 6, starting with Oracle Database 10g, it's possible to leverage RMAN's Transportable Tablespace Sets (TTS) features to transport any self-contained set of tablespaces between different platforms, even when those tablespaces' databases are hosted on OS environments with different endianness.

- Oracle 10*g* also introduced a new migration technique—Transportable Database (TDB)—that leverages RMAN to quickly transport an entire database between OS platforms with the same endianness.

- Whichever method is used, it's important to plan for one crucial requirement: the need to bring the source tablespaces (or the entire database, in the case of TDB) into READ ONLY mode until transport is completed.

Migration with Enhancement/Upgrade

Migrating a database isn't always as simple as moving it from one environment or platform to another. In Part III we presented several techniques that we have found particularly useful when it is also necessary to transform a source database's data during its migration to its final destination.

Export/Import

As discussed in Chapter 7, Export/Import (including Data Pump) is a basic building block for many migration methods. In addition, Export/Import can be used for stand-alone migrations if the situation allows for it. As with all of the migration methods that are covered in this book, the situation and requirements typically dictate the migration method. Export/Import and Data Pump Export/Import can be quite time consuming but allow for maximum flexibility in transforming the database.

- Use this method when you need maximum flexibility.

- Use Data Pump whenever the source database is version 10*g* or newer.

Zero or Minimal Downtime Migrations with Oracle GoldenGate

Oracle GoldenGate is a heterogeneous replication product that allows for a source and target database to be synchronized. As described in Chapter 8, this allows the data migration to take place over a long period of time, after which the two databases can be kept in sync until cutover. At cutover, the downtime can be very short or, in some cases, nonexistent. This allows for minimum or zero downtime migrations.

- Consider other uses for Oracle GoldenGate once the migration is done. GoldenGate can be used for ETL/ELT, general replication, reporting servers, etc.

- Bring in extra expertise if needed. GoldenGate is a great product, but experience is invaluable.

Cross-Platform Tablespace Migration with Incremental Backups

If the source database is at least Oracle Database release 11.2.0.3, you may be able to take advantage of that release's new Cross-Platform Transportable Tablespace (XTTS) utility, as discussed in Chapter 9.

■ XTTS makes it possible to keep the tablespace sets on the source database in READ WRITE mode for an extended period of time because it leverages an initial INCREMENTAL LEVEL 0 backup and several additional INCREMENTAL LEVEL 1 backups until a desirable point in time is reached—say, a brief window during which a READ ONLY state of the tablespace set is acceptable for the application workload—at which point a final INCREMENTAL LEVEL 1 backup is taken against the source tablespaces and then transported to the destination database for application.

■ You might want to consider leveraging XTTS if your application workload requires that it operate in READ WRITE mode a majority of the time and can only accept a narrow window of inopportunity.

Migrating to New Storage Platforms Using ASM

Migrating a database with ASM is another specialty migration that is available only under very specific circumstances. This method allows the database to be migrated to a new storage platform with zero downtime. As described in Chapter 10, it is accomplished by adding the new disks to the disk groups and then removing the old disks. This can all be accomplished with the database still online.

■ Use this method if your migration meets the criteria.

■ This method requires no database downtime.

■ Always do a complete backup before any migration/upgrade.

■ Add and remove as many drives as you can at the same time.

■ Document carefully what ASM disk groups have been created.

■ Script the migration for documentation purposes and accuracy.

■ Monitor carefully.

Optimized Upgrades/Migration

In Part IV, we reviewed some of the more advanced techniques for migrating data to an Oracle database, including using different database technology as a source and transitioning to more advanced database architecture, platforms, and even the cloud.

Database Upgrade Assistant

Chapter 11 described how the DBUA is an awesome tool that can be invaluable in helping you plan for a database upgrade. Database upgrades involve performing an in-place upgrade.

- Beware of the risks involved in an in-place upgrade, since you have no easy way of undoing a failure without significant time.

- Beware of the downtime requirements of an in-place upgrade.

- Always do a complete backup before any migration/upgrade.

- Remember that no modifications or enhancements can be made during an upgrade.

Migrating from Microsoft SQL Server to Oracle

One of the chief benefits of Oracle GoldenGate is that it supports the source and target on different platforms, including database software. Using Oracle GoldenGate, you can perform a near-zero downtime migration to an Oracle database from SQL Server, as presented in Chapter 12.

- Allow plenty of time for application migration.

- Perform sufficient testing.

- Bring in extra resources if needed.

Moving to Oracle Database 12c

Oracle Database 12c's new multitenant features introduce the concept of container databases (CDBs) and pluggable databases (PDB), as described in Chapter 13. Understanding this concept is key to moving to Oracle Database 12c.

- Oracle 12c offers a plethora of methods to clone an existing PDB into another PDB with a few simple SQL commands—an invaluable option for databases that need to be cloned quickly in an on-demand fashion.

■ We provided examples of how simple it is to migrate a pre-12c database (also known as a non-CDB) to a CDB environment and then plug it in as a new PDB.

■ There are additional licensing costs to support the new multitenant architecture, but these may be well worth your IT organization's consideration because of the relative simplicity of creating PDBs from other production sources.

Moving to Oracle Engineered Systems

Oracle engineered systems like the Exadata Database Machine (DBM) are quickly becoming the norm in many larger IT organizations because of their relative cost savings for both CAPEX and OPEX. Chapter 14 provided guidance for moving to Oracle engineered systems.

■ Because Exadata DBMs combine the best of software and hardware solutions for data storage and retrieval, they offer excellent opportunities for consolidating multiple Oracle databases onto one large, powerful hardware platform.

■ Oracle Database 12c's new multitenant features also promote a synergy with Oracle engineered systems like Exadata.

■ It's important to be aware of some simple caveats when migrating to an Exadata environment—for example, the need for objects' segment and extent sizes to comply with the corresponding recommended ASM allocation unit size of 4MB.

■ Whoever is responsible for supporting the Exadata hardware needs to be aware of how to effectively limit consumption of Exadata I/O resources with Database Resource Manager (DBRM) and I/O Resource Manager (IORM) plans.

Migrating to Oracle in the Cloud and Recommendations, Reminders, and Best Practices

This book has provided numerous options for migrating, upgrading, and transforming Oracle databases and even moving to Oracle from another database. It was designed to provide good techniques, tips, and helpful instructions. Each migration is different, and the techniques provided here are not all-inclusive. Take this information and modify it for your particular needs.

Migrating to the Oracle in the Cloud

Cloud computing has become a new way of looking at systems and databases. Migrating to the cloud is just like any other migration, but has some considerations that need to be taken into account, as discussed in Chapter 15.

- Be careful what you sign. You can expect the cloud provider to meet the terms of the SLA, but don't expect more.

- You get what you pay for. Beware of bandwidth and response time.

- Monitor carefully and often.

Summary of Best Practices

This chapter has attempted to provide a summary of the book along with some of the valuable tips and best practices. We hope this and all chapters of this book serve you well.

A Final Word...

Our best hopes and wishes to all who have read this book. Migrating, transforming, and upgrading an Oracle database is not for the faint of heart, but we hope our efforts to alleviate any anxiety over its complexity have been of service to you. Happy computing!

Index

H

Q

R

T

Z

Join the Largest Tech Community in the World

Download the latest software, tools, and developer templates

Get exclusive access to hands-on trainings and workshops

Grow your professional network through the Oracle ACE Program

Publish your technical articles – and get paid to share your expertise

Join the Oracle Technology Network
Membership is free. Visit oracle.com/technetwork

@OracleOTN   facebook.com/OracleTechnologyNetwork

ORACLE®

Copyright © 2014, Oracle and/or its affiliates. All rights reserved. Oracle and Java are registered trademarks of Oracle and/or its affiliates.

Our Technology. Your Future.

Fast-track your career with an Oracle Certification.

Over 1.5 million certifications testify to the importance of these top industry-recognized credentials as one of the best ways to get ahead. **AND STAY THERE.**

START TODAY

ORACLE®

CERTIFICATION PROGRAM

certification.oracle.com

Hardware and Software
Engineered to Work Together

ORACLE®
ACE PROGRAM

Stay Connected

oracle.com/technetwork/oracleace

[f] oracleaces

[t] @oracleace

[B] blogs.oracle.com/oracleace

Need help? Need consultation?
Need an informed opinion?

You Need an Oracle ACE

Oracle partners, developers, and customers look to Oracle ACEs and Oracle ACE Directors for focused product expertise, systems and solutions discussion, and informed opinions on a wide range of data center implementations.

Their credentials are strong as Oracle product and technology experts, community enthusiasts, and solutions advocates.

And now is a great time to learn more about this elite group—or nominate a worthy colleague.

For more information about the Oracle ACE program, go to:
oracle.com/technetwork/oracleace

ORACLE®

Copyright © 2012, Oracle and/or its affiliates. All rights reserved. Oracle and Java are registered trademarks of Oracle and/or its affiliates. Other names may be trademarks of their respective owners. 123022

Reach More than 700,000 Oracle Customers with Oracle Publishing Group

Connect with the Audience that Matters Most to Your Business

Oracle Magazine
The Largest IT Publication in the World
Circulation: 550,000
Audience: IT Managers, DBAs, Programmers, and Developers

Profit
Business Insight for Enterprise-Class Business Leaders to Help Them Build a Better Business Using Oracle Technology
Circulation: 100,000
Audience: Top Executives and Line of Business Managers

Java Magazine
The Essential Source on Java Technology, the Java Programming Language, and Java-Based Applications
Circulation: 125,000 and Growing Steady
Audience: Corporate and Independent Java Developers, Programmers, and Architects

For more information or to sign up for a FREE subscription:
Scan the QR code to visit Oracle Publishing online.

ORACLE®

Copyright © 2012, Oracle and/or its affiliates. All rights reserved. Oracle and Java are registered trademarks of Oracle and/or its affiliates. Other names may be trademarks of their respective owners. 113940

Beta Test Oracle Software

Get a first look at our newest products—and help perfect them. You must meet the following criteria:

- ✔ Licensed Oracle customer or Oracle PartnerNetwork member

- ✔ Oracle software expert

- ✔ Early adopter of Oracle products

Please apply at: pdpm.oracle.com/BPO/userprofile

ORACLE®

If your interests match upcoming activities, we'll contact you. Profiles are kept on file for 12 months.

Copyright © 2014, Oracle and/or its affiliates. All rights reserved. Oracle and Java are registered trademarks of Oracle and/or its affiliates.

Join the Oracle Press Community at
OraclePressBooks.com

Find the latest information on Oracle products and technologies. Get exclusive discounts on Oracle Press books. Interact with expert Oracle Press authors and other Oracle Press Community members. Read blog posts, download content and multimedia, and so much more. Join today!

Join the Oracle Press Community today and get these benefits:

- Exclusive members-only discounts and offers

- Full access to all the features on the site: sample chapters, free code and downloads, author blogs, podcasts, videos, and more

- Interact with authors and Oracle enthusiasts

- Follow your favorite authors and topics and receive updates

- Newsletter packed with exclusive offers and discounts, sneak previews, and author podcasts and interviews

Oracle Press

@OraclePress

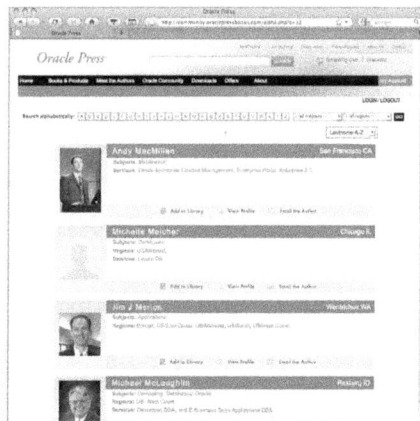

www.ingramcontent.com/pod-product-compliance
Lightning Source LLC
Chambersburg PA
CBHW080130220326
41598CB00032B/5017